Risk in Social Science

Risk in Social Science

Peter Taylor-Gooby and Jens O. Zinn

OXFORD
UNIVERSITY PRESS

OXFORD
UNIVERSITY PRESS

Great Clarendon Street, Oxford ox2 6DP

Oxford University Press is a department of the University of Oxford.
It furthers the University's objective of excellence in research, scholarship,
and education by publishing worldwide in

Oxford New York

Auckland Cape Town Dar es Salaam Hong Kong Karachi
Kuala Lumpur Madrid Melbourne Mexico City Nairobi
New Delhi Shanghai Taipei Toronto

With offices in

Argentina Austria Brazil Chile Czech Republic France Greece
Guatemala Hungary Italy Japan Poland Portugal Singapore
South Korea Switzerland Thailand Turkey Ukraine Vietnam

Oxford is a registered trade mark of Oxford University Press
in the UK and in certain other countries

Published in the United States
by Oxford University Press Inc., New York

British Library Cataloguing in Publication Data
Data available

Library of Congress Cataloging in Publication Data
Data available

Typeset by SPI Publisher Services, Pondicherry, India
Printed in Great Britain
on acid-free paper by
Biddles Ltd., Kings Lynn, Norfolk

ISBN 978-0-19-928595-2 (hb)
      978-0-19-928596-9 (pb)

Preface

Risk and uncertainty have emerged as central themes in social science, for good practical and theoretical reasons. More flexible labour markets, greater freedom to divorce, cohabit and re-partner and greater diversity in life-styles erode the certainty with which people can map out their futures. Step-changes in the complexity and scale of technological innovation enable rapid rises in living standards, and, at the same time, bring the possibility of major catastrophes closer. Unexpected disasters, from the Challenger Space Shuttle to Chernobyl, from the Herald of Free Enterprise to Exxon Valdez remind us of the limits to our capacity for control.

Advances in social science improve understanding of how people perceive and prioritise risks, broaden awareness of the bearing of a range of other issues (trust, experience during the life course, democratic expectations) on people's capacity to manage risks, and facilitate exploration of the ways in which people communicate about and respond to risk and uncertainty. New conceptual and methodological developments create opportunities to extend this work.

In this book, we review recent work on risk, paying particular attention to the way risk and uncertainty have emerged as central themes across a range of areas. We also seek to draw together work from different perspectives in order to improve current understanding of the contribution that social science can make in this field.

The book rests on the active engagement of a number of people, including in particular colleagues from the ESRC *Social Contexts and Responses to Risk* research network and participants in our conference on *Learning about Risk* in Canterbury in January 2005. We are extremely grateful to the ESRC without whose support under grant 336-25001 this work would not have been possible, and also to our project administrator, Ms Mary Mustafa, for collating and preparing the manuscript against a very tight timetable.

University of Kent at Canterbury   Peter Taylor-Gooby
October 2005   Jens O. Zinn

v

Contents

Contents

Notes on the Contributors

David Abbott is a Research Fellow at the Norah Fry Research Centre, University of Bristol. He has a long-standing interest in issues of inequality in Social Policy and has, since 1999, focused on research about the lives of disabled children, young people, and adults with learning difficulties. His latest book is *Secret loves, hidden lives? Exploring issues for people with learning difficulties who are gay, lesbian or bisexual* (with Joyce Howarth, Policy Press 2005).

Andy Alaszewski is Professor of Health Studies and director of the Centre for Health Services Research at the University of Kent. Previously he was director of the Institute of Health Studies (1991–2000) and Professor of Health Studies (1992–2001) at the University of Hull. He is editor of the international journal *Health, Risk and Society* (published by Routledge, Taylor and Francis Group) and has published empirical studies of risk management in health and welfare services (A. Alaszewski, L. Harrison, and J. Manthorpe (eds.) *Risk, Health and Welfare: Policies, Strategies and Practice*, Open University Press, Buckingham, 1998 and A. Alaszewski, with H. Alaszewski, S. Ayer and J. Manthorpe, *Managing Risk in Community Practice: Nursing, Risk and Decision making*, Balliere Tindall, London, 2000), and a methodological text on *Using Diaries for Social Research* (Sage December 2005).

Karen Henwood is Senior Lecturer in Social Science in the Cardiff University School of Social Sciences. She has substantive research interests in the study of identity, culture, and risk. With Nick Pidgeon she has previously studied the meanings and non-economic values people attach to their natural environment. Throughout her career she has explored the role of qualitative methods in psychology and the social sciences. Her published articles have appeared in journals such as *British Journal of Psychology, Feminism and Psychology, Theory and Psychology, Journal of Environmental Psychology, Social Science and Medicine,* and *British Journal of Social Psychology.*

Emma Hughes is a research associate in the School of Journalism, Media and Cultural Studies at the University of Cardiff. She is currently working on an ESRC-funded project on Media Discourse and Framing and on her Ph.D. which is based upon media representations of Genetically Modified Crops. Recent papers include *The Contaminated Risk of Genetically Modified Crops: How threats are merged in the GM debate.*

Bridget Hutter is Professor of Risk Regulation at the London School of Economics (LSE) and Political Science and director of the ESRC Centre for Analysis of Risk and Regulation (CARR). Her research concerns the sociology of regulation and risk management, the regulation of economic life, and the social control of organizations. She is author of numerous publications on the subject of regulation including *Risk and Regulation* (OUP 2001) and *Organizational Encounters with Risk* (ed. with M. Power CUP 2005). She is also the Editor of the *British Journal of Sociology.*

Anwen Jones is a research fellow in the Centre for Housing Policy. Her research interests include homelessness, anti-social behaviour, and sustainable housing. She is currently working with Deborah Quilgars on an EU-funded study of security and insecurity in home ownership and another EU-funded project on cooperation in housing provision for risk groups. Her publications include: Jones, A. and Quilgars, D. (2004) *The Prevention of Homelessness*: an Advice Note Issued by the Welsh Assembly Government, Cardiff: National Assembly for Wales and Fitzpatrick, S. and Jones, A. (2005) 'Pursuing social justice or social cohesion?: Coercion in street homelessness policies in England', *Journal of Social Policy*, 34(3): 389–406.

Hazel Kemshall is currently Professor of Community and Criminal Justice at De Montfort University. She has research interests in risk assessment and management of offenders, effective work in multi-agency public protection, and implementing effective practice with offenders. She has completed research for the Economic and Social Research Council, the Home Office, and the Scottish Office. She is the author of the Home Office risk training materials for probation officers, and the Scottish Office materials for social workers, and has numerous publications on risk. Her most recent publications include: *Risk, Social Policy and Welfare* (Open University Press 2002) and *Understanding Risk in Criminal Justice* (OUP 2003).

Jenny Kitzinger holds a chair in the School of Journalism at the University of Cardiff and is director of the Tom Hopkinson Research Centre and of the Risk, Science and Health Media Research Group. Her work examines power struggles in media production processes and is particularly concerned with questions of media influence and audience reception. Recent publications include *Framing abuse: media influence and public understandings of sexual violence against children* (Pluto 2004), *The Circuit of Mass Communication: media strategies, representation and audience reception in the AIDS crisis* (Sage, co-author), *Developing Focus Group Research: politics, theory and practice* (Sage, co-editor) and *Mass Media and Power in Modern Britain* (Oxford University Press, co-author).

Jane Lewis is Professor of Social Policy at the LSE. She has a long-standing research interest in family change, family policy, and gender issues. Her most recent publications include: *Should We Worry about Family Change? The 2001 Joanne Goodman Lectures.* Toronto: University of Toronto Press, 2003; and *The End of Marriage? Individualism and Intimate Relations.* Cheltenham: Edward Elgar, 2001.

Graham Murdock Reader in the Sociology of Culture at Loughborough University, is well-known both nationally and internationally for his research and writing on contemporary communications. His work has been translated into seventeen languages and he has held visiting professorships in the USA, Belgium, Norway, and Mexico, and most recently in Sweden, as the Bonnier Chair at the University of Stockholm. He has a long-standing interest in the way popular media represent areas of contention and anxiety in social life and has investigated representations of rioting, public disorder and terrorism. His recent and current research examines the relations between media representations and public perceptions across a range of risk areas.

Nick Pidgeon is Professor of Applied Psychology at Cardiff University. He has research interests in people's perception of risk and its communication with particular applications to public policy decision-making, environmental issues (such as biotechnology, nuclear power, and climate change), and industrial safety. A social psychologist by background, he has worked extensively within interdisciplinary teams throughout his career. He is co-author of the book *Man-Made Disasters* (with Barry Turner, 2nd edn. 1997) and *The Social Amplification of Risk* (with R. Kasperson and P. Slovic 2003).

Deborah Quilgars is a senior research fellow in the Centre for Housing Policy at the University of York. Her main research interests are in homelessness, housing and community care, and housing and risk. Deborah is currently working on an EU-funded project on Security and Insecurity in Home Ownership; she was part of the research team involved in the ESRC's 'Risk and Human Behaviour Programme' which looked at families' management of risk in a flexible labour market. Her publications include: Quilgars, A. and Abbott, D. (2000) 'Working in the risk society: families perceptions of and responses to, flexible labour markets and the restructuring of welfare', *Community Work and Family*, 3(1): 15–36 and Abbott, D. and Quilgars, D. (2001) 'Managing the risk of unemployment' in Edwards, R. and Glover, J. *Risk and Citizenship: Key issues in welfare*, London: Routledge.

Sophie Sarre is a research officer currently at the LSE. Her primary research area is families and social policy. She has also carried out evaluations of services managed by the Department for Work and Pensions, The Department for Education and Skills and the Family Welfare Association. Publications include: (with Martin Evans, Jill Eyre, and Jane Millar) *Research Report, New Deal for Lone Parents: Second Synthesis Report of the National Evaluation* (DWP 2003); *Evaluation of the Queensbridge and Dalston Sure Start Programme* (City and Hackney Primary Care Trust 2003); (with Karen Clarke) 'Breaking Down Barriers Between Health and Social Care' in David Taylor (ed.) 2001 Health and Social Policy Research Centre; (with Jane Lewis and Jessica Datta) *Individualism and Commitment in Marriage and Cohabitation* (Lord Chancellor's Department 1999); *A Place for Fathers: fathers and social policy in the post-war period* (LSE Welfare State Programme 1996).

Peter Simmons is a lecturer in the School of Environmental Sciences, University of East Anglia. His main research focus for several years has been the contextual study of public understandings of and responses to environmental and technological risk. He also has a research interest in space, place and risk, and in the use of deliberative processes in risk decision-making. Current research includes a project on narrative approaches to understanding people's experience of everyday risk, part of the ESRC-funded Social Context and Risk Response (SCARR) network.

Peter Taylor-Gooby is Professor of Social Policy at the University of Kent and director of the ESRC Social Contexts and Responses to Risk network. He is a founding academician at ALSiSS, a fellow of the RSA and current president of the Sociology and Social Policy section of the BAAS. Recent publications include: *Ideas and the Welfare State*, Palgrave, 2005; *New Risks, New Welfare*, Oxford University Press, 2004; *Making a European Welfare State?* Blackwell, 2004; and *Risk, Trust and Welfare*, Macmillan, 2000.

John Tulloch is Research Professor of Sociology at Brunel University. His research interests include the media and risk, high culture, television production and Australian film. He directed the Centre for Cultural Risk Research at Charles Sturt University, Australia, and currently directs the Media and Risk Research group at Cardiff University. He is active in areas such as HIV/AIDS research, sexuality and the body, fear of crime, and perceptions of risk. He has obtained a number of grants in these areas from the Australian Research Council and the National Health and Medical Research Council. Recent major publications include: *Risk and Everyday Life* (with Deborah Lupton), Sage, 2003 and *Performing Culture*, Sage, 1999.

Sarah Vickerstaff is Professor in Work and Employment at the School of Social Policy, Sociology and Social Research at the University of Kent. Her main research interests are in changes to the relationship between paid work and the life course, in particular at the beginning and end of 'working life'. She has recently completed work for the Joseph Rowntree Foundation on *Happy Retirement? The impact of employers' policies and practice on the process of retirement* (The Policy Press, 2004), and for the Equal Opportunities Commission on *Older Workers and Options for Flexible Work*, 2005 (with W. Loretto and P. J. White). Sarah is also on the ACAS Panel of Arbitrators.

Jens O. Zinn is a research fellow at the School of Social Policy, Sociology and Social Research at the University of Kent. He worked empirically and theoretically on risk and uncertainty for several years in the Collaborative Research Centre on Status Passages and Risks in the Life Course in Bremen (1995–9) and the Collaborative Research Centre on Reflexive Modernization in Munich (1999–2002). Since 2002 he is working as network fellow in the ESRC SCARR. Recent publications on risk and uncertainty: 2005: 'The biographical approach—a better way to understand behaviour in health and illness?' In: *Health, Risk and Society* 7(1): 1–9; 'Biographical Certainty in Reflexive Modernity'. In: Kelly, N., Horrocks, C., Milnes, K., Roberts, B. and Robinson, D. (eds.) *Narrative, Memory and Everyday Life*, Huddersfield University, 87–95; 2004; 'Health, Risk and Uncertainty in the Life Course: A Typology of Biographical Certainty Constructions', *Social Theory and Health* 2(3): 199–221.

1

The Current Significance of Risk

Peter Taylor-Gooby and Jens O. Zinn

Risk is to do with uncertainties: possibilities, chances, or likelihoods of events, often as consequences of some activity or policy. As such, risk has always accompanied the development of human society (Sahlins 1974; Garnsey 1988; Gallant 1991). Harvest failure, pestilence, migrations, new currents in religion, technological developments, and the unforeseen consequences of urbanization have all exerted a powerful and typically unpredicted influence on the problems and difficulties we face. For much of history, the lack of certainty was largely attributed to agencies beyond human control: the ignorance of imperfect humanity, divine agency, luck, destiny, or fate. In recent years, the idea of risk has attracted intense scrutiny from social scientists—for two main reasons.

The first concerns the increasing complexity of our technologies and of the institutions that govern our lives. Failures of technology and innovation are well publicized. This applies to the Thalidomide tragedy (emerging in 1962), Bhopal (1984), Chernobyl (1986), the Challenger space shuttle in the same year, the Exxon Valdez oil spill in 1989, the continuing arsenic poisoning of some 20,000 people a year in Bangladesh from the early 1990s onwards (Pearce 2001), and more recent pharmaceutical, nuclear, nutritional, and space-related catastrophes (the arthritis drug Vioxx in 2004, the Tokaimura chain reaction in 1999, the BSE outbreak from 1986 to 1996, and the Columbia space shuttle in 2003). These events have all brought home the way in which risk has accompanied technical development and revealed the weaknesses of institutions for managing the resulting uncertainty. Similarly, the shortcomings of a whole range of social projects for improving human well-being, from high-rise estates in big cities to the enormous growth of road transport, from the

1

centralization of the Soviet economy to the Common Agricultural Policy of the EU, from the computerization of social security delivery in the UK to privatization in health care and education, have all demonstrated the difficulties in achieving the goals that had been confidently predicted by their advocates. Issues of uncertainty are part of technical development. It is the increasing complexity of the processes involved, both in terms of the coordination of myriad activities in planning and in terms of the institutions through which risks are governed, and the high level of public awareness of shortcomings in risk management that account for the peculiar modern force of the notion of risk.

Second, alongside the evidence that risk and uncertainty are endemic, and that our technology and social institutions are unable to eliminate it, it is increasingly recognized that risk and uncertainty also involve socio-political questions of acceptability and of contest. Once risk issues become politicized, the scope for resolution through technical means alone is limited. A whole range of innovations including nuclear power, GM food, motorway building and the Ilisu, and Namarda and Yangtse dam projects all provoke vigorous and determined political protest. More broadly, the possible consequences of the pivotal international project to impose a largely market trade structure through the WTO, the shifts in the regulation of intimate relations and family life as gay relationships are formally recognized, the management of cohabitation, divorce and separation, and the technology of fertility treatment and of the application of the new genetics in people's lives, all give rise to debate and conflict.

This has led to a rapid expansion of activity across social science. In Chapters 2 and 3 we review these developments and pay particular attention to the trajectory of new work in economics, psychology, and sociology. In all these disciplines, traditional approaches, based on assumptions about risk calculation through the cool deliberations of rational actors, abstracted from social and cultural settings and influences or from the impact of emotions have been called into question. New developments also seek to find ways of broadening debates originating in decision theory and in the study of risk management into new fields. These include the processes of risk communication, and the extent to which users of mass media can be understood as passive recipients of official messages; the way in which particular responses to uncertainty emerge as normative systems, which constitute a factor in the government of social life; the way the contexts in which judgements are made influence risky choices by both lay-people and experts; and the social and political outcomes in relation to trust or the operation of the institutions intended to manage risks. One result has been experimentation with new approaches and methods, including 'mental modelling' to understand how people variously conceptualize risk issues and ways of coping with them, new qualitative methods intended to provide opportunities to examine the relation between a person's social experience, biography and identity and their conception of risk, and combined research methods, linking together quantitative and qualitative work, to enable the generalization of conclusions informed by detailed and nuanced individual analysis.

A further outcome has been a decline in confidence in technical experts and in policymakers (both in government and in corporations) and the proliferation of pressure groups and other bodies acting as watchdogs and as rallying points for public concern. At the same time, people are much more likely to take legal action when authorities fail to manage risks successfully, leading to defensive constraints in many areas.

Risk has always been important. The increasing scale of the uncertainties surrounding the technical innovations which our society makes available at a breakneck pace and the collapse of confidence in authorities and in official experts as the accredited managers of risk have pushed issues in this field to the forefront in social science. They have also led to a rapid pace of development in the social science concerned to understand risk perception and response. In this book we examine in more detail how risk has been recognized, analysed, and researched and how different disciplines have responded, and provide an overview of the work that has been carried out across a range of different fields.

The Emergence of Risk as a Social and Political Issue

The origins of the notion of risk are subject to debate. Wharton derives it from the Arabic risq ('something from which you draw a profit'—1992), Chambers Dictionary from the Latin *risicum* (the challenge posed to a sailor by a barrier reef—1946), Luhmann dates it in German to the mid sixteenth century and refers to the Latin *riscum* in use earlier (1993), and Giddens suggests it may come from the Spanish *risco* (a rock 1999; see Althaus 2005: 570 for these and other derivations). Risk appears to have emerged as an idea in the Middle Ages, in the context of voyages into uncharted waters (Giddens 1999: ch. 2; Ewald 2002). It referred to the uncertainty about outcomes of the exploratory/trading/imperialist missions of the early mercantile world and was linked to the evolving concept of insurance. It entered the world of moneylending and finance more generally, and then became a useful tool in the conceptualization of the probable consequences of investment decisions. During the eighteenth and nineteenth centuries, the development of a mathematics of probability (from Bernouilli's 'law of large numbers', propounded in 1713, onwards—see Boyne 2003: 4–9) facilitated the application of probabilistic reasoning to risk issues, so that (as Knight puts it in his classic text, written early in the twentieth century) 'results become predictable in accordance with the laws of chance' (1921: 46).

The increasing sophistication of the mathematics of probability and the economics of risk affected investment and market behaviour. The early development of insurance was based on the experience and personal judgement of underwriters (O'Malley 2004: ch. 6). Probability calculation supported the development of a more sophisticated approach, where the more modern notion of risk as 'damage from the event multiplied by the probability of the event occurring' (Adams 1995: 8) leads to more precise estimates of premia in a competitive market. Insurance extended to life insurance in the eighteenth century, and upper working class groups developed mutual insurance and friendly society systems of support during the nineteenth century. The progress of census and mortality statistics enabled a more scientific approach to life insurance, with the foundation of the Institute of Actuaries in 1848. These interlinked developments provided the foundation for modern approaches to banking, investment, and insurance, and led to the growth of the international financial markets that have now become central institutions in a globalized international economy (O'Malley 2000; Baker and Simon 2002).

Techniques of probability assessment were applied across a broad range of areas, including technical risk assessment through the sphere of business and enterprise, epidemiology and the evaluation of the suitability of particular treatments in modern health care, environmental protection, and the management of crime. The method lent itself to risk monitoring and response in virtually any field where evidence on current risk levels is available, and can plausibly be used as a guide to the future. This is discussed in more detail in Chapter 2. An important outcome at the political level where merits more attention is the transition in the role of the state through the developing modern period.

Foucault analyses this as a double process (1991). On the one hand, governments sought to control their citizens by a whole catalogue of measures that include both the means whereby populations can be accurately counted, assessed, judged, disciplined, and categorized. On the other, policy aims at instilling appropriate values to achieve particular outcomes. This is summed up in the compound notion of 'governmentality' (see Dean, M. 1999: ch. 2). The logic of insurance is one means through which both aspects can be linked. It includes the basis for a more precise estimate of the needs and ability to pay of particular groups, and the justification for different treatment of different risk categories.

During the late nineteenth and early twentieth centuries, governments were able to accommodate to political pressures by extending and nationalizing the existing friendly society risk-sharing schemes of the upper working and lower middle class into social insurance. This became the foundation of European welfare states and the most important element in government spending in developed countries in the settlement at the end of the Second World War. The current pressures on welfare spending have led to retrenchment of these systems (Pierson 2001). In some contexts, this has meant a retreat from welfare inclusiveness to precise actuarial calculation, with the denial of benefit to those who is with imperfect contribution records. In others, it has led to the privatization of areas of social insurance and the targeting of state help more accurately on clearly defined groups (Myles 2002).

Risk, uncertainty, and risk-responses have also played a role in the development of the institutions of family and household life. The slow progress through the nineteenth and twentieth centuries of the legal institutions that enabled women to hold property, gain access to employment rights and to independent social security, to the right to divorce, towards control over their own sexuality and child bearing, and towards a recognition of problems of violence and exploitation corresponded to a shift in the status of marriage and sexual relationships (Lewis 2001). Whilst marriage provided a form of security for women in dependence on a male breadwinner (the domestic 'haven in a heartless world'), the development of alternatives raised the question of how to balance the risks of threat, subordination, and lack of opportunity in marriage with those available in other contexts. Population shifts included an increase in the number of older, predominantly female, households, and raising new issues about shifting patterns of poverty and of social need. In turn, a new strand in the politics of personal interests, concerned with how the risks of new and different lifestyles are to be managed, has emerged (see Taylor-Gooby 2004: ch. 9). An increasing flexibility in family and personal life parallels the growing flexibility of employment in a context of rapid technological innovation and ever-intensifying international trade. Uncertainty is brought home at the level of individual life.

More Recent Developments

Risk issues and institutions for managing them have played an important role in modern economics, in the development of the modern state, and in relation to modern political and social institutions. Equally, developments in all these fields have directed attention to risk. Much of the recent debate has been concerned with negative aspects, given impetus by the obvious disasters, failures, and intractable problems referred to at the beginning of the chapter. The core meaning of risk in the Oxford English Dictionary is given as 'a situation involving exposure to danger'. However, in all economic, political, and social life, risks have a positive as well as a negative side. This is also a key element in current conceptions of risk, discussed further in Chapter 3.

A strong element in economic thinking stresses the importance of risk-taking and the role of entrepreneurship (see Knight 1921: 361; Schumpeter 1976). However, as Knight points out, a major direction in the development of business is the prediction, analysis, and containment of risks, so that, over time, risks are converted into certainties (Knight 1921: 347). One might add that large and uncertain projects which offer possible high returns but involve considerable uncertainty have tended to be supported by government, outside the traditional system of speculative entrepreneurship—for example, North Sea Oil exploitation in the 1980s and 1990s or the French nuclear power programme (the most developed in Europe) from the 1970s onwards. As economies become more globalized, and the capacity of nation states and other agencies to regulate national markets diminishes (Scharpf 1997), the positive aspects of economic risk-taking receive greater emphasis. This is summed up in the declaration at the Lisbon EU conference in 2000 that the goal for Europe must be to become 'the most dynamic and competitive knowledge-based economy in the world' (Presidency Conclusions 2000: 3). The action plan on growth and jobs includes 'well-designed and sustainable social protection' to 'minimise social dependency by creating strong incentives to seek work, to take entrepreneurial risks and to be mobile' (EU 2005, Table 8).

In concert with this process, governments have encouraged policies designed to promote 'activism', entrepreneurship, initiative, and risk-taking among their populations, so that flexibility becomes the central concept in the OECD 'jobs strategy' (Casey 2004, Table 1). The shift from passive reliance on benefits to active willingness to seek jobs and to retrain for them has been the leading theme in the 'modernization' of European and US social security systems through the provision of opportunities rather than welfare handouts (EU 1997). At the level of collective innovation, the political pressures on government to reduce risks, running counter to an equal enthusiasm to promote and exploit technical innovation, have led to discussion about the role of government in managing new developments in the public interest. Here the chief outcome has been the adoption of a 'precautionary principle' in regulation (EU 2000: 1).

The problem that immediately emerges from the increased emphasis on the positive as well as the negative aspects of risk is the question of how to balance risk against advantage (Levidow, Carr, and Wield 1999: 307–11). This is intensified in the context of commercial and international pressures, brought home by threats of trade wars and of WTO litigation, to open up markets to new technologies. The most significant example at the European level currently is the debate over the licensing of GM foodstuffs. The EU initially refused to license some GM crops (oilseed rape and maize) appealing to the precautionary principle, despite the balance of scientific research which fails to provide compelling evidence of problems. The refusal of five member states to accept the crops has led to the maintenance of the ban, although the EU Commission's officials argue that it is hard to see how it can be scientifically, and therefore legally, justified. The UK government sought to reconcile scientific evidence and popular disquiet by organizing the *GM Nation?* Debate—the largest consultation exercise about the introduction of a new technology that is a matter of public concern so far in the UK—in 2002–3. The key finding was that contact with experts hardened public opinion against the new technology. The government has not licensed GM organisms, possibly hoping that international commercial pressures at the level of the WTO will resolve the issue. Political pressures prevent diffusion of a new technology despite lack of scientific evidence—a clear demonstration of the importance of political and social issues in policymaking about the risks of innovation.

At the level of individual and intimate life, risk has always been bound up with pleasure, in sexual relationships, eating, drug-taking, and a huge range of other activities. We discuss recent work in this area further in Chapter 3. One area of academic interest has been 'edgework'—deliberate risk-seeking in mountaineering, motor sport, relationships, sexual adventuring, and the new 'extreme' sports such as base jumping or free diving (Lyng 2005). In social life, concerns about security interact with antagonism to paternalism, the nanny state, and over-regulation. This leads to the view that, far from advancing enterprise and edgework, the predominant concerns of modern culture are obsessively over-protective: one controversial perspective argues that current concern with risk produces a damaging 'culture of fear', expressed through a fascination with risk-reduction in every aspect of lifestyle and a determination to find scapegoats for any difficulty or set-back (Furedi 2002 and 2005; but see, for example, Beck 1998; Harkin 1998; Mythen 2004 for contrary views). Cultural shifts, influencing the way people think about risks at the personal level, are brought back to the political level, in the question of how regulatory frameworks should operate in this context.

This brief review of some developments in economic policymaking and in political and social life shows that, for a range of reasons, ideas about risk and uncertainty and the availability of intellectual tools which both claim to advance risk management and demonstrate the limitations of such approaches have become more widespread. Risk concerns are now pervasive and risk issues have become to a considerable extent political and social concerns. In general, the climate of concern is negative: risks are feared. However, there is also a positive side to risk in entrepreneurship, active citizenship, and the excitement of edgework. Recent developments in the social science of risk are now recognizing both dimensions in this developing field.

Approaches in Different Disciplines

Work on risk and uncertainty has advanced rapidly across a number of social science disciplines. We review the impact of the new context of risk research on developments in detail in Chapters 2 and 3. Here, we wish to chart out the main features of the work.

Economists have tended to tackle risk using a rigorous conceptualization of rational action. A number of developments have led to modifications of this core idea. Empirical evidence of paradoxes and inconsistencies in the way people approach risky choices, even when they are relatively well informed and have the opportunity to deliberate, provides a substantial challenge (Hargreaves-Heap et al. 1992). A rational model places stringent requirements on people's capacity to process information and estimate probabilities. Psychologists have demonstrated through experiment and survey that cognitive illusions and distortions influence perceptions of risk. Further work shows that responses to risks are often influenced by the way the issues are presented. In addition, economists have developed the concept of 'bounded rationality' (Simon 1987) to capture the limitations to people's cognitive capacities.

As a result of these developments, work from an economic perspective has increasingly moved from modelling based on assumptions about rational action to attempts to chart precisely the limitations of rational action in different contexts, so that risk responses can be analysed more successfully. This process also reflects back on theory-building in economics, since it provides an impetus for the modification of a simple rational actor paradigm.

From a *psychological perspective*, approaches to risk are typically tackled at an individual level, and experimental methodologies are important, sometimes reinforced by interview and social survey. In addition to the points about the limitations of human risk apprehension mentioned above, work by psychologists has also demonstrated the importance of other factors. For example, the issues of risk and trust, discussed in Chapter 3, emerge from work that charts the interaction of the individual social actors on whom psychology initially focuses. Recent work on mental modelling has sought to analyse the conceptual frameworks in and through which people think about risk and how to respond to it.

Social psychology has had a powerful impact on work from this perspective, bringing in psychometric contributions from social surveys. This approach has demonstrated common features across concerns about risks in a wide range of fields. Of particular importance to popular risk judgements is the extent to which the issue under consideration provokes dread, and conversely the extent to which it is familiar, regardless of the objective extent of the threat involved (Slovic 2001: ch. 2). People who take steps to avoid the dreaded unknown in possible but un-evidenced risks from mobile phones may accept the substantial risks in riding a bike to work on busy city roads. Work from this perspective has also led to interest in the extent to which cultural factors influence risk perceptions and responses, and to attempt at ambitious theory-building which include and seek to reconcile the contribution of both rationality and the limitations of rationality on judgements. In addition, the institutional frameworks which influence communication about risk through the mass media and the opportunities people have to respond to risks have attracted attention (Pidgeon, Kasperson, and Slavic 2003).

Sociological approaches tend to start out from a rather different position, since the background assumption is that social action is best understood as shaped by institutions and culture, rather than directed by rational planning or influenced by individual emotions. Risk approaches have

9

incorporated a strong interest in cultural factors, together with detailed and often ambitious attempts to chart the importance of the institutional changes that have recently brought risk to the forefront of debate. This has led to approaches which link together the rise of the modern state and modern forms of power to changes in the economy, in the experience of work and in family life, and to the continuing impact of new technologies and cultural shifts. A key focus is typically on the distinctive features of modern approaches to risk. Serious analytical problems arise from the fact that the theoretical frameworks used are often insufficiently precise to generate hypotheses that can be tested successfully on the basis of the available information. Cultural perspectives often lead to a case-study approach. Such material requires careful situation in a broader theory of society to support generalization.

This brief overview points to a number of features of social scientific work on risk. All the disciplines have started out from positions which rest heavily on core presuppositions: in economics, rational actor approaches, in psychology, assumptions about the individual as the basic building block of analysis, in sociology, the idea that culture or institutions can be studied as developing in a substantially autonomous way. As research has developed, these assumptions have been modified for two kinds of reasons: first, work from other disciplines has influenced and contributed to understanding, and assisted researchers in coping with the problems they faced. Examples of this process are the importance in current economic analysis of the psychological evidence about the limited capacity of people to deal with risk issues and choices as, in any sense, rational actors; the way in which psychologists have developed interest in ideas about the impact of culture and of social institutions; and sociological interest in the different rationalities of different social groups.

The second point concerns the impact of the experience of dealing with practical issues on analysis of perceptions of and responses to risk. Much of the impetus (and certainly of the research funding) for work in relation to risk has stemmed from the involvement of government and business in attempts to introduce new technologies or new forms of management in areas where risks are involved. Research thus confronts the puzzles and frustrations that arise when people do not respond to risks and to expert judgements and advice in the ways predicted by theory— whether the theory rests on claims about rational action, on assumptions about the culture of different groups, or on other factors. One of the most important contributions to social psychological work arises from the developing ideas of Slovic, driven to a considerable extent by the problems in understanding popular responses to dam and nuclear power projects and by the politicized contests surrounding smoking in the USA (1999). In Europe, the issues of GM food, of transport, of reforms to health care systems, and of nuclear waste disposal have all provoked substantial bodies of research (Royal Society 1992, 1997). These practical concerns have also led risk research in new directions, concerned with trust in government and in experts (raising issues about democratic institutions), with issues of responsibility and with the extent to which research in this field is a tool for popular empowerment or an additional mechanism for official management (Cabinet Office Strategy Unit 2002).

The impact of the theoretical problems experienced in different disciplines and of the practical demands made on risk researchers has been twofold. The trajectory of academic development has led to increased awareness of the limitations and difficulties of research confined within one approach. This has led to greater interest in interdisciplinarity and in hybrid approaches. At the same time there has been stronger recognition of the interaction between academic research, government policymaking, and the practical issues that confront businesses concerned to pursue innovations across a wide range of fields. The outcome has been an escalation of interest in research dealing with topics from crime to the mass media, from public policy regulation to intimate family relations, from employment to the environment, and seeking to situate understanding of the issues within a broader intellectual framework. This book is designed to provide convenient access to this growing body of work and to recent theoretical developments.

We now move on to describe the plan of the book.

The Structure of the Book

Chapters 2 and 3 set out the contributions of different disciplines to risk research, dwelling mainly on psychology and sociology. Chapter 2 examines the main areas of work during the past half century. In Chapter 3, the most recent developments, currently attracting excitement, are discussed. The following ten chapters each focus on a particular field of research and follow a common structure of four main sections:

- A review of the context in which work in the field is situated;
- An account of how risks and uncertainties are understood in the area and why the particular perspective has emerged;

11

- Discussion of the main research themes that have been the focus of work during the past decade; the main findings of recent work; and
- The emerging problems and issues which are the focus of current attention.

In this way, it is possible for the reader to trace developments and to look at how interest has shifted between topic areas over time.

The key themes to emerge from the discussion of risk topics in the chapters fall into six categories:

- A rapid expansion of interest in and awareness of risk;
- A shift from reliance on the perspectives of experts to much greater recognition of the independent value of lay perspectives in understanding of risk;
- An associated move from rational actor to more socially informed approaches;
- Theoretical and related methodological developments, concerned to reconcile realist and constructivist approaches and quantitative and discursive methods;
- A shift away from approaches directed at the elimination or reduction of risk towards interest in the management of risks as they can be identified; and
- New policy approaches which empower or (from another perspective) subject individuals by shifting more of the responsibility for coping with risk from state to citizen, running parallel to greater sophistication in identifying risk factors and in the regulation and governance of particular groups.

First and most obvious, all the chapters chart a rapid expansion of interest in the theme of risk across all the areas examined. Issues have become more complex as a result of technical innovations (e.g. in the environmental field, Chapter 5, and in the problems to be regulated, Chapter 10). At the same time, there is much greater awareness of the difficulties faced by existing social institutions in managing risk, whether in relation to crime (Chapter 4), securing satisfactory employment (Chapter 9), or health (Chapter 8).

Second, approaches which focus on the authority of experts and government have tended to be supplanted by interest in the perspectives of ordinary people, particularly those directly affected by the issue. This is most evident in areas such as crime (Chapter 4) and public policy

(Chapters 13 and 10), where the emphasis was initially on the state imposing particular regimes or implementing particular approaches. Research
focused on the technical value and the public acceptability of these
measures. This perspective has tended to be replaced by a broad range
of approaches which share much greater interest in the individual level
of understanding of risk, both in relation to the processes whereby people
assume responsibility for their behaviour, for example in avoiding crime
(Chapter 4) or in managing health and illness (Chapter 8), and in relation
to issues of trust, empowerment, and participation (see Chapter 5 on the
environment and technical developments).

Outside the immediate field of state regulation (Chapters 13 and 10),
research into family and intimacy (Chapter 7) or diversity (Chapter 11)
or into media and communication (Chapter 12) has moved away from
an understanding of the relevant processes as essentially 'top-down', so
that people tend to follow culturally prescribed roles or behave as passive
recipients of information about risks. These areas are now much more
likely to be investigated as interactive or plural, so that different groups
construct and follow norms and actively choose and assess media messages. This process is discussed in Chapter 6 on *Everyday Life and Leisure
Time*. Here the active construction of risk is conceptualized through the
notion of a continuing interactive 'dialogue' between expert and lay
understanding. The shift in approach has led to advances in research
methods, and the chapter also charts the growing interest in qualitative
and especially ethnographic methods as appropriate tools to study these
issues.

Expert authority is often seen as expressing scientific knowledge and
reasoned judgement. Initial work on risk responses often operated in
rational actor terms which privileged officially sanctioned expertise. The
third development, paralleling the move to value lay perspectives, has
been a shift away from the rational actor standpoint. Thus, approaches
to crime which stress the discipline appropriate to a logic of rational
deterrence have tended to be supplanted by those which focus more
on identifying risks and then on devising rehabilitation and training
programmes within the criminal justice system (Chapter 4). In analyses
of personal and family life, more attention is paid to the role of new
patterns of obligation and of 'gendered moral rationalities' in managing
relationships, as separation and re-partnering give rise to a more complex
set of interconnection (Chapter 7). In risk regulation research, the perspective that stressed technical issues of risk and the processes appropriate to
improving safety has been succeeded by one that also includes the social

factors that influence how people behave in managing systems to gain higher levels of security (Chapter 10).

Fourth, there are new developments at a theoretical level, with implications for research methods that have not yet been fully realized. Many researchers have grown uneasy with simple distinctions between realist and constructivism approaches to risk, the former emphasizing risk as external to and independent from social factors, and the latter seeing the categorization of particular activities or phenomena as risky as itself a product of social processes (Chapters 2 and 6). This leads to conceptualizations which seek to reconcile both approaches. In work on the role of the media in communication and everyday life, researchers increasingly analyse the way in which people reflect on and interact with the messages they receive in constructing and modifying their own recognition of risk (Chapter 12). In areas such as crime (Chapter 4), or health risks (Chapter 8), the official agenda is mediated through popular responses.

The importance of the context of the rapid social changes discussed earlier in this chapter to the intellectual processes which have directed risk research is also significant. In many areas an important factor in research has been the way that, just at the same time as people have become more aware of risks, it has been recognized that the capacity of the state or other authorities to meet them has been curtailed by the pressures of globalization and by the reduced willingness of citizens to accept direction from the authorities. The outcome is a tendency to move towards analyses which consider risk not so much as something to be controlled and removed, but as part of the context in which people live, and to which they must adjust in their everyday activities, in family life, in health behaviour, in seeking work or in planning retirement, and in relation to ethnic diversity or sexuality (Chapters 6–9, and 11).

These theoretical developments raise two important issues in relation to methodology. The first is a shift towards detailed case studies of particular risk issues (the BSE crisis, mobile phones, street crime, unsafe sexual practices, nanotechnology, and MSR vaccination) in order to chart the interactions between the objective and constructed dimensions of risk. Problems then arise in linking the particular to the more general theoretical level of accounts of the social changes which underlie current interest in risk issues. Chapters 6 on everyday life and 12 on communication discuss the way in which the 'cultural turn' in sociology has exacerbated the problem of relating the 'grand narrative' to the everyday. In Chapter 3 some of the recent approaches to this problem are discussed.

These include biographical methodologies, which situate the particular risk issues along an individual's life course, and combined quantitative and qualitative research, which seek to link together the insights into individual understanding of problems derived from interactive interviewing with the generalizability of large, random-sample structured surveys.

The *fifth* area of interest concerns the policy relevance of research. The trajectory of development in a number of areas has been, broadly speaking, from risk reduction to risk management, as mentioned above. Policymakers increasingly recognize that the elimination of all risk is an unlikely goal, and focus on systems that more accurately identify and categorize risks and provide programmes for handling and reducing them (see Chapters 4, 8, 10, and 13). This point corresponds to the argument at the more theoretical level that risks are to be seen much more as part of the way that people construct their social environment, rather than as external and objective. In penal policy and in social services (Chapters 4 and 13), the process of risk assessment is central to the way in which offenders or members of different need groups are classified and managed. Interest in risk factors in epidemiology and in the management of health problems plays a similar role (Chapter 8). Assessment leads to recommendations for custodial or non-custodial sentences, surveillance through probation, provision of home help services, programmes of health visitor contact to check on children's development, and so on (see Kemshall 2002; Warner and Gabe 2004).

Sixth, a number of commentators have suggested that risk has become a central aspect of governance (for example, Dean, H. 1999; O'Malley 2000). This develops in two directions: through the growing individualization of risk and risk responsibilities in the discourse of official statements (mentioned in the second point above), and through the emphasis on regulation and control as policymakers have lost confidence in exclusive reliance on rational actor approaches for changing the behaviour of problematic groups and as new mechanisms for directing such risk-management more accurately towards social problems have developed (the fifth point).

From the first perspective, individuals are encouraged, for example, through the counselling on job prospects included in the New Deal for young unemployed people (Chapter 9), through the lifestyle advice in health promotion programmes (Chapter 8), or through the provision of information on the pension level to which they are currently entitled (Chapter 13), to understand in more detail the risks they currently face. This is understood as both empowering, through the provision of transparent information, and transferring responsibility from a more 'hollowed-out' state to more active citizens. A number of the chapters (9, 11, 13) express concerns that a discourse of individualized responsibility in a context in which inequalities remain stubbornly stratified implies a bleak future for the most vulnerable groups.

Other concurrent developments form part of a more regulatory approach. Examples are the move to prioritize punishment over rehabilitation and to fine-tune the range of custodial and non-custodial alternatives for different groups in relation to crime (Chapter 4); the careful distinctions in mental health policy between those who suffer mental health problems appropriate for community treatment and those which require incarceration (Chapter 8; Rose 1990, 1999); or the use of a complex range of tax-credits for different groups of low-paid workers coupled with lower, closely monitored benefits for unemployed people judged capable of work and more strictly targeted, more generous disability support for those who are not, as part of a 'welfare to work' strategy (Chapter 11).

Conclusion

Risk has moved up the agenda of social science as a result of developments in institutions and in culture. New approaches in research and in analysis have resulted. In the following two chapters we examine the development of risk research and the issues that are currently at the top of the agenda in more detail. We then go on, in the rest of the book, to demonstrate the way in which realization of the significance of risk issues have transformed academic work across a wide range of areas. Risk has become seen much more as a complex matter, involving both real external factors and social construction processes which privilege particular accounts of risk and of how it emerges in people's lives. This has led to the pursuit of richer, more cross-disciplinary approaches, and more hybrid methods of research. It has also led to the recognition of risk as both the object of policy, in the sense that risk reduction is a goal aimed at in a wide range of areas, and an increasingly important ingredient within policy, as the management of continuing risks replaces risk elimination as the major policy concern.

Risk is now at the centre of social science, for good reasons. We hope this book will provide an informed, helpful, and up-to-date introduction to the concept and serve as a guide and directory to the main currents of work within the field.

References

Adams, J. (1995). *Risk*. London: UCL Press.

Althaus, C. (2005). 'A Disciplinary Perspective on the Epistemological Status of Risk', *Risk Analysis*, 25(3): 567–88.

Baker, T. and Simon, J. (2002). *Embracing Risk*. Chicago, IL.: Chicago University Press.

Beck, U. (1998). 'Organised Irresponsibility: Reply to Frank Furedi', *Prometheus*, Winter.

Boyne, R. (2003). *Risk*. Milton Keynes: Open University Press.

Cabinet Office Strategy Unit (2002). *Risk: Improving Government's Capability to Handle Risk and Uncertainty*, Strategy Unit Report, November 2002, COSU, London.

Casey, B. (2004). 'The OECD Jobs Strategy and the European Employment Strategy', *Journal of European Public Policy*, 10(3): 329–52.

Chambers (1946). *Chambers' Twentieth Century Dictionary*. Edinburgh: W and R Chambers Ltd.

Dean, H. (1999). 'Managing Risk by Controlling Behaviour', in Peter Taylor-Gooby (ed.), *Risk, Trust and Welfare*. London: Macmillan.

Dean, M. (1999). *Governmentality: Power and Rule in Modern Society*. London: Thousand Oaks.

EU (1997). 'Employment Agenda for the Year 2000', Paper from the *Luxembourg Council* meeting, EU.

——— (2000). *On the Precautionary Principle*, Com 2000/1, EU, Brussels.

——— (2005). *Lisbon Action* Plan, SEC 192.

Ewald, F. (2002). ' "The return of Descartes" Malicious Demon: An Outline of a Philosophy of Precaution' (trans. by Stephen Utz)', in T. Baker and J. Simon (eds.), *Embracing Risk: The Changing Culture of Insurance and Responsibility*. Chicago, IL: University of Chicago Press, pp. 273–301.

Foucault, M. (1991). 'Governmentality', in G. Burchell et al. (eds.), *The Foucault Effect*. London: Harvester Wheatsheaf, pp. 87–104.

Furedi, F. (2002). *The Culture of Fear*. London: Continuum Press.

——— (2005). *The Politics of Fear*. London: Continuum Press.

Gallant, T. (1991). *Risk and Survival in Ancient Greece*. Cambridge: Polity.

Garnsey, P. (1988). *Famine and Food Supply in the Graeco-Roman World: responses to risk and crisis*. Cambridge: Cambridge University Press.

Giddens, A. (1999). *Runaway World: How Globalisation is Shaping our Lives*. London: Profile Books.

Hargreaves-Heap, S., Hollis, M., Lyons, B., Sugden, R., and Weale, A. (1992). *The Theory of Choice*. Oxford: Blackwell.

Harkin, J. (1998). 'In Defence of the Modernist Project', *British Journal of Educational Studies*, 46: 3.

Kemshall, H. (2002). *Risk, Social Policy and Welfare*. Buckingham, UK: Open University Press.

Knight, F. (1921). *Risk, Uncertainty and Profit*. Boston, MA: Houghton Mifflin.

Levidow, L., Carr, S., and Wield, D. (1999). 'Regulating Biotechnical Risk', *Journal of Risk Research*, 2(4): 307–24.

Lewis, J. (2001). *The End of Marriage? Individualism and Intimate Relations*. Cheltenham, UK: Edward Elgar.

Luhmann, N. (1993). *Risk: a Sociological Theory*. New York: A. de Gruyter.

Lyng, S. (2005). 'Sociology at the Edge: Social Theory and Voluntary Risk Taking', in Stephen Lyng (ed.), *Edgework. The Sociology of Risk-Taking*. London: Routledge, pp. 17–49.

Myles, J. (2002). 'A New Social Contract for the Elderly?' in G. Esping-Andersen, D. Gallie, A. Hemerijk, and J. Myles (eds.), *Why we Need a New Welfare State*. Oxford: Oxford University Press.

Mythen, G. (2004). *Ulrich Beck: A Critical Introduction to the Risk Society*. London: Pluto Press.

O'Malley, P. (2000). 'Risk societies and the government of crime', in M. Brown and J. Pratt (eds.), *Dangerous Offenders*. London: Routledge.

—— (2000). 'Uncertain Subjects: Risks, Liberalism and Contract', *Economy and Society*, 29(4): 460–84.

—— (2004). *Risk, Uncertainty and Government*. London: Glasshouse Press.

Pearce, F. (2001). 'Bangladesh's Arsenic Poisoning: Who is to Blame?', *UNESCO Courier*, January.

Pidgeon, N., Kasperson, R., and Slovic, P. (2003). *The Social Amplification of Risk*. Cambridge: Cambridge University Press.

Pierson (2001). *The New Politics of the Welfare State*. Oxford: Oxford University Press, pp. 410–56.

Presidency Conclusions (2000). *Lisbon European Council 23/24 March 2000*, SE 100/00, EN, European Communities.

Rose, N. (1990). *Governing the Soul*. London: Routledge.

—— (1999). *Powers of Freedom*. Cambridge: Cambridge University Press.

Royal Society (1992). *Study Group on Risk Assessment, Analysis, Perception and Management*. London: Royal Society.

—— (1997). *Science Policy and Risk*. London.

Sahlins, M. (1974). *Stone Age Economics*. London: Tavistock.

Scharpf, F. (1997). 'European Integration, Democracy and the Welfare State', *Journal of European Public Policy*, 4(1): 18–36.

Schumpeter, J. (1976). *Capitalism, Socialism and Democracy*. London: Allen and Unwin.

Simon, H. (1987). 'Bounded Rationality', in J. Eatwell, M. Millgate, and P. Newman (eds.), *The New Palgrave: A Dictionary of Economics*. London: Macmillan.

Slovic, P. (1999). 'Trust, Emotion, Sex Politics and Science—Surveying the Risk Assessment Battlefield', *Risk Analysis*, 19(4): 689–701.

——(2001). *The Perception of Risk*. London: Earthscan.

Taylor-Gooby, P. (2004). *New Risks, New Welfare*. Oxford: Oxford University Press.

Warner, J. and Gabe, J. (2004). 'Risk and Liminality in Mental Health Social Work', *Health, Risk and Society*, 6(4): 387–99.

Wharton, F. (1992). 'Risk Management: Basic Concepts and General Principles', in J. Ansell and F. Wharton (eds.), *Risk Analysis, Assessment and Management*. Chichester, UK: John Wiley.

2

Risk as an Interdisciplinary Research Area

Jens O. Zinn and Peter Taylor-Gooby

Risk issues initially attracted attention as the growing complexity of technical processes and enterprises generated interest in practical problems of risk management. Two factors—the realization that accidents and errors were not simply technical issues, and the increased opposition of members of the public to innovations—directed attention to psychological and sociological approaches to risk. As theoretical and empirical work developed, researchers from different perspectives recognized the importance of the sociocultural embeddedness of risk perceptions. This chapter discusses the variety and complexity of risk issues and the value of the various approaches.

The chapter starts by examining the established procedures of statistical-probabilistic risk calculation in three main areas: insurance, of technical risks, and toxicological and epidemical risks in health and illness. Risks from this perspective are concerned with the extent to which objective hazards can be managed through insurance, prevention, and reduction, in relation, for example, to the reliability of technical processes, the deterioration of machines, the probability of industrial accidents, or the effectiveness of medicine or medical treatment. These strategies are likely to be successful so far as risks and impacts can be specified and a value-consensus on the acceptable level of risk exists.

However, risk decisions involve issues other than technical management. Uncontrollable malfunctions like the Three Mile Island nuclear power plant incident (near Harrisburg in 1979) or the catastrophic accidents in Bhopal (1984) or Chernobyl (1986) revealed the limitations of risk-management systems. In addition, evidence about the ways in which people actually deal with risks indicated the weakness of common research assumptions. Initially, researchers treated responses to existing risks (e.g. traffic accidents, smoking, and drinking) as a benchmark for the acceptability of new risks. Similar assumptions were applied to the introduction of new technologies (Starr 1969). However, it became obvious that people treat established and novel risks in very different ways. A further point is that public concern about the risks attending technical innovation in a wide range of fields, from food safety to nuclear power, from new medicines to fuel additives, and from mobile phones to air pollution raised difficult issues about acceptable risk levels for policymakers.

As a result, researchers became more interested in peoples' perceptions of and decisions about risky issues. Whilst behavioural economists and cognitive psychologists sought to establish universal laws of human decision-making, risk research in the narrower sense examined the problem of public perception of risks through a psychometric paradigm. This approach aims to understand how risk perception is influenced by the characteristics of risks as well as by socio-structural factors. Optimistic expectations that this work would find more or less stable patterns in perceptions and responses, which would allow researchers to predict and to explain risk acceptance and which could be used for decision-making by politicians and business, were not fulfilled. Another stream of research in this area that has attracted more attention recently approaches risk responses by assuming that people interpret their world through 'mental models'.

Researchers inspired by psychological and social psychological perspectives have attempted to integrate different approaches, mainly those concerned with risk perception and risk communication, into an ambitious *Social Amplification of Risk Framework* (Pidgeon, Kasperson, and Slovic 2003). This enterprise built on the assumption that risk perception is mainly determined by risk communication through the media and other routes. Examination of the way these processes work can then explain the amplification or attenuation of risk concerns. However, the model has proved to have weak predictive ability.

Further research indicated that the public framework of risk perception is a complex and socioculturally diverse mixture of stable and unstable patterns. As a result, the more individualistic approaches have tried to integrate sociocultural accounts of risk perception into their models. Simultaneously, sociocultural and more general sociological approaches have attracted attention.

The prelude to the sociological contribution to the risk debate was the 'expert-layman' controversy. In controversies between local laypeople and experts on such issues as how to assess the impact of large-scale industrial accidents, the authorities often found the rejection of official expertise frustrating. Sociological and, increasingly, psychological approaches support the recognition that laypeople's knowledge systems also offer valid interpretations of risk.

One assumption has been that the ways in which people perceive and respond to risk are significantly determined by the social organization or group to which they are attached and their position in it. In later cultural approaches, risk perceptions are often understood as linked to the individual's social identity. Others assume that the current explosion of interest in risk in public discourse is a systematic problem associated with the stage of development of modern societies. The risk society, reflexive modernization approach argues that growing uncertainties have to be accepted, because they can only be managed and not eliminated. In another tradition, risk awareness is interpreted chiefly as the product of society itself. The dominance of a new style of government which shifts risks and responsibility to the subject is responsible for the preoccupation with risk issues.

Statistical-Probabilistic Concepts of Risk

The development of statistical methods to calculate probabilities supported the rapid spread of risk ideas across a wide range of areas. Initially applied in the concept of insurance, it spread into technical risk calculation in an industrializing society and into other domains, including, for example, the estimation of the effects of treatments and lifestyles on health and illness, or the assessment of pension benefits.

All these applications of the idea of risk rest on statistical-probabilistic calculation. A central requirement for the successful calculation of risk is that expected gains and losses can be transformed into an objective measure (most prominent in economics and technical approaches)—for example, money, life expectancy, or, in epidemic and toxicological approaches, death rates. In this way risk can be understood as an objective entity (risk is understood to equal the probability of an occurrence multiplied by the extent of damage) which can be calculated with the help of probability theory.

Insurance

Insurance initially developed at the close of the Middle Ages as a method for managing the risks of trade. Merchants sought to guard against insolvency in the event of losing a ship. The loss was calculated as the value of a cargo, and estimates of the probability of loss based on experience. The quality of risk estimation depends on experience of previous losses. As long as past experience can be applied to the future, insurance is a feasible solution.

In a changing world with an uncertain future, insurance companies need reserves for unexpected events. They are sensitive to shifts in probabilities, and are unable to manage risks where predictions of the future entail a high degree of uncertainty. Examples would be a rapid and unforeseen increase in flooding, or the problems involved in the nuclear industry, where technology is innovative, experience limited, and the possible costs enormous.

Technical Risk Analysis

The point of origin for technical risk research was concern with the controllability, safety, and reliability of technical systems and processes, and with the reasons and outcomes of failures in the context of the rapid expansion of technical innovation during industrialization. Technical risk analysis aims to make a process or technique more reliable and secure. From this perspective, researchers need to develop the necessary routines and techniques in order to identify vulnerabilities and eliminate them in order to reduce the final risk to an acceptable level. The approach is typically based on the principle of cost efficiency, so that the option with the best balance of risk and cost is chosen.

Comprehensive risk analysis and evaluation developed from the middle of the ninteenth century onwards, particularly in major industrial enterprises and the defence industry. Through 'Operations Research' and 'Systems Analysis', an independent stream of research to estimate risk (risk assessment) was established, drawing on a purely technical and economical approach. Typical methods are the analysis of hypothetical accidents, models and scenarios of possible accidents, cost-benefit analysis, probabilistic estimation of safety and credibility, and quantitative risk estimation. This strategy aims to control the uncertainties and insecurities which go along with the application of new techniques (Banse 1996: 31). The approach works well in many cases but also shows systematic deficiencies which may trigger public concerns about new developments.

Epidemiological and Toxicological Risk Analysis

Risk estimations are also relevant to medical contexts. Epidemiological and toxicological research estimates how factors such as lifestyle or diet influence the probability of falling ill (e.g. the connection between smoking and cancer), or whether particular medical treatments significantly reduce the symptoms of an illness. Other aspects concern the probability and seriousness of side effects from a medicine and whether these are acceptable compared with the risk of illness.

  The whole logic of modern orthodox medicine rests on the direction of treatment to tackle the identified causes of symptoms, to produce objectively measurable improvements. This approach was central to the development of scientific medicine, supplanting the former plurality of magical and philosophical belief systems. However, problems may arise. New illnesses with unclear symptoms and no certain treatment strategies, as well as acknowledgement that some illnesses cannot be cured at all, promoted patients' engagement with alternative approaches (Bury 2001). Their involvement is accompanied by the increasing influence of competing more holistic knowledge systems, such as acupuncture or homeopathy, and by new approaches which seek to define health in terms of positive well-being, rather than the absence of illness.

The Crisis of the Statistical-Probabilistic Approach to Risk

A rational and objective approach to risk calculation was successful as long as it was applied to risks where the outcomes could be ascribed, the expected harms, losses, or damages could be measured, and causes and results controlled and isolated. It was sometimes not fully understood that the probability and extent of losses can only be estimated over groups of events and do not strictly apply to individual cases. This approach encountered problems with innovative and large-scale technologies where risks have changed not only quantitatively but also qualitatively. In several other domains the risk logic also came under pressure.[1] The potential threats as well as the growing uncertainty regarding ignorance and knowledge of possible outcomes were prefigured in the Windscale reactor fire in 1957 and attracted growing public attention during the 1970s and 1980s. The accidents mentioned in the first section (including Bhopal, where a gas release from the Union Carbide plant killed more than 2,000 people immediately and many more in the following years, and Chernobyl, with uncounted deaths, injuries, and illnesses caused by contamination) showed the limits of current approaches to risk. The Challenger Space Shuttle accident in 1986 brought home the uncertainties inherent in advanced technology. Perhaps more important than any technical shortcomings of the statistical approach is the fact that the public response to these disasters is a growing suspicion of technical innovations and developments.

These new risks have qualities and dimensions which violate many of the assumptions of risk calculation. They tend no longer to be geographically, regionally, or nationally restricted, but are global. They are complex and increasingly entangled with different areas. New technical risks share the characteristics of catastrophes. The potential material, and financial and personal damage can hardly be estimated and may extend to the elimination of all life on earth. They are mainly invisible and inaccessible by direct means. They produce long-lasting outcomes, and are difficult to determine, and the effects cannot easily be reversed. Not all of these factors are absolutely new. Some were shared by past risks, such as plague or crop failure. It is the extensive public awareness of the new risks that brings home these characteristics in a way that is qualitatively different in its cultural impact.

The disasters and accidents mentioned above graphically illustrate the shortcomings of scientific, technical, and formal strategies in controlling complex technical systems. These failures direct attention to the question of how complex organizations can be managed safely. A series of studies has shown how the rapid development of management systems intended to reduce the scope for disaster often in fact increases it, because complexity introduces greater uncertainty (Perrow 1984). Further work shows how risks which conflict with the range of outcomes expected within an organizational culture may not be effectively tackled (Turner 1978; Pidgeon and O'Leary 2000). Economic and political pressure can also influence an organization's safety culture (Vaughan 1996).

In some fields, the characteristics of new risks make adequate analysis through probability estimations virtually impossible. If we still use such approaches, the extent of subjective weightings and valuations has to be taken into account. Scientifically developed long distance planning and probability risk analyses pursue the successive adaptation of technical systems to situational necessities (e.g. more restrictive safety regulation as a response to accidents). Hypothetical assumptions substitute for practical knowledge (models, ideals, and reductions of complexity), and empirical knowledge is replaced by probability assumptions. Tests of the assumptions cannot be applied, and experiments and observations cannot be repeated adequately. The potential damages and the probability of their occurrence cannot[2] be determined and reduced by the usual strategies of learning by trial and error (Banse 1996: 34). Even though risk calculation in some areas was eroded by uncertainty and estimates were open to interpretation by different scientists, the real crisis of the technical-rational paradigm resulted from a separate socio-political development. In many cases in which the potential damage is irreversible, growing numbers of the public will not in fact accept any probability of risk, however small (Luhmann 1993: 2). Examples are nuclear energy, vaccination resistance, and genetically modified food. Many experts were astonished at public resistance to comparatively small new risks, in contrast to the acceptability of much higher everyday risks (such as those associated with road transport or smoking) without even questioning the dangers. The understanding of the public as 'irrational' was widespread, and gave new impetus to further research on responses to significant political decisions.

The Problem of Predicting the Acceptability of Risk

Politicians and other decision-makers have to act on the basis of available knowledge, even though this knowledge may be limited. The central problem is the acceptability of decisions, rather than the resolution of technical questions. With the shift from technical problems to the questions of acceptability and the prediction of public response, social and psychological issues move to the fore in risk research. How urgent this question had become for technical risk research may be illustrated by the fact that the first attempt to deal with the problem was by a leading engineer turned academic.

Starr, former president of the Atomic Division of Rockwell International, analysed popular responses to risk in a way intended to be of use to decision-makers (Krohn and Krücken 1993: 26). In his lecture *What is our society willing to pay for safety?*, the findings are phrased in precise, statistical terms: the public 'is willing to accept "voluntary" risks roughly 1,000 times greater than "involuntary" risks'; tends to use risk of death as a "psychological yardstick"; and acceptability "appears to be crudely proportional to the third power" of expected benefits' (1969: 1237). He compares the risks of nuclear power with the level of risks associated with the existing conventional power plants that most people apparently find acceptable. The lower risks for nuclear power (estimated at 1 in 200 as against 1 in 40), together with the expected gains, support his optimistic expectation of a high social acceptability of the new technology.

Critics of this approach commented on the equation of acceptable and accepted risks, the restriction to risk of death, the pecuniary calculation of costs and profits, and the focus on quantitative approaches to the exclusion of a qualitative dimension. They also pointed out that Starr derived people's preferences theoretically and not directly. This led to interest in the examination of people's actual risk perceptions, pursued through the psychometric paradigm of risk research.

How Do People Make Decisions and Perceive Risks?

The psychologists who criticized Starr (1969) referred to another stream of research which had already started to develop in decision-making research. This work was pursued mainly by cognitive psychologists, who originally experimented in laboratories with risk behaviour, examining gambling and risky choices. Referring to the economic model of rational action, behavioural economists and cognitive psychologists together examined how people deviate from theoretical assumptions. This interest resembles closely that of technicians and engineers who cannot understand why and how people deviate from what seems the best risk calculation for them, from a rational standpoint. Whilst risk management was, for technicians and engineers, principally a technical problem of calculation and public acceptance, from the perspective of behavioural economists and cognitive psychologists it was understood as a more general problem of decision-making. They were much more interested in the universal laws of decision-making than specific responses to technical innovations.

One stream of research sought to investigate the conceptual models of reality people construct, and how these models differ from those based on expert knowledge. Slovic and colleagues also worked from the assumption that laypeople's perceptions of risk were inadequate ('faulty perceptions of risk could be explained as a result of the cognitive limitations of human beings', Slovic, Fischhoff, and Lichtenstein 1977). They introduced, in response to Starr (1969), a new methodological approach to investigate risk perception, which became at the time the most influential approach in risk research, the 'psychometric paradigm'.

Behavioural Decision-Making

Since the assumptions of rationality seem to be inaccurate in many cases, economists had started to find out how people really decide or judge. Simon's early work on 'bounded rationality' (1957) and further examinations in behavioural economics led Tversky and Kahneman (1974) to the conclusion 'that the deviations of actual behaviour from the normative model are too widespread to be ignored, too systematic to be dismissed as random error, and too fundamental to be accommodated by relaxing the normative system. We conclude from these findings that the normative and descriptive analyses cannot be reconciled' (quoted in Renn et al. 2000: 43). The central finding of Tversky and Kahneman (1974: 35) showed that 'people rely on a limited number of heuristic principles which reduce the complex tasks of assessing probabilities and predicting values to simpler judgemental operations.' Even though these heuristics are in general useful, they sometimes lead to severe and systematic errors. The range of heuristics includes *representativeness, availability, anchoring*, and *adjustment*.

People tend to compare issues with others by superficial indicators assumed to indicate whether an issue belongs to a specific group with corresponding characteristics (representativeness) (Tversky and Kahneman 1974: 36). They often judge the frequency or probability of an event by the ease with which such issues can be brought to mind (availability). 'For example, one may assess the risk of heart attack among middle-aged people by recalling such occurrences among one's acquaintances' (Tversky and Kahneman 1974: 42f.). However, availability is also influenced by factors such as media coverage rather than the frequency of the event itself. This heuristic may produce systematic biases. Another important heuristic shows that judgements are anchored to an initial value, which is then adjusted according to present circumstances (Kahneman, Slovic, and Tversky 1982), so that relative judgements depend crucially on the respective starting points.

Another central result in the field of decision-making is the *framing effect*. Although the concept of rationality assumes that the same problem should always lead to the same result, even though the contexts differ, the formulation (framing) of a problem influences the judgement. How decision-makers frame a problem is partly influenced by the formulation of the problem and by the norms, habits, and personal characteristics of the decision-maker. For example, a problem can be presented as a gain (200 of 600 threatened people will be saved) or as a loss (400 of 600 threatened people will die). In the first case people tend to adopt a 'gain frame', generally leading to risk aversion, and in the latter people tend to adopt a 'loss frame', generally leading to risk-seeking behaviour (Tversky and Kahneman 1981).

A number of criticisms of this research have been made. The experiments were conducted in laboratories under artificial conditions. The subjects had limited information and were under strict time pressures. They may therefore deviate systematically from the real life situations where people already have relevant experiences or can ask others for help and advice. This approach shares with Starr the difficulty that little direct information about people's risk judgements in real life is employed.

At least two main strategies followed from this perspective. One tried to map out the ways in which people think and decide by qualitative experimental methods (*mental modelling*). The other approach, quite influential for risk research, is to simply ask people directly (*psychometric paradigm*).

The Psychometric Paradigm

Following Starr's work, the psychometric paradigm developed rapidly. It promised to give access to the understanding of public risk preferences which was urgently needed by politicians and other decision-makers. It also anticipated the identification of more or less stable factors in risk perception to which risk policy could refer. On this basis, it was hope that policy could be adapted to fit public attitudes and be made acceptable to a wider audience (Krohn and Krücken 1993: 28). The psychometric paradigm to risk perception was principally developed by the 'Decision Research Group' at the University of Oregon (Fischhoff et al. 1978, 1983; Slovic, Fischoff, and Lichtenstein 1982, 1984, 1985, cited in Rohrman and Renn, 2000, 17). Whilst Starr referred to *revealed preferences*, the psychometric paradigm aims at *expressed preferences* which can be approached by standardized questionnaires (Fischhoff et al. 1978; Slovic, Fischoff, and Lichtenstein 1985). It assumes that 'risk is subjectively defined by individuals who may be influenced by a wide array of psychological, social, institutional and cultural factors ... many of these factors and their interrelationships can be quantified and modelled in order to illuminate the responses of individuals and their societies to the hazards that confront them' (Slovic 2001: xxiii). People were asked to rate the risks associated with various sets of hazardous activities, substances, and technologies, such as nuclear power, pesticides, bicycles, or sunbathing.

Also, judgements were recorded about other hazard characteristics which were hypothesized to account for risk perceptions. Several contextual factors were identified to affect the perceived seriousness of risks, for example, the expected number of fatalities (Renn 1983; Jungermann and Slovic 1993) and the catastrophic potential of a risk.

We follow the authoritative introduction to risk perception research of Rohrmann and Renn (2000). The work showed that risks with a low probability but high consequences would be perceived as more threatening than more probable risks with low or medium consequences (von Winterfeldt, John, and Borcherding 1981). Additionally, the perceived characteristics of the risk source or the risk situation, for example, the conviction of having personal control over a risk, familiarity with a risk, the perception of equitable sharing of both benefits and risks, and the opportunity to blame a person or institution responsible for the creation of a risky situation, influence evaluation (Slovic, Fischoff, and Lichtenstein 1981). Finally, beliefs and attitudes about the nature, consequences, history, and justifiability of a risk are also important (Otway and Thomas 1982; Renn and Swaton 1984).

Multivariate analysis of the relations between these variables showed that many of these risk characteristics are related to two or three underlying factors, which explain most of the variance of the judgements. Most important is the factor which represents characteristics which were related to the severity or dreadfulness of the hazard, such as terror, lack of controllability, involuntariness, or concern for future generations (the dreadfulness of risks factor). A second factor comprises knowledge-related characteristics such as whether the risk is observable, known, or new (the degree of knowledge and familiarity with the hazard factor). In some studies the number of exposed people represents another factor, but its influence is weak. This two-dimensional structure appears in a number of articles by Slovic, Fischhoff, and Lichtenstein (1980, 1981, 1985, 1986) and Slovic (1987, 1992). Several studies reproduce similar structures, at least for factors of dreadfulness and degree of knowledge (compare Renn and Rohrmann 2000: 29).

Further research demonstrates the complexity of attitude structures. National patterns of risk perception have been discovered, as well as regional and local differences (Fitchen, Heath, and Fessenden-Raden 1987; Fowlkes and Miller 1987). Social stratification (by gender, ethnicity, or social class) also influences the ways in which people perceive risks (Rohrmann 1999). The central result is the identification of a mixture of stable and unstable patterns of risk perception which generally make overall predictions of the acceptability of risks difficult (Fischhoff, Slovic, and Lichtenstein 1983; Slovic 1992: 127). However, the original hope of discovering the explicit risk estimations and preferences of the public and therefore the urgently needed knowledge for decision-making in politics and economy was disappointed. One of the reasons for this unsatisfying result might be that the study of risk perceptions within this paradigm condenses information which is based on average ratings. The influence of knowledge, values, and feelings, and of individual differences, receives little attention. Before findings could be generalized, the cultural context has to be explicated (Rohrmann 1999: 135–7), and this context is often dynamic rather than stable. Another limitation is the unclear connection between the measured risk perception and the practical response in everyday life (Wilkinson 2001).

The important message of the psychometric approach for risk is that for most (lay)people, risk is not just a combination of the size and the probability of damage, as proposed by the technical-statistical approach, but also has a social and subjective dimension.

Mental Modelling

'Mental modelling' approaches draw on the conventional concept of rational decision-making and the insights of the findings of cognitive psychology about heuristics and cognitive biases in laypeople's decision-making. The core idea is that people develop conceptual structures that correspond to risks as they understand them. These structures may be more or less accurate and may be mapped through psychological investigation. The approach seeks to examine how people construct accounts of reality.

Such models are useful in understanding the world, but as Fischhoff et al. (e.g. 1997) point out, may lead to error if they contain misunderstandings. This approach lends itself to the view that distinguishes expertise and ignorance, and the concern with improving communication to rectify the latter by ensuring that lay models correspond more closely to those of experts. For example: 'whatever the goal of communication, its designers need to address the mental models that recipients bring to it, that is, the pattern of knowledge, overly general understandings, and outright misconceptions that can frustrate learning' (Atman et al. 1994).

Models may typically be elicited through qualitative interviews and then compared with expert understandings in order to identify discrepancies (Weyman and Kelly 1999: 26). Quantitative studies can then be designed to explore the extent of these discrepancies and their relationship to knowledge and other factors. The approach draws on decision-making research on heuristics and biases, and on findings from psychometrics, but differs in the use of qualitative methods to elicit lay understandings of risk, including beliefs both corresponding to and differing from those of experts.

The potential of the approach was judged by the 1992 Royal Society report as 'highly promising' (Pidgeon et al. 1992: 121). A considerable amount of work has been carried out on lay models of specific risks (reviewed in Weyman and Kelly 1999: 12), much of it indicating that laypeople have simpler and more intuitive mental models than experts, often influenced by cognitive biases which appear to result from the use of simplifying heuristics. More recently, a number of writers have questioned the critique implicit in much of the work (and expressed in the Atman quotation above and by MacGregor and Fleming 1996) of the accuracy of lay mental models. One strand concerns the extent to which expert knowledge can be seen as unified and consistent and as having an objective status, in contrast to the presumed subjective nature of lay perceptions. Another raises the issue of the validity of lay knowledge of risk issues in the context in which most people encounter them. This approach effectively claims an equal status for lay understanding with that of experts whilst acknowledging differences in perspective. A third raises the issue of trust in expert accounts and how this contributes to acceptance of the authority of expertise (Weyman and Kelly 1999: 26).

Attempt to Integrate Different Approaches

Some psychologists, unsatisfied with the lack of a dynamic perspective in their models of risk perception and the under-examination of contextual factors, have developed the concept of social amplification. This approach combines risk perception and risk communication perspectives in such a way that other social psychological insights may be integrated in an overall theoretical framework. The social amplification approach (SARF) developed by the Clark University group (Kasperson et al. 1988; Renn et al. 1992) is an ambitious attempt 'to construct a framework which unifies understanding of risk-perception and -communication' (Pidgeon, Kasperson, and Slovic 2003: 2). The point of origin is the assumption that most of our knowledge comes at second hand, and is acquired by communication—mainly understood as information given by the mass media. Risk messages are understood as signals emitted by social events and 'subject to predictable transformations as they filter through various social and individual amplification stations' (Pidgeon, Kasperson, and Slovic 2003: 15).

The first stage of the basic model identifies several social processes which influence risk perception. These include the operation of the channels through which information is disseminated (or not), the role of social institutions in modifying signals, individual factors (e.g. the use of the cognitive heuristics identified by Tversky and Kahneman), and social and institutional behaviour, such as protest actions, or political processes within parliament or public enquiries. In the second stage, 'risk messages' 'ripple out' through a widening range of social groupings from the individual to society as a whole. There is provision for feedback between the various first-stage processes, and it is in the operation of these processes and the interaction between them that amplification or attenuation of risk signals occurs. The established theories dealing with risk institutions, social systems, individual cognition, and so on provide understanding of the various individual processes. Thus, the approach links together existing work and provides a framework within which accounts of the processes which influence the way risk events are perceived and influence society, and in particular the way in which expert judgements fail to carry consistent conviction with the public, are located. Parallels can be drawn between SARF and work in other disciplines, for example, the sociological analysis of the diffusion of 'moral panics' as a process of 'deviance amplification' in the understanding of the 'mods and rockers' seaside riots (Cohen 2002; Murdock, Petts, and Horlick-Jones 2003).

The authors comment that existing research on risk signalling, communications and the mass media, organizational processes, imagery, and stigma contribute to the framework (Pidgeon, Kasperson, and Slovic 2003: 16–30). The approach is eclectic and interacts with other social sciences, especially sociology, in its interest in social institutions and processes, and increasingly with political science in the emerging awareness of how political factors facilitate or obstruct the impact of risk perceptions on policy (see Gowda 2003). However, the operation of ripple effects (which are of most importance in relation to public policy) is less well understood, and proponents argue that this is where more research is needed (Pidgeon, Kasperson, and Slovic 2003: 31–6).

The main criticisms of the framework concern its ontology and its account of social processes. It has also been criticized on the grounds that it is not a theory and does not generate testable hypotheses

(Wåhlberg 2001). This may miss the point, since the approach claims to offer an overall framework, which combines a range of disciplinary backgrounds and middle-range theories (of human cognition and communication, attitude change, the influence of mass media, and so on), rather than a tightly defined theory. It implicitly adopts the realist conception of risk that underlies all work that makes a strong objective, subjective distinction and 'lies at the core of the SARF foundation' (Rosa 2003: 62). This is challenged by those who adopt a more cultural approach and see risks as socially constructed at all levels. The main criticisms of the account of social processes concern the role of feedback, particularly in relation to the media, and the implicit account of power in society. Murdock and colleagues, drawing on the work of Bourdieu, point out that media reporting is not simply a one-way process. The complex interactions between individuals and the media in relation to risk events cannot simply be captured in the account offered in stage one of social amplification, drawing on an electronic engineering metaphor of signals and feedbacks (Petts, Horlick-Jones, and Murdock 2001: ch. 6; see also Murdock, Petts, and Horlick-Jones 2003: 158).

Sociological Approaches to Risk

Sociological theories approach risk questions mainly from the opposite direction to psychologists and economists, moving from societal institutional structures to the level of the individual, rather than the other way about. The main problems tackled from this perspective are the interweaving of culture and individual perception and responses to risk, and the way in which these factors change or develop over time.

The influence of sociological approaches to risk originates with the debate on the lay-expert division of knowledge. Many economists, psychologists, and decision-theory researchers set the objective or rational ideal as the standard for individual decision-making. The assumption was that experts would tend to follow this model whereas laypeople (as the research showed) do not. An alternative tradition in science studies has criticized the claim that experts and science in general always take an objective standpoint as a myth (in the context of risk, 'Wynne 1982; more generally, Latour and Woolgar 1979). The dismantling of positivistic accounts of science and their intrinsic hierarchical political impact on risk problems strengthened the view that citizens' understanding of risk has an equivalent validity and rationality to that of the accredited experts. It also supported a new approach to public responses to the new technologies, especially in the development of social movements opposed to new technologies, such as the nuclear industry, and the promotion of a more ecological lifestyle.

These public responses are explained from the sociological perspective in terms of sociocultural change. The new developments were initially examined, in the US context, through the *cultural approach* of Douglas and Wildavsky, as the result of sociocultural change affecting societal groups differently. In Germany, by contrast, Beck's approach through the concepts of *Risk Society* and *Reflexive Modernization* emphasizes the impact of a general shift within modernity caused by new risks as well as socio-structural changes. This perspective has gained ground rapidly and has also been developed in the UK, whilst the *systems theory* approach to risk, developed by Luhmann, is prominent only in Germany. In Britain, as in other Anglo-phone countries, another perspective has gained ground, explaining growing risk awareness in terms of a shift in how societies are governed or govern themselves. This *governmentality* approach (Foucault 1991) was imported from France and fitted very well the experience of free market liberalism from 1979 onwards.

Expert–Layman Controversy

Much early risk research assumed, either implicitly or explicitly, that scientific and professional knowledge is superior to that of laypeople or embodied in everyday life practices. The difference between lay and expert judgements about risks and uncertainties was explained in terms of limited knowledge and misunderstandings of reality. Despite the evidence that scientists are also influenced by heuristics and biases (e.g. Tversky and Kahneman 1974: 50), the assumption of an objective and superior scientific knowledge, which would lead to an optimum solution if only the confounding influence of policy, values, and ideologies could be discounted, was central to the early risk debate (Wynne 1982).

In accordance with the basic idea of a positivistic science, accidents such as those in nuclear power plants were regularly interpreted as caused by the imperfect behaviour of the staff responsible. This led to recommendations for improved staff selection and training. More recently, social studies of science have argued that objective positivistic knowledge can be illusory, and often serves to disguise social power enshrined as authority (Wynne 1982).

Consequently, the practical sociological contribution to the risk debate aims to acknowledge laypeople's knowledge, values, and cultural positions on the one hand and to show how expert knowledge is involved in social processes of knowledge production on the other. It fills the gap between those psychological approaches which interpret public responses mainly as deviations from correct solutions generated by science and the claims to objective and expert knowledge which ignore the social embeddedness of knowledge.

A key finding in relation to such activities as public participation exercises or the implementation of nuclear technology is that laypeople are not necessarily irrational, but pursue a specific form of knowledge and experience based on value systems which are culturally different from rather than inferior to those of experts. The research of Wynne was highly influential, especially in the UK. He pointed out that the laboratory knowledge of the experts fails repeatedly in attempts to transfer it to real life situations (Wynne 1982, 1987, 1992, 1996). He uses detailed empirical studies to show that experts have their own beliefs, epistemologically similar to laypeople's knowledge, although constructed by following scientific rules rather than through life experience. He showed, for example, that expert framing of the safety problem regarding the production and usage of pesticides was naïve. It assumed, for example, that 'pesticide manufacturing process conditions never varied so as to produce dioxin and other toxic contaminants of the main product stream; drums of herbicide always arrived at the point of use with full instruction intact and intelligible; in spite of the inconvenience, farmers and other users would comply with the stated conditions, such as correct solvents, proper spray nozzles, pressure valves and other equipment, correct weather conditions, and full protective gear' (Wynne 1992).

Wynne also examined the responses of Cumbrian sheep farmers to the claims of government scientists about the impact of radiation from the Chernobyl disaster, and more generally in accounts of the risks from agricultural chemicals (1992, 1996). He points out that the farmers felt themselves 'completely controlled by the exercise of scientific interpretation' (1996: 63) but developed a thorough-going scepticism of scientists pronouncements, because they were aware that the scientists made obvious errors. Official science failed to predict the course of the outbreak of radiation in ways which was financially devastating for the farmers, and made elementary and obvious mistakes in experiments and analysis. This was because they simply did not have the farmers' understanding of sheep behaviour and of local environmental conditions (1996: 65–7).

Subjective and sociocultural beliefs or frames of reference differ. People respond differently to risk and often deviate systematically from the simple assumptions of a generalized rationality which seeks to apply to all people in the same way. In this context, cultural aspects play an important role.

Sociocultural Approaches to Risk

The sociocultural perspective on risk was initially informed by the seminal anthropological work of Douglas (1963, 1966) and was further developed by Douglas (1985, 1992) and Douglas and Wildavsky (1982). A stream of work uses a quantitative perspective (Wildavsky and Dake 1990; Dake 1991; Dake and Wildavsky 1991) whilst another stream follows a qualitative approach (Rayner 1986; Bellaby 1990). In more recent qualitative work, the influence of the functionalistic perspective of Douglas and Wildavsky is supplanted by more descriptive approaches (Tulloch and Lupton 2003).

The core assumption of the cultural approach is that the individual's perception and response to risk can only be understood against the background of their embeddedness in a sociocultural background and identity as a member of a social group, rather than through individual cognition, as is proposed by mainstream economics and cognitive psychologists (Douglas and Wildavsky 1982: 6–7). Risk is interpreted as a socially constructed phenomenon although it has 'some roots in nature' (Thompson and Wildavsky 1982: 148). The different ways in which societies or specific social groups construct risks and dangers are understood as depending on their form of social organization (Douglas and Wildavsky 1982: 8). Douglas and Wildavsky explain the new awareness of risk and the rise of social movements opposing technical innovations in the 1980s through shifts in the organizational culture of society (which they call 'sectarian'), rather than by the occurrence of new risks. Complex historical changes have led to increased mobilization of citizen's organization opposing big government, big money, and market values (Douglas and Wildavsky 1982: 10–1).

Douglas and Wildavsky developed a framework for analysing social organization along the two dimensions of 'grid' and 'group'. Grid stands for the degree to which an individual's life is regulated or prescribed by the roles in a social group. It is high in hierarchical organizations and low in egalitarian organizations. The group dimension stands for the degree of identification with a particular group. It is strong when the individual is a member of a group and weak when the individual does not belong

(Douglas 1992: 192). The result is a four-category typology (Thompson, Ellis, and Wildavsky 1990: 62–6).

The cultural type of competition or individualism, typified by the market and entrepreneurial perspective on risk, interprets risk-taking as an opportunity to pursue personal goals in competition with others. Group cohesion is weak and the normative bonding into the group is low. In contrast, strong group incorporation and low hierarchy characterize the cultural type of egalitarianism or enclave (the earlier sectarian type). People belonging to this type emphasize cooperation and equality, and have a strong sense of solidarity. They tend to focus on the long-term effects of human activities and are more likely to abandon an activity than to take chances. A strong group cohesion and highly regulated social life are associated with hierarchy, or bureaucracy. Cultural types falling into this category rely heavily on rules and procedures as provided by social institutions to manage risks and uncertainties. The last type stands for isolation, fatalism, or atomized respectively stratified individuals which believe in hierarchies but do not identify with the hierarchy they belong to. They rely only on themselves and are very reluctant to accept risks imposed by others. Finally, some researchers have identified a fifth group, located between the others. Hermit or autonomous individuals do not belong to one of the specified types but can flexibly refer to each type, as long as it fits their personal aims and needs (see, for example, Rohrmann and Renn 2000: 34–5). The cultural approach has a major impact on risk research. A mainly quantitative perspective refers to risk perception approaches. Standardized measures for cultural values (worldviews) were developed (Dake 1991, 1992), assumed to correspond to group cultures. This concept of culture also influences the psychometric paradigm, which tries to integrate cultural aspects in their instrument (Slovic 2001).

The influence of cultural values on risk perception and responses is still controversial. Some studies suggest that other attitudes associated with risk sensitivity (specific fears in relation to the particular risk) explain by far the largest part of risk perception, whilst the heuristics and other variables stressed by psychometry (dread and customary risk) explain roughly half as much, and culture even less (Marris, Langford, and O'Riordan 1998; Sjöberg 2000). One problem is that such an approach interprets culture as an additional and independent, not as a general underlying factor. The evidence of dread, for example, is itself understood as strongly influenced by culture. Critics doubt whether cultural approaches can be successfully captured through structured questionnaires as developed by Dake (1991, 1992) or in general (Rippl 2002; Tansey 2004).

Besides the standardized quantitative stream of cultural theory, there is also research in a qualitative tradition which uses the grid/group scheme as a heuristic or a means out of charting sociocultural reality (e.g. Douglas and Calvez 1990). Some researchers argue that the ideal types are too schematic to grasp the complexity of social life (Funtowicz and Ravetz 1985; Johnson 1987). They also claim that the grid/group scheme is little help in understanding how the shift of risk perception, from one type to another, might take place (Bellaby 1990). More recently, research has been influenced by cultural studies. These approaches use the categories of post-structuralism and postmodernism to analyse experience of social change. The work of Tulloch and Lupton is influential (see *Risk and Everyday Life*, 2003). Douglas drew attention to the fundamental distinction between Self and Other running across cultures and interpretations of social contexts, and used it to provide an understanding of the multi-dimensionality of socially available semantics and perception of risk. The main concerns here are the different ways in which risk is understood by different people, how people construct their identities and membership of social (sub-) cultures referring to risk, how the understanding of risk is engaged in 'border crossings' between Self and Otherness, and how people interpret risks as positive Lupton and Tulloch 2002; Tulloch and Lupton 2003)[3] as well as sometimes negative. The concept of risk used in this tradition is a descriptive one ('real definition'), focusing on people's understanding of risk in the context of their everyday lives.

Risk Society and Reflexive Modernization

Beck's work on the *Risk Society* (1992) originally published in German (1986: *Risikogesellschaft*) was influential for theorizing in this field. It was complemented by further publications (1995: *Ecological Enlightenment*, 1999: *World Risk Society*) which respond to earlier criticisms. Several publications critically discuss the initial assumptions (Lash, Szerszynski, and Wynne 1996; Adam, Beck, and Van Loon 2000). The main thesis and controversies about a changing modernity are published in *Reflexive Modernization* (Beck, Giddens, and Lash 1994; Beck, Bonss, and Lau 2003). The growing risk-awareness and societal as well as individual responses to risk are interpreted from the perspective of the risk society thesis in a general framework of social change within modernity. The modern worldview emerged through the interaction of many factors: the critical and scientific spirit of the enlightenment, the technological advances of the European industrial revolution, and the social and political changes that followed the development of a working class, the continuing refinement of the division of labour, the expansion of an international system resting on sovereign nation states, and the political economy of national economic management in the interests of assured growth. Beck's thesis claims modernization undermines its own foundations. He identifies two central developments.

First, qualitatively new risks (or better: dangers, threats, and harms) produced as unforeseen and unintended side effects of industrialized modernity are emerging. A risk logic increasingly replaces the traditional logic of social class. Although some risks and risk-dimensions still follow class patterns (Beck 1992: 35), other and new risks concern people in a way that is relatively independent from their social status. New risks, for example, BSE, smog, radiation, climate change, genetically modified food, and ozone depletion, mainly follow logics of allocation other than those of social class. They are 'democratic' even though some might argue that money and status could partly help to deal with such risks or influence how they are perceived. Whilst these risks appear as unexpected side effects of industrialized modernity, they also cannot be solved easily on the basis of available knowledge. Their effects and causes are typically only partly understood, and science does not provide us with the necessary knowledge to manage them within the current policy framework. The typical strategy used to domesticate uncertainty in modernity, insurance, cannot be applied, it is claimed, since the necessary information on the probability and extent of damages is not available—the risks are too great and there is too little experience of them for prediction. Therefore, uncertainty becomes a fundamental experience of modernity where it was once successfully overcome by science and technique.

Second, understanding of social inequalities shifts from a collective social class to an individual level. Beck (Beck 1992: 91–2) starts out from the puzzle that 'the structure of social inequality in the developed countries displays an amazing stability' whilst 'the topic of inequality disappears almost completely from the agenda of daily life, of politics, and of scholarship'. 'During the past three decades, almost unnoticed by social stratification research, the social meaning of inequality has changed... Social groups lose their distinctive traits, both in terms of their self-understanding and in relation to other groups. They also lose their independent identities and the chance to become a formative political force' (Beck 1992: 100). 'Inequalities by no means disappear. They merely become redefined in terms of an individualization of social risks. The result is that social problems are increasingly perceived in terms of psychological disposition: as personal inadequacies, guilt feelings, anxieties, conflicts, and neuroses. There emerges, paradoxically, a new immediacy of individual and society, a direct relation between crises and sickness. Social crises appear as individual crises, which are no longer ... perceived in terms of their rootedness in the social realm' (1992: 100).

Since the allocation logic of risk does not follow the traditional class logic and the bonds to traditional social groups are weakened or dissolved, political mobilization tends to follow the logic of risk rather than of social class solidarity (1992: 35–6, 100).

The risk society approach claims that risks are real and also socially constructed. Referring to Latour (1993), Beck (1999: 146, 150) claims that risks or hazards are hybrids which are not accessible beyond their social construction but also affect the social. It is not possible to be only on the realist or constructivist side. Rather the distinction between realism and constructivism or nature and culture is seen as a modern idea of reality which never becomes real ('*We have never been modern*' as Latour puts it, 1993). This position can be understood as reconciliation between the strong opposition of realist and constructivist sides of risk, which is theoretically unsatisfying, even though still widely disseminated in risk discourse. Risk society themes have been taken up in the UK by Giddens. Adopting a different approach from that of Beck, who discusses individualization processes on the institutional level (Beck 1992: 128–9), Giddens (1991) pays greater attention to the operation of reflexive modernization at the individual level. This leads to a strong emphasis on the 'cultural turn' away from received authority and expertise and towards a citizenship of 'active trust', rather than taken-for-granted deference to accredited experts (1994). Giddens follows through the implications of a critical citizenry and a decline in the capacity of nation states to manage the political economy for the political order in the context of the 'Third Way' politics of New Labour in the UK (Giddens 1999).

In Giddens' view, the key cultural shift among the citizens of risk society is that individuals are more conscious of their social context and their own role as actors within it. Managing the risks of civilization becomes both a pressing issue and one that is brought home to individuals. At the same time however, confidence in experts and in accredited authorities tends to decline as people are more aware of the shortcomings of official decision-makers and of the range of alternative approaches to problems available elsewhere on the planet. The tendency to breakdown of an established traditional order in the life course provided by work, marriage, family, and community leads to greater individualization and increased uncertainty and anxiety. In this context, the individualized citizens of world risk society are increasingly conscious of the responsibility to manage the risks they perceive in their own lives, and, in this sense, 'self-create their own biographies'.

The risk society approach has been criticized both theoretically (Lash 1994; Alexander and Smith 1996; Lupton 1999; Elliott 2002; Boyne 2003) and on the basis of empirical evidence (Tulloch and Lupton 2003: 132). Rose (1996: 321) points out that Beck's claim 'the prevalence of a language of risk is a consequence of changes in the contemporary existential condition of humans and their world (Beck 1992)' may be misleading. A number of studies (e.g. Ewald 1986; O'Malley 2004: 179) show that risk emerged as a social category and as a concern for government in relation to social insurance at least as early as the nineteenth century (see also Dingwall 1999).

Further comments address the predominance of an individualized notion of identity and agency. Since Beck mainly argues on the institutional level and interprets institutional individualization as a process which can succeed or fail at the individual level, he pays too little attention to differences between social groups. Focusing on the declining role of social class and the importance of personal and active choice, Beck tends to underestimate the continuing explanatory power of social class categories (Mythen 2005). The responsible, confident, self-creating individual may mainly be fulfilled within a particular social stratum (Rose 1999).

Lash (2000) and others stress the significance of culture and an emotional and aesthetic dimension to life, alongside choice in individual action. Beck emphasizes that the cultural construction of risk is not the whole truth. Risk and culture cannot be separated. 'Risk' and the '(public) definition of risk' are one and the same' (1999: 135). He moves from a notion of risks as dangers to risks as (social) expectations, which are necessarily socioculturally constructed. He explicitly opposes the separation of an realist and constructivist side of risk.

From the perspective of risk society and reflexive modernization, the fundamental social changes regarding risk and uncertainty are understood as the result of objective changes in the quality of risks as well as societal transformations. Governmentality studies, however, interpret this change in terms of a shift in strategies of power and domination.

From this perspective, risk is understood as a fundamental social construction referring to a specific social constitution, rather than a change in objective dangers.

Governmentality

Governmentality approaches draw on the path-breaking work of Foucault (1991). Following some early work (Burchell, Gordon, and Miller 1991) an increasing number of books and articles has been published, examining the phenomena of governance in a broad range of societal domains, such as the governance of childhood (Bell 1993; Brownlie 2001; Kelly 2001), crime (Garland 1997; Joyner 2001; O'Malley 2004), health and illness (Turner 1997; Joyce 2001; Brown and Michael 2002; Flynn 2002), and cyberspace (Loader 1997). For an overview, see Dean (1999). Foucault's work on societal governance contributes to the discourse on two levels: he provides an instrument to analyse power and domination in society and offers an historical analysis of how they were transformed during the development of the modern state. Central to Foucault's theorizing is the connection between governing (*'gouverner'*) and mentality (*'mentalité'*), which is united in the term *'governmentality'*. It indicates his broad view regarding issues of power and domination, which are reduced neither to direct external impacts on the subject nor to the governmental practices of the state. It rather includes the construction of realities through practice *and* sense-making, encompassing the multitude of societal organizations and institutions producing social reality.

In his historical analysis of power and domination in societies from the mercantilist nation states in the seventeenth century to the modern capitalist state, Foucault identifies significant changes. Modern states developed new techniques for managing their populations and achieving national goals (Foucault 1977; see Dean 1999: 18–20). Instead of punishment and immediate external control directed at a specific ideal, the strategies refer ever more to populations and abstract categorization to assess national resources and assist planning. These were transformed into sophisticated systems of ordering, a whole rationality of government which saw its role as including the reviewing, planning, structuring, allocating, and regulating of its own population. Authorities developed the use of audit, judicial discipline, economic management and an apparatus of welfare, education, urban planning, and redistributive measures directed at enhanced security during the life course to achieve these ends.

The individual is no longer treated holistically but as a bearer of indicators which qualify his or her affiliation to one or another group (as 'at risk' or 'risky'). Specific 'safety strategies' were developed (most prominently, social insurance), which supplant the former class (or 'estate' in mercantile society) specific organizations. The friendly society, for example, represents the idea of a prudent and responsible working class. Class specific organizations were replaced with systems established by the state which refer to the family or individual rather than to class solidarity. Such historical transformations regarding societal self-constitution were first supported by the analyses of the circle of scholars around Foucault (e.g. Ewald 1986; Donzelot 1997).

Foucault also mentioned a far-reaching change within modern liberal states (Gordon 1991: 19f.). Neo-liberal power strategies change the relation between state and economy. Whilst in early liberalism the state was understood as controlling the liberty of the market, the market became the central regulatory principle of the state itself. Economics is no longer a domain with a specific rationality, laws, and instruments. Rather all human action became characterized by an economic rationality as far as the allocation of limited resources is concerned. The general principle of government is no longer the regulation of natural liberty, which has to be accepted. Instead it constitutes an artificial 'freedom' for economically rational individuals (Burchell 1993: 271; Rose 1996: 50–62; Lemke 2001).

This freedom is produced by linking 'power strategies' and 'technologies of the self' which indicates another important theoretical distinction introduced by Foucault. It allows systematic analysis of the link between the strategies which aim to determine individuals' behaviour directly (*power strategies*) and the ways in which individuals are empowered to manage their bodies, souls, and their way of life in order to attain such goals as perfection, happiness, purity, or exceptional power (*technologies of the self*). The dominant moral model of the liberal project is not the direct control of individuals, but rather the autonomous, self-responsible, prudent subject, weighing rationally the pros and cons of choices. In several societal domains, the governmentality approach shows how responsibility for societal risks such as illness, unemployment, and poverty is transferred to the collective and to individual subjects (individuals, families, clubs, and so on). It thereby becomes a problem of self-provision (see, for example, O'Malley 1996: 199–204; Rose 1996: 50–62; Dean 1999: 191–2).

Within this theoretical framework, risk and security are understood as central elements of power and domination and thus a strategy for the government of societies. Risk does not result directly from objective facts, rather it represents a specific way in which aspects of reality can be conceptualized and rendered controllable. From this perspective the 'objective' decision-making approach of rational choice, mainly used in economics and psychology, is interpreted as a normative societal programme which is linked to the rise of neo-liberal styles of governmentality. The increasing amount of risk communication in society is therefore understood as the result of the growing influence of neo-liberal strategies of government.

One stream of research in the tradition of Foucault refers to François Ewald's work on the development of insurance as a core indicator of the transition to modernity. It stresses that insurance does more than distribute financial risks between insured parties. Insurance constitutes and spreads a moral idea of responsibility. The actor is released from responsibility for the insured event and the person affected entitled to compensation. Insurance also is part of a moral technology which defines correct behaviour. For example, compensation may be limited to motor accidents where the driver is sober.

Even though the theoretical instruments developed by Foucault open up a broad range of analysis, many governmentality studies focus narrowly on the level of national government. For example, Dean starts out from broad definitions ('the conduct of conduct'—1999: 10—embracing the 'government of the self', to include such personal activities as dieting and religious practice—17), but by the end of the book concentrates on 'historically delimited' authoritarian and neo-liberal forms of government (Chapters 7 and 8). In principle, however, the approach can include a cultural account of power at all levels.

Governmentality perspectives have also been criticized as over-reliant on a top-down functionalism that seeks to explain social developments in terms of the exigencies of government and other power-holding institutions, to see people as inherently open to manipulation and to contain an under-developed account of agency. The topic of agency emerges mainly through the notion of a generalized subject constructed by societal discourses. Individual possibilities for resistance are often underestimated (Lupton 1999). One direction for development links together the accounts of shifts at the level of political economy with detailed and nuanced analyses of individual behaviours and responses. Kemshall's work (2002) on young people and perceptions of risks in the context of a more flexible labour market or Hartley Dean (1999) on the changing responses to social security regulation are examples of this approach.

Some Lessons and Perspectives from Interdisciplinary Work on Risk and Uncertainty

All the approaches reviewed in this chapter contribute to the overall understanding of perceptions and responses to risk. The technical and rational calculation of risk is still applied successfully in domains where knowledge of the relevant risk and shared values about its status, priority, and management are available. Psychological approaches show how risk perception deviates from technical scientific rationality, and that it is subjectively constructed but is also influenced by factors such as gender, national culture, age, class, and ethnic group. This corresponds to the sociological insight that people perceive and respond to risks in the context of their sociocultural embeddedness, which is also constituted by other group affiliations, lifestyles, values, and identity constructions in general. Furthermore, people often apply diverse strategies as heuristics in order to simplify choice or to manage the decision-making load of everyday life. This is not best understood as a deviation from a superior, objective scientific rationality. Laypeople have specific knowledge and a perspective which draws on their experience of scientific expertise, but is also linked to local and everyday knowledge and their specific position in society. Our current concerns regarding risk and uncertainty are as much an effect of the evident limits of control by science and technology as they are an outcome of a cultural perspective which tends to interpret uncertainties as in principle controllable by rationality.

Overall, approaches which attempt to explain risk perception and responses only at the level of one of the social science disciplines contributing to work on risk seem inadequate. Nevertheless, the attempt to combine a range of theoretical approaches within the social amplification of risk framework encounters the problem of its limited predictive power. We have available a range of different instruments and methods. The absence of a homogenous approach may be seen as an advantage, enabling us to do justice to the multidimensional reality of risk and uncertainty in current society.

Some of those issues emerged in the very recent past and they still attract research engagement and feed into continuing controversies. The 'precautionary principle' (the idea that if the consequences of an action are unknown, but may have major or irreversible negative consequences, then it is better to avoid it) is promoted in order to manage irresoluble uncertainties and provide a way of deciding which risks we are willing to take. The controversy about the irrationality of public responses to risk as against the development of scientific knowledge continues. In several research domains, there have been real improvements in knowledge in recent years. The link between the media and the public is seen as interactive and complex, rather than just top-down.

People do not generally and automatically place their trust in established institutions. Instead of following an overall objective rationality, people's perceptions and responses to risk are bound up with their cultural and social context. The factors influencing risk responses and their interaction and dynamic development are difficult to predict. In the process of decision-making, rationality as well as trust, emotion, competing perspectives, and the accumulation of risks are interwoven, and further research is needed in all these areas. Finally, discourse is often narrowed to the negative side of risk. The fact that people are willing to take risks in areas such as extreme sports and sexual activities also requires further considerations. In the next chapter we consider how these issues are being tackled in current research.

Notes

1. We explore the growing risk awareness and the erosion of traditional risks through the example of technical risks because of their significance for the development of risk research in general. The objective concept of risk was also questioned in relation to health and illness, crime, environmental issues, and several other domains mentioned in the thematic chapters of the book.
2. They are sometimes not allowed for ethical reasons, for example.
3. Compare the work on edgework and voluntary risk-taking (Lyng 2005).

References

Adam, B., Beck, U., and Loon, J. V. (2000). *The Risk Society and Beyond: Critical Issues for Social Theory*. London, Thousand Oaks, Calif: Sage.

Alexander, J. and Smith, P. (1996). 'Social Science and Salvation: Risk Society as Mythical Discourse', *Zeitschrift für Soziologie*, 25(4): 251–62.

Atman, C. J., Bostrom, A., Fischhoff, B., and Granger Morgan, M. (1994). 'Designing Risk Communications: Completing and Correcting Mental Models of Hazardous Processes, Part I', *Risk Analysis*, 14(5): 779–88.

Banse, G. (1996). 'Herkunft und Anspruch der Risikoforschung', S. 15–72, in Banse, Gerhard (ed.), Risikoforschung zwischen Disziplinarität und Interdisziplinarität. Von der Illusion der Sicherheit zum Umgang mit Unsicherheit. Berlin: edition sigma.

Beck, U. (1986). *Risikogesellschaft: auf dem Weg in eine andere Moderne*. Frankfurt am Main: Suhrkamp.

____(1992). *Risk Society: Towards a New Modernity*. London, Newbury Park, California: Sage.

_____(1999). *World Risk Society*. Malden, MA: Polity Press.

_____(2000). 'Risk Society Revisited: Theory, Politics and Research Programmes', S. 211–229, in Adam, Barbara, U. Beck, and J. Van Loon (eds.), *The Risk Society and Beyond. Critical Issues for Social Theory*. London: Sage.

_____and Beck-Gernsheim, E. (1995). *The Normal Chaos of Love*. Polity Press and Blackwell.

_____Giddens, A., and Lash, S. (1994). *Reflexive Modernization: Politics, Tradition and Aesthetics in the Modern Social Order*. Stanford, CA: Stanford University Press.

_____Bonss, W., and Lau, C. (2003). 'The Theory of Reflexive Modernization. Problematic, Hypotheses and Research Programme, Theory, Culture and Society', 20(2): 1–33.

Bell, V. (1993). Governing Childhood: Neo-liberalism and the Law, *Economy and Society*, 22(3): 390–405.

_____(1996). 'The Promise of Liberalism and the Performance of Freedom', S. 81–97, in Barry, Andrew, T. Osborne, and N. Rose (eds.), *Foucault and Political Reason. Liberalism, Neo-liberalism and Rationalities of Government*. London: UCL Press.

Bellaby, P. (1990). To Risk or Not to Risk? Uses and Limitations of Mary Douglas on Risk-acceptability for Understanding Health and Safety at Work and Road Accidents, *Sociological Review*, 38(3): 456–83.

Boyne, R. (2003). *Risk*. Buckingham; Philadelphia: Open University Press.

Brown, N. and Michael, M. (2002). 'From Authority to Authenticity: The Changing Governance of Biotechnology', *Health, Risk and Society*, 4(3): 259–72.

Brownlie, J. (2001). The 'Being-Risky' Child: Governing Childhood and Sexual Risk, *Sociology*, 35(2): 519–537.

Burchell, G. (1993). 'Liberal Government and Techniques of the Self', *Economy and Society*, 22(3): 267–82.

_____Gordon, C., and Miller, P. (1991). The Foucault Effect. Studies in Governmentality.

Bury, M. (2001). 'Illness Narratives: Fact or Fiction?', *Sociology of Health and Illness*, 23(3): 263–85.

Cohen, S. (2002). *Folk Devils and Moral Panics*. New York: Routledge.

Dake, K. (1991). 'Orienting Dispositions in the Perception of Risk: An Analysis of Contemporary Worldviews and Cultural Biases', *J. Cross-Cult. Psychol*, 22: 61–82.

_____(1992). 'Myths of Nature: Culture and the Social Construction of Risk', *J Soc Issues*, 48: 21–37.

_____and Wildavsky, A. (1991). 'Individual Differences in Risk Perception and Risk-Taking Preferences', S. 15–24, in B. J. Garrick and W. C. Gekler (eds.), *The Analysis, Communication, and Perception of Risk*. New York: Plenum Press.

Dean, M. (1999). *Governmentality: Power and Rule in Modern Society*. London: Sage.

Dingwall, R. (1999). 'Risk Society': The Cult of Theory and the Millennium? *Social Policy and Administration*, 33(4): 474–91.

Donzelot, J. (1997). *The Policing of Families*. Baltimore, MD: Johns Hopkins University Press.

Douglas, M. (1963). *The Lele of the Kasai*. London: Published for the International African Institute by the Oxford University Press.

_____ (1966). *Purity and Danger: An Analysis of Concepts of Pollution and Taboo*. New York: Praeger.

_____ (1985). *Risk Acceptability According to the Social Sciences*. New York: Russell Sage Foundation.

_____ (1992). 'Risk and Blame: Essays in Cultural Theory'. London, New York: Routledge.

_____ and Wildavsky, A. B. (1982). *Risk and Culture: An Essay on the Selection of Technical and Environmental Dangers*. Berkeley, CA: University of California Press.

_____ and Calvez, M. (1990). The Self as Risk Taker: A Cultural Theory of Contagion in relation to AIDS.

Elliott, A. (2002). 'Beck's Sociology of Risk: A Critical Assessment', *Sociology*, 36(2): 293–315.

Ewald, F. (1986). *L'Etat providence*. Paris: B. Grasset.

Fischhoff, B., Slovic, P., and Lichtenstein, S. (1983). 'Labile Werte. Ein schwieriges Problem für die Risikoforschung', S. 60–68, in J. Conrad (ed.), *Gesellschaft, Technik und Risikopolitik*. Berlin: Springer.

_____ _____ _____ Read, S., and Combs, B. (1978). 'How Safe is Safe Enough? A Psychometric Study of Attitudes Toward Technological Risk and Benefits', *Policy Science*, 9: 127–52.

Fischoff, B., Bostrom, A., Jacobs, B., and Quadrel, M. (1997). *Risk Perception and Communication*. Oxford University Press.

Fitchen, J. M., Heath, J. S., and Fessenden-Raden, J. (1987). 'Risk Perception in Community Context. A Case Study', S. 31–54, in B. B. Johnson and V. T. Covello (eds.), *The Social and Cultural Construction of Risk*. Dordrecht, The Netherlands: Reidel.

Flynn, R. (2002). 'Clinical Governance and Governmentality', *Health, Risk and Society*, 4(2): 155–73.

Foucault, M. (1977). *Discipline and punish: the birth of the prison*. New York: Pantheon Books.

_____ (1991). 'Governmentality', S. 87–104, in G. Burchell et al. (eds.), *The Foucault Effect*.

Fowlkes, M. and Miller, P. (1987). Chemicals and Community at Love Canal, S. 55–78, in B. Johnson and V. Covello (eds.), *The Social and Cultural Construction of Risk: Essays on Risk Selection and Perception*. Dordrecht, the Netherlands: Reidel.

Funtowicz, S. and Ravetz, J. R. (1985). Three Types of Risk Assesment: A Methodological Analysis, S. 217–231, in C. Whipple and V. Covello (eds.), *Risk Analysis in the Private Sector*. New York: Plenum.

Garland, D. (1997). 'Governmentality' and the Problem of Crime: Foucault, Criminology, Sociology, Theoretical Criminology', *An International Journal* (1): 173–214.

Giddens, A. (1991). *Modernity and Self-Identity*. Cambridge: Polity Press.

_____ (1994). *Beyond Left and Right: The Future of Radical Politics*. Stanford, CA: Stanford University Press.

_____ (1999). *The Third Way: The Renewal of Social Democracy*. Malden, Mass: Polity Press.

Gordon, C. (1991). 'Governmental Rationality: An Introduction', S. 1–51, in G. Burchell et al. (eds.), *The Foucault Effect*.

Gowda, M. V. R. (2003). 'Integrating Politics with the Social Amplification of Risk Framework: Insights from an Exploration in the Criminal Justice Context', S. 305–25, in N. Pidgeon, R. E. Kasperson, and P. Slovic (eds.), *The Social Amplification of Risk*. Cambridge: Cambridge University Press.

Johnson, B. B. (1987). 'The Environmentalist Movement and Grid, Group Analysis', S. 147–178, in V. T. Covello and B. B. Johnson (eds.), *The social and cultural construction of risk*. Dordrecht, The Netherlands: Reidel.

Joyce, P. (2001). 'Governmentality and Risk: Setting Priorities in the New NHS', *Sociology of Health and Illness*, 23(5): 594–614.

Joyner, M. (2000). Surfing the Crime Net: Probation arid Risk Society, *Crime Prevention and Community Safety: An International Journal*, 2(2): 67–74.

Jungermann, H. and Slovic, P. (1993). 'Characteristics of Individual Risk Perception', S. 85–102, in *Bayerische-Rueck* (ed.), *Risk—A Construct*. München: Knesebeck.

Kahneman, D., Slovic, P., and Tversky, A. (1982). *Judgment Under Uncertainty: Heuristics and Biases*. Cambridge; London; New York; New Rochelle; Melbourne; Sydney: Cambridge University Press.

Kelly, P. (2001). 'Youth at Risk: Processes of Individualisation and Responsibilisation in the Risk Society', *Discourse: Studies in the Cultural Politics of Education*, 22(1): 23–33.

Kemshall, H. (2002). *Risk, Social Policy and Welfare*. Buckingham, UK: Open University.

Krohn, W. and Krücken, G. (1993). Riskante Technologien: Reflexion und Regulation.

Lash, S. (1994). Reflexivity and its Doubles: Structure, Aesthetics, Community, S. 110–173, in U. Beck, A. Giddens and S. Lash (eds.), *Reflexive Modernization: Politics, Tradition and Aesthetics in the Modern Social Order*. Stanford, Calif: Stanford University Press.

Lash, S. (2000). 'Risk culture', S. 47–62, in B. Adam, U. Beck, and J. Van Loon (eds.), *The Risk Society and Beyond. Critical Issues for Social Theory*. London: Sage.

—— Szerszynski, B., and Wynne, B. (1996). *Risk, environment and modernity: Towards A New Ecology*.

Latour, B. (1993). *We Have Never Been Modern*. Cambridge, MA: Harvard University Press.

—— and Woolgar, S. (1979). *Laboratory Life: The Social Construction of Scientific Facts*. Beverly Hills: Sage Publications.

Lemke, T. (2001). '"The Birth of Bio-Politics": Michel Foucault's Lecture at the Collège de France on Neo-Liberal Governmentality', *Economy and Society*, 30(2): 190–207.

Loader, B. (1997). The Governance of Cyberspace: Politics, Technology and Global Restructuring.

Luhmann, N. (1993). *Risk: A Sociological Theory*. New York: A. de Gruyter.

Lupton, D. (1999). *Risk*. London; New York: Routledge.

—— and Tulloch, J. (2002). 'Life would be Pretty Dull without Risk': Voluntary Risk-taking and its Pleasures, *Health, Risk and Society*, 4(2): 113–24.

MacGregor, D. G. and Fleming, R. (1996). 'Risk Perception and Symptom Reporting', *Risk analysis*, 16(6): 773–83.

Marris, C., Langford, I. H., and O'Riordan, T. (1998). 'A Quantitative Test of the Cultural Theory of Risk Perceptions: Comparison with the Psychometric Paradigm', *Risk Analysis*, 18(5): 635–47.

Murdock, G., Petts, J., and Horlick-Jones, T. (2003). 'After Amplification: Rethinking the Role of the Media in Risk Communication', S. 156–178, in N. Pidgeon, R. E. Kasperson, and P. Slovic (eds.), *The Social Amplification of Risk*. Cambridge: Cambridge University Press.

Mythen, G. (2005). 'Employment, Individualization and Insecurity: Rethinking the Risk Society Perspective', *The Sociological Review*, 53(1): 129–49.

O'Malley, P. (1996). 'Risk and Responsibility', S. 189–207, in A. Barry, T. Osborne, and N. Rose (eds.), *Foucault and Political Reason. Liberalism, Neo-Liberalism and Rationalities of Government*. London: UCL Press.

____ (2004). *Risk, Uncertainty and Government*. Glasshouse Press.

Otway, H. and Thomas, K. (1982). 'Reflections on Risk Perception and Policy,' *Risk Analysis*, 2(1): 69–82.

Perrow, C. (1984). *Normal Accidents: Living with High-Riks Technologies*. Princeton, NJ: Princeton University Press.

Petts, J., Horlick-Jones, T., and Murdock, G. (2001). 'Social Amplification of Risk: The Media and the Public'. Research report 329, 01, *Health and Safety Executive*. London.

Pidgeon, N., Hood, C., Jones, D., Turner, B., and Gibson, R. (1992). 'Risk Perception', S. 89–134, in The Royal Society (ed.), *Risk: Analysis, Perception and Management*. Report of a Royal Society Study Group. London.

____ Kasperson, R. E., and Slovic, P. (2003). The Social Amplification of Risk.

Rayner, S. (1986). 'Management of Radiation Hazards in Hospitals. Plural Rationalities in a Single Institution', *Social Studies of Science*, 16: 573–91.

Renn, O. (1983). 'Technology, Risk and Public Perception', *Angewandte System-analyse*, 4: 50–65.

____ and Rohrmann, B. (2000). *Cross-Cultural Risk Perception. A Survey of Empirical Studies*. Dordrecht; Boston; London: Kluwer.

____ and Swaton, E. (1984). 'Psychological and Sociological Approaches to Study Risk Perception', *Environment International*, 10: 557–75.

____ Burns, W., Kasperson, J., Kasperson, R., and Slovic, P. (1992). 'The Social Amplification of Risk: Theoretical Foundations and Empirical Applications', *Journal of Social Issues*, 48(4): 137–60.

____ Jaeger, C. C., Rosa, E. A., and Webler, T. (2000). The Rational Actor Paradigm in Risk Theories: Analysis and Critique, S. 35–61, in M. J. Coehn (ed.), *Risk in the Modern Age: Social Theory, Science and Environmental Decision-Making*. Houndmills; Basingstoke; Hampshire; New York: Palgrave.

Rippl, S. (2002a). 'Cultural Theory and Risk Perception', *Journal of Risk Regulation*, 5(2): 147–66.

____ (2002b). 'Cultural Theory and Risk Perception: A Proposal for a Better Measurement', *Journal of Risk Research*, 5(2): 147–65.

Rohrmann, B. (1999). Risk Perception Research. Jülich: Programmgruppe Mensch, Umwelt, Technik (MUT), Forschungszentrum Jülich.

Rohrmann, B. and Renn, O. (2000). 'Risk Perception Research: An Introduction', S. 11–53, in O. Renn and B. Rohrmann (eds.), *Cross-Cultural Risk Perception. A Survery of Empirical Studies*. Dordrecht; Boston; London: Kluwer.

Rosa, E. A. (2003). 'The Logical Structure of the Social Amplification of Risk Framework (SARF)', in N. Pidgeon, R. E. Kasperson, and S. Paul (eds.), *Meta-theoretical foundations and policy implications*. Cambridge: Cambridge University Press.

Rose, N. (1996). 'Governing "Advanced" liberal democracies', in A. Barry, T. Osborne, and N. Rose (eds.), *Foucault and Political Reason. Liberalism, Neo-liberalism and Rationalities of Government*. London: UCL Press, 37–64.

—— (1999). *The Powers of Freedom*. Cambridge: Cambridge University Press.

Simon, H. A. (1957). *Administrative Behavior: A Study of Decision-making Processes in Administrative Organization*. New York: Macmillan.

Sjöberg, L. (2002). 'Are Received Risk Perception Models Alive and Well?' *Risk Analysis*, 22(4): 665–9.

Slovic, P. (1987). *Perception of Risk, Science*, 236: 280–85.

—— (1992). 'Perception of Risk: Reflections on the Psychometric Paradigm', S. 117–152, in D. Golding and S. Krimsky (eds.), *Theories of Risk*. London: Praeger.

—— (2001). *Smoking: Risk, Perception Policy*. Thousand Oaks, CA: Sage.

—— Fischhoff, B., and Lichtenstein, S. (1977). Cognitive Processes and Societal Risk Taking, S. 7–36, in H. Jungermann and G. de Zeeuw (eds.), *Decision Making and Change in Human Affairs*. Dordrecht: Riedel.

—— —— —— (1980). Facts and Fears—Understanding Risk', S. 181–218, in R. C. Schwing and W. A. Albers (eds.), *Societal risk assessment*. New York: Plenum.

—— —— —— (1981). Perceived Risk: Psychological Factors and Social Implications, S. 17–34, in Royal Society (ed.), *Proceedings of the Royal Society, Report A376*. London: Royal Society.

—— —— —— (1982). 'Facts Versus Fears: Understanding Perceived Risk', S. 463–489, in D. Kahneman, P. Slovic, and A. Tversky (eds.), *Judgment Under Uncertainty: Heuristics and Biases*. Cambridge; London; New York; New Rochelle; Melbourne; Sydney: Cambridge University Press.

—— —— —— (1984). 'Behavioural Decision Theory on Risk and Safety', *Acta Psychologica*, 56: 183–203.

—— —— —— (1985). 'Characterizing Perceived Risk', S. 91–125, in R. W. Kates, C. Hohenemser, and J. X. Kasperson (eds.), *Perilous Progress: Managing the Hazards of Technology*. Boulder, CO: Westview.

—— —— —— (1986). 'The Psychometric Study of Risk Perceptions', in V. T. Covello, J. Menkes, and J. Mumpower (eds.), *Risk Evaluation and Management*. New York: Plenum.

Starr, C. (1969). 'Social Benefits Versus Technological Risk', *Science*, 165: 1232–8.

Tansey, J. (2004). 'If all You Have is a Hammer. Reply to Sjöberg', *Journal of Risk Research*, 7(3): 361–4.

Thompson, M. and Wildavsky, A. (1982). 'A Proposal to Cerate a Cultural Theory of Risk', S. 145–161, in H. C. Kunrreuther and E. V. Ley (eds.), *The Risk Analysis Controversy. An Institutional Perspective*. Berlin: Springer.

____ Ellis, R., and Wildavsky, A. B. (1990). *Cultural Theory*. Boulder, CO: Westview Press.

Tulloch, J. and Lupton, D. (2003). *Risk and Everyday Life*. London: Sage.

Turner, B. A. (1978). *Man-Made Disasters*. London, England: Wykeham Publications (London).

Turner, B. S. (1997). From Governmentality to Risk: Some Reflexiton son Foucault's Contribution to Medical Sociology, in A. Petersen and R. Bunton (eds.), *Foucault, Health and Medicine*. London: Routledge.

Tversky, A. and Kahneman, C. (1981). 'Framing of Decisions and the Psychology of Choice', *Science*, 211: 453–8.

____ and Kahneman, D. (1974). 'Judgment Under Uncertainty', *Heuristics and Biases, Science*, 185: 1127–31.

Vaughan, D. (1996). *The Challenger Launch Decision: Risky Technology, Culture, and Deviance at NASA*. Chicago: University of Chicago Press.

Wåhlberg, A. (2001). 'Theoretical Features of Some Current Approaches to Risk Perception', *Journal of Risk Regulation*, 4(3): 237–51.

Weyman, A. and Kelly, C. (1999). 'Risk Perception and Communication: A Review of the Literature', *Health and Safety Executive*, Research Report, 248: 99.

Wildavsky, A. and Dake, K. (1990). 'Theories of Risk Perception: Who Fears What and Why?' *Daedalus*, 119: 41–60.

Wilkinson, I. (2001). 'Social Theories of Risk Perception: At Once Indispensable and Insufficient', *Current Sociology*, 49(1): 1–22.

Winterfeldt, D. V., John, R. S., and Borcherding, K. (1981). 'Cognitive Components of Risk Ratings', *Risk Analysis*, 1: 277–87.

Wynne, B. (1982). 'Institutional Mythologies and Dual Societies in the Management of Risk', in H. C. Kunreuther and E. V. Ley (eds.), *The Risk Analysis Controversy. An Institutional Perspective*. Berlin; Heidelberg; New York: Springer, 127–43.

____ (1982). Rationality and Ritual: The Windscale Inquiry and Nuclear Decisions in Britain. Chalfont St Giles, Bucks, UK: British Society for the History of Science.

____ (1987). Risk Management and Hazardous Waste: Implementation and the Dialectics of Credibility.

____ (1992). 'Risk and Social Learning: Reification to Engagement', in S. Krimsky and D. Golding (eds.), *Social Theories of Risk*. New York: Praeger.

____ (1996). 'May the Sheep Safely Graze? A Reflexive View of the Expert-lay Knowledge Divide', S. 44–83, in L. Scott, B. Szerszynski, and B. Wynne (eds.), *Risk, Environment and Modernity*. London; Thousand Oaks; New Delhi: Sage.

3

The Challenge of (Managing) New Risks

Jens O. Zinn and Peter Taylor-Gooby

Research in the field of risk has expanded rapidly in recent years, as Chapter 2 shows. Social science approaches have developed from an initial concern with the management of technical issues, drawing on rational actor models of behaviour, to include psychological and sociological perspectives which seek to capture the complexity of the factors that influence risk responses in different settings, and the ways in which thinking about and managing risk is embedded in social and cultural contexts. In parallel to the expansion in the range of disciplines and methods applied to risk, is an expansion of theoretical interest, embracing more sophisticated accounts of mental modelling, lay/expert interactions, and theories of governmentality and of risk society.

This chapter deals with the most recent work and with the current unresolved debates in risk research. The chief areas of interest stem from three developments, both implicit in the argument developed in the previous chapter.

First there is a widespread recognition that risk issues are endemic in any society that relies on complex enterprises, particularly those involving the onward rush of new and untried technologies. Once this point is understood, there is no possibility of returning to a situation in which risks could be understood as simply technical issues, which could be eliminated if the right systems were put in place. The issue becomes much more one of managing an acceptable level of risk.

This leads to the *second* point: if risk is understood as, to a great extent, a matter of judgements about acceptability, a whole range of political issues about trust in authorities, experts, and officials, about social communication and the mass media come into play. Once the views of the lay public are taken seriously, decision-making can no longer be exclusively a preserve of the authorities, but must include processes of interaction and participation between all those involved.

The *third* point follows from this and also draws on the much broader range of social science approaches now included in the analysis of risk. Recent work demonstrates the complexity of the risky choices that people make in their everyday lives. Issues of social identity and group membership are bound up with risk-taking and risk-avoidance. Some people actively seek out some risks, which others just as strenuously avoid. It becomes clear that risk cannot be understood simply in terms of rational judgement. Emotional factors supply the drive necessary to make choices and are often implicated in the process of choosing. Equally, anxiety and stress are associated with risk, and contentment with security.

Risk as a theme in social science has spread to embrace a whole range of issues and approaches. Work in this field includes analyses at the macrolevel, seeking to understand risk and uncertainty as primary elements in modern culture. It also refers at an intermediate level to the question of how risks are to be managed by institutions and organizations in a publicly acceptable way, and, at the micro-level, to the problem of accounting for the way people respond in complex contexts. One major challenge now lies in finding ways to bring together these levels of understanding. Another results from recognition that individual risk experience develops over time, and methods which capture experience, anticipation, and biography are required.

New challenges for risk research result from globalized risks, such as global warming, BSE, influenza epidemics, and international crime and terrorism, and the need for transnational collaboration to manage them. National differences in risk regimes and cultures and the implications of accounts of society in terms of risk become issues for further research and theorizing.

Endemic Risk

The current discussion of risk is permeated by concerns about 'new' uncertainties which cannot be transformed by rational calculation into manageable risks. With the acceptance that there are, in principle, limits to knowledge and control, the question of how to cope with uncertainty rises up the societal agenda. The 'Challenge of Uncertainty'

(Zinn 2005a) emerges across many societal domains. At a technical level, it refers to the problem of coping with the limits of scientific knowledge and with the resulting question of which risks we want to take. These political and ethical issues feed into the political principle of precaution. Here and in other non-technical areas of risk, 'objective' rationality and social and subjective rationalities compete with each other in political controversies and processes.

Precaution

With the growing acknowledgement of the social as an important part of risk management, different values and perspectives on risk are introduced into the technical approach on risk. The 'precautionary principle' offered a solution to the problem of coping with the mixture of limited knowledge and ethical doubts with respect to the uncertain impact of technical developments, particularly in the fields of the environment and health.

Adoption of the principle was driven by the desire for the political management of public concerns rather than as a scientific concept. It promised a systematic way of coping with the irreducible uncertainties of decision-making and thereby providing legitimation for policy. It also seeks to reduce errors caused by ignoring 'early warnings' and to develop procedures for promoting greater awareness of the possible side effects of innovations (EEA 2001).

The precautionary principle has emerged as a general rule for decision-making across many areas of policymaking. The EU Treaty of Nice (2000) declares that all areas of EU policymaking should embrace this principle. Despite its wide application, the definition of the principle is imprecise. A scientific and a 'common sense' approach can be distinguished (Burgess 2004: 158).

The scientific approach accepts precaution only on the basis of scientific knowledge and calculation, whereas the common sense approach accepts everyday life knowledge and concerns as reasons for rejecting innovations where there is uncertainty. It opens up the discourse to 'rationally' unfounded rejections. Some authors interpret that as a necessary brake on innovation required by ecologically informed decision-making (Japp 2000). This approach is criticized by those who claim the principle gives too much power to irrational fears. Consumer organizations and the public often react hysterically (Burgess 2004), and prevent necessary scientific and societal development. This perspective argues that a reactionary 'culture of fear' (Furedi 1997, 2002) has to be overcome in order to support societal (particularly economic) development (Wilsdon and Willis 2004). However, the aspiration that unrestrained innovation will produce the knowledge necessary to solve today's problems (Wildavsky 1988, 1995) also involves risk (Japp 2000).

Competing Rationalities

Awareness of the limits of technical risk assessment and management to control uncertainty within the technical paradigm has led to attempts to improve the quality of calculation and assessment. Additionally the approach attempts to combine objective with social and subjective risk problems. For example, Klinke and Renn (2002) seek to combine precaution and rational assessment as appropriate to specific risk problems. They distinguish ideal types of risks by combining several criteria to generate a typology of six different risk types. Depending on the different characteristics they recommend specific strategies to manage different kinds of risk. *Risk-based management* is suggested for risks where both the probability of occurrence and the extent of damage are relatively well known and can mainly be managed by reducing the catastrophic potential by technical and formal means. *Precaution-based management* is suggested when the risk is connected with a relatively high degree of uncertainty. The first priority of risk management is the application of precautionary measures and the development of substitutes. Finally, *discourse-based management* is appropriate when objective risk knowledge is not used properly, for example, when the potential for wide-ranging damage is ignored (climate change) or harmless effects are perceived as threats (mobile phones).

This approach starts from the identifiable characteristics of a risk problem and provides a systematic strategy for managing new risks and uncertainties (Klinke and Renn 2002: 1082–5, 1090). Limitations emerge when it is difficult to assign a risk to a category in advance. The approach maintains the value of scientific knowledge and implies that on that basis discursive strategies will lead to unambiguous solutions. Some research indicates that this is often an unrealistic expectation (STAGE 2005).

The problem of the limits to the rational management of uncertainty is powerful in other domains as well. For example, in health and illness it is a widely shared norm that uncertainty has to be minimized, particularly regarding the success of treatments (compare Alaszewski, Chapter 8). Formal control structures take responsibility from the individual provided that the rules are followed. However, the success of organizations depends also on informal structures. A doctor who only followed strictly formal rules might, when faced with an unexpected situation, become a risk. At the same time, health knowledge is becoming increasingly diverse and uncertain, as orthodox medicine is questioned by other knowledge systems, such as homeopathy and acupuncture (Zinn 2005).

In criminology the 'key contention is that the modernist disciplinary agenda delivered through the welfare state has been replaced by a welfare-penal agenda based upon risk' (see Kemshall, Chapter 4). Despite the huge range of actuarial risk techniques that are now applied, the more recent concern in research and theorizing is about the implications and the dark side of risk. Risk calculations are interpreted not only as an objective issue but also as a moral concept interwoven with ideas of responsibility and neglecting diversity (as also in the governmentality approach). Concerns about crime cannot be divorced from decisions about the level of uncertainty or deviance we would like to accept and about which crimes provoke concern.

This tension between freedom, autonomy, and uncertainty is also an issue in the context of family and partnership (compare Lewis and Sarre, Chapter 7). When partnership is open to negotiation and decisions, as the individualization thesis implies, it may become uncertain in terms of continuity, but might become more certain in terms of quality. The controversy in research is about how these uncertainties are to be understood as good or bad and how they have to be handled, as something to be supported or prevented by social policy.

Finally, the idea of regulation and management is increasingly infected by the insight that in some high-risk organizations, it is impossible to achieve absolute control (Vaughan 1996). This leads to interest in the management of such pervasive uncertainties, and also in how management and organization itself produce unforeseen risks and how we can control them (see Hutter, Chapter 10).

The Public Acceptability of Risky Choices

The concern of politicians and other decision-makers about the public acceptability of risky decisions generates support for research on good risk governance (TRUSTNET 1999, 2004; PABE 2002; STAGE 2005). In this context and more generally, the media are seen as a decisive framing mechanism, capable of not only reinforcing acceptability but also of destroying it. Public trust in authorities is a major influence on acceptance of decisions, which cannot be overseen in detail. Recent research shows that the issues of risk governance and participation, and media influence and public trust are more complex than often assumed.

Risk Governance

The technical and knowledge-based approach to risk increasingly acknowledges a role for the social and subjective aspects of risk, as the previous chapter showed. These problems are embedded in a more general perspective on risk governance (TRUSTNET 2004), which is mainly about how decisions can be made in a publicly acceptable way. The focus shifts from a technical question of risk to general ideas of democracy and public participation. The central assumption is that participation can increase public acceptance of risky decisions. A range of instruments (such as consensus-conferences, public debates, roadshows, and surveys) have been developed to facilitate public participation. Recent research shows that participation alone is not enough and that attempts to foster acceptance may prove counterproductive. The idea of shaping public opinion may come into conflict with the idea of democracy, which assumes early public involvement in risky decisions, and a highly transparent decision-making process.

The ideal of consensus is not necessarily attainable (STAGE 2005), and it is sometimes necessary to find solutions in such cases. Japp gives a number of examples (2000, compare Zinn 2004a: 17). He suggests that partial interests could become embedded in more general collective interests so that interest groups may accept compromises to promote public welfare. Another strategy is moving from a pure instrumental rationality to a more symbolic rationality, to shift perspectives on the problem and its solution (compare also Hutter, Chapter 10). The pressing question in this area still is how risk governance can be developed in a way which is morally and democratically acceptable to the public.

The Media

Many approaches to risk assume that the media exert significant influence on social identities, risk definitions, risk selection, and the knowledge people have about risks, and are therefore central to risk awareness and to explanations of people's responses to risk.

From an objective perspective, the media were understood as a channel for public information and a means to overcome an irrational risk aversion. Sociological approaches initially also tended to conceptualize the role of the media as framing public understanding of risk or facilitating the development of 'risk consciousness' (Beck 1992: 23, 132f.). Although it soon became clear that the relationship between the media and the public is much more complex, systematic research in this field is comparatively underdeveloped.

Significant changes in understanding of the media during the 1990s had major implications for approaches to risk, risk perceptions, and risk-taking. The classical approach, focused on the objectivity, rationality, and accuracy of media coverage (e.g. Freudenburg et al. 1996; Wilson 2000), encountered serious difficulties. On the one hand, the fundamental assumption that the role of the media was to support the public in making adequate judgements by providing objective information met the problem that often such objective knowledge is not available (Adams 1995: 194f.; Kitzinger 1999; Murdock, Pelts, and Horlick-Jones 2003). On the other hand, the implicit and widely disseminated assumption that media reports have a determining influence upon public risk perception (e.g. Renn et al. 1992; Spencer and Triche 1994) was confronted with evidence that the subject has a relatively more active role concerning the interpretation of and response to risk (compare Kitzinger and Murdock, Chapter 12).

Assumptions like the notion of a general risk consciousness in the risk society approach (Beck 1992) or the determining influence of the mass media on the public (e.g. Adams 1995; Kasperson and Kasperson 1996) contain oversimplifications. Media research as well as sociocultural studies show the ambivalence of audience attitudes towards the information they receive about risk, the range of partial, ambiguous, and contradictory views about the benefits and wisdom of the scientific knowledge individuals hold, and the contradictions, incoherence, and disagreement in the ways in which these groups actively make sense of the threat posed in areas such as environmental hazards (Irwin et al. 1999: 1312).

Sociocultural studies show that risks are discursively constructed in everyday life with reference to the mass media, individual experience and biography, local memory, moral convictions, and personal judgements. The mass media are only one among other important factors (Tulloch 2000: 197; Murdock, Petts, and Horlick-Jones 2003). Quantitative surveys on general risk awareness may well give little information on peoples' individual assumptions about the risks that they face—a point often summed up as the 'impersonal impact hypothesis' (Dickens 1992; Coleman 1993; Wilkinson 2001b: 13).

The wide range of different findings in media studies cannot be explained by a set of general rules or logics. They seem rather to be influenced by the substantive nature of the particular topic under consideration (Kitzinger 1999: 57) and/or to be the result of specific situational constellations. Studies which compare media coverage at different points in time tend to show that the social and political context is essential for understanding risk-reporting and how it changes over time (Kitzinger 1999: 59). This suggests that research on the framing of risk perception by the media can only fully be understood by simultaneous analysis of the context of risk-reports and a careful 'ethnographic' analysis of the individual's embeddedness in cultural and social contexts and biographical experiences.

Trust

Public trust in expertise, science, and politicians has declined, particularly as a result of the major accidents of the 1980s (Chapter 2). The problem for politicians is exacerbated by the evidence that trust is much easier to destroy than to rebuild (Axelrod 1981; Coleman 1986; Fukuyama 1996; Gambetta 1998; Putnam 2000; Le Grand 2003: 29 etc. see Pidgeon, Kasperson, and Slovic 2003, 31–2). Establishing trust has become a topic of central interest for decision-makers and for risk researchers, in order to facilitate the public acceptance of policy decisions (Jungerman et al. 1996). In this section, we review psychological and sociological approaches.

Psychological work on trust relationships between the public and institutions initially identified two main themes: the characteristics of the agency to be trusted and particularly its competence to carry out the role assigned to it (Renn and Levine 1991), and the relationship between the values of the agency and the citizen (Siegrist, Cvetovitch, and Roth 2000). These general dimensions have been subdivided into a number of component factors, including perceived competence, objectivity, fairness, consistency, care, and faith (Hovland et al. 1953; Renn and Levine 1991; Frewer et al. 1996; Metlay 1999). Recent work indicates that trust may be bound up with more general and fundamental attitudes towards an issue, which provides the basis for both trust and risk judgements (Poortinga and Pidgeon 2005). This could also help to explain why some studies show only a limited influence of trust on the understanding of risk (Sjöberg 2001; Viklund 2003).

The support for the existence of more general beliefs or attitudes fundamental to the relationship between trust and risk offers opportunities to link to the more cultural and emotional approaches to trust, even though

61

it is still controversial whether the domain under consideration plays a greater role in influencing trust and risk judgement (Petts 1998; Weyman and Kelly 1999: 30), or is a general attitude which does not vary much across different domains of risk (Poortinga and Pidgeon 2004).

Earle and Cvetovich (1995) argue that in everyday life, most people find complex risk issues too difficult and wearisome to analyse, and resort to a general sense of sympathy with the institution (or otherwise) rather than cognition to guide them. This parallels sociological approaches, which assume that culture plays a central role in trust and risk. It is also supported by transnational research which shows significant cross-national differences in trust (Renn and Rohrmann 2000; Viklund 2003; Delhey and Newton 2005). These require more detailed investigation.

Sociological approaches have adopted a broad conceptualization of trust to include self-confidence as well as trust in worldviews (religion, ideology), in institutions (the family, the state), in abstract systems (money, economy, medicine), or in others (partner, friends, group, neighbourhood). Trust is a fundamental prerequisite of complex modern societies to enable people to act and secure social cohesion (Luhmann 1979; Barber 1983). When societies became more and more complex, the significance of trust in 'abstract systems' became increasingly necessary to manage everyday life (Giddens 1991). Trust exists between knowledge and ignorance (Simmel 1968: 393). In this sense the function of trust can be defined as solving the problem of limited knowledge (Giddens 1995: 48) by reducing its complexity (Luhmann 1979).

Trust may also be understood as a matter of choice when there is a possibility of failure (Crasswell 1993). Because it is actively given and therefore closely linked to the modern idea of risk, Luhmann (1979) distinguishes trust from other forms of non-rational strategies to secure expectations, such as hope or confidence. When there is no possibility of choice, it is confidence or hope rather than trust that is at stake. A small number of writers suggest that trust applies to circumstances where we do not reflect on the issue. Once we make conscious decisions about whether to trust someone or not trust is already threatened. From this perspective, trust reduces to uncritical habit.

Further developments identify a new form of trust emerging within modernity. This is 'active trust' (Giddens 1994) or 'reflexive trust' (Bonss and Zinn 2005) associated with the shift from a class stratified to a functionally differentiated form of society. Giddens (1994) argues that in modernity a routinely given trust in abstract systems (such as the expert systems, represented by scientists, doctors, and other professionals—1991) is increasingly accompanied by active trust. Active trust has to be won; it is not predetermined by status or gender role. It is autonomously given and is therefore a powerful source of social solidarity (Giddens 1994: 14f.). In the more uncertain conditions of late modernity, democratic decision-making rests on the 'clever citizen'—well informed and able to criticize policy—and a dialogic style of governance— in which government must seek to attract active trust. Optimistically, Giddens proposes that clever citizens and open governance will lead to a 'democratization of democracy'. He recognizes, but has not entirely resolved, the problems of uncertainty that such a process involves. Individuals must choose and may revise their choices about trust in personal relationships and in political and social institutions. They must work to build and sustain trust, but there can be no guarantee of success. It is unclear whether such a dialogue will necessarily lead to consensus when the interests, knowledge, and values of experts, politicians, and lay-people systematically differ.

Most research concurs on the importance of trust in the current context and agrees that further research is needed. Unresolved key debates cover a considerable number of areas:

- The complexity and in particular the number of dimensions involved in trust (relating to sources of information about risk, processes by which risk policies are enacted, the relationship between the basic values of the institution trusted and the trusting citizen, and the domains of risk in question);
- The importance of trust in risk perception;
- The relationship between trust, risk judgement, and the acceptability of a risk; the role of cultural differences and of affect;
- The extent to which the problem concerns the factors which influence how a message from a particular source is received, rather than interaction between the risk assumptions of lay-people (derived from cultural and other sources) and those of experts.

New Insights into Factors Affecting Individual Choices in Everyday Life

In several disciplines (economics, psychology, and sociology) and domains of risk research, it became clear that the way people make decisions in the course of their life is much more complex than is understood in terms of rationality and rational deliberation (Elster 1998; Jaeger et al. 2001; Loewenstein et al. 2001; Pixley 2004). When resources are limited and/or no certain knowledge is available, or just in order to manage a broad range of uncertainties in everyday life, individuals refer to different strategies. They use a range of heuristics (Tversky and Kahneman 1982) and refer to emotion, trust, tradition, belief, and other factors. Besides the cultural framing of decision-making and especially recognition of the role of emotions challenged theoretical considerations and empirical research.

Cultural approaches to risk have emphasized at an early stage that emotions and affect are a major issue in relation to identity and group affiliation and thus to the perception and management of risk (Douglas 1966; Lash 2000; Tulloch and Lupton 2003). A positive approach, which interprets risk itself as the motivation to take risks, is outlined in the edgework approach (Lyng 2005) and is also used to explain deviant behaviour in criminology. More remarkable in this context is the tendency in technical, objectivistic, and rational approaches to risk to accept that emotion can be something positive, a prerequisite for decision-making in the first place.

Emotion and Affect

Sociological theorists, cognitive psychologists, and economists traditionally understood emotions as contradicting rationality. Fundamental work done by Elias (1978, 1982, 1994) interprets the process of modernization as the control and domestication of irrational emotions prioritizing rational thinking. In the tradition of these early analyses, emotions are mainly seen as destabilizing modernity (Luhmann 1995) or as the negative outcome of the growing uncertainties of current developments (Giddens 1991). This orthodox perspective was questioned by cultural approaches which introduced a positive interpretation of risk and uncertainty (Lupton and Tulloch 2002; Tulloch and Lupton 2003), especially in the context of 'edgework' (Lyng 2005) and of reflexive modernization (Zinn 2004).

Emotions as the cause of action were also acknowledged in economics thinking. Keynes (1936: 161–2) famously argued 'that a large proportion of our positive activities depend on spontaneous optimism rather than mathematical expectations, whether moral or hedonistic or economic. Most, probably, of our decisions to do something positive, the full consequences of which will be drawn out over many days to come, can only be taken as the result of animal spirits—a spontaneous urge to action rather than inaction, and not as the outcome of a weighted average of quantitative benefits multiplied by quantitative probabilities.'

The need for emotions for entrepreneurial and innovative decision-making was accepted in economics (Pixley 2002: 83); in conventional thinking on judgement emotions were interpreted as disturbances to an otherwise superior rationality. This view was also shared by technical approaches on risk, concerned that the objectively best risk calculations become confounded by values and irrational beliefs.

Decision-making research accommodates emotions mainly as the expected accompaniments of particular courses of action. One reason may be that emotions as expectations can easily be added to the list of items weighed up in the conventional rational choice model. Risky choices then can be predicted by assuming that people assess the severity and likelihood of the possible outcomes of choice alternatives, albeit subjectively and possibly with bias or error, and integrate this information through some type of expectation-based calculus to arrive at a decision.

This perspective differs from the view of researchers engaged in other psychological research domains, as neuroscience and social psychology. They focus much more on how immediate emotions influence decision-making (Loewenstein et al. 2001). In contrast to earlier approaches, emotions and affects are no longer solely interpreted as aberrations in decision-making, but as a prerequisite. For example, Damasio (1996) has argued, referring to research on people with specific brain injuries, that emotions are necessary to value alternatives in the decision-making process (the 'somatic marker' hypothesis). Emotions and rationality necessarily interact in order to direct the decision-making process. In his view, rapid and basic emotional evaluation combined with a rational assessment would produce good decisions in a limited time. In this way, feelings have a direct effect on decision-making. Clore, Schwarz, and Conway (1994) argue that feelings affect people's judgements or choices within a decision-process in those cases where the feelings are experienced as reactions to the imminent judgement or decision.

The research of Alhakami and Slovic (1994) and Finucane et al. (2000) conceptualizes affect[1] as an 'orienting mechanism' (Slovic 1999: 694f.). Affect is prior to the rational evaluation of alternatives. 'It thus appears that the affective response is primary, and the risk and benefit judgments are derived (at least partly) from it' (Slovic 1999: 694). It is easy to imagine a socio-biological account of how rapid 'hard-wired' responses to threats might be highly valued compared with rational ones that took longer to execute. There are also parallels to the notion of 'quick trust' (Alaszewski 2003: 238) or 'facework-based trust' (Cook, ch. 1 in Kramer and Cook 2004) to account for the processes whereby people make decisions whether or not to trust doctors on the basis of brief interviews when they themselves are not competent to judge the technical issues (compare also Eiser and colleagues 2002).

Emotional intensity seems to influence significantly risk perception and risk-taking, as well. Emotions at a comparatively low level of intensity can be understood to play the role of an advisor *in* decision-making. The evaluation of one's feelings is then used to find out how to judge (Loewenstein et al. 2001). Conversely, intense emotions might rule out cognitive consideration. This fits in with the observation that under specific circumstances, risk calculation as a whole is rejected (Japp 2000; Rescher 1983; Loewenstein et al. 2001). One of the reasons to reject risk-taking is that probable outcomes are seen as so horrible or catastrophic that even the smallest probability acquires an unbearable emotional weight (e.g., resistance to vaccination because it is believed to cause autism, or the refusal to deal with nuclear energy as a whole because of the incalculable damages of a serious accident). The problem that emotions and rationality sometimes do not coincide (Loewenstein et al. 2001) is rarely considered in the context of risk research, but is a common topic in research on intrapersonal conflict (Schelling 1984). People are often overwhelmed by their emotions and cannot act rationally, even if they want to (Rolls 1999).

Edgework

Another perspective on emotions interprets them not just as a prerequisite for action in general but emphasizes the thrill which accompanies specific risk-taking activities. This perspective is outlined in the edgework approach (Lyng 2005), which is mainly applied to explain participation in 'manifestly irrational' leisure time activities (Lyng and Snow 1986) such as high-risk sports. It is also used in criminology in order to understand the motivation for some criminal activities (Katz 1988; Ferrell and Sanders 1995). Edgework can also take place in a broad range of activities, including mountaineering, skydiving, some aspects of working life (stock market trading, rigging scenery, and lighting), crime, drug use, and the arts.

Edgework deviates in many respects from other approaches to risk. It is close to recent cultural approaches to issues of identity, in its emphasis on emotions, and related issues such as aesthetics. The main assumption is that risk and uncertainty itself attract people. This attraction is not just explained as an anthropological constant but is understood in two different ways in respect to modern society. From one view, edgework is interpreted as an escape from the normative demands of modern society which determine individual opportunities to shape ones life and gain original experiences. Society is seen as limiting individual activities. From the opposite perspective, exploring the limits of control is understood as an expression of the normative idea of modern society extended into the domain of leisure time activities (Lyng 2005: 5). On this view it can be expected that people who explore the edge in everyday life (e.g. in their work) are also inclined to do so during their leisure time by bungee jumping, sky surfing, or similar activities. The edgework approach helps to explain different styles of risk-taking with the help of emotions. How this behaviour can be embedded in general societal developments is still controversial.

Emotional experiences are often seen as positioned beyond rational, cognitive, and textual approaches to risk. In the context of edgework, the focus is on exciting experiences that people actively seek. Recent research on health and illness has also considered how people manage the experience of involuntary suffering (Wilkinson 2004*a*, *b*).

Challenges in Risk Research

Risk perception, responses to risk, and risk-taking have tended to be analysed through strategies which examine a specific decision or a specific attitude. Approaches which focus attention on context and on the inter-action of different factors in risk perception and response raise questions of how risk issues are to be understood interactively, in relation to other risks and dynamically, over time.

One approach points out that much analysis focuses on risks as isolated instances, whilst in everyday life, people respond to a range of mutually interacting risks. There are indications that the embeddedness of a risk in a range of *competing alternatives* influences how such risks are evaluated. For example, in research on health and illness the risk of an illness tends to be interpreted against the background of other current and previous illnesses (Faircloth et al. 2004; Pound, Gompertz, and Ebrahim 1998). Health issues are generally embedded in common patterns of behaviour regarding life (risks) in general as Cornwell (1984) has shown in research on working class responses to risk of illness.

Second, risk research has benefited greatly from the stronger interest in culture and experience at the individual level in sociology since the 1980s, whilst in psychology a move in the same direction, from methodological individualism to the inclusion of cultural issues, has been apparent in recent years (see Chapter 2). This 'cultural turn' (see also John Tulloch's discussion in Chapter 6) opens up new ways of understanding the richness of the contexts in which people perceive and respond to risks. However, there are real issues about how such approaches are to be linked with the more institutional accounts of risk society theories or the macro-sociology of governmentality approaches.

There is comparatively little research on the dynamics of how people experience risks or how they develop specific ways of approaching risks over time. Whilst at the macro-level there is little progress in theorizing risk processes since the Social Amplification of Risk Framework (see Chapter 2), there have recently been promising developments at the micro-level. In psychology Eiser (2003) attempts to bring together risk research with cognitive and social learning theory. In sociology the biographical approach develops without attracting much attention from mainstream risk research. It focuses on how people develop specific patterns of action and behaviour under changing social conditions. In these processes, risks and uncertainties are central issues (Zinn 2005).

Referring to learning and social learning theory Eiser (2005) explores the range of problems that result from the fact that a successful risk learner needs to gather appropriate feedback from the environment on when to pursue or not to pursue a course of action, and to be able to modify behaviour accordingly. Learning theory deals with how we assimilate information from practical situations, whilst social learning theory (Mischel and Shoda 1995) extends this to the experientially based views that people acquire about the social environment in which they live and how they can handle it with confidence. In practice, many of the risk situations we deal with provide poor feedback. For example, most of the time speeding drivers reach their destinations safely—and learn that the risks associated with speeding do not apply to them (Eiser 2005: 23).

In sociology, there has been considerable interest in new methods which provide nuanced and detailed understanding of the way individual experience and context contribute to people's perceptions of and responses to risk. One important approach now attracting attention is biographical methodology (Chamberlayne et al. 2000, 2002; Rosenthal

2004). 'The purpose of the sociobiographical approach is to avoid the overgeneralization and abstraction of many social research methods, which often reduce individuals to aggregates, averages, or bundles of variables, and which lose sight of the coherence of individual lives' (Chamberlayne, Rustin, and Wengraf 2002: 3). The focus is the subject's interpretation of life situations, and choices in response to them; how individuals maintain their identity or restore an injured identity over time. This approach and other qualitative methods allow researchers to explore how specific interpretations and action patterns develop during their lives. They help to explain why people respond differently to specific risks. They also facilitate examination of how competing risks interact in the way individuals cope with uncertainty and how emotions are interconnected in experiencing, remembering, and learning from the past. In this way, learning and social learning theory and biographical approaches could complement each other.

Another challenge for risk research is globalization. Global warming, epidemics of influenza, the spread of GM food through world trade agreements, or international terrorism attract growing attention. The link between national and transnational factors is not sufficiently theorized and empirically analysed. The predominant focus on western industrialized societies neglects the question of how such countries and their risk practices are linked to those of other nations and cultures and how they mutually influence them.

In this context still under-examined national differences in terms of institutional risk regimes and risk culture(s) become more important in explaining complex transnational interrelationships. It remains unclear why specific risks raise greater concern in some countries than in others and why more general risk awareness is differently developed in different societies. Although some comparative studies exist (e.g. regarding risk perception [Renn and Rohrmann 2000] or trust Delhey and Newton 2005) there is scope for further research.

These sociocultural and institutional differences are linked to another issue which receives little attention. Risk is not just an objective entity but also a specific way of understanding society and placing a value on particular approaches to opportunities and dangers. Social institutional changes bound up with greater international competition, the introduction of new and more flexible technologies, the shift towards a post-industrial society, changes in the status and role of women, and other factors all interact to restructure the agenda of risks that people recognize and confront in their everyday life. This leads to the emergence of 'new social risks' associated with problems in access to employment or satisfactory childcare or lack of appropriate education and training (Taylor-Gooby 2004). Much work on risk and social change analyses risk from perspectives that focus on individual experience and pay little attention to structural social inequalities. At the same time a moral programme of individual responsibility in public policy reinforces discrimination against disadvantaged groups, as social supports are withdrawn in a neoliberal policy context. This raises the issues of how perceptions of risk are used as a resource in different systems of governance and how risk causes different affects in the diverse sociocultural styles of government in Europe and elsewhere.

Such a perspective resembles constructivism in the governmentality perspective. More recently Baker and Simon (2002) diagnosed a fundamental shift in understanding of the role of insurance (social as well as private). The notion of solidarity and risk-pooling through insurance has become increasingly supplanted by a more active and enterprising approach they term 'embracing risk'. They draw on a strong current research tradition in identifying two general cultural trends, which are most evident in Anglophone countries (see Rose 1996; Dean 1999; O'Malley 2004). Increasingly, social problems are conceived and addressed in terms of risk, and various efforts have been made to make people individually accountable for risks. The paradigm of solidarity is being eroded by new developments which return responsibility to the individual and differentiate the population through lifestyle, and exposures to risk and behavioural patterns. The return of the market is associated with a cultural change which accords greater value to success in business enterprise, stock market speculation, and other high-risk financial activities, and promotes wider public engagement in such ventures. This perspective shows how the notion of risk leads to different outcomes in different sociocultural and institution contexts.

Conclusion

This review points out the wide range of new avenues for research resulting from the developments of the past two decades. Risk research is now at a juncture where the interlinking of perspectives and methods from different disciplinary traditions offers excellent opportunities for taking research forward and for developing richer theoretical understanding of risk and uncertainty as central features of how people live their lives in a distinctively modern form of society. We go on to examine these developments in detail across the main areas of research in the following chapters.

Note

1. Affect in this context is 'defined as a positive (like) or negative (dislike) evaluative feeling toward an external stimulus (e.g. some hazard such as cigarette smoking)' (Slovic 1999: 694).

References

Adams, J. (1995 [1998 printing]). *Risk*. London [UK]: Bristol, PA: UCL Press.

Alaszewski, A. (2003). 'Risk, Trust and Health', *Health, Risk and Society*, 5: 235–9.

Alhakami, A. S. and Slovic, P. (1994). 'A Psychological Study of the Inverse Relationship Between Perceived Risk and Perceived Benefit', *Risk Analysis*, 14: 1085–96.

Baker, T. and Simon, J. (2002). *Embracing Risk: the Changing Culture of Insurance and Responsibility*. Chicago, IL: University of Chicago Press.

Beck, U. (1992). *Risk Society: Towards a New Modernity*. London, Newbury Park, Calif: Sage Publications.

Bonß, W. and Zinn, J. (2005). 'Erwartbarkeit, Glück und Vertrauen—Zum Wandel biographischer Sicherheitskonstruktionen in der Moderne', *Soziale Welt*, 56: 79–98.

Burgess, A. (2004). *Cellular Phones, Public Fears, and a Culture of Precaution*. New York: Cambridge University Press.

Chamberlayne, P., Bornat, J., and Wengraf, T. (2000). *The Turn to Biographical Methods in Social Science*. London, New York: Routledge.

——Rustin, M., and Wengraf, T. (2002). *Biography and Social Exclusion in Europe: Experiences and Life Journeys*. Bristol, CT: Policy Press.

Clore, G. L., Schwarz, N., and Conway, M. (1994). 'Affective Causes and Consequences of Social Information Processing', in R. S. Wyer and T. K. Srull (eds.), *Handbook of Social Cognition (1)*. Hillsdale, NJ: Erlbaum, pp. 323–417.

Coleman, J. S. (1990). *Foundations of Social Theory*. Cambridge, MA: Belknap Press of Harvard University Press.

Coleman, C. (1993). 'The Influence of Mass Media and Interpersonal Communication on Societal and Personal Risk Judgments', *Communication Research*, 20: 611–28.

Cornwell, J. (1984). *Hard-Earned Lives: Accounts of Health and Illness from East London*. London, New York: Tavistock Publications.

Damasio, A. (1996). *Descartes' Error: Emotion, Reason and the Human Brain*. Macmillan. London papermac edition.

Delhey, J. and Newton, K. (2003). 'Who Trusts? The Origins of Social Trust in Seven Societies', *European Societies*, 5: 93–137.

Dickens, P. (1992). *Who Would Know? Science, Environmental Risk and the Construction of Theory*.

EEA (European Environment Agency) 2001: Late Lessons From Early Warnings: The Precautionary Principle 1896–2000. Copenhagen.

Eiser, R. J. (2003). *Public Perception of Risk: A Review of Theory and Research*.

Elias, N. (1978). *The Civilizing Process*. New York: Urizen Books.

—— (1982). *The Civilizing Process*. New York: Pantheon Books.

—— (1994). *The Civilizing Process*. Oxford [UK], Cambridge, MA: Blackwell.

Faircloth, C. A., Boylstein, C., Rittman, M., Young, M. E., and Gubrium, J. (2004). 'Sudden Illness and Biographical Flow in Narratives of Stroke Recovery', *Sociology of Health and Illness*, 26: 242–61.

Ferrell, J. and Sanders, C. (1995). *Cultural Criminology*. Boston, MA: Northeastern University Press.

Finucane, M. L., Alhakami, A., Slovic, P., and Johnson, S. M. (2000). 'The Affect Heuristic in Judgments of Risks and Benefits', *Journal of Behavioral Decision Making*, 13: 1–17.

Fischer-Rosenthal, W. (2000). 'Biographical Work and Biographical Structuring in Present-day Societies', in P. Chamberlayne, J. Bornat, and T. Wengraf (eds.), *The Turn to Biographical Methods in Social Science. Comparative Issues and Examples*. London, New York: Routledge, pp. 109–25.

Freudenburg, W. R. (2000). 'The "Risk society" Reconsidered: Recreancy, the Division of Labor, and Risks to the Social Fabric', in M. J. Cohen (ed.), *Risk in the Modern Age. Social Theory, Science and Environmental Decision-Making*. Palgrave, pp. 107–20.

Freudenburg, W., Coleme, C. L., Gonzale, J. and Helgeland, C. (1996). 'Media Coverage of Hazard Events,' *Analysing Assumptions Risk Analysis*, 16(1), 31–42.

Furedi, F. (1997). *Culture of Fear: Risk-Taking and the Morality of Low Expectation*. London, Washington: Cassell.

—— (2002). *The Culture of Fear*. London, New York: Continuum.

Giddens, A. (1991). *Modernity and Self-Identity*. Cambridge: Polity Press.

—— (1994). *Beyond Left and Right: The Future of Radical Politics*. Stanford, Calif: Stanford University Press.

Irwin, A., Simmons, P. and Walker, G. (1999). Faulty Environments and Risk Reasoning: The Local Understanding of Industrial Hazards. *Environment and Planning, A31*, 1311–28.

Japp, K. P. (2000). *Risiko*. Bielefeld, Germany: Transcript Verlag.

Kasperson, R. E. and Kasperson, J. X. (1996). The Social Amplification and Attenuation of Risk. *The Annals of The American Academy of Political and Social Science*, 545, 95–105.

Katz, J. (1988). *Seductions of Crime: Moral and Sensual Attractions in Doing Evil*. New York: Basic Books.

Keynes, John M. (1936). *The General Theory of Employment, Interest and Money*. Macmillan. London.

Kitzinger, J. (1999). 'Researching risk and the media', *Health, Risk and Society*, 1: 55–69.

Klinke, A. and Renn, O. (2002). 'A New Approach to Risk Evaluation and Management: Risk-Based, Precaution-Based, and Discourse-Based Strategies', *Risk Analysis*, 22: 1071–94.

Loewenstein, G., Weber, E., Hsee, C., and Welch, N. (2001). 'Risks as Feelings', *Psychological Bulletin*, 127: 267–86.

Luhmann, N. (1979). *Trust and Power*. Chichester, New York, Brisbane, Toronto: John Wiley.

—— (1995). *Social Systems*. Stanford, CA: Stanford University Press.

Lupton, D. and Tulloch, J. (2002). '"Life would be pretty dull without risk": Voluntary Risk-taking and its Pleasures', *Health, Risk and Society*, 4: 113–24.

Lyng, S. (2005). 'Sociology at the Edge: Social Theory and Voluntary Risk Taking', in S. Lyng (ed.), *Edgework. The Sociology of Risk-Taking*. New York, London: Routledge, 17–49.

Lyng, S. G. and Snow, D. A. (1986). 'Vocabularies of Motive and High-Risk Behaviour: The Case of Skydiving', in E. J. Lawler (ed.), *Advances in Group Processes*, pp. 157–79.

Murdock, G., Petts, J., and Horlick-Jones, T. (2003). 'After Amplification: Rethinking the Role of the Media in Risk Communication', in N. Pidgeon, R. E. Kasperson, and P. Slovic (eds.), *The Social Amplification of Risk*. Cambridge: Cambridge University Press, pp. 156–78.

PABE (Public Perception of Agricultural Biotechnologies in Europe) 2002: Final Report of the PABE research project funded by the Commission of European Communities. Contract number: FAIR CT98-3844 (DG12-SSMI).

Pidgeon, N. F., Kasperson, R. E., and Slovic, P. (2003). *The Social Amplification of Risk*. Cambridge, New York: Cambridge University Press.

Pixley, J. (2002). 'Emotions and Economics', in J. Barbalet (ed.), *Emotions and Sociology*. Oxford, Malden MA: Blackwell Publishing/The Sociological Review, pp. 69–89.

—— (2004). *Emotions in Finance: Distrust and Uncertainty in Global Markets*. Cambridge, UK, New York: Cambridge University Press.

Pound, P., Gompertz, P., and Ebrahim, S. (1998). 'Illness in the Context of Older Age: The Case of Stroke', *Sociology of Health and Illness*, 20: 489–506.

Putnam, R. D. (2000). *Bowling Alone: The Collapse and Revival of American Community*. New York: Simon Schuster.

Renn, O., Burns, W. J., Kasperson, J. X., Kasperson, R. E., Slovic, P. (1992). The Social Amplification of Risk: Theoretical Foundations and Empirical Applications. *Journal of Social Issues*, 48(4), 137–60.

Renn, O. and Levine, D. (1991). 'Credibility and Trust in Risk Communication', in R. E. Kasperson and P. J. M. Stallen (eds.), *Communicating Risks to the Public*. Dordrecht, Boston, London: Kluwer, pp. 175–217.

―――and Rohrmann, B. (2000). *Cross-Cultural Risk Perception. A Survey of Empirical Studies*. Dordrecht, Boston, London: Kluwer.

Rescher, N. (1983). *Risk: A Philosophical Introduction to the Theory of Risk Evaluation and Management*. University Press of America.

Rolls, E. T. (1999). *The Brain and Emotion*. New York: Oxford University Press.

Rose, N. (1995). 'The Death of the Social', *Economy and Society*, 25: 327–56.

Rosenthal, G. (2004). 'Biographical research,' in C. Seale, G. Gobo, J. F. Gubrium, and D. Silverman (eds.), *Qualitative Research Practice*. London, Thousand Oaks, New Delhi: SAGE, pp. 48–64.

Schelling, T. (1984). 'Self-Command in Practice, in Policy, and in a Theory of Rational Choice,' *American Economic Review*, 74: 1–11.

Schumpeter, J. (1976). *Capitalism, Socialism and Democracy*. London: Allen and Unwin.

Siegrist, M., Cvetkovich, G., and Roth, C. (2000). 'Salient Value Similarity, Social Trust, and Risk/Benefit Perception,' *Risk Analysis*, 20: 353–62.

Slovic, P. (1999). 'Trust, Emotion, Sex, Politics, and Science: Surveying the Risk-Assessment Battlefield', *Risk Analysis*, 19: 689–701.

―――Finucane, M. L., Peters, E., and MacGregor, D. G. (2004). 'Risk as Analysis and Risk as Feelings. Some Thoughts About Affect, Reason, Risk, and Rationality', *Risk Analysis*, 19: 689–701.

Spencer, W. J. (1994). Media Construction of Risk and Safety: Differential Framings of Hazard Events. *Sociological Inquiry*, 64(2), 199–213.

STAGE (Science Technology and Governance in Europe: Challenge of Public Engagement) (2005): Science, Technology and Governance in Europe. Final Report.

TRUSTNET (1999). A New Perspective on Risk Governance.

―――(2004). Towards Inclusive Risk Governance. Trustnet 2.

Tullock, J. (2000). ' "Landscapes of Fear", Public places, fear of crime and the media', in A. Stuart, B. Adam and C. Cynthia (eds.), *Environmental Risks and the Media*. London; New York: Routledge, pp. 184–97.

Tulloch, J. and Lupton, D. (2003). *Risk and Everyday Life*. London: Sage.

Vaughan, D. (1996). *The Challenger Launch Decision: Risky Technology, Culture, and Deviance at NASA*. Chicago, IL: University of Chicago Press.

Weyman, A. and Kelly, C. (1999). *Risk Perception and Communication: A Review of the Literature, Health and Safety Executive, Research Report, 248/99*.

Wildavsky, A. B. (1988). *Searching for Safety*. New Brunswick, NJ: Transaction Books.

―――(1995). *But is it True?: A Citizen's Guide to Environmental Health and Safety Issues*. Cambridge, MA: Harvard University Press.

Wilkinson, I. (2001). 'Social Theories of Risk Perception: At Once Indispensable and Insufficient', *Current Sociology*, 49: 1–22.

—— (2004a). *Suffering. A Sociological Introduction*. Cambridge: Polity Press.

—— (2004b). 'The Problem of "Social Suffering". The Challenge to Social Science', *Health Sociology Review*, 13: 113–21.

Wilsdon, J. and Willis, R. (2004). *See-through Science*. London: DEMOS.

Wilson, K. M. (2000). 'Communicating climate change through the media Predictions, Politics and Perceptions of risk', in A. Stuart, B. Adam and C. Carter (eds.), *Environmental Risks and the Media*. London; New York: Routledge, pp. 201–17.

Zinn, J. O. (2004). 'Health, Risk and Uncertainty in the Life Course: A Typology of Biographical Certainty Constructions', *Social Theory and Health*, 2: 199–221.

—— (2004a). *Sociology and Risk*. ESRC-network Social Contexts and Responses to Risk (SCARR) working paper 2/2004 (http://www.kent.ac.uk/scarr/papers/papers.htm), University of Kent, Canterbury.

—— (2005). 'The Biographical Approach—A Better Way to Understand Behaviour in Health and Illness?', *Health, Risk and Society*, 7: 1–9.

—— (2005a). *The Challenge of Uncertainty*. Presentation at the BSA Risk & Society Study Group, 4th Annual Conference (4–6th Sept. 2005), Liverpool Hope University College, Liverpool.

4

Crime and Risk

Hazel Kemshall

Introduction

Crime and risk have become intrinsically linked, and contemporary penal practices have been significantly influenced by the risk society (although just how extensively is a matter of some debate [Pratt 2000a, 2000b; Rose 2000; Sparks 2000]). The key contention is that the modernist disciplinary agenda delivered through the welfare state has been replaced by a welfare-penal agenda based upon risk (Kemshall 2002a). The modernist agenda[1] sought to rehabilitate and normalize offenders, and to discipline the wider population through the 'soft policing' of welfare (Donzelot 1980; Garland 1985, 1996). However, by the close of the twentieth century the modernist agenda was discredited, primarily on the grounds of cost in a shrinking welfare state (see Kemshall 2002a for a full discussion), and as inadequate for the containment of crime (Pratt 2000a). The 'social causes of crime' were dismissed (heralding the 'death of the social' Rose 1996a), and crime management through treatment was seen as a failure (Martinson 1974). The Thatcher years (1979–90) saw an era of 'prison works' and tougher community penalties and the development of what has been labelled a New Right penology (James and Raine 1998). This period saw a severe challenge to the cost and effectiveness of criminal justice and concern with increased crime rates, and discontent with interventions that focused on the 'causes of crime' (McLaughlin and Muncie 1996). This was epitomized by Thatcher's famous statement that there is 'no such thing as society'. The welfare paradigm was replaced by a justice paradigm emphasizing personal responsibility, culpability, and blame, and a prioritization of punishment over rehabilitation. This trend continued throughout the

1980s and 1990s and led many penal policy commentators to argue for a 'new penology'.

A New Penology?

Whilst the terms postmodernity and late modern are open to some debate (see Kellner 1999 for a full review), theoretical insights from the risk society and postmodernity realms have influenced much recent crime research and analyses. Within criminology these theoretical features can be seen in debates about the extent or otherwise of the new 'risk penality' (Feeley and Simon 1994) and the extent to which penal practices have been transformed by conditions of postmodernity (Garland 1996, 2000; Pratt 2000*a*, 2000*b*, 2000*c*). However, whilst there is much evidence of the prevalence of risk concerns and the impact of actuarial practices on criminal justice (Kemshall 2003), there is extensive debate as to whether penal policy and crime management is solely governed by risk (O'Malley 2000, 2004; Hudson 2002). In particular, commentators disagree about the extent to which penal practices are governed by risk, and whether the modernist agenda is really defunct (O'Malley 2004). Whilst disputes continue to rage (see O'Malley 2001) there is some consensus about the main precursors and key themes of the new penology:

- The rise and extension of capitalism, and the development of techniques to discipline and regulate the workforce particularly the 'underclass'.
- The use of actuarial risk practices to ensure civil stability and social order.
- Concerns with the management of the 'dangerous class' and the risk distribution of 'bads'.
- The role of risk in social utility thinking, in particular the influence of modernist reason and rational thought in the development of economic and legal approaches to social and penal policy.
- Economic pressures on crime management and concerns to effectively and efficiently manage criminal justice systems.
- The retreat from liberal crime management and penal policy under conditions of advanced liberalism. (Kemshall 2003: 29)

The major claim of interest here is that the new penality is characterized by a shift from a disciplinary focus on individual behaviour and the possibility of change towards the management of risk distribution and the 'management in place' of those segments of the population not amenable to change (Kemshall and Maguire 2001).

Key Research Themes

Research into crime and risk has tended to be eclectic, both empirically and theoretically, and has drawn on a number of theoretical perspectives, ranging from rational choice theory in studies of situational crime prevention and offender desistance studies (Felson and Clarke 1997); to positivist approaches to the development and evaluation of risk assessment tools (Bonta 1996); and governmentality theories to explore penal practice and the regulation of conduct (Rose 2000). These are discussed in detail below.

Research has also been policy led, with the emphasis upon economic crime risk management leading to a number of initiatives such as the recent Crime Reduction Programme (CRP) requiring evaluation. The CRP initially earmarked £400 million for programmes (although as Maguire [2004] states rather less was spent), and was spawned by 'evidence-based' policy. The CRP reflected particular government interest in the potential of multi-agency partnerships (Morgan 1991), and situational crime prevention techniques (advocated by Ekblom, Law, and Sutton 1996) (see Maguire 2004 for a full review).

Rational Choice Theory, Situational Crime Prevention, and the Rational Choice Actor

The conceptualization of the offender as a rational choice actor was progressed by both research and policy throughout the 1980s and 1990s as part of the New Right agenda of crime management and parallels similar developments in health and social care (Kemshall 2002a, 2002b, 2003). The rational actor is characterized as 'volitional and rational' (Lupton 1999: 21) and the emphasis upon personal choice and responsibility reflected an era in which the 'social' was eschewed (Rose 1996a). The rational actor is represented as an 'information processing unit', and any actor who fails to process information correctly (e.g. towards pre-specified desirable ends) is characterized as irrational (Bloor 1995; Lupton 1999). Research in this area usually takes place within a realist paradigm and is most often investigated using cognitive science (the 'psy' disciplines), and treatment/interventions are shaped by this (e.g. cognitive behavioural therapy). Risk is generally investigated at the individual level, for example, studies of risk perception, risk-taking behaviour (such as drug-taking), and desistance, or by collecting public perceptions of crime (some of which are then deemed 'out of step' with expert views on prevalence rates). Within criminology, the rational choice actor is located within the positivist tradition, and is characterized as a 'free-willed actor who engages in crime in a calculative, utilitarian way and is therefore responsive to deterrent' (Garland 1997: 11).

Crime management and research in this arena has focused on two areas: individual choice and the crime opportunity. Research attention to individual choice has been most discernible in desistance studies (why offenders stop offending), and in the cost-benefit calculations seen to underpin many crime prevention strategies (e.g. the locks and bolts approach to discouraging criminals). Informed by risk research in other areas (Slovic 1992) the rational choice approach frames the offender as a rational, calculative actor capable of making an informed risk decision based upon a cost-benefit ratio if only given the correct information and if only the costs of crime are made to outweigh the benefits. Desistance studies have been focused on how these calculations are made, and what costs and benefits are literally being weighed (Cornish and Clarke 1986). Until recently these studies focused on individual rather than social or structural factors, and have contributed to an individualization of offending distanced from any social causation (Young 1992, 1994). They have produced what Farrall (2002) and Maruna (2000a) have called correlates of desistance, for example, stable employment, but cannot explain the 'precise sequence of events and processes involved' (Farrall 2002: 3) leaving us with an unexplained 'black box' of desistance (Maruna 2000a: 12; Maruna 2000b).

The studies have also reinforced the notion of individual choice and 'wickedness', and vested blame and responsibility for offending solely with individual offenders, thus reinforcing New Right responses to crime. They also confirmed that some offenders would continue to have criminal careers regardless of interventions, and that such careers could be interrupted either by custody or by the reduction of crime opportunities. Rational choice began to take on a new agenda, the 'designing out' of crime (Clarke and Mayhew 1980) and the reduction of crime opportunities through situational crime prevention and the control of environments. In crime prevention terms this resulted in policies that increased the chances of being caught, for example, CCTV, making homes more burglar proof, introducing neighbourhood watch, and making cars more thief proof, literally increasing the cost to the offender. These initiatives were subject to extensive evaluation (Maguire 2004; Raynor 2004), although whether they reduce crime or merely displace it to other less well-regulated areas is a much debated point (Hughes 1998).

Following research into other areas of risk, not least drug use, HIV and condom use (Bloor 1995), and other health related issues (Petersen and Lupton 1996), the rational actor has been much critiqued by the sociological research literature (Lupton 1999). The interaction between knowledge of a risk and subsequent action is seen as much more complex (Lupton 1999), affected by distorted perceptions, constraints on personal choice, limited opportunities to act otherwise, group norms and influences, and so on (Bloor 1995; Grinyer 1995; Rhodes 1997; Kemshall 2003: 60). In the desistance area this has resulted in a more interactive approach concerned with opening the black box (Farrall and Bowling 1999; Farrall 2002), emphasizing the complexity of desistance using Byrne's approach which argues that social processes have multiple causes; that such causes are not merely additive; and that subtle differences in initial conditions may over time produce large differences in outcomes (Byrne 1998: 2–28; Farrall 2002: 42).

Reviewing the Rational Actor: Reintroducing the Social

This reshaping of the rational actor has introduced important notions of context, power (e.g. to act differently), and opportunity (to avoid or resist risky situations) into risk research (see Bloor 1995; Rhodes 1995; Green 1997). In crime management this has led to revisions in both desistance studies and situational crime management. Research in this area focuses on contextual and structural issues and casts the rational actor as a *social* actor, and focus is upon how these processes work and impact upon risk decisions, and how risk decisions vary across different contexts. Social action theories conceptualize risk as the product of social interaction, context specific, and bounded by group norms and values (Douglas 1986). Research studies focus on the interactive notion of risk and seeks to place risk decision-making within context.

In the desistance arena, it has led to a reintroduction of the 'social', with attention to the role of social factors in decisions to desist (May 1999). However, these factors (e.g. accommodation, employment, drug use) have not added that much to the predictive criminal variables of age, gender, and number of previous convictions (May 1999). However, these social factors assist with explanations of the process and choice of desistance (Farrall 2002). More recent studies have been concerned with structural constraints on decision-making and take place within a 'weak constructivist' paradigm in which real risks are seen as 'inevitably mediated through these social processes and can never be known in isolation from these processes' (Lupton 1999: 35). Research focuses on opportunities and power to desist, and the social factors and resources that play a role in such decisions (Maruna 2000*a*, 2000*b*; Farrall 2002). The interaction of agency and structure is increasingly posed as a key theoretical concern of such research (Farrall and Bowling 1999).

In situational crime management routine activity theory (Cohen and Felson 1979) has recast the rational choice actor as an adaptive one and the cost-benefit equation as one that is always changing (Ekblom 1997, 2001). Crime and its attendant opportunities are always changing (e.g. computer fraud, or the growth of internet pornography). For Ekblom the only response to this is a constant anticipationism from policymakers and crime prevention personnel. Crime proofing requires non-criminals to 'think thief' and to constantly anticipate and remove crime opportunities. However, such anticipationism has a built in obsolescence, prevention strategies can never keep up, and they fall into disrepute as they fail. However, the approach has been useful for introducing the interaction between offender, crime opportunity and situation into the risk calculation. How the rational actor interacts with his/her context is seen as crucial to effective crime management.

Risk Tools: The Pursuit of Certainty

Risk tools have been another area subject to much research and evaluation. Such tools have been seen as essential to the proper functioning of actuarial justice providing the mechanism by which offenders can be identified and classified for risk-based interventions (Kemshall 2003). Commentators have associated the development of risk tools within the New Penology and located their use within an economic discourse of crime control (see Kemshall 2003: ch. 3 for a full review). Risk tools have also been inscribed within the responsibilization project of advanced liberal governance (Rose 2000; O'Malley 2004), assisting with the identification of offenders for corrective programmes and moral re-engineering (Gibbs, Basinger, and Fuller 1992; Kemshall 2002*b*). Tool development has generated research into risk factors to predict offending and characterize certain individuals as risky, based largely on meta-analysis and the profiling of risk recidivism factors and more recently harm factors. Research is within the realist paradigm, utilizing quantitative methods, and has produced what has been called a 'risk factorology' for use in criminal justice agencies such as police and probation (Kemshall 2003).

Risk assessment tools have played a key role in regulating the practice of criminal justice personnel and providing a mechanism for allocating offenders to different 'treatment modalities' (Bonta 1996). In essence, such tools provide a rationing mechanism for scarce resources in criminal justice (e.g. intensive behavioural programmes in probation). These assessment tools have focused mainly on the prediction of recidivism rates (the likelihood of reconviction in a particular [usually 2 year] period). The nationally accredited tool for use in probation and prisons in England and Wales is the Offender Assessment System (OASys) derived largely from Home Office reconviction studies and the 'what works' literature (Clark 2002). The quoted figure for the accuracy rate of OASys is 69.2 per cent (Clark 2002). However, the tool has not been specifically designed to predict the risk of harm and this is the least actuarially developed part of the tool (reflecting in part base rate issues in this area). The tool's major contribution is in the area of criminogenic risk assessment and in targeting offenders for intervention programmes in prison and probation (Kemshall 2003). The most common risk of harm tool is MATRIX 2000 used exclusively for the assessment of sex offenders within police and probation. The tool has been validated retrospectively against a 20-year follow-up of reconvictions and found to identify high-risk offenders of whom 60 per cent were reconvicted (Grubin 2000; Thornton 2002; Grubin 2004).

The history of risk tools has been characterized as an attempt to 'tame chance' and reduce uncertainty through the use of formalized risk methods of assessment and calculation (Hacking 1987, 1990; Reddy 1996). Bonta (1996) has presented the development of risk tools as a journey to ever increasing accuracy and reliability. Research in this field has tended to pursue an uncritical and technical approach to risk, framing risk as an 'artefact' in which it is framed as objectively knowable and amendable to probabilistic calculation (Bradbury 1989; Horlick-Jones 1998). Risk tools are embedded in empiricism, scientific canons of proof, probabilistic thinking, and a realist epistemology of risk. Early work is characterized by positivist methods of data collection (statistical methods and meta-analysis) and the collection of risk variables to identify particular segments of the population. Such tools have gained much currency within police, probation, and prisons (Kemshall 1998, 2001, 2003; Robinson 2001), but research into both their use and development has resulted in a number of critiques.

The most common critique is from research into how tools are used by practitioners 'on the ground' that has examined how actuarial practices are mediated by both workers and institutional barriers to implementation (Kemshall 1998; Lynch 2000; Robinson 2001). As O'Malley has put it, actuarial practices are rarely implemented in pure form (2001, 2004). This latter work raises the issue of context in risk practice, and the particular influences of values, culture, organizational structures, and the belief systems of staff and the impact upon risk decision-making (Kemshall 1998; Kemshall and Maguire 2001; Robinson 2001). This has focused some attention on implementation issues (Kemshall 1998) and also on sites of resistance to actuarialism (O'Malley 2001; Robinson 2001, 2002), without characterizing the workforce as irrational.

Criticisms have also been made on methodological grounds (see Kemshall 2001, 2003 for a review), and on the grounds of non-transferability or indeed discrimination against certain groups (e.g women, Hannah-Moffat and Shaw 1999). Such criticisms have also raised research interest in how certain populations are singled out for risk attention, and how certain risks are chosen for attention (Sparks 2000, 2001a, 2001b). This research draws on cultural and social theory and is carried out in the 'strong constructivist' paradigm (Lupton 1999) and is epitomized by work on fear of crime and victimization (Lupton and Tulloch 1999; Lupton 2000; Hope and Sparks 2000; Sutton and Farrall 2005), but also includes work on media coverage and crime (Sparks 2001a, 2001b; Kitzinger 2004; see also Jewkes 2004 for an introduction to the issue), and on the relationship between risk practices and modes of governance (Rose 2000). This is considered in the next section, and sees the definition of risk and criminological attention to it, change from risk factors and calculations of probability to a broader concern with 'social insecurities' (Goodey 2005).

Crime, Risk, and Regulation

Within cultural approaches to risk research in the crime arena, the traditional binary conceptualizations such as 'real' and 'imaginary fears', and 'lay' and 'expert' perceptions of risk are discounted in order to examine how such risks are produced (Lupton 2000). Within this framing of risk the focus is not individual risk decision-making, but on how some risks are chosen for attention whilst others are not (e.g. the attention to 'Stranger-Danger' in child sexual abuse and the relative neglect of sexual abusing within families [Kitzinger 2004]). Such work pays attention to the symbolic and cultural meanings carried by risk (Douglas 1992), and the political rationalities and strategies that underpin them (Sparks 2001b). In essence, risk technologies are not morally neutral but always carry a political and morally infused message (O'Malley 2004). Much work of this type is about 'unpicking' such underlying rationalities.

Governmentality theorists in particular 'explore risk in the context of surveillance, discipline, and regulation of populations, and how concepts of risk construct particular norms of behaviour which are used to encourage individuals to engage voluntarily in self-regulation in response to these norms' (Lupton 1999: 25). This is what Rose has termed responsibilization (Rose 1996a, 2000). Rose (1996a, b) argues that governance in neo-liberal societies is carried out at the 'molecular level' in which the active citizen is required to self-regulate towards the preset norms of society. Those who fail to exercise the prudential risk choice are excluded, marginalized, and demonized. Offenders, particularly those deemed dangerous or intransigent are a case in point, leading to what Garland has called 'a criminology of the Other' (Garland 2001). Governmentality theorists argue that the State's power is dispersed, and that overt power is exercised more subtly through facilitation, education, advice, training, and public health campaigns all seeking to provide the active and risk alert citizen with sound information upon which to make his or her risk choice. Those who fail to make the wise choice are blamed, and deemed to be in need of corrective programmes to alter their faulty thinking. Whilst the rational actor is also at the heart of this approach, the research focus is with how a particular construction of the rational actor is formed and the role it plays in the governance of conduct and the regulation of populations.

In criminology, this social constructivist approach to risk is epitomized by work on fear of crime and victimization in which the 'knowledges, discourses, and experiences used by people to construct their notions of risk and fear' are investigated (Lupton 2000: 23). In this area attention has been given to the gendered nature of victim experiences and fear of crime (Walklate 1997),[2] the risk of repeat victimization and the inequitable distribution of victimization risks (Hope and Walklate 1995), and the relationship between daily lived experiences (what Hope and Sparks 2000 call 'tribulations of place') and fear of crime. The importance of this work is in its ability to 'plot' differences in risk perception across communities, and between public and experts without reducing such differences to irrationality. The British Crime Survey (Budd, Sharp, and Mayhew 2005) now plots differential exposure to risk across differing segments of the population, recording higher levels for British Minority Ethnic (BME) groups (Home Office Findings 237); and much recent research is examining how location and context play a significant role in victimization risks and perception of crime rates (Goodey 2005).

From a broader perspective, the drive towards responsibilization and the creation of an 'active citizen' (Rose 1996) is seen as compounding existing inequalities (Walklate 1998). In brief, some sections of the population do not have the resources to become expert risk managers of their fate and the 'activeness' of some citizens can be heavily curtailed by poverty, social exclusion, and geographic location. The ability to self-risk manage victim risks may be quite different on a 'sink estate' to those deployed in 'fortress middle England' (Stenson 2001).

The concept of responsibilization also raises questions about new techniques of social regulation (although there is some debate about how transformative present conditions currently are, see Garland 2001). This trend can be discerned at two levels: at the level of moral engineering of the individual offender mainly through CBT programmes (Kemshall 2002b) (see discussion above), and at the level of communities through crime prevention (Stenson 2001). As O'Malley puts it, the rational choice offender has become the risky offender, and victims have become 'at risk' citizens (1992, 1994). Crime reduction is now everyone's responsibility (Gamble 1988; O'Malley 1992; Stenson 1993), and responsibility for crime prevention is devolved to public–private partnerships and from the State to local communities (Crawford 2001). Research in this area has tended to be either policy-led, providing evaluations of crime prevention initiatives (Maguire 2004; Raynor 2004), or providing critical analyses of the techniques of responsibilization (Stenson 1999, 2001; Stenson and Edwards 2001). The former research tends towards pragmatic evaluations of 'what works' (Raynor 2004) and is presented as morally neutral from a realist perspective, and the latter investigates the moral assumptions and techniques of regulation underlying crime prevention strategies and operates within a strong constructivist paradigm. This latter focus raises important questions about risk and security, in particular how to provide security within an increasingly diverse and risk-infused society without the use of overt State power (Loader and Sparks 2002). Less risk may mean more surveillance, less justice, and less rights (Hudson 2004).

Recent Key Findings: A Summary

As outlined above, research into risk within the crime arena has been diverse, carried out within differing paradigms and covering a wide range of concerns. However, some key developments can be discerned. The first is the presence of the rational actor and attention to individual risk decision-making. Whilst the characteristics of the rational actor have been subject to revision with increased attention to social and contextual factors, much research takes this actor for granted (or its counterpart, the hedonistic, irrational actor). With the advent of governmentality theorists, the rational actor has been reconstituted and problematized as the active citizen and is now held responsible for personal moral self-regulation—the prudent citizen will act well. The rational actor has also been extended to the rational at risk citizen capable of avoiding crime risky situations if only properly informed and responsible enough, and there has been increased policy and research attention to public perceptions of crime and how to 'deal with' fear of crime.

A further key research development has been interest in whether penology has been transformed by a risk-based approach to justice and the attendant development and use of risk tools and risk practices. This continues to be much investigated and much debated, and empirical studies into actual frontline practices have resulted in some revision of the more general theoretical claims (see, e.g. O'Malley 2004).

As Garland has expressed it, transformations in penality should be evident in the 'material forms' of practice as well as in statements of 'orientation' (1995: 200) and this requires detailed empirical study. Paralleling, but largely distanced from this work, has been research and development of risk assessment tools, with only relatively recent attention to the context of their use and their moral and political implications (Kemshall 2003).

Social regulation in advanced liberal society has also been a growing theme—in effect, how to provide security and effective crime management in societies characterized by diversity, fragmentation, and a shrinking State (Rose 2000; Stenson 2001; Stenson and Edwards 2001; Stenson and Sullivan 2001). This research raises issues of how populations are regulated and managed, how risks are distributed, and the allocation of responsibility for their effective management between communities and the State.

Conclusion: Emerging Problems and Issues

Risk has become 'core business' of the criminal justice system—its management, reduction, and avoidance. Crime has been inscribed as a major risk in the twenty-first century, an ever present risk of everyday life (Garland 2001). How to deal with the risk of crime is now a major policy and research preoccupation. This has spawned quite a research 'industry', much of it policy-led and government funded, but also a large critical industry of commentators and analysts on risk driven penal policy developments.

Whilst it is not possible to review findings from the many studies on crime and risk over the last 10 years it is possible to generalize some major research outcomes. Perhaps the most interesting from the point of view of risk is the increasing challenge to the notion of the rational choice actor and RCT presented by studies on both crime prevention and desistance. Is the concept of a uni-dimensional rational choice actor useful in a society characterized by pluralism and fragmentation? Diversity and the increased contextualization of social life make normative assumptions about the rational actor more problematic. Whose rationality is it? Whose cost and whose benefit? Policy planning based on the rational choice actor has found itself in a position of 'catch up', chasing the 'adaptive actor' and finding situational crime prevention techniques affected by issues of diversity and structural inequality (Hughes 1998). The emphasis upon the local has often reduced national consistency and resulted in 'ghettoization' (Crawford 1998: 264). The rise of 'defensive strategies' such as the use of CCTV and private security has led to the creation of 'fortress cities' based upon exclusionary risk management (Davis 1990; Hughes 1998; Crawford 1999)—those who can afford to do so leave 'threatened places', those who remain assume a higher risk burden with less resources to manage them (Hughes 1998). Whilst policy is largely concerned with the creation of safe spaces, behind this there is an uncritical redistribution of risks that is worthy of further investigation.

In the area of actuarial justice empirical studies into actuarial practices have revised the grand claims of the New Penology by providing evidence of how such practices are often mediated by workers and are embedded in the organizational contexts within which they are used (Kemshall 1998; Lynch 2000; Robinson 2001). This research has shown more variability in risk technologies within the delivery of penality, and has demonstrated that there is no inexorable logic of risk (O'Malley 2001,

2004). This research is also building an empirical evidence base on how risk technologies are actually deployed (see, e.g. Kemshall 2003), and provides a base from which comparative work between differing forms of justice can be made, for example, between actuarial and restorative justice. O'Malley (2004) has argued that risk technologies are not value neutral and that it is important to examine the moral assumptions underlying their construction and deployment. Some risk technologies may be inclusive rather than exclusive, and emphasize rights as well as risks. Such issues raise important questions about the types of risks we wish to avoid and manage, those we deem as bad, and ultimately the type of society we wish to live in.

Notes

1. Most commonly defined as the period of industrialization from the Industrial Revolution to the late 1970s in Western societies. It is characterized by capitalism, industrial expansion, imperialism, representative democracies, and the formation of the welfare state. The modernist agenda is described as the social policy period covered by the formation and operation of the welfare state from the Second World War onwards.
2. The role of gender is now under some dispute—see for example, Sutton and Farrall 2005 who contend that males 'play down' fear of crime and that differences in crime-related anxieties are consequently overstated.

References

Bloor, M. (1995). *The Sociology of HIV Transmission*. London: Sage.

Bonta, J. (1996). 'Risk-needs assessment and treatment', in A. T. Harland (ed.), *Choosing Correctional Options that Work*. Thousand Oaks, CA: Sage.

Bradbury, J. (1989). 'The Policy Implications of Differing Concepts of Risk', *Science, Technology and Human Values*, 14(4): 380–99.

Budd, T., Sharp, C., and Mayhew, P. (2005). *Offending in England and Wales: First Results From the 2003 Crime and Justice Survey*. Home Office Research Study 275. London: Home Office.

Byrne, D. (1998). *Complexity Theory and the Social Sciences*. London: Routledge.

Clark, D. (2002). *OASys—An explanation*. Paper presented to Home Office 'Criminal Justice Conference: Using Risk Assessment in Effective Sentence Management'. Pendley Manor Hotel, Tring 14–15 March.

Clarke, R. and Mayhew, P. (1980). *Designing out Crime*. London: HMSO.

Cohen, L. E. and Felson, M. (1979). 'Social Change and Crime Rate Trends: A Routine Activity Approach', *American Sociological Review*, 44(4): 588–608.

Cornish, D. and Clarke, R. (1986). 'Situational Crime Prevention: Displacement of Crime and Rational Choice Theory', in K. Heal and G. Laycock (eds.), *Situational Crime Prevention: From Theory to Practice*. London: HMSO.

Crawford, A. (1998). *Crime Prevention and Community Safety: Politics, Policies and Practices*. London: Longman.

———(1999). *The Local Governance of Crime: Appeals to Community and Partnerships*. Oxford: Oxford University Press.

———(2001). Joined-up but Fragmented: Contradiction, Ambiguity and Ambivalence at the Heart of New Labour's 'Third Way', in R. Matthews and J. Pitts (eds.), *Crime, Disorder and Community Safety: A New Agenda?* London: Routledge.

Davis, M. (1990). *City of Quartz: Excavating the Future of Los Angeles*. London: Verso.

Donzelot, J. (1980). *The Policing of Families*. London: Hutchinson.

Douglas, M. (1986). *Risk Acceptability According to the Social Sciences*. London: Routledge and Kegan Paul.

———(1992). *Risk and Blame*. London: Routledge.

Ekblom, P. (1997). 'Gearing up Against Crime: A Dynamic Framework to Help Designers Keep up with the Adaptive Criminal in a Changing World', *International Journal of Risk, Security and Crime Prevention*, 214: 249–65.

———(2001). 'Future Imperfect: Preparing for Crimes to Come', *Criminal Justice Matters*, 46 (winter): 38–40.

———Law, H., and Sutton, M. (1996). *Safer Cities and Domestic Burglary. Home Office Research Study 164*. London: Home Office.

Farrall, S. (2002). *Rethinking What Works with Offenders: Probation, Social Context, and Desistance from Crime*. Cullompton, UK: Willan.

———and Bowling, B. (1999). 'Structuration, Human Development and Desistance from Crime', *British Journal of Criminology*, 39(2): 252–67.

Feeley, M. and Simon, J. (1994). 'Actuarial Justice: The Emerging New Penal Law', in D. Nelken (ed.), *The Futures of Criminology*. London: Sage.

Felson, M. and Clarke, R. (1997). 'The Ethics of Situational Crime Prevention', in G. Newman, R. Clarke, and G. Shoham (eds.), *Rational Choice and Situational Crime Prevention: Theoretical Foundations*. Aldershot, UK: Ashgate.

Gamble, A. (1988). *The Free Economy and the Strong State*. London: MacMillan.

Garland, D. (1985). *Punishment and Welfare: A History of Welfare Strategies*. Aldershot, UK: Gower.

———(1995). 'Penal Modernism and Postmodernism', in T. Blomberg and S. Cohen (eds.), *Punishment and Social Control: Essays in Honor of Sheldon Messinger*. New York: Aldine de Gruyer.

———(1996). 'The Limits of the Sovereign State: Strategies of Crime Control in Contemporary Society', *British Journal of Criminology*, 36(4): 445–71.

———(1997). ' "Governmentality" and the Problem of Crime: Foucault, Criminology and Sociology', *Theoretical Criminology*, 1(2): 173–64.

Garland, D. (2000). 'The Culture of High Crime Societies', *British Journal of Criminology*, 40: 347–75.

___(2001). *The Culture of Crime Control: Crime and Social Order in Contemporary Society*. Oxford: Oxford University Press.

Gibbs, J. C., Basinger, K. C., and Fuller, D. (1992). *Moral Maturity: Measuring the Development of Sociomoral Reflection*. Hillsdale, NJ: Erlbaum.

Goodey, J. (2005). *Victims and Victimology: Research, Policy and Practice*. Harlow, UK: Pearson/Longman.

Green, J. (1997). *Risk and Misfortune*. London: UCL Press.

Grinyer, A. (1995). 'Risk, the Real World and Naïve Sociology', in J. Gabe (ed.), *Medicine, Health and Risk: Sociological Approaches*. Oxford: Blackwell.

Grubin, D. (2000). *Risk Matrix 2000*. Paper presented to Risk Assessment and Management Police Conference, Moat House Hotel, Cheltenham, 19–20 October.

___(2004). 'The Risk Assessment of Sex Offenders', in H. Kemshall and G. McIvor (eds.), *Managing Sex Offender Risk*. London: Jessica Kingsley.

Hacking, I. (1987). 'Was There a Probabilistic Revolution 1800–1930?', in I. Kruger, L. Daston, and M. Heidelberger (eds.), *The Probabilistic Revolution*, Vol. 1, *Ideas in History*. Cambridge, MA: MIT Press.

___(1990). *The Taming of Chance*. Cambridge: Cambridge University Press.

Hannah-Moffat, K. and Shaw, M. (1999). *Women and Risk: A Genealogy of Classification*. Paper presented to the British Journal of Criminology Conference, Liverpool, July.

Home Office Findings 237 (2004). *Ethnicity, Victimisation and Worry About Crime: Findings From the 2001/02 and 2002/03 British Crime Surveys*. London: Home Office.

Hope, T. and Sparks, R. (2000). *Crime, Risk and Insecurity*. London: Routledge.

___and Walklate, S. (1995). *Repeat Victimisation: Differentiation or Structuration?* Paper presented to the British Criminology Conference, Loughborough, July.

Horklick-Jones, T. (1998). 'Meaning and Contextualisation in Risk Assessment', *Reliability Engineering and System Safety*, 5: 79–89.

Hudson, B. (2002). 'Punishment and control', in M. Maguire, R. Morgan, and R. Reiner (eds.), *The Oxford Handbook of Criminology*. Oxford: Oxford University Press.

___(2004). *Justice in the Risk Society*. London: Sage.

Hughes, G. (1998). *Understanding Crime Prevention: Social Control, Risk and Late Modernity*. Buckingham, UK: Open University Press.

James, A. and Raine, J. (1998). *The New Politics of Criminal Justice*. London: Longman.

Jewkes, Y. (2004). *Media and Crime*. London: Sage.

Kellner, D. (1999). 'Theorizing the Present Moments: Debates Between Modern and Post-modern Theory', *Theory and Society*, 28: 639–56.

Kemshall, H. (1998). *Risk in Probation Practice*. Aldershot, UK: Ashgate.

—— (2001). *Risk Assessment and Management of Known Sexual and Violent Offenders. Home Office Police Research Series 140*. London: Home Office.

—— (2002a). *Risk, Social Policy and Welfare*. Buckingham, UK: Open University Press.

—— (2002b). 'Effective Practice in Probation: An Example of "Advanced Liberal Responsibilisation"', *Howard Journal of Criminal Justice*, 41(1): 41–58.

—— (2003). *Understanding Risk in Criminal Justice*. Buckingham, UK: Open University Press.

—— and Maguire, M. (2001). 'Public Protection, Partnership and Risk Penality: the Multi-agency Risk Management of Sexual and Violent Offenders', *Punishment and Society*, 3(2): 237–64.

Kitzinger, J. (2004). *Framing Abuse: Media Influence and Public Understanding of Sexual Violence Against Children*. London: Pluto Press.

Loader, I. and Sparks, R. (2002). 'Contemporary Landscapes of Crime, Order and Control: Governance, Risk and Globalisation', in M. Maguire, R. Morgan, and R. Reiner (eds.), *The Oxford Handbook of Criminology*. Oxford: Oxford University Press.

Lupton, D. (1999). *Risk*. London: Routledge.

—— (2000). 'Part of Living in the Late Twentieth Century: Notions of Risk and Fear in Relation to Crime', *Australian and New Zealand Journal of Criminology*, 32(1): 21–36.

—— and Tulloch, J. (1999). 'Theorizing Fear of Crime: Beyond the Rational/ Irrational Opposition', *British Journal of Sociology*, 50(3): 507–23.

Lynch, M. (2000). 'Rehabilitation and Rhetoric: The Ideal of Reformation in Contemporary Parole Discourse and Practices', *Punishment and Society*, 2(1): 40–65.

Maguire, M. (2004). 'The Crime Reduction Programme in England and Wales: Reflections on the Vision and the Reality', *Criminal Justice*, 4(3): 213–37.

Martinson, R. (1974). 'What Works? Questions and Answers About Prison Reform', *The Public Interest*, 10: 22–54.

Maruna, S. (2000a). 'Desistance From Crime and Offender Rehabilitation: A Tale of Two Research Literatures', *Offender Programs Report*, 4(1).

—— (2000b). 'Criminology, Desistance and the Psychology of the Stranger', in D. Canter and L. J. Alison (eds.), *Beyond Profiling: Developments in Investigative Psychology*. Aldershot, UK: Dartmouth.

May, C. (1999). *Explaining Reconviction Following a Community Sentence: The Role of Social Factors. Home Office Research Study 192*. London: Home Office.

McLaughlin, E. and Muncie, J. (1996). *Controlling Crime*. London: Sage.

Morgan, J. (1991). *Safer Communities: The Local Delivery of Crime Prevention Through the Partnership Approach* (Morgan report). London: Home Office.

O'Malley, P. (1992). 'Risk, Power and Crime Prevention', *Economy and Society*, 21(3): 252–75.

—— (1994). 'Responsibility and Crime Prevention: A Response to Adam Sutton', *Australian and New Zealand Journal of Criminology*, 21 (4c), special edition.

—— (2000). 'Risk Societies and the Government of Crime', in M. Brown and J. Pratt (eds.), *Dangerous Offenders: Punishment and Social Order*. London: Routledge.

—— (2001). 'Risk, Crime and Prudentialism Revisited', in K. Stenson and R. Sullivan (eds.), *Crime, Risk and Justice: The Politics of Crime Control in Liberal Democracies*. Cullompton, UK: Willan.

—— (2004). 'The Uncertain Promise of Risk. The Australian and New Zealand', *Journal of Criminology*, 37(3): 323–43.

Petersen, A. and Lupton, D. (1996). *The New Public Health: Health and Self in the Age of Risk*. London: Sage.

Pratt, J. (2000a). 'The Return of the Wheelbarrow Men; Or, The Arrival of Postmodern Penality', *British Journal of Criminology*, 40: 127–45.

—— (2000b). 'Emotive and Ostentatious Punishment: Its Decline and Resurgence in Modern Society', *Punishment and Society*, 2(4): 417–40.

—— (2000c). 'Dangerousness and Modern Society', in M. Brown and J. Pratt (eds.), *Dangerous Offenders: Punishment and Social Order*. London: Routledge.

Raynor, P. (2004). 'The Probation Service "Pathfinders": Finding the Path and Losing the Way?', *Criminal Justice*, 4(3): 309–25.

Reddy, S. (1996). 'Claims to Expert Knowledge and the Subversion of Democracy: The Triumph of Risk Over Uncertainty', *Economy and Society*, 25(2): 222–54.

Rhodes, T. (1997). 'Risk Theory in Epidemic Times: Sex, Drugs and the Social Organisation of "Risk Behaviour"', *Sociology of Health and Illness*, 19(2): 737–48.

Robinson, G. (2001). 'Power, Knowledge and "What Works" in Probation', *Howard Journal of Criminal Justice*, 40(3): 235–54.

—— (2002). 'A Rationality of Risk in the Probation Service: Its Evolution and Contemporary Profile', *Punishment and Society*, 4(1): 5–25.

Rose, N. (1996a). 'The Death of the Social? Re-figuring the Territory of Government', *Economy and Society*, 25(3): 327–56.

—— (1996b). 'Governing "Advanced" Liberal Democracies', in A. Barry, T. Osborne, and N. Rose (eds.), *Foucault and Political Reason: Liberalism, Neo-liberalism and Rationalities of Government*. London: UCL Press.

—— (2000). 'Government and Control', *British Journal of Criminology*, 40: 321–39.

Slovic, P. (1992). 'Perceptions of Risk: Reflections on the Psychometric Paradigm', in S. Krimsky and D. Golding (eds.), *Social Theories of Risk*. Westport, CT: Praeger.

Sparks, R. (2000). 'Risk and Blame in Criminal Justice Controversies: British Press Coverage of Official Discourse on Prison Security (1993–1996)', in M. Brown and J. Pratt (eds.), *Dangerous Offenders: Punishment and Social Order*. London: Routledge.

_____(2001a). ' "Bringing it all Back Home": Populism, Media Coverage and the Dynamics of Locality and Globality in the Politics of Crime Control', in K. Stenson and R. R. Sullivan (eds.), *Crime, Risk and Justice: The Politics of Crime Control in Liberal Democracies*. Cullumpton, UK: Willan.

_____(2001b). 'Degrees of Estrangement: The Cultural Theory of Risk and Comparative Penology', *Theoretical Criminology*, 5(2): 159–76.

Stenson, K. (1993). 'Community Policing as a Government Technology', *Economy and Society*, 22: 373–89.

_____(1999). 'Crime Control, Governmentality and Sovereignty', in R. Smandych (ed.), *Governable Places: Readings in Governmentality and Crime Control*. Aldershot, UK: Dartmouth.

_____(2001). 'The New Politics of Crime Control', in K. Stenson and R. R. Sullivan (eds.), *Crime, Risk and Justice: The Politics of Crime Control in Liberal Democracies*. Cullumpton, UK: Willan.

_____and Edwards, A. (2001). 'Crime Control and Liberal Government: The "Third Way" and the Return to the Local', in K. Stenson and R. R. Sullivan (eds.), *Crime, Risk and Justice: The Politics of Crime Control in Liberal Democracies*. Cullompton, UK: Willan.

_____and Sullivan, R. R. (eds.). (2001). *Crime, Risk and Justice: The Politics of Crime Control in Liberal Democracies*. Cullompton, UK: Willan.

Sutton, R. M. and Farrall, S. (2005). 'Gender, Socially Desirable Responding and the Fear of Crime', *British Journal of Criminology*, 45(2): 212–24.

Thornton, D. (2002). 'Constructing and Testing a Framework for Dynamic Risk Assessment', *Sexual Abuse: A Journal of Research and Treatment*, 14: 139–53.

Walklate, S. (1997). 'Risk and Criminal Victimisation', *British Journal of Criminology*, 37(1): 35–45.

_____(1998). *Understanding Criminology*. Buckingham, UK: Open University Press.

Young, J. (1992). 'Ten Points of Realism', in J. Young and R. Matthews (eds.), *Rethinking Criminology: The Realist Debate*. London: Sage.

_____(1994). 'Incessant Chatter: Recent Paradigms in Criminology', in M. Maguire, R. Morgan, and R. Reiner (eds.), *The Oxford Handbook of Criminology*, 1st edn. Oxford: Clarendon Press.

5

Risk, Environment, and Technology

Nick Pidgeon, Peter Simmons, and Karen Henwood

Although philosophers and social scientists have a long history of raising questions about the appropriate relationship between science and wider society, such questioning is more widespread today as policymakers and members of the public face controversies over the environment, health, and the introduction of new technologies. Disputes that emerged in the 1960s and 1970s over the risks of nuclear power have been followed by concerns in some countries over chemicals and pesticides, industrial and transport related pollution, genetically modified foods, and latterly nanotechnology. Many such controversies involve differing views about the meaning of risk, its acceptance, and distribution across society.

This chapter reviews the wealth of research findings on how people appraise environmental and technological risks. Its scope includes both harm to the quality of the environment from ongoing human activities such as large-scale technological systems and industrial processes, as well as threats to human well-being with environmental/technological origins. The latter, as in the case of climate change, in turn often themselves derive from a close and complex set of interactions between human activities and 'natural' events.

Environmental Risk

Environmental and technological issues are particularly interesting from the point of view of risk research, as they tend to have a number of characteristics which have been shown to be particularly difficult to deal with both in formal risk assessments and in public policy (see Pidgeon and Beattie 1998; Pidgeon and Gregory 2004). This complexity forms the backdrop to discussion of how individuals and social groups represent such risks. For example, many environmental threats, such as major industrial plant accidents, stem from very low probability but high consequence events which are particularly challenging to assess. Not all environmental risks can be described probabilistically, and descriptions often contain such uncertainty that experts themselves disagree about the likelihoods and consequences. Equally, environmental and technological risk invariably presents both hazard and opportunity, and it is now well known that people evaluate outcomes very differently depending upon whether they personally view them as 'losses' as opposed to 'gains'. Many hazards, such as naturally occurring radon gas, will never have been directly experienced by those who must be persuaded to act to mitigate their very real future consequences. And environmental hazards often also involve making difficult trade-offs over time, with consequences possibly very far into the future, such that long-term effects are inequitable in their distribution across different groups or must be anticipated for people not yet born (e.g. burning oil and coal offer benefits now, but brings future risk from climate change). Finally, certain environmental hazards (e.g. nuclear power or biotechnology) are associated with such extreme societal conflicts about risk acceptability that they appear to be a proxy for disagreements less over scientific facts than over different groups' values, politics, or ways of life.

Many of the above issues pose basic and often intractable societal decision problems, both for laypeople and for environmental risk assessment, regulation, and management. This provides the first clue as to why levels of public acceptance (or not) of a hazardous activity may at times diverge from formal expert assessments of risk (the latter tending to emphasize solely probability and consequence in the risk metric), and why resolving such differences is not just a matter of 'knowledge' about the science and technology at hand. Research on the social science of risk and uncertainty also shows us why, in the arena of environmental risk assessment, policy decisions may be particularly prone to conflict and mis-communication between the many and varied stakeholders involved.

Within applied social and experimental psychology there is now a well-established body of empirical (primarily quantitative) work on people's cognitive responses to environmental and technological risks, under the broad umbrella of risk perception research. However, the argument we present in this chapter is that understanding how people respond to risk, and the ways in which they work through their decisions and ways of living with risk, requires that attention be given to a range of wider social and cultural, as well as spatially and temporally patterned dynamics involved in risk issues (Krimsky and Golding 1992; Pidgeon et al. 1992; Pidgeon, Kasperson, and Slovic 2003).

Research Themes and Findings

Psychometric Risk Research

Research on risk perceptions arose during the 1970s and 1980s, initially in response to rising environmental concerns amongst Western populations, in particular about the impacts of nuclear power. For the social and cognitive psychologists of the time, this offered the possibility of an empirical understanding of some of the judgements and beliefs underlying this highly visible and complex social and public policy issue. Since then, of course, risk perceptions research has embraced a more diverse set of both disciplines (anthropology, sociology, and human geography) and hazards (chemicals, electromagnetic fields, ecological hazards, air pollution, and biotechnology). Although the objectives of the researchers themselves are primarily theoretical and empirical, a range of significant public policy issues surround the conflicts over particular technological developments, and hence have been a major driver of much of the research in this field (Pidgeon and Gregory 2004). From the mid-1970s to the mid-1990s, risk perception research was framed either within a cognitive science or a sociocultural approach, with relatively little interaction between the two. As we go on to argue below, more recent theorizing has stressed an increased awareness of and interest in more interpretative approaches which are sensitive to the symbolic qualities of risk perceptions as grounded in context, and which seek to step beyond simple oppositions such as 'cognition' or 'culture'.

Early risk perception studies were dominated by the experimental psychology investigations of Kahneman and Tversky into the mental heuristics or short-cuts which people use in estimating probabilities, in particular, availability, representativeness, and anchoring and adjustment (see, e.g. Kahneman, Slovic, and Tversky 1982; Gilovich, Griffin, and Kahneman 2002, and Chapters 1 and 2). Whilst thought to be generally adaptive, the use of heuristics was argued to sometimes lead to large and systematic errors, so-called 'biases', in people's assessments of uncertainty. However, its foundations in Bayesian decision theory offered a relatively restricted conceptualization of risk (essentially as subjective probability), as well as an uncritical treatment of its use of the core concepts of bias and error (see Einhorn and Hogarth 1981).

In hindsight, it is not difficult to see how the heuristics and biases research came to be interpreted, by some external commentators at least, as apparently demonstrating people's 'irrationality' in the face of 'true' risks. Echoing this, Lupton (1999) describes much of the traditional psychological risk perception research (e.g. as reviewed in Royal Society 1992) as falling within a 'techno-scientific' model. That is, adhering to a set of assumptions that reify the risk object as in some senses being real (as assessed through formal risk analysis), whilst perceptions serve as deviations from that baseline. However, in making this distinction Lupton and others misinterpret the objectives of such research. As Fischhoff (1990) points out, this research tradition has always accommodated a much richer—non-dualistic—view of, on the one hand, formal risk assessment practice (as itself a highly conditional and constructed representation system; see, for example, Fischhoff et al. 1981; Slovic 1998), and, on the other hand, public responses to environmental and technological hazards (as constructions that hold a distinctive logic and meaning of their own). Such a view forms the foundation for much of the work within the classic psychometric paradigm (Slovic, Fischhoff, and Lichtenstein 1980; Slovic 2000). This work, using primarily quantitative questionnaire methodology, suggested that perceived risks were sensitive to a range of qualitative factors above and beyond pure probability and consequence; such things as the controllability of an activity, the fear it evoked, its catastrophic potential, voluntariness of exposure, equity of risk distribution, observability of the risk, and so on. In so doing, risk perceptions were seen as richer and more complex than expert conceptions (see also Wynne 1996; Slovic 1998).

The early psychometric studies provided a model for an extensive research programme and literature (for overviews see Pidgeon et al. 1992; Pidgeon and Beattie 1998; Slovic 2000). However, whilst the basic approach of psychometric risk perception research provided extensive empirical *descriptions* of the psychology of risk perceptions, it did not initially yield substantive *theoretical* progress towards explaining those beliefs, or behaviour, in the face of risks. A major difficulty has been the concepts used in psychometric research, which are proximal rather than distal (close to rather than removed from the object of research): predicting evaluations of risk often precisely because they are in part tautologies of what it means to be hazardous or not (Marris, Langford, and O'Riordan 1998). A second concern has revolved around the extent to which the data analysis techniques used—primarily principal components factor analysis—are descriptive of individual or merely aggregate responses (Langford et al. 1999; Willis et al. 2005). In addition, such concepts, being primarily individual and cognitive, rarely fully articulate with social and cultural framing of risk issues, or until very recently the role of emotions and affect (but see Loewenstein et al. 2001; Slovic et al. 2002; Langford 2002). Also over time we have come to realize, as documented below, that people's intuitive evaluations of hazards include wider questions such as the trustworthiness of the political and institutional arrangements for managing risk in society.

Sociocultural/Socio-Structural Approaches

The 1980s saw a growing interest in the role played by social, cultural, and institutional processes in the construction of perception and other descriptions of risk (see, e.g. Johnson and Covello 1987; Krimsky and Golding 1992). Social and cultural factors are important because the perceiver of risk is rarely an isolated individual, but a 'social being' defined through a range of relationships with others (see Joffe 2003). Hence some aspects of risk beliefs might be socially shared. Early work within social psychology and sociology (Eiser and van der Plight 1979; Buss, Craik, and Dake 1986) suggested that value orientations or 'worldviews' towards the environment were related to attitudes to risk. The best known sociocultural approach to risk, that of Douglas and Wildavsky (1982), develops the worldview idea in conceptual terms, positing that human attitudes towards risk and danger vary systematically according to four cultural 'biases'—individualist, fatalist, hierarchist, and egalitarian. Such biases are held to reflect modes of social organization, thought, and value, all of which serve the function of defending individuals' favoured institutional arrangements and ways of life, and in particular who to blame when those arrangements become threatened from outside (see Chapter 2).

Risk is central to the process of institutional defence, with cultural biases orienting people's selection of which dangers to accept or to avoid, the fairness of distribution of risks across society (Rayner and Cantor 1987), and who to blame when things do go wrong (Douglas 1992). Cultural theory has also been valuable in stressing the neglect, within the early psychometric studies, of a concern for the political dimensions to risk (see also Jasanoff 1998). Despite this, cultural theory suffers from a circularity of argument in the definitions of the four cultural biases, and from the fact that its categories of worldview are both static and top-down in nature

(Marris, Langford, and O'Riordan 19
empirically the cultural biases met wi
and Peters 1998; Rippl 2002). The sur
cultural theory would be consistent wi
people's value orientations are not so
constructed from a set of available soci
as danger, blame, trust, and accountab
the much disputed structural-functional
has pioneered the acceptance of the mai
perspective on risk (e.g. Lupton 1999).

Arguably as important as Douglas has be
Giddens (1990) in their discussion of 'ris   ...ciety theory
starts from an analysis of the macro-structural conditions and consequences of contemporary (late-modern) industrialized Western society.
The claim is that late-modernity has been accompanied by the emergence
of new classes of all-pervasive and 'invisible' risks, experienced only indirectly through expert systems of knowledge. If modernity was defined
by the production and distribution of goods, late-modernity is defined
through the distribution of bads, or risk. Technical and environmental
risks (climate change, nuclear power, pollution, and chemicals) are the
hazards of risk society *par excellence*. According to Beck and Giddens,
consequences for the individual include the emergence of new forms of
anxiety and existential uncertainty (also Langford 2002), alongside the
fragmentation of traditional social categories such as gender, the family,
and class. Risk society theory also emphasizes the processes of reflexive
modernization (i.e., societal questioning of the outcomes of modernity),
greater individualization, and personal responsibility for the control of
risk as a result of the breakdown of established norms, values, and social
ties, personal risk reflexivity (through which people develop an awareness
of risk, and ways of responding to it in everyday life), and an increased
reliance upon risk experts. Risk society theory represents, in essence, a set
of arguments about changing macro-social conditions. Although these are
held to lead to impacts upon people's understandings of risk issues at an
everyday level, the precise empirical consequences may be far less easy to
establish (see Tulloch and Lupton 2003).

Social Amplification of Risk

A criticism of both psychological and traditional sociocultural approaches
to environmental and technological risk research is that they both fail to

layered and dynamic character of the ways that risk
come about. Events such as the Chernobyl disaster, the
w) controversy, the major terrorist attacks in various countries
rld since 2001, and the impacts of global climate change have
home to risk analysts and managers the extensive intertwining of
chnical risk with social considerations and processes. As Erikson (1994)
succinctly puts it, modern disasters present us with a 'new species of trouble'. But social research on risk, despite substantial progress, is still quite
handicapped in seizing the opportunity. In theoretical terms, the risk perception and risk communication literatures remain seriously fragmented:
between the psychometric paradigm and cultural theories of risk perception; between postmodernist and discourse-centred approaches and more
quantitative studies of risk; between economic/utility-maximization and
economic-justice approaches; and between communications and empowerment strategies for risk communication. Meanwhile, a professional and
cultural divide continues to separate the natural hazards and risk analysis
schools of inquiry, despite the obvious and considerable convergence of
interests.

One approach that at least attempts to bridge psychological, social,
and cultural approaches is the social amplification of risk framework
(Kasperson et al. 1988; Kasperson 1992; Pidgeon, Kasperson, and Slovic
2003). The approach adopts a metaphor from communications theory to
explain why certain hazards and events are a particular focus of concern
in society, whilst others receive comparatively little attention. The social
amplification framework posits that whilst hazards and their material
characteristics (e.g. deaths, injuries, damage, and social disruption) are
real enough, these interact with a wide range of psychological, social, or
cultural processes in ways that transform signals about risk. In this way
the social amplification approach moves beyond the relatively static categories of both psychometric and cultural theories to stress the essential
dynamic and symbolic character to risk understandings. A key contention
is that signals may be subject to filtering processes as they pass through
a variety of social 'amplification stations' (scientists, the mass media,
government agencies and politicians, and interest groups) resulting in
intensification or attenuation of aspects of risk in ways predictable from
social structure and context. Kasperson et al. (1988) also argue that social
amplification accounts for the observation that certain events lead to
spreading ripples of secondary consequences, which may go far beyond
the initial impact of the event, and may even impinge upon initially
unrelated hazards.

Risk events, when they undergo substantial amplification and result in unexpected public alarms or what some would call 'social shocks' (Lawless 1977), often surprise policymakers and risk managers. No less remarkable is the extreme attenuation of certain risk events so that, despite serious consequences for the risk bearers and society more generally, they pass virtually unnoticed and untended, often continuing to grow in effect until reaching disaster proportions. For example, Lorenzoni, Pidgeon, and O'Connor (2005) suggest that, until quite recently, the issue of climate change could be viewed in this way. Kasperson and Kasperson (1991) describe such highly attenuated risks as 'hidden hazards' and offer a theoretical explanation for their existence. Hidden hazards, in their view, have to do with both the nature of the hazards themselves and the nature of the societies and cultures in which they occur. The 'hiding' of hazards is at once purposeful and unintentional, life threatening and institution sustaining, and systematic and incidental.

The Kaspersons describe five aspects of such hazards that drive attenuation, each associated with differing causal agents and processes. *Global elusive hazards* involve a series of complex problems (regional interactions, slow accumulation, lengthy time lags, and diffuse effects). Their incidence in a politically fragmented and unequal world tends to mute their signal power in many societies. *Ideological hazards* remain hidden principally because they lie embedded in a societal web of values and assumptions that attenuates consequences, elevates associated benefits, or idealizes certain beliefs. *Marginal hazards* befall people who occupy the edges of cultures, societies, or economies where they are exposed to hazards that are remote from or concealed by those at the centre or in the mainstream. Many in such marginal situations are already weakened or highly vulnerable whilst they enjoy limited access to entitlements and few alternative means of coping. *Amplification-driven hazards* have effects that elude conventional types of risk assessment and environmental impact analysis and are often, therefore, allowed to grow in their secondary consequences before societal intervention occurs. And, finally, *value-threatening hazards* alter human institutions, lifestyles, and basic values, but because the pace of technological change so outstrips the capacity of social institutions to respond and adapt, disharmony in purpose, political will, and directed effort impede effective responses and the hazards grow. The presence of such hidden hazards has been documented in subsequent analyses of environmental degradation and delayed societal responses in varied regions around the world (Kasperson, Kasperson, and Turner 1995; also Kasperson and Kasperson 2005).

Critics of the amplification idea suggest that it might be taken to imply that there exists a baseline or true risk, which is then distorted in some way by the social processes of transformation (echoing the techno-scientific critique levelled at much of the psychometric research). However, its proponents (Kasperson et al. 2003) have stressed that their conceptualization of risk does not make this assumption: risk is associated with objective hazards of the world, but is also firmly seen in terms of signs, symbols, and images, a view more compatible with a more constructionist approach to the topic. For example, Rosa (2003) argues that the framework steers a course between social constructivist and realist representations, and can be understood in relation to sociologist Luhmann's distinction between risk and danger, and to lay ontologies of hazards. A more significant critique advanced by Murdock, Petts, and Horlick-Jones (2003) is that the social amplification framework relies too heavily upon a one-way 'source-message-receiver' framework derived from communications theory, and that this fails to account for the complex arenas of power, agency, and interpretation that typically surround any environmental or technological risk controversy (cf. also Molotch and Boden 1985). It certainly is the case that the social amplification framework does not itself address the basic political, sociological, or psychological processes which might underlie amplification or attenuation of risk signals and perceptions in any *specific* context. However, it does remain an important conceptual device for understanding how the dynamics of risk controversies and communications can play out.

Interpretive Risk Research

An argument running throughout this chapter is that all of the 'traditional' approaches to environmental risk perception above can be critiqued for a lack of attention to the framing and construction of the 'risk object' (Hilgartner 1992) within the terms of people's everyday lives and local contexts. Each, in their own way, impose a-contextual frames of meaning derived from other than the everyday: whether the 'qualitative' hazard dimensions of the psychometric approach, the macro-cultural or structural concerns of cultural theories, or the classical communications paradigm in the case of social amplification. It is not surprising therefore to find that empirical attempts to explore the interface between cultural and psychological approaches have produced mixed results (see, e.g. Sjöberg 1997; Marris, Langford, and O'Riordan 1998; Slovic and Peters 1998). In methodological terms, it has also become increasingly clear that questionnaire-based research alone does not capture the complexity of risk perceptions in specific hazard locations, suggesting that methods more sensitive to context are needed. Equally, the macrostructural concerns of risk society theory—as the most recent meta-narrative of risk—run a similar danger of imposing reified external categories (reflexive modernity, 'trust' in expert systems) upon people's private reflections about risk issues.

It is against this backdrop that a range of interpretative approaches to risk have arisen, stressing the symbolic and locally embedded nature of the sociocultural element to risks, as well as the active interpretation of people in the generation of risk understandings. Drawing on hermeneutic and phenomenological traditions, such perspectives recognize the central roles of meaning and interpretation in structuring social interactions and being. According to this approach, it might be anticipated that the concepts risk and 'environment' could assume complex roles and multiple and symbolic meanings in lay discourse and action. Approaches within such a tradition take a more locally grounded approach to both the content and origins of risk perceptions (see studies such as Fitchen, Heath, and Fessenden-Raden 1987; Irwin, Dale, and Smith 1996; Irwin, Simmons, and Walker 1999; Bickerstaff and Walker 2001; Horlick-Jones, Sime, and Pidgeon 2003; Poortinga et al. 2004; Simmons and Walker 2004). As Horlick-Jones, Sime and Pidgeon (2003) point out, within the interpretative tradition, situation specificity and context have emerged as important aspects of the processes of risk sense-making, as have shared interpretative resources: the taken for granted 'stock of knowledge' as phenomenologists describe it (Schutz 1970). Such approaches are predominantly qualitative or mixed-method in nature (Jasanoff 1993), seeking to explore talk about, and understandings of, risk where people are directly exposed to a hazard (such as industrial environmental pollution, a chemical or nuclear facility) within their everyday lives. The emphasis is upon the logics and rationalities that local people bring to bear upon an issue (cf. also Irwin and Wynne 1996) rather than with reference to an externally imposed concept of technical, psychological, or culturally determined risk. As such, interpretive approaches share some common ground with more psychologically based approaches to perceptions and risk communication design that are based upon the mental models technique (Morgan et al. 2002; Cox et al. 2003).

A recent development in this area is the use of more narrative-based approaches to understand environmental conflicts and risk. In particular, Satterfield has begun to think through the possibilities of a narrative approach to eliciting the values that attach to environmental risk (Satterfield and Gregory 1998; Satterfield, Slovic, and Gregory 2000; Satterfield 2001, 2002). Working initially within a decision analysis framework, Satterfield has opened up new questions about more context sensitive methodologies for exploring and eliciting people's environmental values (see also Burgess and Limb 1988; Henwood and Pidgeon 2001). Related work by Tulloch and Lupton (2003) explores the role of risk biography in everyday life, and that of Hollway and Jefferson (2000) the use of narrative within a psychoanalytic frame to understand how anxieties and fear raise in the face of everyday risk.

Technological Risk and Organizations

As yet, limited attention has been paid to the role of organizations and institutions in the social generation of environmental and technological risk. Kasperson et al. (2003) suggest that linking social amplification effects to the considerable empirical base of knowledge concerning organizational processes intended to prevent large-scale failures and disasters might yield important theoretical and empirical insights. Most contemporary risks originate in socio-technical systems rather than natural phenomena so that risk management and internal regulatory processes governing the behaviour of institutions in identifying, diagnosing, prioritizing, and responding to risks often become key parts of the broader amplification process. As Short (1992) points out, large organizations increasingly set the context and terms of debate for society's consideration of risk. Understanding such amplification dynamics, then, requires insight into how risk-related decisions relate to organizational self-interest, messy inter- and intra-organizational relationships, economically related rationalizations, and 'rule of thumb' considerations that often conflict with the view of risk analysis as a scientific enterprise (Short 1992: 8). Since major accidents are often preceded by smaller incidents and risk warnings, how signals of incubating hazards are processed within institutions and communicated to others outside the institution do much to structure society's experience with technological and industrial risks.

Noting the relative void of work on organizational risk processing, Freudenburg (1992, 2003) has examined characteristics of organizations that serve to attenuate risk signals and ultimately to *increase* the risks posed by technological systems. These include such attributes as the lack of organizational commitment to the risk-management function, the bureaucratic attenuation of information flow within the organization (and particularly on a 'bad-news' context), specialized divisions of labour that create 'corporate gaps' in responsibility, amplified risk-taking by workers, the atrophy of organizational vigilance to risk as a result of a myriad of factors (e.g. boredom and routinization), and imbalances and mismatches in institutional resources. Freudenburg concludes that these factors often work in concert to lead even well meaning and honest scientists and managers to underestimate risks. In turn, such organizational attenuation of risk serves systematically and repeatedly to amplify the health and environmental hazards that the organization is entrusted to anticipate and to control.

In her analysis of the *Challenger* accident in the USA, Vaughan (1992, 1996) also found communication and information issues to be critical but argued that structural factors, such as pressures from a competitive environment, resource scarcity in the organization, vulnerability of important subunits, and characteristics of the internal safety regulation system, were equally important. Evidence of a range of broad social and organizational preconditions to large-scale accidents is available in the work of Turner (1978; see also Turner and Pidgeon 1997). As a result of a detailed analysis of 84 major accidents in the UK, Turner concluded that such events rarely come about for any single reason. Rather, it is typical to find that a number of undesirable events accumulate, unnoticed, or not fully understood, often over a considerable number of years, which he defines as the *disaster incubation period*. Preventive action to remove one or more of the dangerous conditions or a *trigger event*, which might be a final critical error or a slightly abnormal operating condition, brings this period to an end. Turner focuses in particular upon the information difficulties, which are typically associated with the attempts of individuals and organizations to deal with uncertain and ill-structured safety problems, during the hazard-incubation period.

The work on organizational processing of risk is important for two reasons. It forms the foundation for an important critique of formal quantitative risk analysis, in that human and organizational processes are rarely open to direct measurement in the same way some technical components of hazardous systems might be (e.g. Toft 1996). It also helps to begin to map out a logic of *why* members of the public might view the issue of trust (in risk regulators and managers) as a core concern. If the main preconditions of technological and environmental disaster are human and organizational one is probably right to be sceptical about any claims to ultimate 'safety'. However, as Power points out (2004), this should not lead to a situation where organizations become over-focused upon risk control (particularly solely through compliance to rules and procedures) rather than a more 'intelligent' attention to safety issues.

Emerging Issues

Environmental Risk Management and Trust

The last decade has seen a surge in interest in the role of trust in people's responses to environmental and technological risks from both the academic and policy communities. In Europe, the BSE crisis in particular was seen as an event that had reduced public trust in risk-management processes. Accordingly, 'rebuilding' trust in the science policy process has been seen as a core policy objective of risk communication and stakeholder engagement processes (House of Lords 2000; Beierle and Cayford 2002; Royal Society 2004). The question of trust and risk perception is not a new one however, being first raised by Wynne (1980). He hypothesized that differences between expert and lay constructions of risk might depend on the evaluation of the trustworthiness of risk management, and of the authorities to act both in the public interest and with regard to best possible technical standards and practice. And indeed one interpretation to be placed upon several of the qualitative dimensions of risk identified in the psychometric studies (e.g. control over risk, equity of impacts, whether a risk is known to science) is that they tap concerns about *institutional* processes of hazard management.

Several early quantitative studies have also shown that trust in institutions is correlated with the perception and acceptability of various environmental risks. For example, Pijawka and Mushkatel (1991–2) found a strong negative relationship between trust in general institutions of government and in specific agencies of government to protect public safety and the perceived risk of a high-level nuclear waste repository. As this was accompanied by high levels of opposition, they came to the conclusion that public opposition to the siting of the repository, as well as their perceptions of risk of the facility, was a result of a lack of trust in the US Department of Energy. Freudenburg (1993) demonstrated that while several socio-demographic and ideological variables were only weakly related to concern about a potential nuclear waste repository, trust variables had substantial higher predictive power. People having high levels of trust in science and technology, and business and federal government to build and manage the nuclear repository safely were much less concerned about the repository than were people who did not trust these groups with specific risk management responsibilities. Bord and O'Connor (1992) found that trust in government and trust in industry were both significantly related to concern about hazardous waste sites. Likewise, Flynn et al. (1992) found that the level of trust in (radioactive) repository management and risk perceptions were closely connected. Trust in repository management was mainly indirectly linked to opposition to the proposed siting of the Yucca mountain radioactive waste repository, via the perceived risk of the waste site.

In conceptual terms trust cuts across all of the five main approaches to environmental risk described above, while a number of recent risk controversies have made policymakers aware that the public have become key players in many controversial risk issues, and that (dis)trust may be a core component of this (House of Lords 2000; Cabinet Office 2002). However, there is currently little agreement on the definition, meaning(s), and properties of trust. Accordingly, the last fifteen years have seen a growing body of both conceptual and empirical work on the determinants and consequences of trust (see, e.g. Renn and Levine 1991; Slovic 1993; Frewer et al. 1996; Cvetkovich and Löfstedt 1999; Johnson 1999; Poortinga and Pidgeon 2003, 2004, 2005).

Three main approaches to trust in environmental risk management can be identified. First, it can be conceptualized as a set of cognitive judgements along discrete dimensions that are primarily related to the (presumed) behaviour of risk managers. In particular care, competence and vested interest (e.g. Frewer et al. 1996; Johnson 1999; Metlay 1999; Poortinga and Pidgeon 2003). However, as Walls et al. (2004) point out, seen from a more discursive perspective, different components of trust—whilst conceptually distinct—can exist in tension, with social trust likely to emerge as multidimensional and fragmented, as a product of a reconciliation of competing ideas, knowledges, and impressions. They propose the concept of *critical trust* as an organizing principle, something which lies on a continuum between outright scepticism (rejection) and uncritical emotional acceptance. Such a concept attempts to reconcile the actual *reliance* by people on risk managing institutions whilst simultaneously possessing a *critical attitude* towards the effectiveness, 'motivations' or independence of the agency in question (also Langford 2002; O'Neill 2002; Poortinga and Pidgeon 2003).

A second approach to trust, initially proposed by Earle and Cvetkovich (1995), is theoretically informed by social psychology, and suggests that trust may be predominantly based on identity-based concepts of value similarity rather than carefully reasoned arguments or direct knowledge of the behaviour of an institution or individual. Recent empirical support for this second view has also been gained (Siegrist, Cvetkovich, and Roth 2000; Siegrist, Cvetkovich, and Gutscher 2001; Poortinga and Pidgeon 2006).

A third, emerging model of trust, stresses the importance of people's prior attitudes (Eiser, Miles, and Frewer 2002; White et al. 2003; Poortinga and Pidgeon 2005). The associationist view starts from the premise that it is a core belief, attitude, or affective association with an issue that forms the basis for other judgements about a technological or environmental risk, including risks and benefits and trust in risk management. It is also worth noting here that the associationist model is compatible with important emerging work on the operation of emotion and 'affect', which are increasingly seen as a part of the way in which laypeople construct risk issues (Loewenstein et al. 2001; Slovic et al. 2002). For example, Poortinga and Pidgeon (2005) found evidence that people's general affective evaluation of GM food serves as a powerful anchor for other more specific risk judgements, among which trust in risk regulation was one. They conclude that the conventional interpretation of trust (or distrust) as the prior determinant of risk acceptability judgements (cf. Pijawka and Mushkatel 1991–2) may need, at least in part, some revision. The findings of this study also hold important implications for risk policy. Although for many policymakers the 'reclamation of trust' has become an explicit objective, this study suggests that risk communication efforts that are aimed at *directly* increasing trust may not be universally effective in solving risk controversies (cf. also Fischhoff 1995). Such policies could well be counterproductive where they are based on the incorrect assumption that trust can be simply manipulated in order to increase the acceptance of a controversial technology. Where trust in risk regulation is strongly dependent on someone's general prior attitude, it seems more important to understand and then address the underlying drivers of concerns about that particular environmental issue.

Public 'Engagement' and Policy

A key shift in focus currently occurring within this research domain concerns the potential contribution that social sciences approaches to environmental risk can offer for societal decision-making and resolving environmental conflicts. Accordingly, a significant policy debate now exists over whether people's perceptions and beliefs *should* form one input, directly or indirectly, to processes of public policy resource allocation (see contributions to Okrent and Pidgeon 1998). This debate touches upon a range of philosophical issues, in particular, regarding the epistemological status of competing 'expert' and 'public' evaluations of risk as well as the appropriateness of making a distinction between 'objective' and 'subjective' depictions of risk (Pidgeon 1998; Slovic 1998).

Social science understandings of risk may require attention by policymakers simply because, as Sunstein comments (2002), perceptions can lead to real consequences, such as secondary social amplification impacts (see Kasperson et al. 2003). For example, Frewer (2003) reports that the public announcement by the UK Health Minister in 1996 of a potential link between eating British beef, 'mad cow' disease, and deaths from CJD (Creutzfeld-Jakob Disease) triggered major consumer avoidance of British sources of beef. Equally, a possible contribution to policy is suggested whenever ethical or value based concerns are implicated in beliefs about risk (as many of the sociocultural approaches, noted above, would suggest is the case).

The debate over public participation in risk policy shifts the technical focus away from one-way risk communication approaches to a more dialogic, two-way relationship between science and society, where learning is possible on both sides of that relationship. Methods of public participation in environmental decisions are typically grounded in local contexts— such as siting or planning disputes—and have accordingly traditionally employed techniques such as consensus conferences, planning cells, or more decision analytic approaches (see Renn, Webler, and Wiedemann 1995; POST 2001; Beierle and Cayford 2002). However, public participation is also being used with more nationally relevant environmental issues, as in the case of agricultural genomics (see Pidgeon et al. 2005). And very recently, proposals to extend participation methods to more upstream areas of emerging technologies—such as nanotechnology— have been made (Royal Society 2004; Wilsdon and Willis 2004; Wilsdon, Wynne, and Stilgoe 2005). However, we do not yet know enough about the consequences of participation processes, particularly where the context is national rather than local or the time frame of impacts stretches far into the future, to say with confidence whether this new approach can meet the ambitious objectives being set for it. Above all there is a challenge to link the operation of analytic-deliberative processes more closely to the needs of decision-makers and ordinary people, since one of the expectations of deliberation (particular amongst people who participate) is that it should indeed lead to concrete policy outcomes.

As a concluding comment, the example of environmental and technological risk is particularly instructive because it illustrates how research framed by a seemingly unproblematic question—why do people object, or not, to certain technologies?—has led to a transformation of the question itself over a period of time as more empirical evidence has accumulated. Mirroring thinking that has come out of the critique of the now discredited 'deficit model' of public understanding of science (Irwin and Wynne 1996), the evidence suggests that public risk perceptions exhibit a complexity and rationality that may be sensitive to a range of factors that go beyond, and are indeed typically ignored in expert risk analyses.

Acknowledgements

Work reported in this chapter was supported through a grant from the Economic and Social Research Council under its 'Risk In Social Contexts' (SCARR) network, and partly by the Programme on Understanding Risk funded by a grant from the Leverhulme Trust (RSK990021).

References

Beck, U. (1992). *Risk Society: Towards a New Modernity* (trans. M. Ritter). London: Sage.

Beierle, T. C. and Cayford, J. (2002). *Democracy in Practice: Public Participation in Environmental Decisions*. Washington, DC: Resources for the Future.

Bickerstaff, K. and Walker, G. (2001). 'Public Understandings of Air Pollution: The "localisation" of Environmental Risk', *Global Environmental Change*, 11: 133–45.

Bord, R. J. and O'Connor, R. E. (1992). 'Determinants of Risk Perceptions of a Hazardous Waste Site', *Risk Analysis*, 12(3): 411–16.

Burgess, J. and Limb, M. (1988). 'Exploring Environmental Values through the Medium of Small Groups 1: Theory and Practice', *Environment and Planning A*, 20: 309–26.

Buss, D. M., Craik, K. H., and Dake, K. M. (1986). 'Contemporary Worldviews and the Perception of the Technological System', in V. T. Covello, J. Menkes, and J. Mumpower (eds.), *Risk Evaluation and Management*. New York: Plenum, pp. 93–130.

Cabinet Office (2002). *Risk: Improving Government's Capability to Handle Risk and Uncertainty*. London: HMSO.

Cox, P., Niewöhner, J., Pidgeon, N., Gerrard, S., Fischhoff, B., and Riley, D. (2003). 'The Use of Mental Models in Chemical Risk Protection: Developing a Generic Workplace Methodology', *Risk Analysis*, 23: 311–24.

Cvetkovich, G. T. and Löfstedt, R. E. (eds.) (1999). *Social Trust and the Management of Risk*. London: Earthscan.

Douglas, M. (1992). *Risk and Blame*. London: Routledge.

____ and Wildavsky, A. (1982). *Risk and Culture: An Analysis of the Selection of Technological Dangers*. Berkeley, CA: University of California Press.

Earle, T. C. and Cvetkovich, G. T. (1995). *Social Trust: Towards a Cosmopolitan Society*. London: Praeger.

Einhorn, H. and Hogarth, R. (1981). 'Behavioral Decision Theory: Processes of Judgment and Choice', *Annual Review of Psychology*, 32: 53–88.

Eiser, J. R., Miles, S., and Frewer, L. J. (2002). 'Trust, Perceived Risk and Attitudes Towards Food Technologies', *Journal of Applied Social Psychology*, 32(11): 2423–33.

____ and van der Plight, J. (1979). 'Beliefs and Values in the Nuclear Debate', *Journal of Applied Social Psychology*, 9: 524–36.

Erikson, K. T. (1994). *A New Species of Trouble: Explorations in Disaster, Trauma, and Community*. New York: Norton.

Fischhoff, B. (1990). 'Psychology and Public Policy: Tool or Toolmaker?', *American Psychologist*, 45: 647–53.

____ (1995). 'Risk Perception and Communication Unplugged: Twenty Years of Process', *Risk Analysis*, 15: 137–45.

____ Lichtenstein, S., Slovic, P., Derby, S. L., and Keeney, R. L. (1981). *Acceptable Risk*. Cambridge: Cambridge University Press.

Fitchen, J. M., Heath, J. S., and Fessenden-Raden, J. (1987). 'Risk Perception in Community Context: A Case Study', in B. Johnson and V. Covello (eds.), *The Social and Cultural Construction of Risk*. Dordrecht, The Netherlands: Reidel, pp. 31–54.

Flynn, J., Burns, W., Mertz, C. K., and Slovic, P. (1992). 'Trust as a Determinant of Opposition to a High-Level Radioactive Waste Repository: Analysis of a Structural Model', *Risk Analysis*, 12(3): 417–29.

Freudenburg, W. R. (1992). 'Nothing Recedes Like Success? Risk Analysis and the Organizational Amplification of Risks', *Risk*, 3: 1–35.

____ (1993). 'Risk and Recreancy: Weber, the Division of Labor, and the Rationality of Risk Perceptions', *Journal of Social Issues*, 71(4): 909–32.

____ (2003). 'Institutional Failure and the Organisational Amplification of Risks', in N. F. Pidgeon, R. K. Kasperson, and P. Slovic (eds.), *The Social Amplification of Risk*. Cambridge: Cambridge University Press, pp. 102–22.

Frewer, L. J (2003). 'Trust, Transparency and Social Context: Implications for Social Amplification of Risk', in N. F. Pidgeon, R. K. Kasperson, and P. Slovic (eds.), *The Social Amplification of Risk*. Cambridge: Cambridge University Press, pp. 123–37.

____ Howard, C., Hedderley, D., and Shepherd, R. (1996). 'What Determines Trust in Information About Food-related Risks? Underlying Psychological Constructs', *Risk Analysis*, 16(4): 473–85.

Giddens, A. (1990). *The Consequences of Modernity*. Cambridge, UK: Polity Press.

Gilovich, T., Griffin, D., and Kahneman, D. (eds.) (2002). *Heuristics and Biases: The Psychology of Intuitive Judgment*. New York: Cambridge University Press.

Henwood, K. L. and Pidgeon, N. F. (2001). 'Talk About Woods and Trees: Threat of Urbanisation, Stability and Biodiversity', *Journal of Environmental Psychology*, 21, 125–47.

Hilgartner, S. (1992). 'The Social Construction of Risk Objects', in J. Short and L. Clarke (eds.), *Organizations, Uncertainty and Risk*. Boulder, CO: Westview, pp. 39–53.

Hollway, W. and Jefferson, T. (2000). *Doing Qualitative Research Differently: Free Association, Narrative and the Interview Method*. London: Sage.

Horlick-Jones, T., Sime, J., and Pidgeon, N. F. (2003). 'The Social Dynamics of Risk Perception; Implications for Risk Communication Research and Practice', in N. F. Pidgeon, R. K. Kasperson, and P. Slovic (eds.), *The Social Amplification of Risk*. Cambridge: Cambridge University Press, pp. 262–85.

House of Lords Select Committee on Science and Technology (2000). *Third Report: Science and Society (Session 1999–2000)*. London: HMSO.

Irwin, A. and Wynne, B. (eds.) (1996). *Misunderstanding Science*. Cambridge: Cambridge University Press.

——Dale, A., and Smith, D. (1996). 'Science and Hell's Kitchen: The Local Understanding of Hazard Issues', in A. Irwin and B. Wynne (eds.), *Misunderstanding Science? The Public Reconstruction of Science and Technology*. Cambridge: Cambridge University Press, pp. 47–64.

——Simmons, P., and Walker, G. (1999). 'Faulty Environments and Risk Reasoning: The Local Understanding of Industrial Hazards', *Environment and Planning A*, 31: 1311–26.

Jasanoff, S. (1993). 'Bridging the Two Cultures of Risk Analysis', *Risk Analysis*, 13: 123–9.

——(1998). 'The Political Science of Risk Perception', *Reliability Engineering and System Safety*, 59: 91–100.

Joffe, H. (2003). 'Risk: From Perception to Social Representation', *British Journal of Social Psychology*, 42: 55–73.

Johnson, B. B. (1999). 'Exploring Dimensionality in the Origins of Hazard Related Trust', *Journal of Risk Research*, 2(4): 325–54.

——and Covello, V. T. (eds.) (1987). *The Social and Cultural Construction of Risk*. Dordrecht, The Netherlands: Reidel.

Kahneman, D., Slovic, P., and Tversky, A. (1982). *Judgement Under Uncertainty: Heuristics and Biases*. Cambridge: Cambridge University Press.

Kasperson, J. X. and Kasperson, R. E. (2005). *The Social Contours of Risk*. London: Earthscan.

————and Turner, B. L. (eds.) (1995). *Regions at Risk: Comparisons of Threatened Environments*. Tokyo: United Nations University.

————Pidgeon, N. F., and Slovic, P. (2003). 'The Social Amplification of Risk: Assessing Fifteen Years of Research and Theory', in N. F. Pidgeon,

R. K. Kasperson, and P. Slovic (eds.), *The Social Amplification of Risk*. Cambridge: Cambridge University Press, pp. 13–46.

Kasperson, R. E. (1992). 'The Social Amplification of Risk: Progress in Developing an Integrative Framework', in S. Krimsky and D. Golding (eds.), *Social Theories of Risk*. Westport, CT: Praeger, pp. 153–78.

——and Kasperson, J. X. (1991). 'Hidden Hazards', in D. G. Mayo and R. D. Hollander (eds.), *Acceptable Evidence: Science and Values in Risk Management*. New York: Oxford University Press, pp. 9–28.

——Renn, O., Slovic, P., Brown, H. S., Emel, J., Goble, R., Kasperson, J. X., and Ratick, S. (1988). 'The Social Amplification of Risk: A Conceptual Framework', *Risk Analysis*, 8: 177–87.

Krimsky, S. and Golding, D. (1992). *Social Theories of Risk*. Westport, CT: Praeger.

Langford, I. H. (2002). 'An Existential Approach to Risk Perception', *Risk Analysis*, 22(1): 101–20.

—— Marris, C., McDonald, A.-L., Goldstein, H., Rasbash, J., and O'Riordan, T. (1999). 'Simultaneous Analysis of Individual and Aggregate Responses in Psychometric Data using Multilevel Modeling', *Risk Analysis*, 19(4): 669–77.

Lawless, E. T. (1977). *Technology and Social Shock*. New Brunswick, NJ: Rutgers University Press.

Loewenstein, G. F., Weber, E. U., Hsee, C. K., and Welch, N. (2001). 'Risk as Feelings', *Psychological Bulletin*, 127(2): 267–86.

Lorenzoni, I., Pidgeon, N. F., and O'Connor, R. (2005). 'Dangerous Climate Change: The Role for Risk Research', *Risk Analysis*, 1387–98.

Lupton, D. (1999). *Risk*. London: Routledge.

Marris, C., Langford, I. H., and O'Riordan, T. (1998). 'A Quantitative Test of the Cultural Theory of Risk Perceptions: Comparisons with the Psychometric Paradigm', *Risk Analysis*, 18(5): 635–48.

Metlay, D. (1999). 'Institutional Trust and Confidence: A Journey into A Conceptual Quagmire', in G. T. Cvetkovich and R. E. Löfstedt (eds.), *Social Trust and the Management of Risk*. London: Earthscan.

Molotch, H. and Boden, D. (1985). Talking Social Structure: Discourse, Domination and the Watergate Hearings', *American Sociological Review*, 50: 272–88.

Morgan, M. G., Fischhoff, B., Bostrom, A., and Atman, C. (2002). *Risk Communication: The Mental Models Approach*. Cambridge: Cambridge University Press.

Murdock, G., Petts, J., and Horlick-Jones, T. (2003). 'After Amplification: Rethinking the Role of the Media in Risk Communication', in N. F. Pidgeon, R. K. Kasperson, and P. Slovic (eds.), *The Social Amplification of Risk*. Cambridge: Cambridge University Press, pp. 156–78.

Okrent, D. and Pidgeon, N. F. (eds.) (1998). 'Risk Assessment Versus Risk Perception', Special Volume of *Reliability Engineering and System Safety*, 59: 1–159.

O'Neill, O. (2002). *A Question of Trust*. Cambridge: Cambridge University Press.

Pidgeon, N. F. (1998). 'Risk Assessment, Risk Values and the Social Science Programme: Why We Do Need Risk Perception Research', *Reliability Engineering and System Safety*, 59: 5–15.

____ and Beattie, J. (1998). 'The Psychology of Risk and Uncertainty', in P. Calow (ed.), *Handbook of Environmental Risk Assessment and Management*. Oxford: Blackwell Science, pp. 289–318.

____ and Gregory, R. (2004). 'Judgment, Decision Making and Public Policy', in D. Koehler and N. Harvey (eds.), *Blackwell Handbook of Judgment and Decision Making*. Oxford: Blackwell, pp. 604–23.

____ Hood, C., Jones, D., and Turner, B. A. (1992). 'Risk Perception', in *Risk: Analysis, Perception and Management*. The Royal Society, London, pp. 89–134.

____ Kasperson, R. K., and Slovic, P. (2003). *The Social Amplification of Risk*. Cambridge: Cambridge University Press.

____ Poortinga, W., Rowe, G., Horlick-Jones, T., Walls, J., and O'Riordan, T. (2005). 'Using Surveys in Public Participation Processes for Risk Decision-Making: The Case of the 2003 British GM Nation? Public Debate', *Risk Analysis*, 25(2): 467–80.

Pijawka, K. D. and Mushkatel, A. H. (1991/1992). 'Public Opposition to the Siting of a High-Level Nuclear Waste Repository: The Importance of Trust', *Policy Studies Review*, 10(4): 180–94.

Poortinga, W. and Pidgeon, N. F. (2003). 'Exploring the Dimensionality of Trust in Risk Regulation', *Risk Analysis*, 23: 961–72.

____ ____ (2004). 'Trust, the Asymmetry Principle, and the Role of Prior Beliefs', *Risk Analysis*, 24(6): 1475–86.

____ ____ (2005). 'Trust in Risk Regulation: Cause or Consequence of the Acceptability of GM Food?', *Risk Analysis*, 25: 199–209.

____ ____ (2006). 'Prior Attitudes, Salient Value Similarity and Dimensionality: Towards an Integrative Model of Trust in Risk Regulation', *Journal of Applied Social Psychology*, 26(7): 1673–99.

Poortinga, W., Bickerstaff, K., Langford, I., Niewöhner, J., and Pidgeon, N. F. (2004). 'The British 2001 Foot and Mouth Crisis: A Comparative Study of Public Risk Perceptions, Trust and Beliefs About Government Policy in Two Communities', *Journal of Risk Research*, 7(1): 73–90.

POST (2001). *Open Channels: Public Dialogue in Science and Technology* (Report 153). London: Parliamentary Office of Science and Technology.

Power, M. (2004). *The Risk Management of Everything: Rethinking the Politics of Uncertainty*. London: Demos.

Rayner, S. (1992). 'Cultural Theory and Risk Analysis', in S. Krimsky and D. Golding (eds.), *Social Theories of Risk*. Westport, CT: Praeger, pp. 83–116.

____ and Cantor, R. (1987). 'How Fair is Safe Enough? The Cultural Approach to Social Technology Choice', *Risk Analysis*, 7: 3–9.

Renn, O. and Levine, D. (1991). 'Credibility and Trust in Risk Communication', in R. E. Kasperson and P. J. M. Stallen (eds.), *Communicating Risks to the Public*. Dordrecht, The Netherlands: Kluwer, pp. 175–210.

—— Webler, T., and Wiedemann, P. (1995). *Fairness and Competence in Citizen Participation*. Dordrecht, The Netherlands: Kluwer.

Rippl, S. (2002). 'Cultural Theory and Risk Perceptions: A Proposal for Better Measurement', *Journal of Risk Research*, 5(2): 147–66.

Rosa, E. A. (2003). 'The Logical Structure of the Social Amplification of Risk Framework (SARF): Metatheoretical Foundations and Policy Implications', in N. F. Pidgeon, R. K. Kasperson, and P. Slovic (eds.), *The Social Amplification of Risk*. Cambridge: Cambridge University Press, pp. 47–79.

Royal Society (1992). *Risk: Analysis, Perception and Management*. London: The Royal Society.

Royal Society and Royal Academy of Engineering (2004). *Nanoscience and Nanotechologies: Opportunities and Uncertainties*. London: RS/RAE.

Satterfield, T. (2001). 'In Search of Value Literacy: Suggestions for the Elicitation of Environmental Values', *Environmental Values*, 10: 331–59.

—— (2002). *Anatomy of a Conflict: Identity, Knowledge and Emotion in Old Growth Forests*. Vancouver, Canada: UBC Press.

—— and Gregory, R. (1998). 'Reconciling Environmental Values and Pragmatic Choices', *Society and Natural Resources*, 11: 629–47.

—— Slovic, P., and Gregory, R. (2000). 'Narrative Valuation in a Policy Judgment Context', *Ecological Economics*, 34: 315–31.

Schutz, A. (1970). *Reflections on the Problem of Relevance*, edited by R. Zaner, New Haven, CT: Yale University Press.

Short, J. F., Jr. (1992). 'Defining, Explaining, and Managing Risk', in J. F. Short, Jr. and L. Clarke (eds.), *Organizations, Uncertainties and Risk*. Boulder, CO: Westview, pp. 3–23.

Siegrist, M., Cvetkovich, G. T., and Gutscher, H. (2001). 'Shared Values, Social Trust, and the Perception of Geographic Cancer Clusters', *Risk Analysis*, 21(6): 1047–53.

—— —— and Roth, C. (2000). 'Salient Value Similarity, Social Trust, and Risk/Benefit Perception', *Risk Analysis*, 20(3): 353–62.

Simmons, P. and Walker, G. (2004). 'Living with Technological Risk: Industrial Encroachment on Sense of Place', in Å. Boholm and R. Löfstedt (eds.), *Contesting Local Environments*. London: Earthscan, pp. 90–106.

Sjöberg, L. (1997). 'Explaining Risk Perception: An Empirical Evaluation of Cultural Theory', *Risk, Decision and Policy*, 2: 113–30.

Slovic, P. (1993). 'Perceived Risk, Trust and Democracy', *Risk Analysis*, 13(6): 675–82.

—— (1998). 'The Risk Game', *Reliability Engineering and System Safety*, 59, 73–7.

—— (2000). *The Perception of Risk*. London: Earthscan.

Slovic, P. and Peters, E. (1998). 'The Importance of Worldviews in Risk Perception', *Risk Decision and Policy*, 3(2): 165–70.

—— Fischhoff, B., and Lichtenstein, S. (1980). 'Facts and Fears: Understanding Perceived Risk', in R. Schwing and W. Albers (eds.), *Societal Risk Assessment: How Safe is Safe Enough?*. New York: Plenum Press, pp. 181–214.

—— Finucane, M., Peters, E., and MacGregor, D. G. (2002). 'The Affect Heuristic', in T. Gilovich, D. Griffin, and D. Kahnman (eds.), *Heuristics and Biases: The Psychology of Intuitive Judgment*. New York: Cambridge University Press, pp. 397–420.

Sunstein, C. R. (2002). 'The Laws of Fear', *Harvard Law Review*, 115: 1119–68.

Toft, B. (1996). 'Limits to the Mathematical Modelling of Disasters', in C. Hood and D. K. C. Jones (eds.), *Accident and Design*. London: UCL Press, pp. 99–110.

Tulloch, J., and Lupton, D. (2003). *Risk and Everyday Life*. London: Sage.

Turner, B. A. (1978). *Man-Made Disasters*. London: Wykeham.

—— and Pidgeon, N. F. (1997). *Man-Made Disasters*. 2nd ed. Oxford: Butterworth-Heinemann.

Vaughan, D. (1992). 'Regulating Risk: Implications of the Challenger Accident', in J. F. Short, Jr. and L. Clarke (eds.), *Organizations, Uncertainties and Risk*. Boulder, CO: Westview, pp. 235–54.

—— (1996). *The Challenger Launch Decision: Risky Technology, Culture, and Deviance at NASA*. Chicago, IL: University of Chicago Press.

Walls, J., Pidgeon, N. F., Weyman, A., and Horlick-Jones, T. (2004). 'Critical Trust: Understanding Lay Perceptions of Health and Safety Risk Regulation', *Health, Risk and Society*, 6(2): 133–50.

White, M. P., Pahl, S., Bühner, M., and Haye, A. (2003). 'Trust in Risky Messages: The Role of Prior Attitudes', *Risk Analysis*, 23(4): 717–26.

Willis, H. H., DeKay, M. L., Fischhoff, B., and Morgan, G. M. (2005). 'Aggregate, Disaggregate and Hybrid Analyses of Ecological Risk Perceptions', *Risk Analysis*, 25: 405–28.

Wilsdon, J. and Willis, R. (2004). *See Through Science: Why Public Engagement Needs to Move Upstream*. London: Demos.

—— Wynne, B., and Stilgoe, J. (2005). *The Public Value of Science*. London: Demos.

Wynne, B. (1980). 'Technology, Risk and Participation: On the Social Treatment of Uncertainty', in J. Conrad (ed.), *Society, Technology and Risk*. New York: Academic Press, pp. 167–202.

—— (1996). 'May the Sheep Safely Graze? A Reflexive View of the Expert-Lay Divide', in S. Lash, B. Szerszynski, and B. Wynne (eds.), *Risk, Environment and Modernity*. London: Sage, pp. 104–37.

6

Everyday Life and Leisure Time

John Tulloch

Theoretical Context

The context of risk debate in this book and elsewhere is generally taken to be a shifting away from modernist 'welfare' paradigms to those of personal responsibility and 'justice' (see *Crime and Risk*). An equivalent shift is noted from interventionist state policies to those of either risk society or new 'governmentality' (see *Risk and Social and Public Policy*). Yet these contexts—especially when we look at theorizing risk, everyday life, and leisure—need to be explored in the context of wider intellectual debate.

Discussing theorization of the leisure industry and risk, Aitchison has contrasted 'Structuralist discourses ... that focus on the big picture or the grand narratives of capitalism, patriarchy, racism or ableism in explaining social and cultural relations' and post-structural analyses of the productive consumption of leisure which focus on 'the micro-level of the everyday where difference and diversity may be visible *within* class, gender, race and (dis)ability categorisations in addition to being identifiable *between* such categories' (2004: 98–9). She adds that 'What has come to be known as the "cultural turn" of the 1980s and 1990s' redirected sociocultural analysis 'from social structures to cultural symbols and from the macro-analyses of global power relations to the micro-analyses of everyday life' (2004: 107).

In fact the 'cultural turn' was evident earlier as part of the 'ethno-graphic turn' in academic research during the 1970s and early 1980s, bringing an 'everyday life' focus to a wide range of disciplines. Every-day practices had, of course, historically been of continuing central concern in anthropology and sociology, though as Denzin and Lincoln indicate, always encapsulated within one or other theoretical-political paradigm. Especially in the later (1970s to 1990s) stages of ethnographic turn, 'linguistic turn', and reflexive anthropology, researchers faced an ever-changing mix of quantitative and qualitative methodologies, and of critical and traditional theories. The ethnographic turn was especially marked by its 'blurred interpretive genres' of paradigms, methods, and theories, even though 'thick descriptions' of detailed everyday events, rituals, and customs, and a conjuncture of both 'expert' and 'lay' narratives about 'local situations' became the preferred methodological focus (Denzin and Lincoln 1998: 19).

The Ethnographic Turn: Culture as 'Ordinary'

The growing field of cultural studies presented itself during the 1970s as an anti-discipline and as the field of 'blurred genres' par excellence in impacting on new studies of everyday life. In the space available it is important to note two key movements here—the notion of culture as 'ordinary' and the importance of dialogic language. These were fundamentally to affect everyday life and 'leisure' research. I will illustrate each of them via a symptomatic but creative cultural thinker.

By the late 1950s, in *Culture and Society*, Williams was already speaking of the everyday yet holistic *ordinariness* of culture and during the 1960s/1970s developed his theory of culture both in terms of aesthetic excellence and as an entire way of life. This encouraged analysis of texts as significant symbolic action far beyond the normal 'Engl.Lit' canon within high culture, and paved the way for later cultural/media studies of everyday consumption of the leisure industries. Couldry notes, however, the centrality to Williams' thinking in holding '*both* notions of culture—as specific works and as ongoing life process—*in tension*' (2000: 23). 'A culture ... is always both traditional and creative; that it is both the most ordinary common meanings and the finest individual meanings' (Williams 1989: 4).

On the one hand, in everyday life extra-aesthetic arguments are made about issues of quality and value, as when 'we say that media or other cultural representations do not ... match our own experience, in the social situations we know' (Pickering 1997: 61, 65). On the other hand, Williams' emphasis on the 'deep personal meanings' within a culture which is 'ordinary, in every society and in every mind' (1989: 4) has opened out social theory in general, and risk theory in particular, to the possibility of examining *every* creative individual response to risk and leisure in this 'everyday' way. For example, Alaszewski discusses how after the 'fateful moment' of a stroke, many survivors construct narratives of their ensuing lives in order to try and rebuild trust in the ordinary, and to re-establish a new sense of identity. Thus, as Alaszewski makes clear, narratives about 'everyday activities such as cooking a meal for friends or going out for a walk' (2005: 23) provide more than the replacing of new uncertainties by heightened risk-taking (e.g., the risk of falling whilst walking), but also can provide the kinds of creative leisure-time pleasure in achieving contact and control that others might find in extreme sports or surfing.

This emphasis on deep personal meanings in everyday narratives has become a regular feature of risk research. Whereas Alaszewski makes use of Giddens' notion of 'fateful moments', Thomson et al. contrast this with their own usage of 'critical moments' in teenagers' narratives of agency and biographical choice, where critical moments are the rhetorical device of 'complication' within narratives of social inclusion and exclusion (2002: 351). Similarly, Tulloch and Lupton (2003) explore edgework as a pleasure in extreme sports, as well as adults' biographical narratives about the risk of 'border crossings' (of geography, sexual preference, and age), as liminal experiences situated in everyday life. Developing his edgework paradigm, Lyng (2005) speaks of personal 'limit experience' in sky and BASE jumping, Courtney examines the 'restorative dynamic of transcendent experience' (2005: 111) which links the competent art viewer/listener to the edgework skydiver, and Simon explores the momentary contemplation of risk and the sublime among English nineteenth century mountaineering lawyers (2005: 222). Further, Gillespie (2002) explores alternative liminalities and fateful moments by comparing alcohol and automotive edgework in young Australian rural men (situated in everyday terms of economic and social marginality and 'hard masculinity') with urban dance party and chemical risk-taking young males who reflexively share their transgression of normative boundaries with young women as they negotiate new masculinities. There is also a growing literature on risk rumours as 'less organized, more spontaneous, and surprising' stories (Nerlich and Wright 2005: 2) working between knowledge sanctioned by those in power and those who felt powerless during the British foot and mouth epidemic (see also Burgess 2005 on internet rumours about mobile phones). In all of these studies, risks and pleasures constructed as everyday narratives (drawing as much on affect as cognition) are as key an element in the 'tension' between Williams' 'known meanings and directions' and 'new observances' as are the kinds of texts studied by literary critics. These everyday risk narratives are fine examples of Coward's point, from within cultural studies, that rather than making a hierarchy of 'high' and 'popular' texts and genres, our interest in 'value' should be in 'how certain texts criticize our everyday perceptions and make us see our surroundings and our emotions in new and critical ways' (1990: 91).

Dialogic Theory

For Williams the democratic communication of culture was dialogic, a matter not only of 'transmission; [but] also reception and response' (Williams 1958: 301). An ongoing implication of the work of Williams and others in the new, broader cultural studies (including history, geography, English, critical psychology, sociology, and anthropology) was an ethical commitment to resisting instrumental reductions of the human (Slack and Whitt 1992: 576). The psychologist Shotter makes this especially clear in *Cultural Politics of Everyday Life* where he quotes Bakhtin in arguing that, 'With a monologic approach ... *another person* remains wholly and merely an *object* of consciousness. Monologue is finalized and deaf to the other's response, does not expect it and does not acknowledge in it any *decisive* force' (Bakhtin 1984: 292–3, cited in Shotter 1993: 197). Thus, the 'traditional analytic view of things' (1993: 197)—for example, the scientific-monological separation of expert analysis and lay object—must give way. A new 'politics of identity' was needed:

citizenship cannot simply be instituted as a new ideology in a top-down power-play by an elite group. It must emerge as a 'living ideology', a new 'tradition of argumentation', consisting in a whole diversity of interdependent arenas. . . a great 'carnival' (Bakhtin, 1968) of different ways of socially constituting *being* in which everyone can have a 'voice'—in which they can play a part in the shaping and reshaping of their lives. (Shotter 1993: 202)

At the same time, feminist theorist Ang was writing within cultural/media studies about the problem of relegating the leisure audiences of television 'to the status of exotic "other"—merely interesting in so far as "we" as researchers use "them" as "objects" of study, and about whom "we" have the privileged position to know the perfect truth' (1987: 20). In a re-thought ethnography 'our deeply partial position as storytellers ... should be ... seriously confronted ... as an inevitable state of affairs which circumscribes the ... responsibility of the researcher/writer as a producer of descriptions which, as soon as they enter the uneven, power-laden field of social discourse, play their political roles as particular ways of seeing and organizing an ever-elusive reality' (Ang 1995: 75–6).

In this context the 'ethnographer's authority remains under assault. A double crisis of representation and legitimation confronts qualitative researchers in the social sciences' (Denzin and Lincoln 1998: 21). The linguistic turn—of which Shotter's re-appropriation of the dialogic in Bakhtin is an important part—has thrown doubt on the ability of qualitative researchers to ever capture lived experience directly, since such experience is created in the social text that the researcher her/himself writes. Theories 'are now read in narrative terms, as "tales of the field" (van Maanen 1988). The concept of the aloof researcher has been abandoned. The search for grand narratives will be replaced by more local, small-scale theories fitted to specific problems in specific situations' (Denzin and Lincoln 1998: 22).

Crucially, this critical cultural-ethnographic conjuncture emphasizing, first, the 'ordinariness' of cultural creation and, second, the researcher/professional as storyteller has drawn attention to narrative reflexivity and empowered a rich body of recent risk research on the construction of local-everyday and professional narratives. An example is Sharland's call for a critically reflexive, dialogic focus in social work where we 'look not only to what risk taking means in young people's lives, but to what we "make it" in our professional minds and actions' (2005: 13). Similarly Warner, in her analysis of homicide inquiry reports, emphasizes the need for dialogic interplay of 'active texts' with (professional and lay) voices, and for a (a cultural/media studies' focus on) 'how readers use text in everyday life' (2005: 4).

Research Themes

The thematic developments within the 'everyday culture' and dialogic tradition of risk research include (i) developments directly within the dialogic discursive and narrative analysis approach to risk; (ii) work that draws on the dialogic in terms of research method and professional policy; (iii) approaches that work empirically to theorize the expert/lay distinction; (iv) theoretical inquiries that draw on the substantive expert/lay focus and a dialogic narrative/discourse methodological approach to ask epistemological questions about the analytical object of risk; (v) 'risk cultures' approaches that focus on affect and emotion; (vi) work on risk, audiences, and media as leisure.

Research Findings

Dialogic Discursive Analyses of Risk

Hassin's analysis of the impact of AIDS on the social identity of intravenous drug users is symptomatic of the importance of dialogic, Bakhtinian narrative approaches to early 1990s risk research. She notes that 'Life stories are often constructed in dialogue', producing research narratives that bring together 'different aspects of the individual's experience' and allowing the person 'to integrate his or her story' (1994: 393). Thus, Hassin analyses her long interview with Roberta, an IV drug-using woman with a baby, as her narrative voices of responsibility and irresponsibility 'are juxtaposed within a dialogic exchange that is "... agitated, internally undecided and two faced" (Bakhtin 1984 [1929], 198)' (1994: 394). 'Through her telling, Roberta openly presents herself as the irresponsible junkie but also the innocent faithful wife of the unfaithful husband: responsible for contracting HIV yet the victim of her husband's sexual promiscuity' (1994: 395). Roberta's narrative goes through several other moves, including the claim that her baby's addiction was not the result of her being on heroin, but—as socially responsible mother—because she took a course of methadone to kick the habit (i.e. state sanctioned legitimation). In her dialogical narrative 'she was able to reconstruct a new identity out of her experiences and the reactions of people surrounding her' (1994: 396).

Another early piece in health risk research, focusing on the dialogic in media programming, was Tulloch and Chapman's analysis of the framing of radio talk between experts about the risk of AIDS to heterosexuals. The focus was radio debate around Michael Fumento's controversial book, *The Myth of Heterosexual AIDS*. At first the Australian medical HIV specialist Professor Dwyer, and then US political scientist Fumento were positioned via intertextual authenticating devices as experts and framed by the radio interviewers' discursive procedures to display neutrality whilst being interviewed singly. However, once they were on line together in direct scientific empiricist/culturalist paradigm debate, Dwyer worked to regain the status of sole expertise by positioning the audience within a 'scientific consensus' via a range of semantic and rhetorical strategies.

Other more recent risk research has emphasized the significant *absence* of dialogic 'talk', especially with children. Scott, Jackson, and Backett-Milburn work through Giddens' and Beck's emphasis on increasing lack of trust in both the project of modernity and expert knowledges, to examine the embeddedness of risk anxiety in the context of parent/child everyday consciousness and practices. They argue that the 'sexualization of risk anxiety focuses on risks which are relatively rare as opposed to the all-too-common dangers posed by abusive fathers and other male carers. . . . How do children make sense of these when they are bounded by what cannot be said, when the sexual aspects of danger are not made explicit, when children themselves do not have access to sexual scripts which might enable them both to understand the warnings they are given and apply them to situations in which risk may be a factor' (1998: 702).

Similarly, drawing on Giddens' and Beck's notions of trust and late-modern reflexivity, and focusing on the everyday monologic and by-rote practices of school sexual health classes, Lupton and Tulloch explore teenagers wanting to 'talk it over' with people living with AIDS and with sexual health counsellors, rather than with more monological doctors and teachers. 'What they wanted was to talk through the issues with people who have experiential knowledge, to view the manifestations of HIV/AIDS as it affects the body' (1998: 29). Girls in particular were also comfortable about their ability to talk with each other, whilst they contrasted this with the macho uncertainty of boys. 'For many of the girls, the two discourses of the project of the body and trust were . . . connected, since it is in "open", "face-to-face" talk that you avoid "skimming the surface" and get to understand "what actually happens to *you*"'(1998: 30).

Dialogic Risk Research Methods and Policies

A key theme in risk research has been dialogue between policymaking bodies and various publics' everyday practices. An early (1993) piece in the tradition that draws on 'everyday voices' in relation to risk campaigns and policy was Venables and Tulloch's work for the New South Wales Family Planning Authority in response to the 'scientifically' driven HIV public health advertisements on television. The researchers constructed a low-tech, 'below-up' campaign based on 17 focus group interviews with Australian builders' labourers who had already been cued about 'safer-sex' by a visiting community theatre group (the research thus combining Williams' 'high cultural' and everyday approaches to cultural change). Via the focus groups, the researchers explored both the leisure-time sexual 'pick-up' sites nominated by the builders' labourers (rugby league and working-men's clubs) and the sexual narratives used by the men at the time of pick-up. The workers were, for example, asked at what point in meeting and having sex with a new acquaintance at the club they might insert discussion about condoms. A consensus emerged from the focus group discussions that raising 'safe-sex' whilst having drinks in the bar after the first meeting on the dance floor would be the best time, by way of specially produced cartoon beer coasters. Consequently, an HIV/AIDS campaign was developed in which the builders' labourers were consulted (at a barbecue that brought the various groups together) about the design of the cartoon beer-mats, and this low-tech medium of safer-sex was then run successfully at one of Sydney's largest rugby league clubs (Penrith Panthers) in a predominantly working-class/migrant area of the city's outer-west (Venables and Tulloch 1993).

This research also worked within the linguistic-dialogic tradition of health risk analysis. One of the focus group interviewers was an expert (female) sexual health counsellor (Venables) and the other a well-liked 'layman'—a (male) builders' labourers' union organizer, who asked all of the 'sexual narrative' questions. The gendered dialogic relationship between the interviewed men and these two different discursive power positions (the one as 'scientific' authority, the other as strongly hetero-sexist male) were analysed as *part of the meaning* of the focus group conversation about everyday safer-sex (Tulloch 1999: ch. 2).

In more recent work, Flynn, Bellaby, and Ricci comment on the intervention by the Royal Society and Royal Academy of Engineering's (2004) report on nanoscience and nanotechnologies which called for 'upstream' dialogue and engagement with publics 'before critical decisions about the technology become irreversible' (2004: 65, cited Flynn, Bellaby, and Ricci 2005: 18). They note that this intervention followed several years of important analysis in Europe, including Renn (1998), Grove-White, McNaghton, and Wynne (2000), Horlick-Jones et al. (2004), and Hunt, Littlewood, and Thompson (2003) who all argued for more communicative interaction between official stakeholder and lay publics. The notion of an upstream process 'designates the idea of conducting participatory consultation early and before the "waters have become muddied" by institutional commitments to a particular course of action' (Hunt, Littlewood, and Thompson 2003: 6). However, Flynn, Bellaby, and Ricci's own work in comparing case studies of carbon storage and sequestration, genetically modified food and nanotechnology indicates that even attempting to move public consultation upstream does not avoid a wide variation in perceiving the uncertainties of science, 'as the framing of risks and benefits is necessarily embedded in a cultural and ideological context, and is subject to change as experience of the emergent technology unfolds' (Flynn, Bellaby, and Ricci 2005: 19).

Flynn, Bellaby, and Ricci comments draw attention to *both* policy-driven *and* theory-driven problems of risk society thinking in the context of everyday 'dialogic' and 'common culture' approaches. As regards policy, Mitchell, Bunton, and Green argue that there have recently been a number of national and European policy developments which engage with young people as risky, while often taking their 'technical and scientific knowledge ... from disciplines such as: epidemiology, medicine, economics, and engineering' (2004: 2), thus differentiating objective from subjective (i.e. supposedly misplaced) notions of risk. As regards theory, Mitchell et al. note the repeated criticisms of Beck's risk society thesis for itself being 'objectivist' (Alexander 1996), remaining embedded in 'cognitive realism' (Lash and Urry 1994), and for missing the 'hermeneutical, aesthetic, psychological, and culturally bounded forms of subjectivity and inter-subjectivity in and through which risk is constructed and perceived' (Elliot 2002, cited in Mitchell et al. 2004: 4). They argue for far more understanding at both policy and epistemological levels 'of the situated, "everyday" reasoning and management of risk in order to begin to address some of these problems with the risk society thesis' (2004: 6). In this context, Mitchell et al. introduce studies which relate to expert policy-driven discourse at the level of regulation (by health promoters, Gillen, Guy, and Banim 2004; by community action programmes to redesign leisure space, Foreman 2004; by rail authorities, Tulloch 2004; by police and traffic authorities, Lupton 2004; and by government and education authorities 'as an enticement for encouraging boys to engage in learning as well as sport', Pratt and Burn 2004: 251).

But always these recent studies are grounded 'in the specific social and economic contexts in which they are embedded: local spaces and places where risk taking is perceived as part of the "normal everyday"' (Mitchell et al. 2004: 15). Frequently, these situated studies of young people engage directly with dialogic negotiation of multiple identities in the process of risk management. Thus Mitchell (2004) discusses the play in identity-construction among young mothers in a deprived northern English city, between the different discourses of risk society (in this case, 'othering' representations of risky paedophiles, joyriders, and needle users), 'responsible motherhood' (differentiating themselves from other mothers who leave their children at risk to the dangerous 'outsiders'), and shifting concepts of childhood as 'work' and 'leisure'. Similarly, in a study of prostitution in north-east England, Green (2004) explores 'the complexity of young people's risk narratives, which are interwoven with the "voices" of different and (often contradictory) identities' (2004: 57)—not only between their own 'risky bodies' and their identity as mothers who care, but also between prostitutes who work to support their children's lifestyle and those supporting a drug habit.

The Dialogic Relation of Expert and Lay Knowledges: Epistemological Debate About 'Risk'

Responding to Beck's risk society thesis about scientific uncertainty, the tradition of consultative public/policy-oriented risk research draws also on two other major areas of risk theory: the focus on lay knowledge by Wynne, and on 'risk culture' (rather than risk society) by Lash. In his empirical study, 'May the sheep safely graze?', Wynne argues (in the tradition of both Williams and Shotter) that 'the fundamental sense of risk in the "risk society" is risk to identity engendered by dependence on expert systems which typically operate with ... unreflexive blindness to their own culturally problematic and inadequate models of the human' (1996: 68). He challenges the 'dismissive modernistic view of indigenous knowledges' conveyed by powerful sciences whose main epistemic principles are 'instrumentalism, control, and alienation' (Wynne 1996: 70), and argues that farmers' everyday, practical knowledge is 'adaptive coping with multiple dimensions in the same complex area .... This kind of knowledge is manifestly local and contextual rather than decontextual and "universal"' (1996: 69–70). Wynne's ultimate critique is of the supposed 'objective boundary between science and the public domain' (1996: 75). 'In Beck's ... view, the ... "out-there" risks are identified by counterexperts [hence] the problems of trust and risk are only raised by expert contestation, and as in Giddens' account the public is only represented by different expert factions. The human dimensions of such natural knowledges, whether contested or not by other *experts*, is not recognised or problematised as a public issue' (Wynne 1996: 76). Like Williams and Shotter, Wynne is arguing for a new kind of public citizenship based on 'collective self-conceptions'.

Wynne takes this argument further in his epistemologically focused work, where he draws attention to the embedding of his own field of the sociology of scientific knowledge within 'the reflexive turn in the humanities and social sciences', and the resulting 'impossibility to ignore the ways in which propositional statements about the environment, risks, or technologies, be these critical or not, embody and project the tacit performance of corresponding models of the human subject, that is, of human-culture-in-the-making' (2002: 471). Thus, Wynne critiques the

top-down 'monovalent simple-realist discourse' (2002: 460) of institutionalized science that has subverted and marginalized the 'essential human-
cultural political dimension—about what kind of human we aspire to
be, and in what kind of human world' (2002: 460). By confining all risk
debate to *consequences*, rather than to 'public epistemic debate about purposes ... not only of technology but of scientific knowledge itself' (2002:
473), institutional risk discourse imposes 'not so much a prepositional
straitjacket on the public domain, but, more perniciously, a *hermeneutic*
one, where the supposedly objective meaning is left unquestioned—risk
and consequences', and the citizen subject (the public) is constructed as
'having a common objective instrumental frame of meaning—risk and
consequences' (2002).

Shotter's 'citizenship ... as a "living ideology", a new "tradition of
argumentation", consisting in a whole diversity of interdependent arenas'
reappears in Wynne's emphasis on the need 'to sustain the hybrid epistemic networks spanning multiple subcultures and local frames of meaning' (2002: 460), where local subcultural frames are deeply enmeshed in
everyday 'lay knowledges'. This is Wynne's epistemology of constructivist
realism—'a natural-social-artefactual hybrid', 'contingent', 'unfinished,
always in the making', and 'forever incompletely represented' (2002: 472);
or, to put it another way, 'a great "carnival"' (Bakhtin 1965) of different
ways of socially constituting *being* in which everyone can have a "voice"—
in which they can play a part in the shaping and reshaping of their lives'
(Shotter 1993, 2002). As with Raymond Williams' emphasis on ordinary
creativity, Wynne's central point is to 'focus on innovation, its proper
human purposes and conditions' (2002: 464).

Wynne's epistemological insistence is that policy oriented to public
participation needs to be much more reflexive 'about the human purposes
and visions which shape front-end innovation commitments' (2002:
463). This position is reflected in a range of current risk research, from
Poortinga and Pidgeon's finding that 'in situations of distrust one must
begin with listening to the concerns of the public before giving them new
information' (2005: 20), to Durodié's generalized view of Western culture
where the appropriation of risk itself has led to 'technical fixations' on
security solutions rather than 'significant public debate as to our aims and
purposes as a society' (2005: 4). For Durodié, 'by framing the discussion in
the fashionable language of risk, an element of passivity and inevitability
has been built into the solutions proffered.... The urgent need to engage
in a broader debate as to social aims and direction, based upon clearly
principled beliefs and the desire to engender amongst the population a

sense of purpose that would truly make it resilient to acts of terror is ...
not even considered' (2005: 16, 17).

Risk and Everyday Cultural Affect

Lash's notion of a reflexive risk culture has critiqued Beck's risk society for
being trapped by the 'legislation of cognitive reason' (Lash 2000: 54). 'Risk
cultures, in contrast, presume not a determinate ordering, but a reflexive
or indeterminate disordering ... Their fluid quasi-membership is as likely
to be collective as individual, and their concern is less with utilitarian
interests than the fostering of the good life. ... Risk cultures ... are based
less in cognitive than in aesthetic reflexivity' (Lash 2000: 47).

Like Wynne's emphasis on '*ambiguous* knowledge' involved in the plurality of different public meanings, Lash refers to 'indeterminate disordering' opposing the top-down monologism of rational-instrumentalist
normative orderings. But his emphasis leads him further into the aesthetic
and the affective than Wynne. Aesthetic reflexivity itself is of two kinds in
Lash's formulation. First there is 'judgement of the beautiful' (including
'the possible future bads which are risks') which 'we intuit ... through
imagination ... [as] schemata [that] are "representations" or "presentations"' (2000: 56). Second, there is the 'terrible sublime', when 'the event
or object is so powerful that the imagination cannot make a presentation. ... Sensation is raw ... Aesthetic judgements of the sublime expose
bodies with lack, expose open bodies to the ravages of contingency, to
darkness to fear and trembling' (Lash 2000: 57).

Important work examining media images both as imaginative schemata
and as the embodied terrible sublime has been done by Boholm analysing
Chernobyl as metaphoric and symbolic representation in newspapers (see
below). Similarly, in theatre studies there have been analyses of 'fans'
and risk which explore these two aesthetics of risk highlighted by Lash
(Tulloch 2005). In both cases, what is being considered is the importance,
in terms of affect, of sects or 'affinity groups', which, Lash argues, typically
'are without hierarchy; they bond through intense affective charge' in
the shifting multiple-identities of everyday life—'not subsumed under
narratives of self-identity' but 'with that part of ourselves in which we
are incomplete and unfinished subjectivities, unfinished, lacking bodies'
(Lash 2000: 59).

Lash's focus on sects in everyday lives has been extended in quite
diverse risk research fields. For example, Wild's reflexive discussion of the
othering of New-Age Travellers (2005); Ferrell, Milovanovic, and Lyng's

study of the hyperreal enterprise of once-a-year legal BASE jumping (2001); Reith's emphasis on the Bakhtinian 'chemical carnival' among the 'rapidly growing subcultural group of soft drug users' (2005: 242); Tulloch's analysis of 'liveness', cognition, and affect among theatre fans faced with embodied representations of risk crossing all of Lash's discursive and aesthetic dimensions (2005); and Courtney's discussion of high art 'competent viewers and listeners' in developing an 'impulsive self' in contrast to an 'institutional self' (2005: 103). Symptomatically, in discussing Caravaggio's indeterminately gendered paintings and Robert Mapplethorpe's erotic photographs, Courtney combines the main themes that this paper has been discussing—of culture as ordinary but also creative, and language as dialogic—in his analysis of both queer theorists and competent viewers/listeners of high art.

Media, Leisure, and Risk

A key intervention of Lash's approach to risk cultures is his emphasis that individual and social reflexivity encompasses more than rationalist self-monitoring. For Lash (2000), reflexivity must also be seen to include evaluation of social processes by way of aesthetic and hermeneutic understandings via everyday membership of a shared community or affinity group. In this area Mary Douglas' emphasis on individual ideas about danger and risk serving to bolster *symbolic* notions of a shared community's boundaries has been an influence. Within modernity the media have been key symbol-making institutions engaging with a diverse range of communities' everyday leisure lives. Hence, a significant development in this theme has been a focus on aesthetic reflexivity in terms of the media. For example, Boholm's analysis of several countries' media coverage of the Chernobyl disaster and her research team's analysis of media coverage of the Hallandsas tunnel-building environmental crisis in southern Sweden draw directly on Douglas, via the 'socially amplified hazards' tradition, to examine 'risk understanding as intuitive and non-probablistic' (Ferreira, Boholm, and Lofstedt 2001: 284).

Ferreira, Boholom, and Lofstedt examined newspaper images of the Hallandsas Tunnel pollution, showing a close-up of a dead, deformed cow, a man pointing to a stream of polluted water, a farmer dumping milk into a urine reservoir, and a family standing next to their defiled drinking well. They noted of this 'testimony of disorder' (contrasting with the conventional 'countryside' media representations of working farmers, cows in fields, and gentle streams):

The kind of photographs that 'witness' the collapse of dairy farm imagery do not rely on notions of rationality ... but in the relation between how the imagery of order is culturally constructed and how its disruption is visualized. ... Like the mixing of water and poison, the mixing of milk and urine ... plays upon one of the strongest "taboos" in every society. ... The theory of rational choice ... overlooks the fact that choices are made according to available alternatives that are themselves symbolic constructs. (2001: 291, 295)

In the case of the Chernobyl media images, Boholm argues that the accident brutally forced the Ukrainian people, without the help of culturally available symbols, to reconsider their own mortality, their changed perception of their own bodies, and their failure to fulfil their everyday life projects as parents and grandparents. This failure—as we contemplate the newspaper image of a little girl smiling happily into camera while her mother and grandmother stare blankly beside her, surrounded by their radioactive village—is a new imagistic 'theatre of mortified flesh' and 'bodies that gaze' (1998: 138).

However, the main approaches to risk, media, and leisure do not derive directly from Douglas. To take two examples, if we look (*a*) at risk analysis of media in the area of fear of crime and (*b*) at leisure and edgework analysis, we can see the way in which critical discourses working within Denzin and Lincoln's blurred genres of everyday life analysis merge, engage, and contest.

(*a*) As elsewhere in risk research, sociocultural analysis of fear of crime has challenged attempts by institutional-administrative risk research to measure the 'rationality' of response. In important early research, Young (1987) focused on the cultural frames through which crime 'makes sense' within specifically (and materially) located communities. Taylor and colleagues drew on Williams' notion of 'structure of feeling' to examine the lived local experience of fear of crime by examining the 'symbolic locations of crime' in two very different post-industrial cities, the multinational corporation 'headquarters city' of Manchester and the 'module production' city of Sheffield (1996). An important feature of this and other work by Taylor (such as his exploration of the emotions and anxieties related to fear of crime in an affluent 'village-style' Manchester suburb, Taylor 1995) is his identification of *different everyday channels of discourse* (gossip overheard at the supermarket check-out, anxious playground talk children bring home to parents, local newspapers' speculation about drug dealing in the park) which engage dialogically as interwoven 'noises', 'talk', 'rumour', and 'myths' of crime that circulate in a very specific local community. They become the everyday 'media' which, historically and geographically, represent a particular politics at a particular time. This tradition continues in other areas of current risk research—e.g. Nerlich and Wright's study of rumour among farmers and in parliament during the British 2001 foot and mouth epidemic (2005), and Tulloch and Lupton's study of everyday narratives, risk biographies, and media use in differently situated 'post-industrial' cities (as in the Taylor et al. 1996 study), in this case Cardiff, Coventry, and Oxford. For example, drawing on Beck's 'risky underemployment' thesis, they examine the differentiated use of media (local radio, works website, holiday- and health-related websites, environmental and community media, television, national newspapers) by 'traditional' and 'high-tech' workers in dealing with work crises, technologically generated risks (e.g. the GM food debate), fear of crime, and leisure-time pleasures and risks. Tulloch and Lupton embed their media analysis in situated, everyday life methodologies, whereas a more 'media-studies' textually focused exploration of the emotive and expressive aspects of crime via metaphorical and figurative representations underpins Sparks argument that fear of crime among those minimally threatened should not be seen as 'irrational', but rather as 'intelligibly summarizing a range of more diffuse anxieties about one's position and identity in the world' (1992: 14). Hollway and Jefferson took this further psychoanalytically in arguing that anxiety is the product of the repression of what is threatening the integrity of the self (like physical ageing and existential boredom) via displacement and then projected onto other targets such as fear of crime. Lupton and Tulloch critiqued Hollway and Jefferson's focus on unconscious displacement for ignoring the conscious strategies and dialogically mobilized circuits of communication adopted in people's everyday biographies, where fear of crime is often a material phenomenon not simply a displacement of less definable and manageable worries (1999).

(b) A similar reflexive engagement and contestation of analytical discourses has recently become evident in edgework analysis of leisure and voluntary risk-taking. For example, Lyng (2005) revisits his earlier Marxian/Meadian analysis of high-risk leisure sports by way of a variety of intellectual paradigms: Weber's disenchantment/enchantment distinction, as in Ritzer's 'cathedrals of consumption' (e.g. shopping mall leisure) in late capitalism (2005: 22); Baudrillard's postmodernist emphasis on consumption practices as a direct conduit to corporeal desire (as in sky diving and the mediated edgework of BASE jumping); and Foucault's post-structuralist account of edgework and the transgressing of limits 'as "acts of liberation" in the face of the micro-politics of power operating in the modern world' (Lyng 2005: 47).

Emerging Problems and Issues

Key problems associated with the persistence of rational choice theory in risk research and policy is taken up in other chapters. Here the focus is on problems and issues associated with post 'ethnographic-turn' understandings of cultures of risk as ordinary and everyday. In her conclusion on theorizing leisure, Aitchison calls for a new conceptual synergy that recognizes the interaction of 'productive' (everyday-transgressive) and 'determined' (structural power) relations of risk. The problems of achieving this are multi-layered.

First, there is the epistemological issue of the 'reality' of risk. Too often in risk research the over-simple binary of *either* (a naïve-materialist concept of) the 'realist paradigm' *or* constructivism operates. However, there is now a considerable tradition of exploring positivist empiricism and more relativist constructivisms in the context of materialist realism (Bhaskar 1978; Lovell 1980; Young 1987; Tulloch 1990), as well as the tradition of 'structuration' and agency (Giddens 1984). This has led to specific debates about risk and constructivist realism (Wynne 2002), the epistemology of risk and critical realism (Tulloch 1999), and a pragmatic choice of realism and constructivism as 'the appropriate means for a desired goal' (Beck 2000: 211). In citing Beck's pragmatic position, Irwin argues that 'there is little point in attempting to calculate whether social and institutional understandings are "real" or "imagined". A more appropriate sociological task is to consider the multiple experiences and constructions of environmental hazard—including, very importantly, the manner in which risk constructions interact with self-identities and wider social understandings' (2001: 177). This is sensible. But it also pushes the problem back to the theoretical/conceptual level: how best to understand the ontological and epistemological status of self-identity construction and 'wider social understandings'?

Thus, it seems clear that current research is positively engaged with the construction of self-identities in conditions of risk, that these frequently take account of the reflexive concern for dialogic negotiation within and between everyday 'lay voices' and professionals, and that by and large this work (often criticizing Beck) embeds 'wider social understanding' analysis in quite traditional understandings of the 'otherness' of age, gender, sexual preference, class, and (dis)ability (Cartmel 2004; Murdock, Petts, and Horlick-Jones 2003). At the same time, it remains a puzzle that whilst media/cultural studies has had a good deal of influence in helping establish the parameters of 'everyday life and leisure' in risk research, it is still the case as Kitzinger notes that 'some researchers display little knowledge of the extensive debate within media studies about media effects and audience reception processes' (1999: 57). Kitzinger concludes that risk research is needed 'which combines rigorous in-depth methodologies, with theoretically reflexive approaches and multi-level research designs that give due attention to production processes and audience reception alongside analysis of media content' (1999: 67). Murdock, Petts and Horlick-Jones would add that this content should include a revived attention to image analysis, since 'mediated communication is as much about symbolic exchange as it is about information transfer' (2003: 172).

Third, then, we need to consider the 'problems' of post-ethnographic turn risk research in the context of carefully replicated methodological procedures. Here Murdock, Petts, and Horlick-Jones argue 'in-depth interviews, biographical narratives, and modes such as focus groups which approximate as closely as possible to the conditions of everyday conversation are likely to produce richer insights into the negotiation of media meanings than standard questionnaires or self-completion tests' (2003: 175). To this should be added Ang's point about reflexive analysis of the already empowered researcher herself, dialogically managing research interviews with research subjects who are themselves negotiating narratives of multiple subjectivity. As we have seen, the current condition of risk research in relation to cultures, everyday life, and leisure is strong in its qualitative telling of 'tales of the field', though still not always articulate about the reflexive (speaking/writing) role of the researcher her/himself.

Fourth, if risk research has recently begun to engage empirically and locally with the 'grand theories' of 'moral panics' (Cohen 1972), 'risk amplification' (Kasperson et al. 1988) or the 'Risk Society' (Beck 1995) (Kitzinger 1999: 67), it is important not to forget the creative *tension* in Raymond Williams' work on ordinary cultures and everyday life. If on the one hand, everyday narratives of stroke victims, prostitutes, people living with AIDS, differently disadvantaged young people, etc. are valuably being analysed both as 'most ordinary common meanings' and as 'the finest individual meanings' (Williams 1989: 4), where on the other hand are the analyses of art/popular cultural works now engaging with Beck's risk society? What are the 'structures of feeling' (Williams)—of combined cognition and affect—which people are expressing as they contemplate, for example, the words and images of contemporary risk conveyed by the 2004 series of British theatrical performances adapting Greek tragedy to the invasion of Iraq one year previously? Or, at the 'popular' end of image-making (following Murdock, Petts, and Horlick-Jones), where are the analyses of the leisure-style-images taken by soldiers at Abu Ghraib prison in Iraq (Best 2004)? Here risk theory needs to revisit its own 'grand theories', and explore, beyond its concern with governance theory, other paradigms around globalization, such as the 'new insecurity' research by political scientists, international relations specialists, sociologists and communication scholars examining our era of 'new wars' (Kaldor 2001; Duffield 2001; Feldman 2004; Humphrey 2004). This will not efface recent developments in situated work on everyday life and leisure, but would reconsider Murdock et al.'s emphasis on 'negotiations between "situated" and "mediated" knowledge' (and affect) within 'private/public' assemblage of policies. This is needed internationally (as in the 'war against terror') and nationally (as the post-Cold War international 'humanitarian' agenda is replicated in 'third way' domestic agendas of 'social capital', Roberts 2004). To begin to examine our own, situated everyday leisure responses to the new mediated imagery of 'shock and awe' and 'collateral damage' (Best 2004) would be one important new phase in reconsidering 'hegemonic social relations and transgressive gender-leisure relations in everyday life' (Aitchison 2004: 211).

References

Aitchison, C. (2004). 'From Policy to Place: Theoretical Explorations of Gender-leisure Relations in Everyday Life', in W. Mitchell, R. Bunton, and E. Green (eds.), *Young People, Risk and Leisure: Constructing Identities and Everyday Life*. Basingstoke, UK: Macmillan, pp. 97–114.

Alaszewski, A. (2005). 'Risk, Uncertainty and Life Threatening Illness: Analysing Stroke Survivors' Accounts of Life after a Stroke', Paper presented at 'Learning About Risk' conference, ESRC Social Contexts and Responses to Risk Network, 28–29 January.

Alexander, J. (1996). 'Critical Reflections on "Reflexive Modernization",' *Theory, Culture and Society*, 13(4): 133–8.

Ang, I. (1996). *Living Room Wars: Rethinking Media Audiences for a Postmodern World*. London: Routledge.

Bakhtin, M. (1965). *Rabelais and his World.* trans. H. Iswolsky. Cambridge, MA: MIT Press.

_____(1984). *Problems of Dostoevsky's Poetics.* Edited and trans. By C. Emerson. Minneapolis: University of Minnesota Press.

Beck, U. (1995). *Ecological Politics in an Age of Risk.* Cambridge: Polity Press.

_____(2000). 'Risk Society Revisited: Theory, Politic and Research Programmes', in B. Adam, U. Beck, and J. Van Loon (eds.), *The Risk Society and Beyond: Critical Issues for Social Theory.* London: Sage, pp. 211–29.

Best, K. (2004). 'Visual Imaging Technologies, Embodied Sympathy and Control in the 9/11 Wars', First International Sources of Insecurity Conference, RMIT University, 17–19 November, 2004.

Bhaskar, R. (1978). *A Realist Theory of Science.* Brighton, UK: Harvester Press.

Boholm, A. (1998). 'Visual Images and Risk Messages: Commemorating Chernobyl', *Risk, Decision and Policy*, 3(2): 125–43.

Burgess, A. (2005). 'Risk, Rumour and Precaution: The Myth of Mobiles Causing Petrol Station Explosion', Paper presented at 'Learning About Risk' conference, ESRC Social Contexts and Responses to Risk Network, 28–29 January.

Cartmel, F. (2004). 'The Labour Market Inclusion and Exclusion of Young People in Rural Labour Markets in Scotland', in W. Mitchell, R. Bunton, and E. Green (eds.), *Young People, Risk and Leisure: Constructing Identities and Everyday Life.* Basingstoke, UK: Macmillan, pp. 75–93.

Cohen, S. (1972). *Folk Devils and Moral Panics: the Creation of the Mods and Rockers.* London: McGibbon and Kee.

Couldry, N. (2000). *Inside Culture: Re-imagining the Method of Cultural Studies.* London: Sage.

Courtney, D. (2005). 'Edgework and the Aesthetic Paradigm: Resonances and High Hopes', in S. Lyng (ed.), *Edgework: The Sociology of Risk Taking*, New York: Routledge, pp. 89–115.

Coward, R. (1990). 'Literature, Television and Cultural Values', *The Yearbook of English Studies*, 20.

Denzin, N. and Lincoln, Y. (1998). *Collecting and Interpreting Qualitative Materials.* Thousand Oaks, CA: Sage.

Duffield, M. (2001). *Global Governance and the New Wars: The Merging of Development and Security.* London: Zed Books.

Durodié, B. (2005). 'Cultural Precursors and Psychological Consequences of Contemporary Western Responses to Acts of Terror', Paper presented at 'Learning About Risk' conference, ESRC Social Contexts and Responses to Risk Network, 28–29 January.

Feldman, A. (2004). 'Deterritorialized Wars of Public Safety', *Social Analysis*, 48(1): 73–80.

Ferreira, C., Boholm, A., and Lofstedt, R. (2001). 'From Vision to Catastrophe: A Risk Event in Search of Images', in J. Flynn, P. Slovic, and H. Kunreuther (eds.), *Risk, Media and Stigma: Understanding Public Challenges to Modern Science and Technology*. London: Earthscan.

Ferrell, J., Milanovic, D., and Lyng, S. (2001). 'Edgework, Media Practices, and the Elongation of Meaning', *Theoretical Criminology*, 5(2): 177–202.

Flynn, R., Bellaby, P., and Ricci, M. (2005). 'Risk Perception of an Emergent Technology: The Case of Hydrogen Energy', Paper presented at 'Learning About Risk' conference, ESRC Social Contexts and Responses to Risk Network, 28–29 January.

Foreman, A. (2004). 'Sites of Contention: Young People, Community and Leisure Space', in W. Mitchell, R. Bunton, and E. Green (eds.), *Young People, Risk and Leisure: Constructing Identities and Everyday Life*. Basingstoke, UK: Macmillan, pp. 142–57.

Gillen, K., Guy, A., and Banim, M. (2004). 'Living in My Street: Adolescents' Perceptions of Health and Social Risks', in W. Mitchell, R. Bunton, and E. Green (eds.), *Young People, Risk and Leisure: Constructing Identities and Everyday Life*. Basingstoke, UK: Macmillan, pp. 43–55.

Gillespie, G. P. (1992). *Playing on the edge: young men, risk-taking and identity*. PhD dissertation, Bathurst, Charles Sturt University.

Green, E. (2004). 'Risky Identities: Young Women, Street Prostitution and "Doing Motherhood"', in W. Mitchell, R. Bunton, and E. Green (eds.), *Young People, Risk and Leisure: Constructing Identities and Everyday Life*. Basingstoke, UK: Macmillan, pp. 56–74.

Grove-White, R., McNaughton, P., and Wynne, B. (2000). *Wising Up: The Public and New Technologies*. Centre for the Study of Environmental Change, Lancaster University.

Hassin, J. (1994). 'Living a Responsible Life', *Social Sciences and Medicine*, 39(3): 391–400.

Hollway, W. and Jefferson, T. (1997). 'The Risk Society in an Age of Anxiety: Situating Fear of Crime', *British Journal of Sociology*, 48(2): 255–66.

Horlick-Jones, T. et al. (2004). 'A Deliberative Future?', Understanding Risk Working Paper, Cardiff University.

Humphrey, M. (2004). 'Postmodern Wars: Terrorism, The Therapeutic State and Public Safety', First International Sources of Insecurity Conference, RMIT University, 17–19 November, 2004.

Hunt, J., Littlewood, D., and Thompson, B. (2003). 'Developing Participatory Consultation', Lancaster University.

Irwin, A. (2001). *Sociology and the Environment*. Cambridge: Polity Press.

Kaldor, M. (2001). *New and Old Wars: Organized Violence in a Global Era*. Cambridge: Polity Press.

Kasperson, R., Renn, O., Slovic, P., Brown, H., Emel, J., Goblie, R., Kasperson, J., and Ratick, S. (1988). 'The Social Amplification of Risk: A Conceptual Framework', *Risk Analysis*, 8: 177–87.

Kitzinger, J. (1999). 'Researching Risk and the Media', *Health, Risk and Society*, 1(1): 55–69.

Lash, S. (2000). 'Risk Culture', in B. Adam, U. Beck, and J. Van Loon (eds.), *The Risk Society and Beyond: Critical Issues for Social Theory*. London: Sage, pp. 47–62.

____ and Urry, J. (1994). *Economies of Signs and Space*. London: Sage.

Lovell, T. (1980). *Pictures of Reality: Aesthetics, Politics and Pleasure*. London: British Film Institute.

Lupton, D. (2004). 'Pleasure, Aggression and Fear: The Driving Experience of Young Sydneysiders', in W. Mitchell, R. Bunton, and E. Green (eds.), *Young People, Risk and Leisure: Constructing Identities and Everyday Life*. Basingstoke, UK: Macmillan, pp. 27–42.

____ and Tulloch, J. (1998). 'The Adolescent "Unfinished Body", Reflexivity and HIV/AIDS Risk', *Body and Society*, 4(2): 19–34.

____ ____ (1999). 'Theorizing Fear of Crime: Beyond the Rational/Irrational Opposition', *British Journal of Sociology*, 50(3): 507–23.

Lyng, S. (2005). 'Sociology at the Edge: Social Theory and Voluntary Risk Taking', in *Edgework: The Sociology of Risk Taking*. New York: Routledge, pp. 17–49.

Mitchell, W. (2004). 'Risk, Motherhood and Children's Play Spaces: The Importance of Young Mothers' Experiences and Risk Management Strategies', in W. Mitchell, R. Bunton, and E. Green (eds.), *Young People, Risk and Leisure: Constructing Identities and Everyday Life*. Basingstoke, UK: Macmillan, pp. 180–202.

____ Bunton, R., and Green, E. (eds.) (2004). *Young People, Risk and Leisure: Constructing Identities and Everyday Life*. Basingstoke, UK: Macmillan.

Murdock, G., Petts, J., and Horlick-Jones, T. (2003). 'After Amplification: Re-thinking the Role of the Media in Risk Communication', in Pidgeon, N., Kasperson, R., and Slovic, P. (eds.), *The Social Amplification of Risk*. Cambridge: Cambridge University Press, pp. 156–78.

Nerlich, B. and Wright, N. (2005). 'Viral Cows and Viral Culture: The Function of Rumour During the 2005 Foot and Mouth Disease Outbreak in the UK', Paper presented at 'Learning About Risk' conference, ESRC Social Contexts and Responses to Risk Network, 28–29 January.

Pickering, M. (1997). *History, Experience and Cultural Studies*. Basingstoke, UK: Macmillan.

Pratt, S. and Burn, E. (2004). 'Every Good Boy Deserves Football', in W. Mitchell, R. Bunton, and E. Green (eds.), *Young People, Risk and Leisure: Constructing Identities and Everyday Life*. Basingstoke, UK: Macmillan, pp. 243–55.

Reith, G. (2005). 'On the Edge: Drugs and the Consumption of Risk in Late Modernity', in S. Lyng (ed.), *The Sociology of Risk-Taking*. New York: Routledge, pp. 227–45.

Roberts, J. (2004). 'What's "Social" About "Social Capital"?', *British Journal of Politics and International Relations*, 6: 471–93.

Scott, S., Jackson, S., and Backett-Milburn, K. (1998). 'Swings and Roundabouts: Risk Anxiety and the Everyday Worlds of Children', *Sociology*, 32(4): 689–705.

Sharland, E. (2005). 'Young People and Risk Making: Perspectives for Social Work', Paper presented at 'Learning About Risk' conference, ESRC Social Contexts and Responses to Risk Network, 28–29 January.

Shotter, J. (1993). *Cultural Politics of Everyday Life*. Buckingham, UK: Open University Press.

Simon, J. (2005). 'Edgework and Insurance in Risk Societies: Some Notes on Victorian Lawyers and Mountaineers', in S. Lyng (ed.), *Edgework: The Sociology of Risk Taking*. New York: Routledge, pp. 203–26.

Slack, J. and Whitt, L. (1992). 'Ethics and Cultural Studies', in L. Grossberg, C. Nelson, and P. Treichler, *Cultural Studies*, 571–92.

Sparks, R. (1992). *Television and the Drama of Crime: Moral Tales and The Place of Crime in Public Life*. Buckingham, UK: Open University.

Taylor, I. (1996). 'Fear of Crime, Urban Fortunes and Suburban Social Movements: Some Reflections from Manchester', *Sociology*, 30(2): 317–37.

——Evans, K., and Fraser, P. (1996). *A Tale of Two Cities: Global Change, Local Feeling and Everyday Life in the North of England. A Study in Manchester and Sheffield*. London: Routledge.

Thomson, R., Bell, R., Holland, J., Henderson, S., McGrellis, S., and Sharpe, S. (2002). 'Critical Moments: Choice, Chance and Opportunity in Young People's Narratives of Transition', *Sociology*, 36(2): 335–54; *Discourse and Society*, 3(4): 437–67.

Tulloch, J. (1990). *Television Drama: Agency, Audience and Myth*. London: Routledge.

——(1999). 'Fear of Crime and the Media: Sociocultural Theories of Risk', in D. Lupton (ed.), *Risk and Sociocultural Theory*. Cambridge: Cambridge University Press, pp. 34–58.

——(2005). *Shakespeare and Chekhov in Production and Reception: Theatrical Events and their Audiences*. Iowa: University of Iowa Press.

——(1999). *Performing Culture: Stories of Expertise and the Everyday*. London: Sage.

——(2004). 'Youth, Leisure Travel and Fear of Crime: An Australian Case Study', in W. Mitchell, R. Bunton, and E. Green (eds.), *Young People, Risk and Leisure: Constructing Identities and Everyday Life*. Basingstoke, UK: Macmillan, pp. 115–28.

——and Chapman, S. (1992). 'Experts in Crisis: The Framing of Radio Debate About the Risk of AIDS to Heterosexuals', *Discourse & Society*, 3(4): 437–67.

——and Lupton, D. (2003). *Risk and Everyday Life*. London: Sage.

Venables, S. and Tulloch, J. (1993). *Your Little Head Thinking Instead of Your Big Head: the Heterosexual Men's Project*. Sydney: Family Planning New South Wales.

Warner, J. (2005). 'Homicide Inquiry Reports as Active Texts', Paper presented at 'Learning About Risk' conference, ESRC Social Contexts and Responses to Risk Network, 28–29 January.

Wild, L. (2005). 'Transgressive Terrain: Nomadism, Ontological Security and Risk Identity', Paper presented at 'Learning About Risk' conference, ESRC Social Contexts and Responses to Risk Network, 28–29 January.

Williams, R. (1958). *Culture and Society*. Harmondsworth, UK: Penguin.

___ (1989). 'Culture is Ordinary', in *Resources of Hope: Culture, Democracy, Socialism*. London: Verso.

Wynne, B. (1996). 'May the Sheep Safely Graze? A Reflexive View of the Expert-lay Knowledge Divide', in S. Lash, B. Szersynski, and B. Wynne (eds.), *Risk, Environment and Modernity*. London: Sage, pp. 44–83.

___ (2002). 'Risk and Environment as Legitimatory Discourses of Technology: Reflexivity Inside Out?', *Current Sociology*, 50(3): 459–77.

Young, J. (1987). 'The Tasks Facing a Realist Criminology', *Contemporary Crises*, 11: 337–56.

7

Risk and Intimate Relationships

Jane Lewis and Sophie Sarre

Context

Interrelated changes in the labour market and in family formation have resulted in what many have termed 'new' social risks for those in intimate relationships (e.g. Bonoli 2004). The traditional, married, male breadwinner family was long believed to offer protection against risk, particularly for women and children. Normative prescriptions as to the gendered contributions men and women were expected to make to families in respect of earning and caring were clearly understood and were underpinned by social welfare provision and family law. Core social programmes such as social insurance made provision for dependants (usually women and children) and family law sought to establish fault and hence entitlement to alimony on divorce. Thus, social policies and family law rested on basic assumptions as to what the family should look like and how it worked. This traditional family model made provision for the support of the unpaid work of care for young and old, albeit, as a generation of feminist analysts of social policies have pointed out, at the price of female economic dependence.

Labour market change and the even more dramatic pace of family change over the last 20 years have resulted in the substantial erosion of the traditional family model (Crompton 1999; Lewis 2001) and have changed the configuration of social risk. High rates of family instability, much greater fluidity in intimate relationships (such that cohabitation may precede marriage and post-date divorce, and rates of extramarital childbearing are high in many western countries), and rising rates of female labour market participation, especially among mothers of young children, have made it impossible to sustain the traditional gender settlement that underpinned social provision and regulation in modern welfare states. Family forms are more fluid and the individual's life-course looks increasingly messy, with the increased possibility of multiple episodes of cohabitation, marriage, and divorce (Haskey 1999).[1] Above all, the rising proportion of lone mother families have made considerable claims on social provision, while rising rates of cohabitation, the driver of so much family change, have raised issues for family law, which has historically maintained a firm separation between the treatment of marriage and cohabitation.

The male breadwinner model family has been substantially eroded in two key respects: the changing pattern of women's and to a much lesser extent men's contributions to the family in respect of cash (more than care), and the changing structure of the family itself. In both respects there has been increasing individual economic independence, but nowhere has a fully fledged dual adult worker model replaced the traditional family model. Greater female economic independence, but not full autonomy, is possible via the wage. Indeed, while in Western Europe there is evidence of substantial movement away from the male breadwinner model towards an adult worker model (Crompton 1999), it is most common to find some form of transitional dual breadwinner model than a full dual career model. As Yeandle (1999: 142) has observed, a complex relationship between individuals and labour markets is emerging across the life course, which is 'fraught with risk' and which 'requires skilful negotiation'. The rapid pace of family change also means that the nature of what constitutes risk in relationships has changed. Oppen-heimer (1994) has argued that with the decline of the male breadwin-ner model family the whole meaning of marriage and partnership has changed. Given that two incomes are usually now necessary to meet household expenditure (particularly, in the UK context, mortgage pay-ments), relationships in which men and women continue to 'specialize' as earners and as carers may be more at risk of breakdown than ones in which men and women make a more equal contribution of money and time.

People have more choice in respect of partnering, reproduction, and, to a lesser extent, the kind of contributions they make to families. Men no longer have to marry in order to have sex and children. Women no longer have to marry to gain economic support. In line with the possi-bility of more individualistic behaviour, Inglehart (1997) has also docu-mented a shift towards more individualistic attitudes. Indeed, as Beck and

Beck-Gernsheim (1995) have argued, the norm is now that there is no norm, whether in respect of partnering or the extent of female employment. The erosion of the traditional family model has opened up the possibility of more choice, but this has been accompanied by greater uncertainty, both material and emotional, due particularly to the high rates of relationship breakdown and the lack of firm expectations about the nature of the contributions that men and women should make to households. Indeed, it is no longer clear, for example, whether marriage is perceived to protect against risk, or, in a society where relationships are fluid, to constitute a risk because of the legal entanglements it entails.

There is a large literature that seeks to make sense of changes in family form and in the contributions that men and women make to families, and to explore the reasons for them. Social theorists have conceptualized these trends in terms of individualization, whereby people's lives come to be less constrained by tradition and custom and more subject to individual choice, which in turn means that people take more individual responsibility for planning their lives and evaluating the risks to themselves (Giddens 1990, 1992; Beck 1992, 1995; Beck and Beck-Gernsheim 1995; Beck-Gernsheim 2002). This literature sees individualization in terms of processes that are not inherently good or bad. Thus, while intimate relationships have become more contingent, they may also have become more democratic (Giddens 1992). However, most English-speaking commentators have focused on what they see as the negative outcomes of the changes, particularly in terms of the effects on child welfare, and have concluded (often by reading off causes from the aggregate statistics of behavioural and attitudinal change) that adults are acting as selfish individualists, seeking what is best for themselves rather than others (e.g. Bellah et al. 1985; Popenoe 1993; Dnes and Rowthorne 2002). In the first part of the chapter, we explore these two influential positions, neither of which is based on empirical investigation of how relationships work, and some of the criticisms directed towards them.

Risk, as opposed to uncertainty, is held to be calculable (Knight 1921). In respect of intimate relationships, it is generally known that there is a high rate of relationship breakdown, although the precise figure may not be known and the differences between the rates for cohabitants and married people may also be unknown. It is also generally appreciated that adult women, married and unmarried, mothers and non-mothers, are now more likely to be employed; indeed, there is evidence of attitudinal shifts among men and women approving this (Scott 1999). In addition, in the UK, it is also generally known that the arrival of children is likely to pose problems for 'work-life balance', particularly for women. However, it is much more difficult to be sure of the extent to which people think about their own decisions regarding their relationships in the context of aggregate statistics. The powerful western idea of romantic love (de Rougemont 1940; Luhman 1986) tells us that people 'in love' are 'swept off their feet' such that 'feelings' overwhelm 'rational calculations'. If this is the case, and as we shall see, the evidence suggests that it may not be for all groups, then it is most likely to dominate perceptions of risk at the point of entry into a relationship. Later in any relationship, uncertainties that emerge as a result of changes in feelings, or changes in economic and social circumstances, including the arrival of children must be 'managed' in some way. In the second part of the chapter, we examine some of the more empirical work on intimate relationships that has explored perceptions of risk and uncertainty, and the ways in which uncertainty is managed. This work has also been important for the additional questions it has raised regarding both the positions outlined in the first section of the chapter. Finally, we look at the policy and research issues that have emerged.

Research Themes I: Individualisation and Individualism

Individualisation

The concept of 'individualization' endeavours to locate the choices made by individuals. It refers to the way in which people's lives come to be less constrained by tradition and customs and more subject to individual choice, which can only be understood against the background of changes in the family, the labour market, and the welfare state. Beck-Gernsheim (1999: 54) has described the effects of individualization on the family in terms of a 'community of need' becoming 'an elective relationship'. Elias (1991: 204) expressed a similar idea in the following:

The greater impermanence of we-relationships, which at earlier stages often had the lifelong inescapable character of an external constraint, puts all the more emphasis on the I, one's own person, as the only permanent factor, the only person with whom one must live one's whole life.

As more opportunities open up and less and less is 'given' individual choice (and responsibility) also increase. Beck-Gernsheim (2002) has argued that with the relaxation of social norms and greater individualization and self-reflexivity, people are more likely to see life as a planning project, and to write their own 'personal biographies', or to work on the 'project of the self' (Giddens 1992). So, people will make more deliberate choices about whether to live together, to marry, to have children, and how to combine employment and household work. They also feel a greater personal responsibility for the outcomes of their choices, that is, for evaluating and managing the risks.

Giddens (1992: 35) argued that by the late twentieth century, relationships had become 'pure', that is, they are

... entered into for [their] own sake, for what can be derived by each person from a sustained association with another; and which is continued only in so far as it is thought by both parties to deliver enough satisfactions for each individual to stay within it.

These relationships are, in Giddens' view, contingent: if a particular relationship does not provide one of the partners with what he or she seeks, then that partner will move on. A Canadian study that attempted to operationalize Gidden's concept of the 'pure relationship', in which the partners are committed only for so long as they feel that they personally benefit, concluded that cohabitants came closest to matching the criteria developed (Hall 1996).

(Selfish) Individualism

This is in large measure what those who regard the rapid pace of family change with dismay fear. Giddens suggested that the emergence of the pure relationship signalled the democratization of the family. However, the majority of commentators on family change, whose interest lies in examining the outcomes of the changes and who are fundamentally concerned about the stability of the family, see it more negatively as an expression of selfish individualism that poses risks above all to the welfare of children. American sociologists, drawing conclusions primarily on the basis of statistics showing the increasing instability of the family, warned that marriage might become 'so insecure that no rational person will invest a great deal of time, energy, and money and forgone opportunities to make a particular marriage satisfactory' (Glenn 1987: 351). Bellah et al.'s influential study (1985: 85) of 'middle America' argued that the individual is realised only through the wider community and read off similar pessimistic conclusions from the statistics of family change:

'if love and marriage are seen primarily in terms of psychological gratification, they may fail to fulfil their older social function of providing people with stable, committed relationships that tie them into the larger society'. Popenoe (1993: 528) expressed this view most clearly, arguing that the statistics of family change showed that 'people have become less willing to invest time, money, and energy in family life, turning instead to investment in themselves.' This interpretation of what lies behind the statistics of family change in terms of individuals sizing up risks and opportunities for themselves, without taking the interests of other family members into consideration has dominated the American literature. It has also resonated in the UK, where a polemical policy-oriented literature has warned against the idea of family relationships becoming seen as merely another 'lifestyle change' (Davies 1993).

Criticisms

Both the proponents of individualization and selfish individualism assume that actors can exercise choice, manage risk, and shape their lives. Both have been criticized for taking insufficient account of the context in which actors make their choices. At the macro-level, as critics of Beck and Giddens' approach have pointed out, people's capacity to make choices, for example, in respect of separation and divorce, depends in some measure on their environment, for example, on the constraints of poverty, social class, and gender, or, more positively, on the safety net provided by the welfare state (Lash 1994; Lewis 2001a), although Giddens (1984) acknowledged the importance of structures and structural change in constraining as well as enabling action. Nevertheless, the question posed by Lash (1994: 120) regarding the importance of structural constraints for particular groups of the population in particular contexts is pertinent:

Just how 'reflexive' is it possible for a single mother in an urban ghetto to be?... Just how much freedom from the 'necessity' of 'structure' and structural poverty does this ghetto mother have to self-construct her own 'life narratives'?

In other words, the context in which people make choices and evaluate risks and opportunities matters.

Other people are part of the individual's context, and critics of both individualization and selfish individualism have argued that relationships and networks still matter and that the social theory of individualization has paid insufficient attention to the pulls of 'relationship' and of the needs and welfare of others that compete with the individual's own desires. Askham (1984), in one of the few qualitative, in-depth explorations of marriage, concluded that married men and women faced a conflict between the pursuit of identity and stability. In the view of those concerned about selfish individualism, the pursuit of identity in the form of self-gratification has won. However, people's choices may depend in part on the consideration they give to the welfare of others (what might be perceived as opportunity by the actor may be perceived as unwelcome uncertainty by another person), and on how far others influence the way in which they frame their choices. Feminists have long insisted upon the importance of connection and the relational self to women's moral sense (Gilligan 1982; Held 1993; Griffiths 1995). Svenhuijsen (1998) makes the case for an 'ethic of care', taking a relational view of the self, and viewing the individual as living in a network of relationships that are interdependent. The matter at hand then becomes, not the individual pursuing a pure relationship, but rather how the individual can achieve some freedom within the web of his or her responsibilities. Empirical research has demonstrated the extent to which people take the issue of their obligations to other kin seriously (Finch and Mason 1993; Smart and Neale 1999; Lewis 2001). The more recent attention to social capital represents a wider appreciation of the extent to which no one is an 'unencumbered self' (Sandel 1996), and also stresses interdependence and hence the obligations people have towards one another (Etzioni 1994).

Finally, whether the emphasis is on individual agency or relationship, the twin issues of power and inequality constitute another important limitation to the notion of individuals 'writing' their own biographies, assessing opportunities, and evaluating risks. Feminist analysis has long drawn attention to the inequalities of what Bernard (1976) called 'his and her marriage'. Unequal power not only makes full individualization unlikely, but also, like the structural constraints emphasized by Lash, pose risks that must be *negotiated*. Given that we are still far from fully individualized relationships (in the sense of adult economic independence), and that contributions of money and time within married and cohabiting relationships remain gendered and unequal (increasingly so with the arrival of children), the power that results from control over resources is likely to be a particularly important factor in determining how individuals are able to make choices and avoid risks.

Furthermore, those who find themselves more dependent within marriage may have less bargaining power, although Gottman (1994) has stressed that women may wield emotional power within the home, even if they lack control over material resources. However, economists using economic bargaining models have recognized that resources are not shared equally and that marital investment and exchange must therefore offer both husbands and wives more than they obtain outside the marriage (Lundberg and Pollak 1996). According to these theories, a rise in women's employment or an increase in their wages will threaten the stability of marriage, because it will no longer offer women unequivocal gains, but this is again to assume a model of self-interested economic rationality in decision-making about relationships that takes no account of context, the power of 'connection', and the ethic of care. Nevertheless, the issue of resources and investments in a relationship is important. Working within a neoclassical economic framework, Cohen (1987) pointed out that investments in marriage are front-loaded for women because of childbearing. The relative decline in the value of women on the marriage market thus exposes them to the risk of the expropriation of their greater investment in marriage—their 'quasi-rents'—by their husbands. However, power and inequality in intimate relationships and the effects they may have on the capacity of the individual to act is an extremely complex subject. Qualitative research exploring the workings of relationships has shown the extent to which the kind of risks posed by the inequality in resources between partners may nevertheless be accepted, justified, and managed. Hochschild (1989) has suggested that each partner in a couple may attach a different value to a particular resource, giving it a different meaning.

Thus, whilst there is a measure of agreement that there is a trend towards greater individualization, first, this cannot be conceptualized simply in terms of increasing atomization. Context in terms of the couple's own relationship and their wider connections to kin and friends, as well as their structural position in society, is crucial in constraining the individual's calculations as to opportunities and risks. Nevertheless, there is also evidence that people relish the much greater choice that they have in entering and exiting a wide range of heterosexual and homosexual intimate relationships. In the next section, we explore further the mainly qualitative literature on heterosexual relationships that has addressed various ways in which risks and uncertainties are perceived and managed.

Research Themes II: People Perceiving and Managing Risk

Perceptions of Risk

The nature and extent of the risks that people in intimate relationships perceive is difficult to estimate; we have already raised the issue of how far people think about (and take steps to avoid) the possibility of relationship breakdown. Whitehead (1997) has referred to the existence of a 'culture of divorce' and Beck Gernsheim (2002) has suggested further that if a couple has doubts about the durability of their relationship they will invest less in it, making breakdown more likely. However, in a study of American student lawyers who were about to marry and who had a good knowledge of the divorce statistics, Baker and Emry (1993) found that they denied that these statistics had any relevance for their own relationships. In other words, it was possible for them to believe in the unique qualities of their own relationships, notwithstanding widely publicized evidence of high rates of breakdown.

Nevertheless, Hackstaff's study (1999) of 'marriage in a culture of divorce', which compared couples married in the 1950s with those married in the 1970s, noted ways in which the divorce culture had permeated the lives of the younger couples. Younger couples were surprised by their own marital endurance, and unexpected divorces among their peers made them feel that 'it could happen to us'. Wynne (1996) has emphasized the way in which lay actors' perceptions of risk draw upon their own situated knowledge of the world, which are in turn based on individual, local, and contextual experience. This makes it more likely that couples will be influenced by what happens to friends and family in terms of relationship breakdown, than by aggregate statistics.

Smart and Stevens (2000) and Macgill (1989) have highlighted the way in which circumstances that would commonly be seen as risky can bring benefits to particular individuals. Such individuals therefore live with a high degree of ambiguity about their risk position. Smart and Stevens (2000) have argued on the basis of a qualitative study of cohabiting women with children, who in the UK are disproportionately poor, that cohabitation represents a rational response to low male wages and economic insecurity (see also McRae 1993 using UK data; and Edin and Kefalas 2003; and Moffitt 2000 for similar conclusions from US data). Given that the father of her child is likely to be low-waged or unemployed, a young woman who will likely also be poorly educated may decide that cohabitation is a 'better bet' than either the legal entanglement of marriage or trying to raise the child alone. Smart and Stevens termed this 'rational risk-taking'. These mothers operated in a context of poverty and low educational achievement. Each option—marriage, cohabitation, or single motherhood—was perceived to carry attendant risks. As Macgill (1989: 58) has concluded:

People's risk perceptions are determined by their interpretations of what they recognise as the attributes, material and symbolic, or the risk source... What attributes people identify and what they then mean depend on people's prejudices and values and their experiences of everyday economic and social life... To speak in terms of irrationality and misperception... is plainly to misunderstand how people, all of us, cope with conflicting realities.

We might add that to speak solely in terms of the pursuit of selfish individualism is also to misunderstand how people cope with conflicting realities. Indeed, it is impossible to attribute choices and a particular evaluation of risk in intimate relationships to any one source, whether the pursuit of self-interest, or the 'alternative moral rationality' (Duncan and Edwards 1999) of connectedness and care. As the French economist Thevenot (2001) has argued, we inhabit different kinds of rationality simultaneously. Depending on the ways in which our social, economic, and ideational context enables or constrains our actions—which will vary over the life course—we may act more with the self or other in mind. Indeed, recent research at the level of the household has highlighted the importance of first understanding what individuals in couple relationships actually perceive as risk and what they are prepared to 'take a chance on'. The risk of 'getting hurt' in a personal relationship is widely understood and accepted, but the search for personal happiness is felt to depend in large part on taking this risk (Lewis 2006). The issue then becomes how people seek to manage this risk.

Managing Risk

While romantic love may effectively counter a more calculative approach to entry into an intimate relationship, as Seligman (1997) has pointed out, love requires trust. In the case of decisions to marry or cohabit, there is good reason to suppose that trust in the partner makes it possible to ignore generalized knowledge about the risks. Furthermore, as Guseva and Rona-Tas (2001) have pointed out in their analysis of the way in which the Russian credit card market works, trust may prove an effective alternative to more tangible modes of calculating the possible risks.

Indeed, Lupton (1999) has suggested that people may seek to 'pool risk' in their intimate relationships, which immediately moves us away from the idea of individuals taking the responsibility for and evaluating risks. In intimate relationships that are working well, Berger and Kellner's (1964), idea of marriage as the writing of a 'joint script', developed more than a generation ago, or Morgan's (1996, 1999) characterization of family life in terms of 'family practices', implying that individuals are actively engaged in 'doing' family, may be more accurate depictions than the idea of increasingly autonomous individuals.

But even in love matches individuals may look for more tangible signs of commitment, particularly later on in the relationship during times of strain and difficulty. Most writers on the subject now agree that commitment involves behaving in ways that support the maintenance and continuation of a relationship, even though the concept has proved difficult to define. Thus, the promotion of commitment is seen as key to permanence and stability in relationships, and, by extrapolation, to the successful negotiation of risk and uncertainty. Furthermore, a strong argument has been made that commitment is antithetical to selfish individualism and is therefore difficult to sustain in cohabiting relationships, because they are more contingent (e.g. Cherlin 1992).This view is linked to that of those who are concerned that family change is a matter of concern because it signifies a growth in selfish individualism and is controversial because it infers that commitment will only be found in marriage.

Other research findings are much more cautious on this score. Mansfield (1999) has suggested that there are two forms of commitment: to what she terms the relationship, which is personal and now-oriented; and to what she terms the partnership. The partnership consists of a 'structure of understanding' which serves to link purposes to expectations and is future-oriented, thus amounting to a notion of commitment to the 'institutional aspects' of the relationship that encompasses a shared understanding of the kind of investments that will be made in it. Commitment to the *partnership* is crucial to long-term stability (see also Lewis 2001). However, it is not easy to separate personal commitment from commitment to the relationship, as many social psychologists have sought to do (e.g. Johnson 1991; Adams and Jones 1997). It may be, as Smart and Stevens (2000) have argued on the basis of their study of cohabitation, that commitment should be viewed as a continuum, with 'mutual' commitment (to the other person and the relationship) at one end, and 'contingent' commitment (dependent on any number of issues to do with the behaviour of the other person) at the other. It is less clear how to promote commitment. Those who start from the fact that breakdown is more likely among cohabitants than married people are likely to promote marriage as a solution (see Waite and Gallagher 2000), but there is also empirical evidence that commitment does not inhere in a particular civil status (Smart and Stevens 2000; Lewis 2001; Jamieson et al. 2002).

Nevertheless, it may be that for some couples marriage is perceived as a welcome, additional manifestation of commitment, which in turn serves to provide protective security against the risk of breakdown. A generation ago the legal status of marriage with a traditional gendered division of labour may have been perceived to provide the best protection. But today, whether or not marriage is thought to provide additional security is likely to be decided by individual temperament and social context (e.g. whether marriage is preferred by family and friends). A measure of economic independence may as likely be thought to provide a secure basis for taking the risky step of entering a relationship, as it was once believed to be inimical to the success of a traditional relationship (Lewis 2006).

However, well-established relationships, whether married or cohabiting, will (usually) face challenges and difficulties along the way, which must be managed. Recent research has stressed the importance of negotiation in accomplishing this. For example, Weeks, Donovan, and Heaphy (1999) have shown that while at the demographic level families and family building are becoming ever more diverse, there is convergence in terms of the negotiated nature of commitment and responsibility across homosexual as well as heterosexual family forms. Lewis (2001) showed the extent to which married and cohabiting couples were prepared to negotiate the investment of time and money in households in a search for balance and commitment, in terms of both personal dedication and attachment, and investment in the family on the one hand, and independence in terms of time, career, and own money on the other. This is particularly important given the well-documented unequal division of material resources in families (Pahl 1989; Vogler and Pahl 1994). Older studies of marriage have demonstrated the ways in which the partners in a relationship seek to balance their own needs with those of the relationship (Askham 1984), and to develop 'coping mechanisms' to bridge the gap between the ideal and the reality of the relationship (Backett 1982; Hochschild 1989).

Thus, the ways in which people seek to manage intimate relationships are often delicate, sometimes convoluted, and difficult for the researcher to unpack. However, later on in a relationship people must be prepared to re-assess, re-negotiate, and re-balance risk, especially at times of major

transition, such as the arrival of children, which poses emotional challenges and usually entails a change in the division of labour. At this
point, the attempt to balance and negotiate uncertainties becomes more
complicated because there is a third party—the child—to consider (Lewis
2006). Indeed, collective support may be particularly important at these
points of transition, as we argue in the next section.

Thus, we can see the extent to which empirical research at the level
of the household reveals a complicated picture of the way in which
risk is perceived and managed. The partners to a relationship may have
different perceptions of risk to themselves and to the relationship, which
depend in turn on their social contexts. These must be assessed, balanced,
and negotiated throughout the duration of the relationship, particularly
at times of major transition, such as parenthood. The research findings about the ways in which relationships are managed demonstrate
the extent to which people are neither selfish individualists nor fully
individualized.

Emerging Issues for Policy and Research

The traditional family model was built on the legal obligations incurred
via marriage and a firm notion of what men and women should contribute to families. Stable families and stable employment for men were
both crucial for the operation of the model. With much greater fluidity
in families and labour markets, the major issues that have been raised
by academic commentators and policymakers centre on the nature of
the shifting relationships between the individual, the family, and the
state. These have always been a source of difficulty, but the traditional
family model made it possible to elide individual and family in the
person of the male breadwinner, the 'head of household'. If there is a
trend towards greater individualization in the sense of greater economic
autonomy on the part of adults, female, as well as male, and if family
formation is likely to get more rather than less unpredictable, with people
moving in and out of different kinds of relationships, then should not
adults be treated on an individual basis, for example, in respect of cash
transfers and pensions? If people are more actively choosing what they
want to do and whom they want to be with, and evaluating the risk
to themselves, then should not responsibilities also be individualized?
But what about the stability that is commonly perceived to be needed
by children and provision for the unpaid work or care more generally?

In short, the erosion of the traditional family model has arguably brought with it 'new social risks' (Bonoli 2004). Moreover, these are profoundly gendered in nature because even if the trend is towards individualization, the division of paid and unpaid contributions to families remains gendered and becomes critical at points of transition, such as the arrival of children.

In fact, changes in social policies and family law have for the most part sought to privatize responsibility to individuals in families, in their capacity as parents and as workers (Eekelaar 1991; Brush 2002; Lewis 2002; Taylor Gooby 2004). Some have characterized these trends as the deregulation of 'the private', citing, for example, the relaxation of divorce laws (Glendon 1981; Seligman 1997). But at the same time, there has been an increase in what might be termed 'regulation at a distance', so that, for example, those wishing to divorce are freer to do so, but must make arrangements for their children. The responsibility is passed to the individual, which makes the individual's evaluation of risks a more difficult task. A good example from the field of social policy is that of pensions: cohabiting or married people may negotiate a new 'work-life balance' when they become parents, weighing up a variety of issues including personal career goals and what is considered best for the child, but responsibility for oneself as a worker has increasingly been extended to self-provisioning in old age. Thus again, making choices and evaluating risks may be getting more difficult. But is this sufficient to make a case for state intervention to tackle new social risks, and if so, what kind?

There have been two particularly strong sets of arguments, one relating to family law and one relating to family policy, that have considered specific ways of addressing the new social risks arising from the erosion of the traditional family model. The first seeks to 'put the clock back' and to encourage marriage as a means to promoting greater commitment, family stability, and personal health, wealth, and happiness (e.g. Morgan 2000; Waite and Gallagher 2000; Ormerod and Rowthorn 2001; Dnes and Rowthorne 2002; Wilson 2002). However, the assumption in these arguments is that resources in marriage are pooled, which ignores the problem of unequal control over resources. Furthermore, any attempt to dictate 'family values' and to tell people how to conduct their private relationships, whether by one person to another or by government to people, is very difficult for liberal democratic states, particularly in the English-speaking countries, which have historically drawn a firm line between the public and private spheres. Commitment in intimate relationships is increasingly understood as voluntary and personal matter, rather than as a matter of duty or sacrifice. It may therefore be both easier and more effective to treat cohabitants with children in the same way that married people are treated than to use carrots and/or sticks to promote marriage.[2]

Second, and in contrast to this first set of arguments, which tend to rely on sanctions (against the unmarried) in order to promote marriage, it has been argued that there should be more collective responsibility for addressing the new social risks arising from family and labour market change, particularly in relation to supporting the unpaid work of care as a means to easing difficult transitions that couples must make over the life course, especially to parenthood. Neo-liberals wish to confine the role of the state to that of providing advice and encouragement to the free and active citizen engaged in evaluating and avoiding risk (Lupton 1999). But, as Taylor Gooby (2004) has argued in relation to social risks such as the need for long-term care, there is evidence that people would welcome more state support. In particular, the risk posed by transitions between paid and unpaid work can only be met by attention to the policies that address time, to work, and to care; proper compensation for care work; and policies to encourage a fairer gender division of care work. Kittay (2001) has argued strongly that public recognition of the value of care work is the ethical response to these new risks, and not the privileging of the traditional, heterosexual, nuclear family (see also Fraser 1997; Lewis and Giullari 2005).

The issues thrown up by changes in family form and in the contributions that adults make to families are large and it is unlikely that they can be addressed within the old frameworks of family law and policy. State intervention in the private world of the family has always been a sensitive issue. People expect to make their own choices and, in large measure, to take responsibility for them, but it is a major challenge for policymakers to work with the grain of change. If they are to do so, they need more information about the nature of change at the household level, in different kinds of heterosexual couples, which we have focused on in this chapter, and in homosexual couples. In particular we need to know more about perceptions of risk, and the way in which it is balanced, negotiated, and managed in the very diverse family forms that now characterize most western societies. For a better understanding of the nature of new social risks, it is as important to know how people perceive and understand their vulnerabilities and their obligations as it is to know the statistics of family change.

Notes

1. There are signs that these patterns are becoming further complicated by periods of 'living-apart-together', particularly among the young and the separated/divorced (Haskey 2005).
2. In the USA, the 1996 welfare reform provided substantial incentives to State Governments to encourage marriage in respect of welfare recipients (Horn and Sawhill 2001).

References

Adams, J. M. and Jones, W. H. (1997). 'Conceptualization of Marital Commitment: An Integrative Analysis', *Journal of Personality and Social Psychology*, 72(5): 1177–96.

Askham, J. (1984). *Identity and Stability in Marriage*. Cambridge: Cambridge University Press.

Backett, K. C. (1982). *Mothers and Fathers: A Study of the Development and Negotiation of Parental Behaviour*. London: Macmillan.

Baker, L. and Emry, R. (1993). 'When Every Relationship is Above Average: Perceptions and Expectations of Divorce at the Time of Marriage', *Law and Human Behaviour*, 17(4): 439–50.

Beck, U. (1992). *Risk Society: Towards a New Modernity*. London: Sage.

—— (1995). *Ecological Politics in the Age of Risk*. Cambridge: Polity Press.

—— and Beck-Gernsheim, E. (1995). *The Normal Chaos of Love*. Oxford: Polity Press.

Beck-Gernsheim, E. (1999). 'On the Way to a Post-familial Family: From a Community of Need to Elective Affinities', *Theory, Culture and Society*, 15(34): 53–70.

—— (2002). *Reinventing the Family: In Search of New Lifestyles*. Cambridge: Polity Press.

Bellah, R., Madsen, R., Sullivan, W., Swidler, A., and Tipton, S. M. (1985). *Habits of the Heart: Middle America Observed*. Berkeley, CA: University of California Press.

Berger, P. and Kellner, H. (1964). 'Marriage and the Construction of Reality', *Diogenes*, 46: 1–25.

Bernard, J. (1976). *The Future of Marriage*. Harmondsworth, UK: Penguin.

Bonoli, G. (2004). 'The Politics of New Social Risks and Policies Mapping the Diversity and Accounting for Cross-national Variation in Post-industrial Welfare States', Paper given to RC19 Conference, Paris, 2–4 September.

Brush, L. D. (2002). 'Changing the Subject: Gender and Welfare Regime Studies', *Social Politics*, 9(2): 161–86.

Cherlin, A. (1992). *Marriage, Divorce, Remarriage*. 2nd edn. Cambridge, MA: Harvard University Press.

Cohen, L. (1987). 'Marriage, Divorce and Quasi-rents; or, "I Gave Him the Best Years of My Life"', *Journal of Legal Studies*, XVI(2): 267–304.

Crompton, R. (ed.) (1999). *Restructuring Gender Relations and Employment: The Decline of the Male Breadwinner*. Oxford: Oxford University Press.

Davies, J. (ed.) (1993). *The Family: Is it Just Another Lifestyle Choice?* London: Institute for Economic Affairs.

De Rougemont, D. (1940). *Passion and Society*. London: Faber and Faber.

Dnes, A. and Rowthorne, R. (eds.) (2002). *The Law and Economics of Marriage and Divorce*. Cambridge: Cambridge University Press.

Duncan, S. and Edwards, R. (1999). *Lone Mothers, Paid Work and Gendered Moral Rationalities*. London: Macmillan.

Edin, K. J. and Kefalas, M. J. (2003). 'Is Marriage the Solution to the Poverty Problem? How Poor Single Mothers talk about Men, Motherhood and Marriage'. Unpublished Paper. Department of Sociology, Northwestern University.

Eekelaar, J. (1991). 'Parental Responsibility: State of Nature or Nature of the State?' *Journal of Social Welfare and Family Law*, 37(1): 37–50.

Elias, N. (1991). *The Society of Individuals*. Oxford: Blackwell.

Etzioni, A. (1994). *The Spirit of Community: The Reinvention of American Society*. New York: Touchstone Books.

Finch, J. and Mason, J. (1993). *Negotiating Family Responsibilities*. London: Tavistock/Routledge.

Fraser, N. (1997). *Justice Interruptus. Critical Reflections On The 'Post-Socialist' Condition*. London: Routledge.

Giddens, A. (1984). *The Constitution of Society*. Oxford: Blackwell.

—— (1990). *The Consequences of Modernity*. Cambridge: Polity Press.

—— (1992). *The Transformation of Intimacy: Sexuality, Love and Eroticism in Modern Societies*. Cambridge: Polity Press.

Gilligan, C. (1982). *In a Different Voice*. Cambridge, MA: Harvard University Press.

Glendon, M. A. (1981). *The New Family and the New Property*. Toronto: Butterworths.

Glenn, N. (1987). 'Continuity Versus Change, Sanguiness Versus Concern: Views of the American Family in the Late 1980s', *Journal of Family Issues*, 8(4): 348–54.

Gottman, J. M. (1994). *What Predicts Divorce? The Relationship between Marital Processes and Outcomes*. Hillsdale, NJ: Lawrence Erlbaum Associates.

Griffiths, M. (1995). *Feminisms and the Self: The Web of Identity*. London: Routledge.

Guseva, A. and Rona-Tas, A. (2001). 'Uncertainty, Risk and Trust: Russian and American Credit Card Markets Compared', *American Sociological Review*, 66(5): 623–46.

Hackstaff, K. B. (1999). *Marriage in a Culture of Divorce*. Philadelphia, PA: Temple University Press.

Hall, D. R. (1996). 'Marriage as a Pure Relationship: Exploring the Link between Premarital Cohabitation and Divorce in Canada', *Journal of Comparative Family Studies*, 27(1): 1–12.

Haskey, J. (1999). 'Cohabitation and Marital Histories of Adults in Great Britain', *Population Trends*, 96 Summer: 1–12.

Haskey, J. (2005). 'Living Arrangements in Contemporary Britain: Having a Partner who usually lives elsewhere and Living Apart Together (LAT)', *Population Trends*, 122 (Winter): 35–46.

Held, V. (1993). *Feminist Morality. Transforming Culture, Society and Politics*. Chicago, IL: University of Chicago Press.

Hochschild, A. (1989). *The Second Shift*. London: Piatkus.

Horn, W. G. and Sawhill, I. V. (2001). 'Fathers, Marriage, and Welfare Reform', in R. M. Blank and R. Haskins (eds.), *The New World of Welfare*. Washington, DC: Brookings Institution Press.

Inglehart, R. (1997). *Culture Shift in Advanced Industrial Society*. Princeton, NJ: Princeton University Press.

Jamieson, L., Anderson, M., McCrone, D., Behhofer, F., Stewart, R., and Li, Y. (2002). 'Cohabitation and Commitment: Partnership Plans of Young Men and Women', *Sociological Review*, 50(3): 356–77.

Johnson, M. P. (1991). 'Commitment to Personal Relationships', in W. H. Jones and D. Perlman (eds.), *Advances in Personal Relationships: A Research Annual*. London: Jessica Kingsley vol. 3, pp. 117–43.

Kittay, E. Feder (2001). 'A Feminist Public Ethic of Care Meets the New Communitarian Family Policy', *Ethics*, 111(3): 523–47.

Knight, F. H. (1921). *Risk, Uncertainty and Profit*. Chicago, IL: Chicago University Press.

Lash, S. (1994). 'Reflexivity and its Doubles: Structure, Aesthetics, Community', in U. Beck, A. Giddens, and S. Lash (eds.), *Reflexive Modernisation: Politics, Tradition and Aesthetics in the Modern Social Order*. Cambridge: Polity Press.

Lewis, J. (2001). 'The Decline of the Male Breadwinner Model: The Implications for Work and Care', *Social Politics*, 8(2): 152–70.

——— (2001a). *The End of Marriage? Individualism and Intimate Relations*. Cheltenham, UK: Edward Elgar.

——— (2002). 'Gender and the Restructuring of Welfare States', *European Societies*, 4(4): 331–57.

——— and Giullari, S. (2005). 'The Adult Worker Model Family, Gender Equality and Care: The Search for New Policy Principles and the Possibilities and Problems of a Capabilities Approach', *Economy and Society*, 34(1): 76–104.

——— (2006). 'Perceptions of Risk in Intimate Relationships', *Journal of Social Policy*, 35(1): 39–57.

Luhman, N. (1986). *Love as Passion: The Codification of Intimacy*. Cambridge: Polity Press.

Lundberg, S. and Pollak, R. A. (1996). 'Bargaining and Distribution in Marriage', in I. Persson and C. Jonung (eds.), *Economics of the Family and Family Policies*. London: Routledge.

Lupton, D. (1999). *Risk*. London: Routledge.

Macgill, S. (1989). 'Risk Perception and the Public: Insights from Research around Sellafield', in J. Brown (ed.), *Environmental Threats: Perception, Analysis and Management*. London: Belhaven Press.

Mansfield, P. (1999). 'Developing a Concept of Partnership', Paper given to the ESRC Seminar Group on Marriage and Divorce, LSHTM, London, Dec. 10.

McRae, S. (1993). *Cohabiting Mothers: Changing Mothers and Motherhood?* London: Policy Studies Institute.

Moffitt, R. A. (2000). 'Female Wages, Male Wages, and the Economic Model of Marriage: The Evidence', in L. J. Waite (ed.), *The Ties that Bind: Perspectives on Marriage and Cohabitation*. New York: Walter de Gruyter.

Morgan, D. (1996). *Family Connections*. Cambridge: Polity Press.

____(1999). 'Risk and Family Practices: Accounting for Change and Fluidity in Family Life', in E. B. Silva and C. Smart (eds.), *The New Family*. London: Sage.

Morgan, P. (2000). *Marriage-lite: The Rise of Cohabitation and its Consequences*. London: Institute for the Study of Civil Society.

Oppenheimer, V. (1994). 'Women's Rising Employment and the Future of the Family in Industrialised Societies', *Population and Development Review*, 20(2): 293–342.

Ormerod, P. and Rowthorn, B. (2001). 'For Marriage', *Prospect* (April): 34–8.

Pahl, J. (1989). *Money and Marriage*. London: Macmillan.

Popenoe, D. (1993). 'American Family Decline, 1960–1990: A Review and Appraisal', *Journal of Marriage and the Family*, 55(August): 527–55.

Sandel, M. (1996). *Democracy's Discontent: America in Search of a Public Philosophy*. Cambridge, MA: Belknap Press of Harvard University Press.

Scott, J. (1999). 'Partner, Parent, Worker: Family and Gender Roles', in *British Social Attitudes Survey*, 15th Report. Aldershot, UK: Ashgate.

Seligman, A. B. (1997). *The Problem of Trust*. Princeton, NJ: Princeton University Press.

Smart, C. and Neale, B. (1999). *Family Fragments*. Cambridge: Polity Press.

____and Stevens, P. (2000). *Cohabitation Breakdown*. York: Joseph Rowntree Foundation.

Svenhuijsen, S. (1998). *Citizenship and the Ethics of Care*. London: Routledge.

Taylor-Gooby, P. (ed.) (2004). *New Risks, New Welfare: The Transformation of the European Welfare State*. Oxford: Oxford University Press.

Thevenot, L. (2001). 'Conventions of Co-ordination and the Framing of Uncertainty', in E. Fulbrook (ed.), *Intersubjectivity in Economics*. London: Routledge.

Vogler, C. and Pahl, J. (1994). 'Power and Inequality with Marriage', *Sociological Review*, 42(2): 263–88.

Waite, L. J. and Gallagher, M. (2000). *The Case for Marriage*. New York: Doubleday.

Weeks, J., Donovan, C., and Heaphy, B. (1999). 'Everyday Experiments: Narratives of Non-heterosexual Relationship', in B. Silva and C. Smart (eds.), *The New Family*. London: Sage.

Whitehead, B. Defoe (1997). *The Divorce Culture*. New York: Knopf.

Wilson, J. Q. (2002). *The Marriage Problem*. London: Harper Collins.

Wynne, B. (1996). 'May the Sheep Safely Graze? A Reflexive View of the Expert-Lay Knowledge Divide', in S. Lash, B. Szerinsky and B. Wynne (eds.), *Risk Environment and Modernity: Towards a New Ecology*. London: Sage.

Yeandle, S. (1999). 'Gender Contracts, Welfare Systems and Non-Standard Working: Diversity and Change in Denmark, France, Germany, Italy and the UK', in A. Felstead and N. Jewson (eds.), *Global Trends in Flexible Labour*. London: Macmillan.

8

Health and Risk

Andy Alaszewski

In this chapter, I review current research on health and health care. In the opening section I consider the importance of risk in the development of health care, especially the ways in which the medical profession has used it to establish a dominant role, and the development of epidemiology as the main method of health risk analysis. In the second section I examine the current risk research agenda and the ways in which this is shaped by health policy agenda. In the third section I review four areas of health risk research: patient safety, medical knowledge, risk communication, the media. In the final section I identify two emerging areas of risk research, trust, and health futures.

Health, Health Care, and Risk

The study of risk in relationship to health is well established and can be traced back to the beginning of the nineteenth century. The development of risk studies in health was closely associated with and linked to the development of the medical profession as a modern science or evidence-based occupation developing using expertise and technologies to identify, prevent, and manage the threats posed by disease and illness. However, trust in the medical profession's ability to effectively assess and manage risk has been undermined and risk management has been separated from clinical management with the development of systems designed to identify and manage risk.

Risk and Health Care

The medical profession has developed a dominant position within the provision of health care by claiming the authority and technical expertise to identify and manage risk, for example, in the early nineteenth century in the care of the insane (Alaszewski 2006), at the start of the twentieth century in the use of the new imaging technology, X-rays (Larkin 1978), and in the latter part of the twentieth century in management of childbirth (Rivett 1998: 153–4). Foucault noted in relation to mental health (1971: 270), this privileged status was based as much on the social standing and trustworthiness of medicine as its science- or knowledge-base. In the late twentieth century a number of developments at global, societal, and individual levels have undermined the medical profession's claim to monopolize the assessment and management of health risk. Global processes such as mass tourism, international drug trafficking, and the development of new technologies have resulted in new threats that are proving difficult to manage such as drug resistant strains of malaria, HIV, and drug misuse (Prothero 2001; Wallman 2001; Yi-Mak and Harrison 2001). The BSE disaster highlighted the limitations of medical and other expertise in identifying a major threat to human health (Van Zwanenberg and Millstone 2005). At a societal level in advanced industrial democracies the State's uncritical acceptance of doctors as the experts who recognize and manage risk has been replaced by a more cautious even critical approach. This relates to a general concern with cost and quality that underpins the 'audit culture' of performance review and specific failings in the health care system and the costs of medical errors (Fenn et al. 2000).

Investigations into health care disasters have found that experts have failed to identify and effectively manage dangers and in some cases even been a cause of harm (Alaszewski 2006; BRI 2001; The Shipman Inquiry 2004). A common theme in these inquiry reports was the failure to effectively assess and manage risk and all made recommendations that greater prominence should be given to risk assessment and management. Risk management is now central to the drive in the UK to modernize public services including health and social care which is designed to restore public confidence and create 'high-trust' organizations (DoH 2000a, para 6.1). Increased awareness of the uncertainty of medical knowledge and evidence from failures of such knowledge can be seen as undermining the relationship of trust which provides patients with a sense of security. For example, the uncertainties and threats associated with conventional medicine and the belief that non-orthodox medicine is 'safer' as it is 'natural' (Cant and Sharma 1996) and provides more control for patients (Killigrew 2000) are factors in its growing popularity (Goldbeck-Wood 1996).

Risk and the Health of the Population

The actuarial model of risk prominent in many parts of the public sector within the health field is closely associated with development of the public health perspective. It focuses on harm and loss. Applied to the future it is used to identify and minimize harm and loss (Kemshall 2000: 146) but when applied to the past it functions to allocate blame (Douglas 1992: 27). This approach has underpinned the development of public health and is evident in its reliance on epidemiology to map the distribution of disease and its determinants in human populations (Silman and Macfarlane 2002) and to identify the specific factors that put individuals at risk. Epidemiology has generated a substantial body of scientific knowledge on the nature of health risks.

This epidemiological evidence is now regularly communicated to the public through the media and forms the basis of health promotion campaigns. The emphasis is on 'refocusing up-stream' to identify and prevent the causes of ill health. In Canada the concept of health promotion, providing information on risk factors so that individual citizens could reduce their personal level of risk, formed the central element of an influential report (Lalonde 1974). In the UK the Departments of Health (1975) responded with Prevention *and health: everybody's business* which formed the basis of the Health of the Nation strategy (Department of Health 2004). To achieve its targets the government has made a commitment to develop a new relationship with the public over risk by providing information so that individuals can make informed decisions.

Comment

In the late twentieth century, risk has become a major issue. With the loss of state confidence in the medical profession, risk has been separated from clinical decision-making and forms the basis of institutional mechanism whilst in public health the growing awareness of 'self-destruction' plus the emergence of new infectious diseases such as HIV and SARS has meant that identifying and communicating information on risk factors has become central to improving the health of the populations.

Research Themes During Last Decade

Given the importance of government bodies in funding health research, research themes in the past decade have been shaped by policy and practice concerns. With the speed of policy development much research has been responsive, evaluating changes after they have taken place, rather than providing an evidence-base for such changes. In relation to health care systems, it is possible to identify funding for research on patient safety and the development of evidence-based practice. In public health issues of risk communication have been prominent with interest in why individuals do not respond rationally to risk information and the role of media in shaping risk perceptions.

Organizations and Regulation: Patient Safety

In the UK, the Department of Health (2000 and 2001) has responded to concerns about clinical errors and harm to patients by developing systems to identify and minimize risk. An important example is the National Patient Safety Agency whose function is to create a process of learning from adverse events and near misses 'to improve patient safety by reducing the risk of harm from error' (DoH 2001: 31).

Research fenders in the USA, Australia, and the UK have responded to policymakers' concerns about errors and negligence by developing programmes to identify ways of ensuring patient safety. In the UK the Chief Medical Officer for England and Wales invited three research councils (the Medical Research Council, the Economic and Social Research Council, and the Engineering and Physical Sciences Research Council) to examine the ways in which the research-base could be developed. The research councils held a joint workshop then funded a number of interdisciplinary networks to 'increase and promote high-quality multidisciplinary patient safety research' (MRC 2003*a*). The consensus at the workshop was that the focus of such research should be broader than evaluation of systems designed to reduce errors and near misses. It should identify the broader cultural and health service changes needed to enhance safety including the ways in which staff and patient perceptions of and attitudes to risk influence behaviour (MRC 2003*b*).

Knowledge and Clinical Practice

The government has recognized that managing risk effectively involves restructuring the decision-making process and in particular ensuring professional practice is research or evidence based. For example, at Bristol Royal Infirmary the key decision-makers consistently disregarded evidence of harmful practice relying heavily on their own experience and custom and practice (BRI 2001, synopsis paras 3 and 8). The policy response to such failures has been to develop systems that generate evidence-based knowledge and ensure it is implemented. In the UK, the system has three components to

- *Develop the evidence-base* by encoding current knowledge in National Service Frameworks and clinical guidelines;
- *Implement evidence-based practice* through a combination of professional self-regulation plus local managerial control of clinical outcomes;
- *Ensure* compliance through routine external inspection.

Flynn noted the ways in which this system is changing the type of knowledge used in clinical practice:

Medicine combines aspects of both 'embrained' and 'embodied' knowledge, and ... current schemes of clinical governance represent a drive to transform medicine into 'encoded knowledge' (especially through the promulgation of Clinical Guidelines by NICE ...) (Flynn 2002: 168).

This new system is generating a substantial body of research funded by the government (NPSA 2006). However, much of this research is of relatively limited interest to social scientist. It involves the development and encoding of medical knowledge and systematically reviewing evaluations. Rather less attention has been given to the implications of the changing nature of knowledge for social and economic relations although the ESRC/MRC Programme on Innovative Health Technology is an exception.

Individual Behaviour and Health: The Importance of Risk Communication

Despite the investment in health promotion and public health, which is targeted at both the general population and at-risk groups, there is little evidence that such campaigns have achieved their goals: see, for example, sexual health behaviour (Alder 1997) or smoking and young adults (Denscombe 2001). There is currently little evidence that expert assessments of risk influence the ways in which non-experts perceive and respond to risks and dangers (Slovic 2000). Many individuals and groups persist with 'high-risk' behaviours (Stroebe and Taylor 1995).

Within the health policy community, the problem has been conceptualized in terms of risk communication. For example, the former Chief Medical Officer of the Department of Health, Sir Kenneth Calman brought together a team to review the current evidence of risk communication and identify ways of improving it (Bennett and Calman 1999). This interest in and concern about the effective communication of risk information has stimulated research on this aspect of risk.

Media, Risk, and Health

Whilst experts can measure risk and (attempt to) communicate their measurements to the public, this information is filtered through various media and interpreted by social groups and individuals (Pidgeon, Kasperson, and Slovic 2002). There is concern that the mass media undermine and distort risk communication. Furedi (2002) has argued that the media exaggerates certain hazards such as those associated with new technologies, foodstuffs, and dangers to children. This in turn can create public panics with scares about issues as diverse as childhood immunization programmes, mobile phones, global warming, foot and mouth disease in livestock, and the risks of long haul flights.

In the UK there have been concerns about the ways in which media have amplified certain risks creating panics about hazards associated with certain foods such as 'listeria hysteria'. Such public concerns have at times undermined public health measures, such as the MMR vaccination campaign. There has been evidence of public concerns in the UK that babies' immune systems can safely cope with the MMR vaccine (Boseley 2002: 9) and media reports of a link between MMR and autism have reduced take-up rates increasing the likelihood of a measles epidemic. Given the centrality of the mass media, researchers have been interested in exploring the ways in which it influences risk communication.

Comment

Policymakers in industrial democracies are committed to ensuring that patients are safe and not harmed by health care systems and that the delivery of services is based upon the latest evidence. They are also committed to communicating information on health hazards and risk so that citizens can make informed choices. However, given the evidence of harm, of variation in practice and the failure of much information to alter behaviour, they have funded research to increase understanding of the process that underpins the effective identification and management of risk.

Recent Findings on Risk and Health

Whilst research on risk and health has been stimulated by policy concerns such as how to reduce the number of clinical errors or how to alter professional, patients, and public behaviour and thereby increase safety and reduce harm, a great deal of social science research is critical of the responses to such concern and identifies the ways in which these responses are unlikely to achieve their desired outcomes. This research does provide important insights into the ways in which risk is created and managed in both health and other key areas of contemporary society.

Clinical Governance and Risk: Recognizing the Importance of the Informal

In the past decade governments have sought to re-engineer health care systems to ensure that they effectively identify risk. In the UK the government wants the NHS to become a learning organization. These developments draw social science research. Turner and Pidgeon's (1997) analysis of man-made disasters has identified organizational failures which result in a collective failure to identify 'incubating' hazards. Hood, Jones, and Pidgeon (1992) have identified ways in which the organizational systems can be redesigned using internal incentive systems to identify and manage hazards. The redesign has emphasized the importance of learning rather than punishing mistakes, in the context of a shift from a blaming to a learning culture, in which employees are encouraged to report adverse events and near misses (DoH 2001: ch. 3).

Research on the development of systems to manage risk more effectively shows that the transfer of organizational models from industries such as air travel into health care is not simple or straightforward. It tends to underestimate the complexity of health care both in terms of the range of skills and expertise required to deliver health care safely and the difficulty of identifying 'near misses' and even accidents.

The delivery of health care involves a diverse range of professional and occupational groups. Whilst formal organizational structures seek to control the relationship between groups and the ways in which risks are identified and managed, actual practice often bears little relationship to formal prescription. My own study of nurses working in the community (Alaszewski et al. 2000) showed the limits of organizational control. When working in clients' homes, nurses were working in spaces controlled and managed by clients. The practicalities of managing everyday interactions meant that these workers developed their own routines and practices to 'control clients and reduce the consequences of uncertainty' (Lipsky 1980: 86) and that such routines existed and functioned independently of agency policy.

Similar 'working practices' have developed within hospital settings. Lankshear, Ettore, and Mason (2006) analysed the social processes that made it difficult to introduce structured decision-making systems in NHS delivery systems. Such decision-making systems are grounded in formal definitions of key decision-makers, for example, the hierarchy of senior doctors, junior doctors, and midwives. In reality risk assessments are usually group decisions resulting from informal group workings. Midwives played a key role in making the judgement that a labour was no longer 'normal'. They tested their judgements within a community they trusted, such as their midwife colleagues.

As Horlick-Jones (2003) has pointed out in a review of professional decision-making, the role of formal systems designed to structure or control the decisions made by professionals tends to emerge more in the justification of a course of action which a professional has decided to take on the basis of 'experience-based practical reasoning' than in actually controlling practice (p. 225). Indeed risk can be invoked to justify overriding the formal system. For example, Horlick-Jones noted how in borderline cases or ambiguous conditions

Professionals routinely 'play safe' and use a variety of accounting practices—the need to 'seek clarification' or an observation that the assessment 'only just don't fit'—to rationalize their decision to override the formal criteria. (p. 225)

Whilst major reforms are taking place in health care systems designed to enhance patient safety by managing risk more effectively, their impact is likely to be limited since such reforms do not appear to take into account the complexity of the health care systems and the centrality of informal relations and processes in delivering health care. In the next section,

I consider in more detail issues related to changing use of knowledge in health care.

Research on Knowledge and Health

Current government moves to develop a more systematic knowledge-base for clinical practice represents a major challenge to the autonomy and power of the medical profession. As Jamous and Peloille (1970) observed in their classic analysis of the nature of knowledge in professional practice, uncertainty is a key resource. The lower the level of uncertainty, the easier it is to encode knowledge and transfer the skills outside the profession. Medicine has traditionally protected its knowledge base by emphasizing risk and uncertainty and the limits of encoded knowledge (Jamous and Peloille 1970). In the UK, the government has overcome institutional resistance to such developments by co-opting key elements of the professions, for example, the Royal Colleges are taking the lead in developing clinical guidelines, and substantially increasing the rewards for individual practitioners.

The shift to encoded knowledge in decision-making and risk management may not achieve the desired policy goals. The difference between formal prescription of decision-making and actual practices is a major impediment. Harper, O'Hara et al. (1997) undertook an ethnographic examination of the use of preoperative risk assessment forms by anaesthetists. They found that the real-world practical use of documents by the medical professional was fundamentally at odds with how the organization prescribed their use. French (2005) examined the ways in which nurses used research evidence and identified unarticulated rules of risk management that influenced the uptake of evidence. Risk was unacceptable 'if it is unpredictable, avoidable, if the nurse causes the damage, if they are held responsible without authority, or if there is no support system for dealing with the consequences' (French 2005: 188).

Even where there is a major shift to the use of encoded knowledge, research has found that such knowledge is not adequate or sufficient as a basis for decision-making. In an analysis of two projects designed to promote patient safety and reduce risk by reducing drug errors and preventing falls, Proctor found that developments only took place when the technical developments grounded in the use of encoded knowledge were combined with a recognition of the broader social context, especially engaging patients and carers and professionals recognizing their experiential knowledge (Proctor 2002: 57). Similar findings have come from research on NHS Direct, a telephone advice service in which nurses use knowledge encoded within computerized decision support software or algorithm to advise callers about self-care and use of other services (DoH 2000a, paras 1.9 and 1.11). In an observational study Ruston and her colleagues found that following an intial conversation with a caller, nurses often made an intial judgement on the best course of action. They then checked this against that prescribed by the algorithm, overriding the algorithm if there was disagreement (Ruston 2006).

Whilst there are few areas of health care in which there has been such a complete shift to encoded knowledge, in many areas of practice there is increased use of computer-based systems designed to 'support' clinical decision-making. Such systems provide a new context and set of resources but they do not remove judgement or negotiation from decision-making. Prior et al. (2002) examined the ways in which clinicians used Cyrillic, a computer-based programme, to estimate patients' risk of cancer. Cyrillic made risk 'visible' by using inputted data on relatives to draw a family tree of cancer and providing a numerical estimate of personal risk (p. 248). Prior et al. found that clinicians had to make 'sense' of results and images, and this involved craftwork especially in the laboratory. Such craftwork meant that there was 'always a large chunk of "tacit knowledge" embedded in professional decision making' (p. 256).

Researchers have identified the move towards evidence-based practice and the use of encoded knowledge in clinical practice but this shift is unlikely to improve the quality of clinical decision-making (however that is judged) unless there is recognition of the organizational contexts which shape responses to new knowledge. As Ferlie (2005) noted in his review of development of evidence-based practice, knowledge by itself does not change practice. The application of new knowledge requires changes in the current relationship between staff and the development of new ones. Without organizational leadership the necessary changes in work practice will not take place and the anticipated benefits of the new knowledge will not be realized. In particular change needs to acknowledge the complexity of such decision-making, the influence of informal power relations, and the use of tacit knowledge.

Communication and Risk: Limitations of Current Approaches

The current approach to risk communication is heavily influenced by the rational actor model and health promotion campaigns attempt to make target groups aware, even anxious, about a specific hazard, so that they will be responsive to information on the ways in which they can change their behaviour to reduce their risk. This rational model can be found in a variety of areas (for communication about risks associated with the triple vaccination for Measles, Mumps, and Rubella, see Hobson-West 2003 and for risk communication with young drug users, Duff 2003). Communication grounded in the rational actor model emphasizes the role and position of experts, such as doctors, who have the ability to identify relevant risk knowledge.

One clear research finding is that the 'rational actor' approach to risk communication is not very effective. Individuals may understand the message and may even respond with concern or anxiety, but then filter out the behavioural implications. Ruston and Clayton (2002) showed the ways in which women disregarded information and conceptually distance themselves from the risk of coronary heart disease—even to those admitted to hospital for heart treatment. Thirlaway and Hegg (2005) analysed the ways in which women responded to an article in a UK national newspaper identifying a health risk, namely, that 'drinking a single glass of wine a day increases a woman's chance of developing breast cancer by 6 per cent'. The information did create personal anxiety and the women use a variety of means to dissipate this anxiety. Most of these strategies did not involve changing behaviour in areas such as alcohol consumption.

One of the key research findings is that citizens and patients are not passive recipients of risk information but actively seek information on risks from many different sources, especially when they are aware that they are facing a crucial decision. Whilst they can use traditional sources such as friends and relatives, if they have the skills and resources they can, through media such as the Internet, access highly sophisticated risk knowledge. For example, Carrier, Laplante, and Bruneau (2005) found that public health messages about Hepatitis C targeted at injecting drug users assumed that drug users adopt a homogeneous vision of Hepatitis C and of its risk. Drug users in their study did access public health messages but they set them alongside other sources of data and other visions of Hepatitis C.

Trust is central to risk communication. Individuals give particular credibility to sources that they know, which may include family and friends but also medical advisers with whom they have developed a relationship. They are particularly concerned about the trustworthiness of particular sources. As Frewer and Miles (2003) argued in their discussion of communication about food risks, individuals use their personal experience to evaluate the trustworthiness of personal sources, such as a particular relative or doctor, and often use contextual information to judge the trustworthiness of impersonal sources. Information provided by a source that has an identifiable commercial interest, such as a company marketing a food product, will be considered as less trustworthy than a source without such an interest, for example, an expert committee of scientists (see also Walls et al. 2004: 140).

Individuals are neither passive recipients of information nor do they respond to risk information in a simplistic rationale way. People actively engage in looking for and using information, but may also make conscious decisions to avoid certain forms of information. Their response to information is shaped by social context, which in health must include individual and group perceptions of threats to health and how these can be addressed. Thus, risk communication is part of the overall process of managing health and illness and will be shaped by the same processes. Zinn (2005) has drawn attention to biographical experiences and resources which individuals develop over their life course and the influence of biography in the response to chronic illness such as multiple sclerosis. For example, men of the 'unbending' type do 'not incorporate the illness in their self-conception' and are therefore less likely to seek and accept information than women of the 'legitimated' type who actively develop an 'identify as multiple sclerosis sufferer' (Zinn 2005: 5).

The Social Amplification of Risk and the Media

The development of new media such as the Internet and of facilities such as NHS Direct has created easier access to medical knowledge. This has undermined the position of medical practitioners as the sole source of expertise and increased awareness of uncertainty in medical knowledge (Miller, Kitzinger et al. 1998). This was particularly evident in the uncertainties surrounding new health risks such as vCJD and HIV. These in their early stages were 'virtual risks' which created considerable debate between experts. Politicians, policymakers, and the public did not have reliable sources of information on which to base their decisions.

Many regard the mass media as playing a major role in the development of anxiety about risk. Amplification of specific hazards by the media appears to play an important role in shaping perceptions of risk and associated behaviour (Miller, Kitzinger et al. 1998). Philo, for example, showed how individuals gave precedence to media accounts of people with mental illness as dangerous and violent over their own contradictory experiences even when they recognized that the media accounts were fictional, as in soap operas (Philo 1999). Given the key role of various media in shaping societal and individual assessment and responses to risk, most of the risk research initiatives have included research on the role of various media.

Researchers have focused on the ways in which the mass media has influenced the identification of and response to risk. Burgess (2002) in a study of new telecommunications technology such as mobile phones and mobile phone masts found that the societal responses were highly varied. In Scandinavian countries, despite high levels of mobile phone usage and masts, there was little evidence of media concern and regulation. In contrast, in Australia and Italy, there were high levels of concern plus close regulation of masts. One explanation for these variations is that institutions such as the mass media act as stations that amplify or attenuate risks. Barnett and Breakwell (2003), for example, have explored the ways in which social amplification has influenced responses to BSE, AIDS, and the 1995 'Pill Scare'. However, critics have observed that this framework fails to take full account of the diversity of the media and its dynamic role as a symbolic information system, or of the active nature of the accomplishment of associated sense-making by lay audiences (Horlick-Jones, Sime, and Pidgeon 2002).

Given the opportunities and threats of new diseases or technological changes, it is important to develop a measured approach to avoid either a false sense of security or a panic response. In this context, analysis of the ways in which the media and other institutions operate to amplify or attenuate specific threats has provided a starting point for a more sophisticated understanding of societal responses to health risks.

Comment

Risk study is a well-established area of health research. However, much of this research is of limited interest to social scientists as it focuses on the identification of hazards which can cause harm. It operates within the positivistic tradition of risk analysis. Given government involvement in the provision of health care and the funding of health research, it is hardly surprising that the research agenda closely reflects policy developments with issues such as patient safety, use of knowledge, risk communication, and societal responses to risk featuring prominently. A major social science contribution has probably been to demonstrate that managing risk involves complex social process operating at individual, group, and societal levels and is not a simple straightforward process of objectively measuring probability and consequence of specific hazards and using rational decision-making systems to take action to minimize harm.

Emerging Problems and Issues

There is clearly scope for developing current research themes such as the ways in which organizational processes can be developed to enhance patient safety (Westwood, Rodgers, and Sowden 2002). There are however two issues that emerge out of current research and could be given more prominence in research, trust and 'health futures'.

Trust and Health

Trust is an issue evident in a number of different areas. For example, in patient safety; reporting systems only work when staff trust assurances that they will not be blamed if they report errors; in risk communication patients are receptive to information from sources which they trust. The restructuring of public services is reconfiguring trust. Traditionally, public services have been delivered through hierarchical structures such as the NHS which aimed to provide a standardized service to patients who were treated as passive recipients who could either take or leave the service. In such services the key issues relate to the ways in which trust relates to asymmetrical or power relations. For example, Cook et al. (2004) showed how patients tended to trust doctors who treat them as equals, individuals not cases, whilst Brehm and Gates (2004) explored ways in which trust lubricated the potentially difficult relationships between supervisor, social worker, and client.

However, it is possible to identify a shift towards new forms of public services based on networks or partnerships. These new networks or partnerships involve a range of alternative, even competing, providers and users have to be active citizens using their social capital to engage with services, make choices, and even negotiate their own package of services from a variety of providers. These new services reconfigure trust; it is less about power and more about information and agreements or contracts. With the development of new and competing sources of information such as the World Wide Web, individuals have to decide which sources they trust and use as the basis of their decisions. In such contexts, new modes of trust develop. For example, McEvily and Zaheer (2004) identified the role of network facilitators in developing trust within dispersed geographic clusters. Nissenbaum (2004) explored the issues associated with trust on the Internet and other digital media in which long-term face-to-face relations are replaced by short-term disembodied interactions.

Future and Uncertainty, New Technology

As Webster (2002), Director of the ESRC/MRC programme on Innovative Health Technologies, noted such technologies can destabilize traditional notions of medical authority and trust and create new dilemmas over the meaning of health and illness. They are reshaping major areas of human experience, for example, facilitating individual construction and manipulation of body (Featherstone 2000), and creating ethical and commercial impacts (Glasner and Rothman 2001; Petersen and Bunton 2001). There are major concerns about the risks and acceptability of these technologies (Siegrist 2000), and the government is seeking to address these concerns by increasing public participation and improving the transparency of decision making (HMG 1999).

The global impact of technological and economic change and the changing pattern of and responses to risk was initially conceptualized in terms of environmental changes. Beck's analysis (1992) of emerging features of contemporary society focused on globalization, risk, and the environment. Whilst this area remains important (O'Riordan and Timmerman 2001) there is increased awareness of the impact of changes on health and health care. For example, the development of new infectious diseases (30 previously unknown since 1970s including HIV/AIDS, DoH 2002), the spread of diseases such as malaria, normally associated with the tropics, to temperate areas as a result of tourism or migration (Prothero 2001) or the development of strains of micro-organisms immune to normal drug therapies such as MRSA (Andersen, Lindemann, and Bergh 2002). The development of biotechnology such as the genetically modified organisms has major implications for ethics (Almond 2000) and the environment and health (Achyra 1999). These developments have drawn attention to the role of science and expertise in predicting and managing future change and potential risks.

Final Comment

Health provides major opportunities for social science research on risk. Such opportunities are shaped by medical and health policy agendas. Researching in this area presents challenges, for example, working with or for policymakers who want quick and easy solutions to policy problems and medical researcher who have little understanding or sympathy with some aspects of social science research. Such challenges are also opportunities; policymakers are also willing to fund social science research on risk and are eager to make use of the findings of such research, and medical colleagues can and do find social science complements their work.

References

Achyra, R. (1999). *The Emergence and Growth of Biotechnology. Experience in Industrialised and Developing Countries*. Cheltenham, UK: Edward Elgar.

Alaszewski, A. (2006). 'Managing Risk in Community Practice: Nursing, Risk and Decision-making', in P. Godin (ed.), *Risk and Nursing Practice*. Palgrave, pp. 24–61.

Alaszewski, A., Alaszewski, H., Ayer, S., and Manthorpe, J. (2000). *Managing Risk in Community Practice*. Edinburgh, TX: Balliere Tindall.

Alder, M. W. (1997). 'Sexual Health—A Health of the Nation Failure', *British Medical Journal*, 314: 1743–6.

Almond, B. (2000). 'Commodifying Animals: Ethical Issues in Genetic Engineering of Animals', *Health, Risk and Society*, 2: 95–105.

Andersen, B. M., Lindemann, R., and Bergh, K. (2002). 'Spread of Methicillin-Resistant Staphylococcus Aureus in a Neonatal Intensive Unit Associated With Understaffing, Overcrowding and Mixing of Patients', *J. Hosp. Infect.*, 50: 18–24.

Barnett, J. and Breakwell, G. M. (2003). 'The Social Amplification of Risk and the Hazard Sequence: the October 1995 Oral Contraceptive Pill Scare', *Health, Risk and Society*, 5: 301–13.

Beck, U. (1992). *Risk Society: Towards a New Modernity*. London: Sage.

Bennett, P. and Calman, K. (eds.) (1999). *Risk Communication and Public Health*. Oxford: Oxford University Press.

Boseley, S. (2002). 'Multi-jabs Pose no Risk to Babies, say US researchers', *The Guardian*, Tuesday 8th January: 9.

Brehm, J. and Gates, S. (2004). 'Supervisors as Trust Brokers in Social-Work Bureaucracies', in R. M. Kramer and K. S. Cook (eds.), *Trust and Distrust in Organizations: Dilemmas and Approaches*. New York: Russell Sage Foundation, pp. 41–64.

BRI (2001). *Learning from Bristol: The Report of the Public Inquiry into Children's Heart Surgery at the Bristol Royal Infirmary 1984–1995*, Command Paper: CM 5207, The Stationery Office, London.

Burgess, A. (2002). 'Comparing National Responses to Perceived Health Risks from Mobile Phone Masts', *Health, Risk and Society*, 4: 175–88.

Cant, S. and Sharma, U. (eds.) (1996). *Complementary and Alternative Medicine: Knowledge in Practice*, London and New York: Free Association.

Carrier, N., LaPlante, J., and Bruneau, J. (2005). 'Exploring the Contingent Reality of Biomedicine: Injecting Drug Users, Hepatitis C Virus and Risk', *Health, Risk and Society*, 7: 107–40.

Cook, K. S., Kramer, R. M., Thom, D. H., Stepanikova, I., Mollborn, S. B., and Cooper, R. M. (2004). Trust and Distrust in Patient-Physician Relationships, in R. M. Kramer and K. S. Cook (eds.), *Trust and Distrust in Organizations: Dilemmas and Approaches*. New York: Russell Sage Foundation, pp. 65–98.

Denscombe, M. (2001). 'Uncertain Identities: The Value of Smoking for Young Adults in Late Modernity', *British Journal of Sociology*, 52: 157–77.

Department of Health (2000a). *The NHS Plan*, CM 4818-I, London: HMSO.

Department of Health (2000b). *An Organisation with a Memory*. London: DoH.

—— (2001). *Building a Safer NHS for Patients: Implementing an Organisation with a Memory*. London: DoH.

—— (2002). *Getting Ahead Of The Curve: A Strategy for Combating Infectious Diseases (Including Other Aspects of Health Protection)*. London: Department of Health.

—— (2004). *Choosing Health: Making Healthier Choices Easier*. CM 6374, London: The Stationery Office.

Department of Health and Social Security (1976). *Prevention and Health: Everybody's Business, A Reassessment of Public and Personal Health*. London: HMSO.

Douglas, M. (1992). *Risk and Blame: Essays in Cultural Theory*. London: Routledge.

Duff, C. (2003). 'The Importance of Culture and Context: Rethinking Risk and Risk Management in Young Drug Using Populations', *Health, Risk and Society*, 5: 285–99.

Featherstone, M. (2000). *Body Modification*. London: Sage.

Fenn, P., Diacon, S., Gray, A., Hodges, R., and Rickman, N. (2000). 'Current Cost of Medical Negligence in NHS Hospitals: Analysis of Claims Database', *British Medical Journal*, 320: 1567–71.

Ferlie, E. (2005). 'Conclusion: From Evidence to Actionable Knowledge?' in S. Dopson and L. Fitzgerald (eds.), *Knowledge to Action? Evidence-Based Health Care in Context*. Oxford: Oxford University Press, pp. 182–97.

Flynn, R. (2002). 'Clinical Governance and Governmentality', *Health, Risk and Society*, 4: 155–73.

Foucault, M. (1971). *Madness and Civilization: A History of Insanity in the Age of Reason*. London: Tavistock.

French, B. (2005). 'Evidence-based Practice and the Management of Risk in Nursing', *Health, Risk and Society*, 7: 177–92.

Frewer, L. J. and Miles, S. (2003). 'Temporal Stability of the Psychological Determinants of Trust: Implications for Communications About Food Risks', *Health, Risk and Society*, 5: 259–71.

Furedi, F. (2002). *Culture of Fear: Risk-Taking and the Morality of Low Expectations*. 2nd edn. London: Cassell.

Glasner, P. and Rothman, H. (2001). 'New Genetics, New Ethics? Globalisation and Its Discontents', *Health, Risk and Society*, 3: 245–59.

Goldbeck-Wood, S. (1996). 'Complementary Medicine is Booming World-Wide', *British Medical Journal*, 313: 131–3.

Harper, R., O'Hara, K., Sellen, A. et al. (1997). Toward the Paperless Hospital? *British Journal of Anaesthesia*, 78: 762–7.

Her Majesty's Government (1999). *Modernising Government*, CM 4310, London: HMSO.

Hobson-West, P. (2003). 'Understanding Vaccination Resistance: Moving Beyond Risk', *Health, Risk and Society*, 5: 273–83.

Hood, C., Jones, D., and Pidgeon, N. (1992). 'Risk Management', in The Royal Society (ed.), *Risk, Analysis, Perception and Management, Report of a Royal Society Study Group*. London: The Royal Society.

Horlick-Jones, T. (2003). 'Managing Risk and Contingency: Interaction and Accounting Behaviour', *Health, Risk and Society*, 5: 221–8.

—— Sime, J., and Pidgeon, N. (2002). 'The Social Dynamics of Environmental Risk Perception: Implications for Risk Communication Research and Practice', in N. Pidgeon, P. Slovic, and Kasperson, R. (eds.), *Social Amplification of Risk and Risk Communication*. Cambridge: Cambridge University Press.

Jamous, H. and Peloille, B. (1970). 'Professions or Self-perpetuating systems? Changes in the French University-Hospital System', in J. A. Jackson (ed.), *Professions and Professionalization*. Cambridge: Cambridge University Press, pp. 111–52.

Kemshall, H. (2000). 'Conflicting Knowledges on Risk: The Case of Risk Knowledge in the Probation Service', *Health, Risk and Society*, 2: 143–58.

Killigrew, S. G. (2000). 'Emotions, Boundaries and Medical Care: The Use of Complementary Therapies by People with Cancer', in N. Malin (ed.), *Professionalism, Boundaries and the Workplace*. London: Routledge.

Lalonde, M. (1974). *A New Perspective on the Health of Canadians*. Ottawa: Information Canada.

Lankshear, G., Ettore, E., and Mason, D. (2006). 'Decision-Making, Uncertainty and Risk: Exploring the Complexity of Work Processes in NHS Delivery Suites', *Health, Risk and Society*, 7 (forthcoming).

Larkin, G. V. (1978). 'Medical Dominance and Control: Radiographers in the Division of Labour', *Sociological Review*, 26: 848–88.

Lipsky, M. (1980). *Street-level Bureaucracy: Dilemmas of the Individual in Public Services*. New York: Russell Sage Foundation.

McEvily, B. and Zaheer, A. (2004). 'Architects of Trust: The Role of Network Facilitators in Geographic Clusters', in R. M. Kramer and K. S. Cook (eds.), *Trust and Distrust in Organizations: Dilemmas and Approaches*. New York: Russell Sage Foundation, pp. 189–213.

MRC (Medical Research Council, 2003*a*). *Cross Research Council Networks in Patient Safety Research—call for proposals* (http://www.mrc.ac.uk/doc-patient_safety_call_closed.doc) accessed 8 August 2005.

_____ (2003*b*). *Report on the Patient Safety Workshop* (http://www.mrc.ac.uk/patient.safety.research_workshop_report.pdf) accessed 8 August 2005.

Miller, D., Kitzinger, J. et al. (1998). The Circuit of Mass Communication: Media Strategies, Representation and Audience Reception in the AIDS Crisis. London: Sage.

NPSA (National Patient Safety Agency, 2006). *Building a Safer NHS for Patients*, http://www.npsa.nhs.uk.consulted8.6.06.

Nissenbaum, H. (2004). 'Will Security Enhance Trust Online, or Supplant It?', in R. M. Kramer and K. S. Cook (eds.), *Trust and Distrust in Organizations: Dilemmas and Approaches*. New York: Russell Sage Foundation, pp. 65–98.

O'Riordan, T. and Timmerman, P. (2001). 'Risk and Imagining Alternative Futures', in J. X. Kasperson and R. E. Kasperson (eds.), *Global Environmental Risk*. London.

Petersen, A. and Bunton, R. (2001). *The New Genetics and Public Health*. London: Routledge.

Philo, G. (1999). 'Media and Mental Illness', in G. Philo (ed.), *Message Received*. Harloco, UK: Addison Wesley Longman, pp. 54–61.

Pidgeon, N., Kasperson, R., and Slovic, P. (eds.) (2002). *Social Amplification of Risk and Risk Communication*. Cambridge: Cambridge University Press.

Prior, L., Wood, F., Gray, J., Pill, R., and Hughes, D. (2002). 'Making Risk Visible: The Role of Images in the Assessment of (Cancer) Genetic Risk', *Health, Risk and Society*, 4: 241–58.

Proctor, S. (2002). 'Whose Evidence? Agenda Setting in Multi-Professional Research: Observations From a Case Study', *Health, Risk and Society*, 4: 45–59.

Prothero, R. M. (2001). 'Migration and Malaria Risk', *Health, Risk and Society*, 3: 19–38.

Rivett, G. (1998). *From Cradle to Grave: Fifty years of the NHS*. London: King's Fund.

Ruston, A. (2006). 'Interpreting and managing risk in a machine bureaucracy: professional decision-making in NHS Direct', *Health, Risk and Society*, 8(3).

Ruston, A. and Clayton, J. (2002). 'Coronary Heart Disease: Women's Assessment of Risk—A Qualitative Study', *Health, Risk and Society*, 4: 125–37.

Siegrist, M. (2000). 'The Influence of Trust and Perceptions of Risk and Benefits on the Acceptance of Gene Technology', *Risk Analysis*, 20: 195–203.

Silman, A. J. and Macfarlane, G. J. (2002). *Epidemiological Studies: A Practical Guide*, Cambridge: Cambridge University Press.

Slovic, P. (2000). *The Perception of Risk*. London: Earthscan.

Stroebe, M. and Taylor, S. (eds.) (1995). 'Social Psychology and Health: Special Issue', *British Journal of Social Psychology*, 31(1).

The Shipman Inquiry (2004). *Safeguarding Patients: Lessons from the Past—Proposals for the Future*, Fifth Report, CM 6394-I, II, III, The Stationery Office, London.

Thirlaway, K. J. and Heggs, D. A. (2005). 'Interpreting Risk Messages: Women's Responses to a Health Story', *Health, Risk and Society*, 7: 107–21.

Turner, B. A. and Pidgeon, N. (1997). *Man-Made Disasters*. Oxford: Butterworth-Heinemann.

Van Zwanenberg, P. and Millstone, E. (2005). *BSE: Risk, Science and Governance.* Oxford: Oxford University Press.

Wallman, S. (2001). 'Global Threats, Local Options, Personal Risk: Dimensions of Migrant Sex Work in Europe', *Health, Risk and Society*, 3: 75–87.

Walls, J., Pidgeon, N., Weyman, A., and Horlick-Jones, T. (2004). 'Critical Trust: Understanding Lay Perceptions of Health and Safety Risk Regulation', *Health, Risk and Society*, 6: 133–50.

Webster, A. (2002). 'Risk and Innovative Health Technologies: Editorial Special Issue', *Health Risk and Society*, 4: 221–6.

Westwood, M., Rodgers, M., and Sowden, A. (2002). Patient Safety: A Mapping of the Research Literature.

Yi-Mak, K. and Harrison, L. (2001). 'Globalisation, Cultural Change and the Modern Drug Epidemics: the Case of Hong Kong', *Health, Risk and Society*, 3: 39–57.

Zinn, J. (2005). 'The Biographical Approach: A Better Way to Understand Behaviour in Health and Illness', *Health, Risk and Society*, 7: 1–9.

9

Life Course, Youth, and Old Age

Sarah Vickerstaff

In this chapter we consider how theorizations of the risk society have impacted upon the sociological understanding of the life course, we take current analyses and controversies about 'youth' and 'old age' as examples to illustrate contemporary debates. The discussion is divided into six parts. First, we provide a brief introduction to the idea of the life course and its traditional conceptualization and how risks and uncertainties are understood in the area of life course studies. In the next two sections we review ongoing debates about how the life course has and is changing with particular reference to the nature of 'youth transitions' and 'retirement transitions' in contemporary western societies. In the fourth and fifth sections, we consider recent major findings and evidence for the extent of change within the life course. Finally, we conclude by considering the emerging problems and issues in current life course analysis.

Conceptualizing the Life Course and its Attendant Risks

The sociological concept of the life course is a shorthand for the way in which the biological process of ageing is structured and given meaning by the social context in which the individual lives. A typical definition is given by Elder:

The life course refers to pathways through the age-differentiated life span, to social patterns in the timing, duration, spacing, and order of events. (Elder 1991: 21)

The significance of chronological age as social marker is seen as a specifically modern phenomenon emerging with industrial society (Featherstone and Hepworth 1991: 372), in particular 'childhood or youth' and old age have become distinct and specific stages with related roles, expectations, and duties. As to why this is the case the dominance of work is seen as key to structuring the modern life course. With the move from domestic production to factory employment, related changes in the family and the accompanying development of the state and the education system, the stages of the life course became institutionalized and defined in terms of labour market participation. In this process the young and the old were excluded from selling their labour (Hockey and James 2003: 64; on the evolution of retirement see Atchley 1976). Kohli refers to this development as the tripartition of the life course into 'a phase of preparation, one of economic activity, and one of retirement' (1986: 275).

This is of course a stylized picture of the male life course. For women the relationship between the transitions from education to work, through work, and into retirement are mediated by the complicating relationship between family and work (Heinz 2001: 4). Hareven, who is interested in the relationship between family time and industrial time, defines the task of life course analysis more broadly:

The crucial question is how people plan and organise their roles over their life course and time their transitions both on the familial and non-familial level in such areas as migration, starting to work, leaving home, getting married, and setting up an independent household. (1982: 6)

Hareven defines the 'life-course paradigm' as being concerned with the 'synchronization of individual time, family time and historical time' (2000: 128–9) and hence the timing of events and movements over the life course (or 'transitions') becomes a critical factor:

Members of different cohorts undergo transitions, which are processes of individual change within socially constructed timetables. (Hareven 2000: 129)

The modern western life course has come to be seen as a set of prescribed stages and transitions, which are not only reflected in social institutions and processes, such as compulsory schooling up to a certain age, the age at which one is entitled to a state pension, but also importantly in individuals' self-identity. The chronologization of the life course has come to be seen as normal, prescribing what individuals' expect for themselves and others (Kohli 1986: 276).

Writers on the postmodern era or the risk society have suggested that recent social and economic changes have disrupted the traditional modern life course. In the work of Beck changes in the labour market and in particular the insecurity associated with changing employment patterns are a key marker for the risk society:

the specificity of the risk regime is that it firmly rules out, beyond a transition period, any eventual recovery of the old certainties of standardized work, standard life histories, an old–style welfare state, national and economic and labour policies.... Whereas the Fordist regime brought about the standardisation of work. The risk regime involves the individualisation of work. (Beck 2000: 70)

As a result of these processes it is argued that the assumptions and certainties of the modern life course are being overturned, and we are witnessing the 'erosion of a work-centred life course' (Heinz 2001: 7). There are a number of different elements to this: first that age cohorts are no longer likely to make key transitions en masse at the same ages (i.e. all leave education at 16, all retire at 65) and second, that work itself has become insecure and unpredictable and hence an unreliable source for sustaining individual identity. The experience of education, work, and retirement has become individualized, changeable, and risky.

Individuals experience a greater range of choices or possibilities, and hence individual or biographical characteristics appear more significant in determining the routes people take. The 'normal' life course can no longer be assumed:

Individualization is understood as a historical process that increasingly questions and tends to break up people's traditional rhythm of life—what sociologists call a normal biography. As a result, more people than ever before are being forced to piece together their own biographies and fit in the components they need as best they can. They find themselves bereft of unquestionable assumptions, beliefs or values and are nevertheless faced with the tangle of institutional controls and constraints which make up the fibre of modern life (welfare state, labour market, educational system etc.). To put it bluntly, the normal life-history is giving way to the do-it-yourself life-history. (Beck-Gernsheim 1998: 56–7)

This conception of risk links to wider debates about the extent to which in late modern (or postmodern) western societies patterns of consumption have displaced patterns of work as the fulcrum for the social expression of individual identity. Ransome points out that the difference between work and consumption as the bases for social identity is that work placed people in existing structures and routines over which they had relatively little control whereas exercising one's identity through consumption appears to involve much greater choice and discretion. The individual is more of an agent in consumption rather than receiving an already given work identity (Ransome 2005: 100–1). If work loses its centrality as an anchor for forging identity then clearly transitions into and out of work lose their resonance as markers in the life course and Kohli's characterization of the tripartition of the life course breaks down; there is the potential for the blurring of stages (Featherstone and Hepworth 1991: 372) with attendant effects on identity formation:

> processes of de-institutionalisation and de-differentiation within the lifecourse are, it is argued, currently destabilising the age-bound categories of childhood, adolescence and adulthood and working to overturn the notion that identity is produced within the process of 'scheduled development'. (Hockey and James 2003: 100)

As Brannen and Nilsen have summarized in this conception the 'choice biography' takes over from the 'standard biography' (2005: 415).

The Changing Life Course: Youth

The changes to the life course hypothesized by the heralds of the risk society are nowhere more keenly seen to prevail than at the beginning and end of working life in youth transitions and retirement transitions. Youth transition is usually seen as composed of three interrelated elements: the transition from school to work, the transition from family of origin to family of destination, and the transition from family home to independent living. In the traditional modern western life course the majority of people left school at the end of compulsory schooling, entered the labour market, and then subsequently left the parental home to establish a family of their own. Looking back, these transitions are seen as linear and relatively unproblematic because jobs were plentiful. This picture is provided by Ashton and Field (1976) who disputed that transitions for most young people were stressful or difficult, pointing to the way in which family background and school conditioned or socialized most young people into a largely unquestioning acceptance of the niche destined for them. Such a characterization is premised, to a degree, upon an assumed golden age of unproblematic transitions in the 1940s, 1950s, and early 1960s. When, by implication, young people easily made the related domestic and work transitions. Furlong and Cartmel (1997: 12) refer to young men making 'mass transitions from the classroom to the factories and building sites, while young women followed pathways leading straight from school to shops, offices and factories'. This conjures up an image of largely predetermined and unconscious transitions. In this sense we can talk about normative transitions, where a significant proportion of a population undergoes a particular transition (i.e. into work) at the same time and 'in conformity with established norms of timing' (Hareven 2000: 129).

However, from the 1970s onwards young people in many parts of Europe are much more likely to stay in full- or part-time education after compulsory schooling and as a result their full entry into the labour market is typically later and for many this combines with a period of extended youth dependency between childhood and adult social status (Iacovou and Berthoud 2001). It is argued that the traditional youth transition from school to (training to) work has been progressively fragmented and individualized in this period resulting in less certainty, more risk, and a variety of possible (and impossible) transitions for young people (see, e.g. Chisholm 1995; Evans and Furlong 1997; Nagel and Wallace 1997; EGRIS 2001; Evans 2002). These changes are argued to have resulted in a period of extended youth dependency (Coles 1997) with attendant consequences for identity formation (Nagel and Wallace 1997). In addition to changes in the pathways to paid work other transitions such as partnering and child-rearing have also undergone significant change with the rise in divorce, the postponement of marriage, the rise of cohabitation, and increases in single parenthood (Furlong and Cartmel 1997; Bynner et al. 2002: 9–11). The traditional pattern that young people left the parental home on marriage no longer fits reality.

All this suggests that the contemporary paths to adulthood differ radically from the experience of previous generations in a number of crucial ways. First, the precise timing and sequence of events is more individualized and cohorts cannot expect to follow the same paths as their immediate contemporaries. Second, the outcomes of transitions are no longer safely predicted, will there be a job or not, will they establish a new household, in what context might they have their own children? Pais argues against a linear view of the life course, arguing that young people now experience a 'labyrinth of life' in which status passages are reversible (2003: 119–22). Thus, the individual is faced apparently with many choices but also with their concomitant risks such as long-term unemployment, lone parenthood, and the failure to find a partner (although it must be said that there is a strong evaluative judgement in seeing these as risks). Third, individuals accept responsibility for making their own paths in the sense that they see success or failure as arising from their own efforts (Ball, Maguire, and Macrae 2000: 4). Travel through the life course is experienced by the voyagers as individualized.

The implication is that the increasing individuation of pathways into and out of paid labour means that individuals have to do more to negotiate these transitions successfully.

The Changing Life Course: Old Age and Retirement

It is similarly hypothesized that transitions out of the labour market have become fragmented and individualized. In the period after the Second World War retirement briefly became for some a predictable, age-patterned end to working life (Phillipson 1982, 1999; Harper and Thane 1989). Defined by state and private pension policies there developed firm expectations about the end of working life, especially for men.

Historically, in so far as the majority of the British workforce faced compulsory retirement at the statutory age, this decision [when to retire] was taken out of their hands. (Maule, Cliff, and Taylor 1996: 178)

More recently, in many parts of Europe, the early exit of men from the labour market (before state pension age) has led to a re-examination of retirement and the theorization of its fragmentation as a homogenous, age-related experience. The trend towards early retirement (in particular for men) appears to have destabilized the traditional life course notion of a 'set' retirement age of 60 or 65, with the result that the concept of 'retirement' itself has become more unpredictable and difficult to define (Vickerstaff and Cox 2005: 78). This provides a parallel with the discussion of the break up of mass transitions for young people. Routes into retirement and older age and their timing have also apparently become more complex and varied. This is what Guillemard refers to as 'the decline of age-based criteria as markers of the life course' (1997: 454).

Theorists of post-modernity and the risk society have come to see the third age or older age as a prime site of the new agency, choice, and reflexivity that contemporary society allows (Giddens 1991; Beck 2000; Gilleard and Higgs 2000). In the post traditional life course older people have the opportunity (and the risk) of decisions about who they want to be in retirement and how they will live.

Retirement has been reinvented as a time of transition to a new life, rather than simply the end of an old one. (Hockey and James 2003: 102)

Once again this links to debates about the significance of consumption for social identity. For those who are relatively well-off in retirement it may be possible to maintain patterns of consumption after stopping paid work leading Gilleard and Higgs to pose the question as to whether 'continuities of consumption mask the changes from working to post-working life?' (2000: 31). Research on retirement aspirations and activities reveals that for some retirement is an eagerly awaited opportunity to spend more time on hobbies, migrate to spend their winters abroad, or simply enjoy the opportunity to take up a range of new activities (Scales and Scase 2000; see Vickerstaff et al. 2004).

This produces a very benign picture of old age in contemporary western societies; however, at the same time there is a climate of risk and uncertainty surrounding pensions and retirement, and many older people, especially women in the UK, live in poverty. In addition to the pressure on state pension systems as the number of older aged members of society increases we have also seen changes in occupational and private pension arrangements. In the UK, as in the USA previously, many private sector organizations have shifted their occupational pensions from final salary to money purchase schemes. These pensions shift the burden of financial risk from the employer to employee and mirror the British government's recent efforts to encourage individuals to take out private or stakeholder pensions. But many of those who have taken out personal pensions have watched as the value of their savings diminishes in a declining stock market (Vickerstaff and Cox 2005: 77–8). This experience of risk is no respecter of class, income, or status. Where companies become insolvent all employees who have paid into their pension schemes stand to lose. These seem on the face of it to be classic examples of the ways in which risk in late modern societies is being redistributed across traditional lines of relative advantage and disadvantage such as class, race, and gender. Not least the risk of living longer, with attendant possible consequences for health and wealth. As Phillipson has put it: 'Old age has been progressively displaced from the institutional framework created by retirement and the welfare state' (2003: 2.4).

All this suggests that the prospect, planning for, and experience of retirement are becoming more individualized. As Gilleard concludes:

Both the status ascribed to older people and the lifestyle created during retirement are less structured than before. (1996: 495)

From this discussion of both youth and older age we have reviewed how theorists of risk make a strong case for significant restructuring of the traditional modern life course. In the next section we review the evidence for these changes.

The Evidence: Youth

Evidence on how youth transitions are changing comes from two main, contrasting sources: longitudinal studies, which map transitions of cohorts across a time span and more micro-based research which looks at individual biographies to uncover the experience of growing up (for a wider discussion of the 'two traditions' in youth research see Heinz et al. 1998; MacDonald et al. 2001; Evans 2002). Typically (but not exclusively) the first kind of study uses more quantitative techniques to interrogate large data sets, and the second focuses on qualitative methods to uncover and explore individual experiences. Perhaps unsurprisingly these different approaches reach different conclusions as to the current state of youth.

There is plenty of evidence from longitudinal studies in Europe, the US, and Canada that class, family background, educational level of parents, gender, and race (summarized as socialization frameworks) continue to significantly structure the educational careers of young people and thus, the opportunities that may be available to them in the labour market (e.g. Furlong and Cartmel 1997; Heinz et al. 1998; Schoon 2001; Bynner et al. 2002; Evans 2002; Andres and Grayson 2003; Plug, Zeijl, and du Bois Reymond 2003; Glaesser and Lauterbach 2004; Lehman 2004; Furlong et al. 2005). In Britain despite the massive expansion in educational opportunities (the increase in numbers staying on after 16 and the increase in those going to University) young people from disadvantaged backgrounds still lose out to the middle classes (Thomson, Henderson, and Holland 2003: 33; Webster et al. 2004). There is evidence of growing polarization in both work and non-work transitions. Those without qualifications face an increased risk of intermittent or long-term unemployment; for young women, especially in Britain and USA this may translate into an accelerated transition to motherhood (Bynner et al. 2002: 10–11).

Although the routes into the labour market have undoubtedly become more varied the majority of young people, even in the difficult circumstances of major social change as in Eastern Europe, do make a transition into employment and do leave the parental home. In a study comparing the transitions of two birth cohorts in Britain from 1958 and 1970 it was found that the two groups were virtually identical with respect to leaving home and that by age 26 a similar proportion of young men were working full time (1958 cohort: 89 per cent, 1970 cohort: 84 per cent and the proportion of young women working full time had increased from 56 per cent to 65 per cent across the cohorts (Bynner et al. 2002: 14). As Roberts put it 'Life goes on!.... Young People continue to fall in love, marry and become parents' (2003: 492).

Research, which focuses on the individual experiences of these processes, is more likely to highlight the risks, discontinuities, and uncertainties of educational and work careers and in particular stresses the non-linear nature of the transition from youth to adulthood:

traditional patterns of transition have all but disappeared (with some class variations), or become extended in ways that create an ambiguous relationship to adulthood for young people. (Thomson et al. 2004: 218; see also, e.g. Ferguson et al. 2000; Thomson et al. 2002; Pais 2003)

Changes in the youth labour market and especially the collapse in the demand for unskilled manual workers are seen as critical in having tipped many young people into an arena of labour market uncertainty and risk. The consequences of poor educational qualifications are now greater. The picture derived from this research is of the individual young person dealing with choice, chance, and opportunity with uncertain outcomes; a set of experiences very different to those of their parents as young people. They may seesaw back and forth between education and work, semi-independence and independence blurring the statuses of 'youth' or 'adult'. In a study of 800 16–18-year-old researchers concluded that at least a third 'were engaged in a series of multiple trajectories', which defied any sense of linearity or 'transition':

Movement seems opportunistic rather than purposive. It is characterised by ad hoc, multiple and diverse experiences rather than any semblance of 'career'. And above all it is powered by a market-driven provision of 'choices' which allows for continual 'drift' between part-time work, full-time work, training, further education, school, college and unemployment. (Ferguson et al. 2000: 293)

In this context many young people are seen to go with the flow and in the face of an unpredictable future invest more in the present (Pais 2003: 125).

This vision of a radical change in the experience of youth transitions in the last 30 years has recently been contested by some writers who have revisited the 'golden age' of the 1950s and 1960s to test whether our contemporary view of the period bears scrutiny. This work, based on interviews undertaken in the 1960s and current accounts of remembered transitions, suggests that the smoothness of youth transitions in the past may have been exaggerated (Vickerstaff 2003; Goodwin and O'Connor 2005).

In work reanalysing interviews undertaken in the early 1960s Goodwin and O'Connor conclude that many of the young people in their sample experienced frequent job changes and uncertainty about their futures, leaving them to rely heavily on family for support and encouragement. Not a picture that sits well with the assumptions about easy or smooth transitions from school to work (2005: 216–17). Similarly, Vickerstaff (2003) in a study of apprenticeship in the 1950s and 1960s found that the experience of leaving school and going into the workplace was traumatic for many. This study came to the conclusion that perhaps the key difference between current cohorts of young people and those interviewed about their apprenticeships in the post-war period is the extent to which young people in the past largely accepted that they had little choice and few supports for resisting adult authority; whereas in research today young people regularly assert that they do have choices (see, e.g. Ball, Maguire, and Macrae 2000). They perceive their paths to have been individualized, even if the common reality is of relatively circumscribed possibilities conditioned by their class, race, and gender.

Work on the degree of complexity of current youth transitions using a longitudinal data set from Scotland found six main clusters of transitions, and that 52 per cent of their sample could be characterized as having followed a linear transition, the most disadvantaged young people had a much higher likelihood of a non-linear transition of the type argued by others to be the general experience of all young people now (Furlong et al. 2005). The authors conclude that: 'linear transitions [are] just as characteristic of the modern age as non-linear transitions' (Furlong et al. 2005: 21).

If one combines this finding with recent work, reanalysing the past (Vickerstaff 2003; Goodwin and O'Connor 2005; O'Connor and Goodwin 2005), it seems to suggest that youth transitions have always varied within a cohort, some young people having a relatively easy and linear transition to adult status, others experiencing a range of difficulties in their paths to independence. What has changed is how as sociologists we examine these processes. In the 1960s and 1970s research focused upon the underlying structures which determined the likely course a young person would take, so explanations focused around class and family background, quality of schooling, and/or structure of the local labour market, for example. By the late 1990s researchers became much more interested in the individual's experience of their own youth and hence biographical factors assumed a much greater significance in our explanations (Goodwin and O'Connor 2005: 217–18). These two traditions in youth studies focus on different

189

groups: the transition theorists on the general trends and the 'normal' groups, and the biographers on the marginalized and more exceptional.

The Evidence: Old Age and Retirement

The retirement transition has not, until very recently, attracted the same level of academic interest as we witness in the youth transitions arena (Hirsch 2000: 2; Phillipson 2002: 2). However, the wave of early retirement or labour market withdrawal (defined as before state pension age) amongst men in many parts of Europe (see Phillipson 2002: 4–7) has led to debates about the nature of the third age in contemporary western societies. Has the shrinking working life opened up opportunities for the pursuit of new interests and lifestyles or merely reinforced patterns of inequality laid down through working life? The more optimistic literature on early retirement presents a picture of individuals choosing to leave work in their fifties to spend more time in leisure activities. Others have suggested that we may need to recognize a new phase in the life course: 'beyond work but not yet into old age' (Phillipson 2002: 2).

To review the evidence on these trends we need to consider first the reasons why people are 'retiring' earlier than they did 30 years ago. In the USA the study of retirement transitions has been dominated by labour economists and gerontologists who focus on what Feldman (1994: 286) has called individual difference variables. These studies, especially those associated with the longitudinal Health Retirement Study, model factors such as health, income, level of education, and domestic circumstances to determine correlations between these factors and labour market participation or timing of retirement. This body of research typically finds that financial position and health status are the two key predictors of individual retirement timing. A similar tradition in the British literature confirms these findings (see, e.g. Disney, Grundy, and Johnson 1997; Meghir and Whitehouse 1997; Tanner 1998; Bardasi, Jenkins, and Rigg 2000; Humphrey et al. 2003). European social policy researchers have focused more on the impact of state pension policies and other benefit regimes in encouraging or discouraging retirement (see, e.g. Kohli et al. 1991; Taylor and Walker 1993: 15–24; Bonoli 2000; Gelissen 2001; de Vroom and Guillemard 2002).

Evidence on the British case suggests that the majority of people who leave the labour market before state pension age cannot be said to have chosen to do so. Donovan and Street concluded in their review of the literature that 'early retirement is in large part a function of management practice and organizational culture' (2000: 31). People leave their jobs through redundancy, early retirement, or ill health (Campbell 1999; Hayden, Boaz, and Taylor 1999; PIU 2000; Arthur 2003). Early retirement may be more or less voluntary and even ill health, which might be seen as an individual factor, is a variable mediated by organizational practice, in that changes to work routine or job modifications could enable some health issues to be accommodated at work (Vickerstaff et al. 2004: 26–7; Vickerstaff 2006, forthcoming). The extent to which early retirement is forced or voluntary has been highlighted as a factor in retirement satisfaction (McGoldrick and Cooper 1994; Dench and Norton 1996; Maule, Cliff, and Taylor 1996). As Guillemard reminds us:

> The principles providing for an orderly passage from work to leisure have vanished. The end of work life is now flexibly organized; ever more subject to both conditions in the labour market and company employment policies. . . . This could be described as an 'individualization' of the life course. But such a description misleads us into thinking that the individual has more room for choice, whereas early exit is usually imposed upon him or her. . . . A sudden break, over which the individual has little control, now marks the passage towards economic inactivity. (1997: 455)

Researchers have identified at least two nations in retirement: those relatively well-paid managers and professionals with a decent pension who may have chosen to retire early and those on much lower incomes, with or without a private pension who left the labour market because of unemployment, ill health, redundancy, or encouraged early retirement. In Britain there is proof of growing economic polarization with increasing age (Scales and Scase 2000: 22). It is clear that lifetime earning trajectories vary considerably according to class and gender and that 'work history matters' (Bardasi and Jenkins 2002) for income in later life.

It is hardly surprising to find that those with higher earnings throughout working life are financially more secure in older age and this fact does not of itself prove or disprove that retirement transitions have changed in response to the wider social changes that have affected the life course more generally. Phillipson argues that the transition to retirement has become extended and more complex (2002: 10–11) notwithstanding the continuing structural effects of class and gender. To examine this assertion we can look for two sorts of evidence: first, data about the extent to which people take longer to retire or the very status of 'being retired' itself has become more fluid and reversible and second, the degree to which individuals have reconceptualized retirement and its significance.

In the continental European literature the increased complexity of possible pathways is often stressed:

The process of early retirement has destabilized the life course by substituting functional categories for chronological categories. The effect was to increase uncertainty, to decrease the retirement system's control over the process, and weaken the intergenerational contract. The growth of bridging pathways converted a standardized, orderly, predictable transition from work to retirement based primarily on age criteria into a de-standardized, heterogeneous process based on functional criteria. Since the chronological markers are becoming less visible, the end of the life course has, for individuals, been blurred. (Jacobs and Rein 1994: 44)

In the USA, the flexible route to full retirement has more of a history with many older Americans taking so-called 'bridge jobs', or becoming self-employed between leaving their career job or employer and retiring fully (Feldman 1994; Bruce, Holtz-Eakin, and Quinn 2000; Benitez-Silva 2002; Taylor 2002: 23; Davis 2003). There is evidence here for retirement having become a more drawn out process, with changes in status from working, semi-retired, part-time working to fully retired.

In the British case there is much talk about the desirability of 'gradual retirement' from an economic, social, and personal point of view; however, its practice still seems to be limited. The majority of older workers in the 50–65 age range work full time, although part-time work is increasing amongst men it is still a comparative rarity along with other forms of flexible working arrangement (Loretto, Vickerstaff, and White 2005: 16–36). Using data from the British Household Panel Survey Bardasi and Jenkins found that although the number of hours worked and income declined for both men and women in the period before retirement there was still a marked fall in income in the year of retirement itself (2002: 41). This suggests that retirement from work still marks a dramatic shift in income at least with attendant implications for individuals' ability to maintain existing consumption patterns.

Research on bridge employment in Britain shows that older workers with more advantaged work histories, in terms of income and skills, are more likely to enter flexible employment on leaving full-time careers and are, unsurprisingly, better placed to obtain higher quality flexible employment (Lissenburgh and Smeaton 2003: 30). A high proportion of those who leave the labour market early through redundancy and ill health find it difficult to get back into the labour market and are more likely to have a range of benefit statuses between working and retiring at state pension age (Beatty and Fothergill 2003). There is every reason to hypothesize that if more flexible working options were available greater numbers of older workers would take the opportunity to retire gradually; however, such options are still likely to privilege those with a more secure income (Loretto, Vickerstaff, and White 2005: 74).

The second area of evidence to consider is whether the experience of retirement has changed dramatically and whether individuals find the end of working life more risky and unpredictable. There is considerably less research in this area. Studies suggest that men and women in managerial posts have developed a firm expectation that they will retire early: increasing workplace pressures and increasing job dissatisfaction have served to entrench such expectations (Scales and Scase 2000: 7). It is also clear from research that retirement timing may be a joint decision between couples: 'There is a strong correlation between spouses' activity rates' (Banks and Casanova 2003: 133–4). From a financial point of view, couples may be balancing the opportunities and threats of retiring in respect of joint earnings and pensions entitlement, but also in terms of the opportunities to enjoy other activities in retirement together (Vickerstaff et al. 2004: 20–1). There are also the risks, especially for women, of marital breakdown and loss of expected access to a spouse's pension.

In recent research on retirement transitions in three organizations it was found that people experienced retirement as an individual project, which they were trying to manage. They had access to a range of experiences of family members, work colleagues, and friends that seemed to suggest that there were very variable outcomes and not a common retirement pathway: retirement timing was to a degree unpredictable (Vickerstaff et al. 2004). This appeared to confirm the individualization and deinstitutionalization theories that chronological age markers no longer structure the life course in the way they once did and that people must, in Beck-Gernsheim's definition, construct their own do-it-yourself life histories. However, an individual's ability to construct their preferred post-working life was in reality severely constrained by their income, their health, and their domestic circumstances.

For some commentators the consumption patterns of older people are a marker for how this stage in the lifecourse has changed:

Those whose lives have been influenced by the cultures of consumption, and whose participation in occupational and personal pension schemes has provided the means to continue a consumer-led lifestyle, form part of a social vanguard. (Gilleard 1996: 490)

Retirement is often seen and marketed as a consumption good; the private pension industry spends considerable amounts of time and money presenting positive images of a consuming third age fuelled by wise pension saving (Mann 2001: 86–92).

However, in practice there are considerable differences in the consumption patterns and possibilities for those on high incomes as opposed to those on low incomes. The lifestyle choices associated with good private pensions are not available to the majority without them (Mann 2001: 95–101). For those on very low incomes there is unlikely to be any sense of choice at all.

There does seem to be evidence for more complex and protracted retirement transitions than in the period 1945–75 (Henretta 2003: 94–5), although historical material on the retirement process in that period is thin. However, evidence on incomes confirms a more traditional picture of a sharp break between working life and retirement.

Conclusion

In relation to youth transitions and the movement from paid work into retirement, assertions about the diminishing effects of traditional structures of disadvantage such as class, gender, race, and location seem premature. These structural features of society still have considerable predictive value in assessing the kinds of life course transitions individuals will make. Having said this, it is clear that there are social changes, not least in the labour market and family structures, which have and will continue to affect the specific patterns of entry into and exit from paid work that individuals experience. These transitions may well be 'choppier' for a higher proportion of an age cohort than was previously the case, though it is important not to rely on a golden age argument that assumes that life course transitions were easy in the past. There is also evidence from both studies of youth and old age that there is greater polarization within age cohorts, making the risks of poverty and social exclusion greater for the disadvantaged. To argue that a linear view of the life course is redundant also, on the evidence, seems unproved. Nevertheless, it is clear that individual biography includes not only the effects of social structure but also individual responses to them through personality, motivation, and identity formation. Those writers who have argued for a biographical approach to understanding the life course have put the need to understand the exceptions, the cases of individuals who do not end up where one might have predicted them to, on the agenda. They have also focused a spotlight on the strategies and understandings that individuals' use to respond to the risks they face.

In the field of youth transitions there is now a growing recognition of the need to combine both the theoretical suppositions and the methodologies that have divided researchers in the past. Evans explores how different writers have grappled with the structure-agency debate in explaining youth transitions and makes an argument for a middle ground theory, which recognizes the usefulness of concepts of both bounded agency and structured individualization:

agency operates in differentiated and complex ways in relation to the individual's subjectively perceived frames for action and decision. Thus, a person's frame has boundaries and limits that change over time, but that have structural foundations in ascribed characteristics such as gender and social/educational inheritance. (Evans 2002: 262)

One challenge in the field of life course study is to combine longitudinal and micro, quantitative, and qualitative methods successfully to develop a richer picture of how people travel through the different stages or phases of their lives (for an example of a study which combines qualitative and quantitative methodologies see Heinz et al. 1998; Kelle and Zinn 1998; for a discussion of some of the methodological issues that arise from mixed methodologies see Zinn 2002).

One of the key themes to emerge from this review of the life course and risk is that the ways in which people define their own roles, their own agency, appear to have changed. Many young people and those approaching retirement articulate a sense of individual responsibility for outcomes. They perceive themselves to have choices and be responsible even when their individual room for manoeuvre is small. This may be evidence for the individualization thesis or merely the impact of political ideology, which for a number of decades has stressed the sovereignty of the individual consumer and her market choices (see Zinn 2002; Brannen and Nilsen 2005: 422–3). The range of scripts and narratives available to the individual has expanded. More young people have been exposed to education and career guidance that has encouraged them to develop personalized expectations about work (Anderson et al. 2002: 5.5). Young people are held more responsible for their success in education and the labour market, and this may force them to be more reflexive about the paths they take (Plug, Zeijl, and du Bois Reymond 2003: 142). It may also be that the more turbulent or choppier quality of transitions into and out of the labour market leads individuals to experience change and agency more sharply than earlier generations (Webster et al. 2004). As the range of routes from school to work and from work to retirement has become more varied the complex interaction between social structures and individual agency may have become more obscure but not necessarily less important (Furlong and Cartmel 1997: 109; Lehmann 2004: 393–5; Brannen and Nilsen 2005).

References

Anderson, M., Bechhofer, F., Jamieson, L., McCrone, D., Li, Y., and Stewart, R. (2002). 'Confidence Amid Uncertainty: Ambitions and Plans in a Sample of Young People', *Sociological Research Online*, 6(4): http://www.socresonline.org.uk/6/4/anderson.html

Andres, L. and Grayson, J. P. (2003). 'Parents, Educational Attainment, Jobs and Satisfaction: What's the Connection? A 10-year Portrait of Canadian Young Women and Men', *Journal of Youth Studies*, 6(2): 181–202.

Arthur, S. (2003). *Money, Choice and Control The financial Circumstances of Early Retirement*. Bristol, CT: The Polity Press/ Joseph Rowntree Foundation.

Ashton, D. and Field, D. (1976). *Young Workers from School to Work*, London: Hutchinson.

Atchley, R. C. (1976). *The Sociology of Retirement*. Boston, MA: Schenkman Publishing.

Ball, J., Maguire, M., and Macrae, S. (2000). *Choice, Pathways and Transitions Post 16 New Youth, New Economies in the Global City*. London: RoutledgeFalmer.

Banks, J. and Casanova, M. (2003). 'Work and Retirement', in M. Marmot, J. Banks, R. Blundell, C. Lessof, and J. Nazroo (eds.), *Health, Wealth and Lifestyles of the Older Population in England: The 2002 English Longitudinal Study of Ageing*. London: Institute for Fiscal Studies.

Bardasi, E. and Jenkins, S. P. (2002). *Income in Later Life: Work History Matters*. Bristol, CT: The Policy Press.

———— and Rigg, J. A. (2000). *Retirement and the Economic Well-being of the Elderly: A British Perspective*, Working paper, University of Essex: Institute for Social and Economic Research.

Beatty, C. and Fothergill, S. (2003). 'Incapacity Benefit and Unemployment', in P. Alcock, C. Beatty, S. Fothergill, R. Macmillan, and S. Yeandle (eds.), *Work to Welfare: How Men Become Detached from the Labour Market*. Cambridge: Cambridge University Press.

Beck, U. (2000). *The Brave New World of Work*. Cambridge: Polity Press.

Beck-Gernsheim, E. (1998). 'On the Way to a Post-Familial Family from a Community of Need to Elective Affinities', *Theory Culture and Society*, 15: 3–4, 53–70.

Benitez-Silva, H. (2002). 'Job Search Behavior at the End of the Life Cycle', Working Paper 2002–10. Boston, MA: Center for Retirement Research at Boston College.

Bonoli, G. (2000). *The Politics of Pension Reform*. Cambridge: Cambridge University Press.

Brannen, J. and Nilsen, A. (2005). 'Individualisation, Choice and Structure: A Discussion of Current Trends in Sociological Analysis', *The Sociological Review*, 53(3): 413–28.

Bruce, D., Holtz-Eakin, D., and Quinn, J. (2000). 'Self-employment and Labor Market Transitions at Older Ages', Working Paper 2000–13. Boston, MA: Centre for Retirement Research at Boston College.

Bynner, J., Elias, P., McKnight, A., Pan, H., and Pierre, G. (2002). *Young People's Changing Routes to Independence*. York: YPS and Joseph Rowntree Foundation.

Campbell, N. (1999). *Decline of Employment Among Older People in Britain*. Centre for Analysis of Social Exclusion Paper 19, London: LSE.

Chisholm, L. (1995). 'Youth Transitions in the European Union', in L. Bash and A. Green (eds.), *Youth, Education and Work*. London: World Yearbook of Education, Kogan Page, pp. 203–17.

Coles, B. (1997). 'Vulnerable Youth and Processes of Social Exclusion: A Theoretical Framework, Review of Recent Research and Suggestions for a Future Research Agenda', in J. Bynner, L. Chisholm, and A. Furlong (eds.), *Youth, Citizenship and Social Change in a European Context*. Aldershot, UK: Ashgate.

Davis, M. (2003). 'Factors Related to Bridge Employment Participation Among Private Sector Early Retirees', *Journal of Vocational Behavior*, 63: 55–71.

Dench, S. and Norton, R. (1996). *Leaving Employment Early*, Report no. 322, Brighton: Institute of Employment Studies.

Disney, R., Grundy, E., and Johnson, R. (eds.) (1997). *The Dynamics of Retirement*. Department of Social Security Report No. 72, London: HMSO.

Donovan, N. and Street, C. (2000). 'Older People and Paid Work', in D. Hirsch (ed.), *Life After 50 Issues for Policy and Research*. York: Joseph Rowntree Foundation.

Elder, G. H. (1991). 'Lives and Social Change', in W. R. Heinz (ed.), *Theoretical Advances in Life Course Research*. Bremen, Germany: Deutscher Studien Verlag.

European Group for Integrated Social Research (EGRIS) (2001). 'Misleading Trajectories: Transition Dilemmas of Young Adults in Europe', *Journal of Youth Studies*, 4(1): 101–18.

Evans, K. (2002). 'Taking Control of Their Lives? Agency in Young Adult Transitions in England and the New Germany', *Journal of Youth Studies*, 5(3): 245–69.

——and Furlong, A. (1997). 'Metaphors of Youth Transitions: Niches, Pathways, Trajectories or Navigations', in J. Bynner, L. Chisholm, and A. Furlong (eds.), *Youth, Citizenship and Social Change in a European Context*. Aldershot, UK: Ashgate.

Featherstone, M. and Hepworth, M. (1991). 'The Mask of Ageing and the Postmodern Life Course', in M. Featherstone, M. Hepworth, and B. S. Turner (eds.), *The Body Social Process and Cultural Theory*. London: Sage.

Feldman, D. C. (1994). 'The Decision to Retire Early: A Review and a Conceptualization', *Academy of Management Review*, 19(2): 285–311.

Ferguson, R., Pye, D., Esland, G., McLaughlin, E., and Muncie, J. (2000). 'Normalized Dislocation and New Subjectivities in Post-16 Markets for Education and Work', *Critical Social Policy*, 20(3): 283–305.

Furlong, A. and Cartmel, F. (1997). *Young People and Social Change*. Buckingham, UK: Open University Press.

—— —— Biggart, A., Sweeting, H., and West, P. (2005). 'Complex Transitions: Linearity and Labour Market Integration in the West of Scotland', in C. Pole, J. Pilcher, and J. Williams (eds.), *Young People in Transition Becoming Citizens?*. Basingstoke, UK: Palgrave Macmillan, pp. 12–30.

Gelissen, J. (2001). 'Old-Age Pensions: Individual or Collective Responsibility?', *European Societies*, 3(4): 495–523.

Giddens, A. (1991). *Modernity and Self-identity*. Oxford: Polity.

Gilleard, C. (1996). 'Consumption and Identity in Later Life: Toward a Cultural Gerontology', *Ageing and Society*, 16: 489–98.

—— and Higgs, P. (2000). *Cultures of Ageing*. Harlow: Pearson Education.

Glaesser, J. and Lauterbach, W. (2004). 'Opportunities and risk factors in labour market entry: results from a longitudinal study', Paper presented at the *European Research Network on Transitions in Youth 2004*, Workshop, Nurnberg, Germany: http://www.roa.unimass.nL/TIY2004/papers/TIY200_glaesserALauterbach.pdf

Goodwin, J. and O'Connor, H. (2005). 'Exploring Complex Transitions: Looking Back at the 'Golden Age' of From School to Work', *Sociology*, 39(2): 201–20.

Guillemard, A.-M. (1997). 'Re-writing Social Policy and Changes Within the Life Course Organisation. A European Perspective', *Canadian Journal on Aging*, 16(3): 441–64.

Hareven, T. K. (1982). *Family Time and Industrial Time*. Cambridge: Cambridge University Press.

—— (2000). *Families, History, and Social Change Life-Course and Cross-Cultural Perspectives*. Boulder, CO: Westview Press.

Harper, S. and Thane, P. (1989). 'The Consolidation of "Old Age" as a Phase of Life, 1945–1965', in M. Jeffreys (ed.), *Growing Old in the Twentieth Century*. London: Routledge.

Hayden, C., Boaz, A., and Taylor, F. (1999). *Attitudes and Aspirations of Older People: A Qualitative Study*. Department for Social Security Research Report No. 102, London: HMSO.

Heinz, W. R. (2001). 'Work and the Life Course: A Cosmopolitan-Local Perspective', in V. W. Marshall, W. R. Heinz, H. Kruger, and A. Verma (eds.), *Restructuring Work and the Life Course*. Toronto: University of Toronto Press.

———Kelle, U., Witzel, A., and Zinn, J. (1998). 'Vocational Training and Career Development in Germany: Results from a Longitudinal Study', *International Journal of Behavioural Development*, 22(1): 77–101.

Henretta, J. C. (2003). 'The Life-course Perspective on Work and Retirement', in R. A. Settersten (ed.), *Invitation to the Life Course Towards New Understandings of Later Life*. New York: Bayward Publishing.

Hirsch, D. (2000). *Life After 50*. York: Joseph Rowntree Foundation.

Hockey, J. and James, A. (2003). *Social Identities Across the Life Course*. Basingstoke, UK: Palgrave Macmillan.

Humphrey, A., Costigan, P., Pickering, K., Stratford, N., and Barnes, M. (2003). *Factors Affecting the Labour Market Participation of Older Workers*. Research Report No. 200, Department of Work and Pensions, Leeds, UK: HMSO.

Iacovou, M. and Berthoud, R. (2001). *Young People's Lives: A Map of Europe*. Colchester, UK: University of Essex, Institute for Social and Economic Research.

Jacobs, K. and Rein, M. (1994). 'Early Retirement: Stability, Reversal, or Redefinition', in F. Naschold, and B. de Vroom (eds.), *Regulating Employment and Welfare*. Berlin: De Gruyter, 1–17.

Kelle, U. and Zinn, J. (1998). 'School-to-Work Transition and Occupational Careers—Results From a Longitudinal Study in Germany', in T. Lange (ed.), *Understanding the School-to-Work Transition: An International Perspective*. New York: Nowa Science, pp. 71–89.

Kohli, M. (1986). 'Social Organisation and Subjective Construction of the Life Course', in M. Kohli, M. Rein, A.-M. Guillemard, and H. Van Gunsteren (eds.) (1991), *Time for Retirement*. Cambridge: Cambridge University Press.

———Rein, M., Guillemard, A.-M., and Van Gunsteren, H. (eds.) (1991). *Time for Retirement*. Cambridge: Cambridge University Press.

Lehman, W. (2004). 'For Some Reason, I Get a Little Scared: Structure, Agency and Risk in School-Work Transitions', *Journal of Youth Studies*, 7(4): 379–96.

Lissenburgh, S. and Smeaton, D. (2003). *The Role of Flexible Employment in Maintaining Labour Market Participation and Promoting Job Quality*. York: Joseph Rowntree Foundation.

Loretto, W., Vickerstaff, S., and White, P. (2005). *Older Workers and Options for Flexible Work*, Equal Opportunities Commission, Working Paper Series No 31.

MacDonald, R., Mason, P., Shildrick, T., Webster, C., Johnston, L., and Ridley, L. (2001). 'Snakes and Ladders: In Defence of Studies of Youth Transition', *Sociological Research Online*, 5(4).

Mann, K. (2001). *Approaching Retirement Social Divisions, Welfare and Exclusion*. Bristol, CT: The Policy Press.

Maule, A. J., Cliff, D. R., and Taylor, R. (1996). 'Early Retirement Decisions and How They Affect Later Quality of Life', *Ageing and Society*, 16: 177–204.

McGoldrick, A. and Cooper, C. (1994). 'Health and Ageing as Factors in the Retirement Experience', *European Work and Organizational Psychologist*, 4(1): 1–20.

Meghir, C. and Whitehouse, E. (1997). 'Labour Market Transitions and Retirement of Men in the UK', *Journal of Econometrics*, 79: 327–54.

Nagel, U. and Wallace, C. (1997). 'Participation and Identification in Risk Societies: European Perspectives', in J. Bynner, L. Chisholm, and A. Furlong (eds.), *Youth, Citizenship and Social Change in a European Context*. Aldershot, UK: Ashgate.

O'Connor, H. and Goodwin, J. (2005). 'Girls' Transitions to Work and Adulthood in the 1960s', in C. Pole, J. Pilcher, and J. Williams (eds.), *Young People in Transition Becoming Citizens?*. Basingstoke, UK: Palgrave Macmillan, pp. 52–73.

Pais, J. M. (2003). 'The Multiple Faces of the Future in the Labyrinth Life', *Journal of Youth Studies*, 6(2): 115–26.

Performance and Innovation Unit (PIU) (2000). *Winning the Generation Game Improving Opportunities for People Aged 50–65 in Work and Community Activity*. Cabinet Office, London: HMSO.

Phillipson, C. (1982). *Capitalism and the Construction of Old Age*. London: Macmillan.

—— (1999). 'The Social Construction of Retirement: Perspectives from Critical Theory and Political Economy', in M. Minkler and C. L. Ester (eds.), *Critical Gerontology*. New York: Baywood Publishing Company.

—— (2002). *Transitions from Work to Retirement*. Bristol, CT: The Policy Press for the Joseph Rowntree Foundation.

—— (2003). 'Globalisation and the Future of Ageing: Developing a Critical Gerontology', *Sociological Research Online*, 8(4), at http://www.socresonline.org.uk/8/4/phillipson.html

Plug, W., Zeijl, E., and du Bois-Reymond, M. (2003). 'Young People's Perceptions on Youth and Adulthood. A Longitudinal Study from The Netherlands', *Journal of Youth Studies*, 6(2): 127–44.

Ransome, P. (2005). *Work, Consumption and Culture*. London: Sage.

Roberts, K. (2003). 'Change and Continuity in Youth Transitions in Eastern Europe: Lessons for Western sociology', *The Sociological Review*, 51(4): 484–505.

Scales, J. and Scase, R. (2000). *Fit and Fifty?* Swindon, UK: ESRC.

Schoon, I. (2001). 'Teenage Job Aspirations and Career Attainment in Adulthood: A 17-year follow-up study of teenagers who aspired to become scientists, health professionals, or engineers', *International Journal of Behavioural Development*, 25(2): 124–32.

Tanner, S. (1998). 'The Dynamics of Male Retirement Behaviour', *Fiscal Studies*, 19(2): 175–96.

Taylor, P. (2002). *New Policies for Older Workers*. Bristol, CT: The Policy Press for the Joseph Rowntree Foundation.

—— and Walker, A. (1993). 'The Employment of Older Workers in Five European Countries', in Institute of Personnel Management (IPM), *Age and Employment Policies, Attitudes and Practice*. London: IPM.

Thomson, R., Bell, R., Holland, J., Henderson, S., McGrellis, S., and Sharpe, S. (2002). 'Critical Moments: Choice, Chance and Opportunity in Young people's Narratives of Transition', *Sociology*, 36(2): 335–54.

—— Henderson, S., and Holland, J. (2003). 'Making the Most of What You've Got: Resources, values and inequalities in young people's transitions to adulthood', *Educational Review*, 55(1): 33–46.

—— Holland, J., McGrellis, S., Bell, R., Henderson, S., and Sharpe, S. (2004). 'Inventing Adulthoods: A Biographical Approach to Understanding Citizenship', *The Sociological Review*, 52(2): 218–39.

Vickerstaff, S. (2003). 'Apprenticeship in the "Golden Age": Were Youth Transitions really Smooth and Unproblematic Back Then?', *Work Employment and Society*, 17(2): 269–87.

—— (2006). ' "I'd rather keep running to the end and then jump off the cliff". Retirement Decisions: who decides?', *Journal of Social Policy*, 35(3): 1–18.

—— and Cox, J. (2005). 'Retirement and Risk: The Individualisation of Retirement Experiences?', *Sociological Review*, 53(1): 77–95.

—— Baldock, J., Cox, J., and Keen, L. (2004) *Happy Retirement: The Impact of Employers' Policies and Practice on the Process of Retirement*. Bristol, CT: The Policy Press/Joseph Rowntree Foundation.

de Vroom, B. and Guillemard, A. M. (2002). 'From Externalisation to Integration of Older Workers: Institutional Changes at the End of the Worklife', in J. G. Andersen and P. H. Jensen (eds.), *Changing Labour Markets, Welfare Policies and Citizenship*. Bristol, CT: The Policy Press, pp. 183–208.

Webster, C., Simpson, D., MacDonald, R., Abbas, A., Cieslik, M., Shildrick, T., and Simpson, M. (2004). *Poor Transitions Social Exclusion and Young Adults*. Bristol, CT: Policy Press.

Zinn, J. (2002). 'Conceptual Considerations and an Empirical Approach to Research on Processes of Individualization', *Forum Qualitative Sozialforschumg*, 3(1): 156 paragraphs.

10

Risk, Regulation, and Management

Bridget M. Hutter

Risk has emerged as an important concept in academic discussions and also in the worlds of business and government. In many respects it has become a new lens through which to view the world. For some commentators this is consequential upon transformations in modern societies, so risk is related to substantive changes in the worlds we inhabit and to re-conceptualizations of the dangers surrounding us (Giddens 1990; Beck 1992). It is argued that there is a class of risks peculiarly associated with modern societies. These are involuntary, manufactured risks, that is, those risks resulting from enormous advances in technology, the growth of large-scale organizations, and globalization. These are the by-products of legitimate and sometimes exciting new developments which carry with them unintended dangers, such as pollution, threats to worker health and safety, and the capacity to upset financial markets at great speed across the globe. Such risks affect the food we eat, the air we breathe, our health and safety at work, the stability of our economic systems, and so on. It is these risks which are associated with regulation. Indeed, some regard government intervention to regulate these economic activities as another defining characteristic of modern societies (Hancher and Moran 1989). The research area focusing on the regulation of the risks associated with modern economic life is the subject of this chapter.

Basic Concepts: Regulation

The past 50 years have witnessed changes in social science definitions of regulation. Early sociological definitions were broadly drawn and synonymous with notions of social control. Between the 1950s and the 1970s, the term regulation took on a much more technical and narrowly defined meaning relating specifically to state intervention in the economy. This was particularly associated with the work of economists, political scientists, and lawyers. In the 1980s and 1990s its conceptual boundaries once again expanded to encompass both non-legal forms of regulation and supranational regulation. So now there are many definitions of regulation reflecting varying disciplinary backgrounds and changes in regulatory practice (Mitnick 1980; Baldwin 1997; Black 2002).

Table 10.1 maps out four broad perspectives on regulation. This is not intended to be an exhaustive typology but one which covers the main approaches. The first two categories, 'regulation as rules' and 'regulation as the efforts of state agencies to steer the economy', follow the distinctions drawn by Baldwin, Hood, and Scott (1998: 3). These categories reflect the work of economists, lawyers, and political scientists who were particularly active in developing a definition of regulation which refers to state efforts to regulate economic activities. Lawyers have, not surprisingly, concentrated on regulation as state intervention through law, which is backed by criminal sanctions and implemented by public agencies. This is commonly referred to as the 'command and control' approach to regulation, referring to the command of the law and the legal authority of the

Table 10.1. The four broad perspectives on regulation

1. Regulation as the promulgation of authoritative rules	State: legislative	Typically economic activity Markets Organizations Individuals within organizations	Law Socio-legal studies
2. Regulation as the efforts of state agencies to steer the economy	State: legislative, economic policies	Economy Economic activities Markets Organizations	Economics Political science
3. Regulation as organized social control	State Non-state A mix of state & non-state	Typically economic activities Markets Organizations Individuals within organizations	Sociology Socio-legal studies
4. Regulation as the control of risk	State Non-state A mix of state & non-state	Individuals Organizations Markets Society	Political Science Socio-legal studies Sociology Social Psychology

state. Meanwhile political scientists and economists often take regulation to refer to a wider range of state interventions, such as broad economic policy, nationalization, and disclosure requirements.

The third category 'regulation as organized social control' reflects developments in the sociology of social control literature.[1] These differ from the early very broad definitions of social control which embraced all forms of social control regardless of their intentionality, formality, or institutionalization. These more contemporary definitions take a more specific institutionally based focus, exemplified by Cohen's definition of social control as

the organized ways in which society responds to behaviour and people it regards as deviant, problematic, worrying, threatening, troublesome or undesirable in some way or another (1985: 1).

He continues:

My focus is those organized responses to crime, delinquency and allied forms of deviant and/or socially problematic behaviour which are actually conceived of as such, whether in the reactive sense (after the putative act has taken place or the actor has been identified) or in the proactive sense (to prevent the act). These responses may be sponsored directly by the state or by more autonomous professional agents in, say, social work and psychiatry. Their goals may be as specific as individual punishment and treatment or as diffuse as 'crime prevention', 'public safety' and 'community public health' (1985: 3).

Such a definition embraces the social control of organizations and individuals, and focuses on responses which are *intended* to regulate, rather than on a much broader range of responses which may regulate but do so unintentionally. Moreover, it considers both state and non-state sources and means of social control whilst keeping the focus firmly on *organized* responses.[2]

A crucial feature of regulation is that it 'attempts to control risk' (Hood, Rothstein, and Baldwin 2001: 3) and this is the key to the fourth and most recent perspective on regulation, namely, regulation as the control of risk. This perspective again focuses on organized responses to risk control, whether they be state or non-state centred. It embraces the risks generated by economic organizations broadly conceived, that is businesses and industries, but it also considers the control of individuals unattached to organizational or market loci. A notable example is the recent work of Hood, Rothstein, and Baldwin (2001) who consider a number of examples involving risks located at the level of the individual. These include attacks by dangerous dogs outside the home, attacks on children from convicted paedophiles, and injuries and deaths from motor vehicles on local roads (see also Hutter 2001).

As one moves from the first to the fourth definition the sources of regulation multiply and expand, and perspectives become ever more inclusive. Whereas perspectives 1 and 2 are entirely focused on state centred regulation, perspectives 3 and 4 embrace state and a variety of non-state sources of regulation, such as industry and professional associations, self-regulation, and third party regulation.

The changing perspectives on regulation have in many respects emerged alongside changes in regulatory practice, that is, they have emerged from action and scholars' developing understandings of the practice of regulation. Thus, regulation has come to be defined as controlling and also as a way of managing risks, but whilst the language of risk may be relatively new the task of regulation as a way of managing risks is not.

Basic Concepts: Risk

Studies of regulation have long recognized that regulation and risk are inextricably connected; however, the relationship between the two was until recently assumed rather than explored. Accounts of the emergence of regulation discussed the reasons for regulation in terms of protection and intervention on behalf of consumers, the public, and the environment. The harms were seen as being associated with a rapidly changing society but the language of risk was seldom used. Regulatory law was recognized as ambivalent and contradictory, attempting to accommodate conflicting interests and balance the harms created by otherwise desirable activities. The law was seen as 'tolerant'—too tolerant maybe— and reasonable—too reasonable even (Hutter 1988). Tensions between these factors were a fundamental characteristic of regulation and ones which were typically left largely unresolved by governments, the crucial decisions being taken by field-level regulatory officials (Otway 1985).

The relatively unsophisticated discussion of risk in early studies of regulation is not entirely surprising, reflecting the state of academic discussions of risk at the time. The situation has, however, changed rapidly in the past decade which has witnessed a massive growth in academic studies of risk and the rapid development of a risk industry (Gabe 1995). There are a variety of disciplinary approaches to the study of risk and a range of different foci of interest, from the individual to cultural. Discussions of the problems of industrialization have been replaced with broader discussions about modernization, and relatively simple discussions of harm have been replaced by increasingly sophisticated discussions of risk and uncertainty. Risk is now seen as a characteristic of modernization, with all aspects of modern life being interpreted in terms of risk and the private spheres of business and industry becoming politicized (Beck 1992; Power 2004*a*).

Risk Analysis

Risk analysis, which embraces both the assessment and management of risk, emerged as a defined area early in 1970s. Short, writing in 1984, commented on its fast growth as a new discipline. The literature distinguishes between the two components of risk analysis, namely, risk assessment and risk management. The former refers to the scientific, calculable component of risk regulation whereas the latter refers to the policy component (Pollak 1995). Early conceptions of risk assessment focused on identifying, measuring, and evaluating outcomes from both natural and technological hazards. The concern was to estimate the probability of these events happening and to estimate their likely effects (Tierney 1999). The assumptions were essentially realist, so it was assumed that there is an objective world of risks which is discoverable, measurable, quantifiable, and controllable by science (Gabe 1995). Policymakers saw risk assessment as a way of systematizing their approach to risk, prioritizing actions, and thereby hopefully diminishing exposure to risks and optimizing the balance between risks and benefits (Rimmington 1992).

The 1970s and early 1980s witnessed a growing recognition that risk management, which involves the choice of policy options, necessarily requires the assignment of values and politicized decision-making. There was also increasing public awareness of scientific disagreements. Douglas and Wildavsky (1982), in an influential book, commented '... substantial disagreement remains over what is risky, how risky it is and what to do about it'. They pointed to scientific disputes over how to interpret data and how to then decide what is acceptable and pointed to a paradox 'better measurement opens more possibilities, more research brings more ignorance to the light of day' (1982: 64). Commentators noted that values differed between countries, between successive administrations, within countries and within the research community (Otway 1985). Moreover, the tools of technical risk analysis came under much criticism for being too simplistic, making too many assumptions and for not recognizing the values which may surround them (Renn 1992).

A fundamental divide emerged in the mid-1970s as a gap between expert and lay opinions became increasingly apparent (Plough and Krimsky 1987). The term 'risk-perception' emerged and psychological risk analyses aimed at explaining why public reactions to risks are not always in proportion to 'objective risks' (Otway 1985; Krimsky 1992). As some observers have commented these studies do share similarities with technical risk assessments to the extent that their aims are purportedly scientific, objective, and quantitative (Gabe 1995: 4). Indeed the notion of risk-communication was introduced in an attempt to bridge the gap between expert views and lay perceptions, and, as some authors indicate, this typically means 'information transmission' and 'persuasion' as the underlying assumption is that the expert view is indeed the correct one to follow.

There were variable consequences of these developments. One was an exacerbation of the challenge to expert opinion and an accompanying growth of mistrust in science and technology which were increasingly seen as the cause of many of the risks in the everyday modern world. There were some attempts to combine social science and scientific approaches to risk analysis. These were referred to by some authors as the 'hard' and 'soft' approaches to risk analysis, the former referring to technical approaches to risk analysis and the latter to social science approaches which take into account the human factors influencing risk (Blockley 1996). Some risk management practices incorporated both approaches, for example, Hazard and Operability Studies (HAZOP) (Hood and Jones 1996: 86). Indeed the influential Royal Society Report on risk, published in 1983, differentiates between 'technical risk estimation' and 'political risk decision', arguing that interaction between the two is necessary.

Social Science Approaches

Although there are examples of social scientists showing an interest in risk prior to the 1970s this was the point at which social science approaches to risk really started to emerge in any significant way. Psychological and social psychological studies of risk perception emerged in the 1970s and anthropology, building on the early work of Douglas (1985), developed cultural theory in the early 1980s. This related concepts of danger and risk to cultures, in particular to varying social and group values. Sociological interest in risk dates from the mid-1980s, before this there was very little sociological interest. This is emphasized by Short Jr, who in his 1984 ASA Presidential Address, urged sociologists to pay more serious attention to risk analysis, arguing that this was the preserve of technical discussion but there were important normative, social, and political dimensions which demanded consideration.

In the late 1980s/early 1990s a number of significant macro-level risk theories emerged—the work of European social theorists such as Beck (1992), Giddens (1990), and Luhmann (1993). Beck's *Risk Society*, which has been especially influential, argues that contemporary western societies are characterized by risks which are distinctive in a number of respects. First, they are manufactured as opposed to natural. Second, they transcend social and national barriers and may be global in their effects. And third, these modern risks are closely but ambivalently associated with science which is seen as responsible for the creation and definition of modern risks but is also seen to have failed to control these risks, thus leading to the emergence of a risk society characterized by global risk situations. One consequence of this, claims Beck, is that there has been a growing scepticism of science which has led to a demystification of science itself. These theories have been criticized for their exclusive focus on technological risks (Tierney 1999; Turner 2001). It has also been claimed that they are too abstract to be useful for empirically oriented research (Tierney 1999: 216). The concentration on technological risk has been a continuing difficulty but with this proviso these theories have, contrary to their critics, spawned numerous grounded studies of risk. These studies have also succeeded in moving discussion beyond the 'hazard' based focus which characterized much of the US-based early work (see below).

Many middle and micro-range sociological studies have adopted a social constructionist approach to risk considering, for instance, the differential definition of risks as risks and varying perceptions of risk amongst different social groups. Of particular interest has been the influence of social structures and social interests upon these definitions and perceptions, for example, the role of organizations and the state (Gabe 1995; Vaughan 1996; Tierney 1999). Other sociological work has focused on the social construction of formal risk analysis, and so has examined the social processes and organizational influences upon formal risk analysis (Perrow 1984; Shrader-Frechette 1991; Vaughan 1996).

There are of course many ways of making sense of the world and coping with risk. Science uses quantitative risk techniques as a way of ordering the world, making sense of it, and rendering some sense of control (Hood and Jones 1996). The law is another way of classifying danger and setting up requirements for its recognition and management, and of communicating about risk (Ericson and Haggerty 1997: 90). These different systems 'talk in different languages' (Luhmann 1993) and may well clash with each other (Smith and Wynne 1989). Discussions of these various systems and their impacts on organizations have emerged at the core of risk regulation debates since the 1980s. In the remainder of this chapter we will focus in particular on risk regulation.

Risk and Regulation: Research Themes

Discussions of regulation have reflected the broader literature on risk but this has happened in a rather piecemeal way. Risk has become incorporated into some aspects of the regulation literature more than others. The early 1990s witnessed the first real wave of work relating risk to regulation issues. Areas which received particular attention were the importance of the relationship between expert knowledge, risk, and regulation, in particular the relationship between regulation and science (Nelkin 1992; Jasanoff et al. 1995) and the role of political factors in determining risk tolerance levels (Jasper 1992). These debates have been especially important in research on policymaking (Brickman, Jasanoff, and Iilgen 1985; Jasanoff 1991; Rayner 1991). Indeed Golding (1992) relates the growth of risk analysis to early 1970s American regulatory legislation, for example, the Environmental Protection Act. He argues that this prompted the professionalization of risk analysis which was largely funded by government agencies, especially regulatory agencies.

Other aspects of regulation examined with reference to risk in the 1990s focused on the role of organizations in the mediation of regulation. Short and Clarke (1992, 1993) were especially important in moving forward these discussions (see also Perrow 1984; Reiss 1984). Whilst their 1993 paper maintained a primary focus on disasters[3] their 1992 book *Organizations, Uncertainties, and Risk* progressed the debate by mapping out the importance of a broader range of organizational risk issues, some of which were routine, some contextual, and other regulatory.

Social science discussions of risk and regulation during the 1990s were muddled in their development. A lack of unifying theory concerned some authors whilst others took a more sanguine view and others simply regarded a single unifying theory as implausible/unnecessary (Clarke and Short 1993; Tierney 1999). Yet all yearned for a more systematic approach and by the turn of the century more systematic analyses of risk and regulation were indeed appearing.

By 1990 the concept of 'risk regulation' was appearing in the social science literature (Otway 1985: 5; Krier et al. 1990: 747). The term has been used increasingly since the 1990s in legal, economic, political science, public policy, psychology, and science studies literatures. Interestingly many authors using the term risk regulation take its meaning for granted and do not define what they mean by the term. Those who do offer an explanation (e.g. Krier et al. 1990; Breyer 1993; Noll 1996; Hood, Rothstein, and Baldwin 2001) refer to state action to reduce health and environmental risks. The main areas of discussion under the risk regulation heading have been

- which risks the state responds to and how one might explain different responses (Noll 1990; Hood, Rothstein, and Baldwin 2001; Vogel 2001);

- the influence of risk debates on regulatory policy, for example, the influence of debates upon scientific expertise on regulatory policy and the effects of government responses to risk upon public confidence in government—and related debates about public participation in risk regulation (Poortinga and Pidgeon 2003);

- business risk management and its responses to state risk regimes (Hutter 2001);

- international, trans-boundary risk regulation (Tait 2001).

Since the 1990s there has been a concerted effort to delineate a new interdisciplinary area of risk regulation studies which would bridge regulation and risk management studies across a number of social science disciplines. This has involved a slow coming together of risk *and* regulation studies to create a more hybrid risk regulation studies. We now turn to the findings of these studies.[4]

Risk Regulation Research Findings

Risk regulation studies have two main foci: the first and main focal point is upon risk and governance and the second is upon risk regulation and organizations. The literature examines the circumstances and ways in which risk has become an organizing concept for regulation within and beyond the state (Power 1997; Clark 2000; Moran 2003).

Variation: Risk Regulation Regimes

State regulation remains a central focus for risk regulation studies. The key work on variations in state handling of risks, particularly variations between domains and states, is Hood et al.'s *The Government of Risk*. This study developed the notion of risk regulation regimes in order to explain variation and focuses on risks to health, primarily with reference to the UK. Their analytical framework for describing and comparing risk regulation regimes distinguishes between regime context (e.g. public preferences, organized interests) and regime content (e.g. policy settings), and analyses components of regulatory control (standard-setting, information-gathering, behaviour-modification). They considered nine domains and found substantial variation. Their results challenged any widespread claim about the emergence of a risk society and called for more nuanced examination of regulatory developments and ones which considered in greater detail the relationships between different components of regimes.

Hood, Rothstein, and Baldwin's (2001) study of risk regulation regimes is important for a number of reasons. It brings together risk regulation in a systematic way. It develops a middle range examination of risk regulation (2001: 12) which complements the broader macro-theories of risk society, regulatory state, and audit society. Moreover, this work gives us an organizing template for developing risk regulation studies. Apart from drawing out the implications for regulatory theory this approach can be used to examine other risk regulation regimes from institutional and comparative perspectives. It provides us with a mapping device for analysing and ultimately explaining variations in standard setting, for instance, why some areas are dominated by quantitative risk assessments and others are not (2001: 7) or why some institutional arrangements result in risk bureaucracies staffed by risk experts whereas others are much more generalist. So the approach is open to methodological, theoretical, and empirical development across domains, time, and cross-culturally. As the authors stress, this is one way of examining the issues as there is '...no single correct way of conceiving risk regulation regimes' (2002: 12).

Much current risk regulation work contributes to the study of risk regulation regimes but not in any particularly systematic way. Historical case studies contribute to our understandings of the emergence of particular examples of regulation and also the ways in which third party actors such as insurance companies have managed risks. There is also work on the exposure of particular sectors of the population to risks but this

211

historical work seldom uses risk regulation approaches nor does it focus on historical understandings of risk (Gourvish 2003).

Continuing research focuses on the factors which influence different parts of risk regulation regimes in determining regulatory responses to risks. There is work, for example, on the influences upon policymakers at the governmental work. An example would be work on the influence of public opinion upon regulatory policy which includes work on the participation of civil society organizations in policymaking (see below). Other work is being done on the factors influencing regulatory officials. Examples would include work on institutional attenuation which considers factors which reduce regulatory awareness of risks both at an everyday enforcement level and at the level of institutional policymaking (Rothstein 2003). Also important is the 'social amplification' literature which develops the risk-perception literature (see above) and examines how risks may become magnified and acted upon disproportionately or attenuated (Pidgeon et al. 2003). The focus of this work is on issues of communication, stigma, trust and blame, and the ways in which organizations process risk. Indeed, an important research finding is the differential understandings of risk which may exist between nation states, policymakers, and the general population (Jasanoff 2005) or between different groups in organizations (Nelkin 1985; Krimsky and Golding 1992). Research findings to date have found that these processes are highly contextualized, making policy recommendations and more general theorizing difficult. A key risk-management message seems to be on the importance of risk communication, often involving participative mechanisms.

The Democratization of Risk and Regulation

Work on democratization, risk and regulation covers a number of interrelated issues. Most emphasis is upon the democratization of risk regulation rather than risk (see below) and these debates are linked to earlier work on the role of experts and expertise and the democratization of politics.

Generally, the process of democratization may be taken to include greater open debate, greater public access to power centres, and greater participation in decisions of government.

So democratization of regulation may be indicated by an increased openness of state regulatory institutions to listen to and incorporate a wide range of people in regulatory debates, and it may also indicate a more active role for the citizenry in regulatory decision-making (Held 1987: 4).

A number of mechanisms have been found to be central here, namely, greater rights and obligations upon the citizenry, greater accountability of state actors, and increased governance of the government. Thus, accountability and transparency appear as central to the democratization process. One of the features of the move from the paternalistic nanny state to a constitutive model of regulation has been the incorporation of a wider range of groups into the regulatory process. So regulation is no longer the preserve of employers and directors but has been extended to involve a broader range of participants including those 'protected' by regulation. This would include, for example, employees, consumers, and the local and global community. Increasingly, it has also involved interest groups (see below).

Work on participative risk regulation has considered the nature of this participation. Much of the work which has been done on this topic has been preoccupied with the rights and wrongs of participation and the processes by which it may be achieved (National Research Council 1996; Owens 2000). Rights have been found to typically be confined to particular stages of the regulatory process such as the policymaking stage or implementation stage. Moreover, some groups are more privileged than others in their inclusion and/or ability to participate. The involvement of non-governmental organizations in regulatory processes (NGOs) has been hotly debated with controversy surrounding the possibility of selecting representative NGOs and issues of internal governance and transparency (Bruyn 1999; Weale 1999).

Democratization includes greater openness of government and greater accountability of its executive. Generally state regulation has been found to be more open to public scrutiny and the activities of state regulators have been subject to greater accountability over time. The key questions here concern calls for greater participation and also for greater legitimacy of regulators. In part, the explanations offered relate to broader governmental scrutiny of the public service (see below). They also relate to earlier discussions about trust in the risk experts and risk expertise (Wynne 1996; Turner 2001). Indeed one key argument for greater participation is that it may increase the legitimation of policymaking processes (Rothstein 2003).

Debates about the relationship between science and regulation increasingly focus on the contention that the relationship between science and society is changing, in particular that it is marked by apparently increasing public distrust of science, companies, and governments (see below). There seem to be a number of reasons for this. It is partly related to the rapid spread of IT and alternative sources of knowledge which fosters a greater appreciation of the contestation of knowledge amongst scientists; enables the fast and often dramatic news of any risk regulation failures; and thus leads to greater scepticism. Coupled with this are reported levels of distrust of government and corporate pronouncements. A real concern here is that there is a fear that adequate risk management is not in place and that scientists are not always in control of their creations. There are thus concerns about the regulation of science and its application, with the public in general having little knowledge of or faith in the regulatory framework.

These debates have been fuelled by a number of regulatory and policy failures, some of which have become the subject of much academic debate. In Britain, BSE and GM foods are key examples. In the case of BSE, trust in government regulatory decisions was severely damaged when the government erroneously assured the public that BSE was not the problem it turned out to be (Phillips 2000). The GM food debate in Britain is another example of a government failure to understand the views of the public on a risk regulation issue—government, along with scientists and industry, did not appreciate that there may be serious public concern about a new technology which its critics feared might have detrimental effects involving future generations (Gaskell and Bauer 2001). These debates of course feed into work on risk regulation regimes (Vogel 2001), and also into the debate about widening participation, some of this work doubting that such increasing participation does in fact increase trust in government (GM Nation 2003; Poortinga and Pidgeon 2004). Discussions about the possibility and effects of greater openness in scientific debates are controversial, with disagreement about the desirability of public involvement in these decisions and also about the outcomes of such involvement (Jasanoff 1990; Irwin and Wynne 1996; Hilgartner 2000; Gurabardhi, Gutteling, and Kuttschreuter 2005).

Changing Patterns of Risk Regulation: The Governance of Risk and Risk as a Form of Governance

Contemporaneous with the broadening participatory base of state regulation has been a more general conceptualization of regulation. Regulation is no longer regarded as the exclusive domain of the state and governments, and the role of non-state actors in regulation is now widely acknowledged (Baldwin, Hood, and Scott 1998; Moran 2003; Black 2002). Some non-state sources are new and represent a growth of regulation, but many of the sources of regulation are well established and have existed for a very long time in one form or another. What is new is the growing recognition of these alternative sources as regulation, their formal co-option by the state and an increasing coordination of activities between various regulatory sources.

This decentring of the state involves a move from public ownership and centralized control to privatized institutions and the encouragement of market competition. It also involves a move to a state reliance on new forms of fragmented regulation, involving the existing specialist regulatory agencies of state but increasingly self-regulating organizations, regimes of enforced self-regulation (Braithwaite 1982), and American style independent regulatory agencies.[5] More broadly these changes represent a move from government to governance, where the state attempts to 'steer' or 'regulate' economic activities through co-opting non-governmental actors (Osborne and Gaebler 1992). Moran's (2000) view is that in Britain we are witnessing a move from a 'club-like' pattern of regulation characterized by informality, flexibility, and cooperation, to something more contractual which is codified, procedural, and specialized.

These changes have led to a growing body of research on the changing concept of regulation (Black 2002) and also different forms of decentred regulation (Grabosky 1995; Hutter, forthcoming). This includes groups in the economic sector, such as industry or trade organizations, companies themselves, and businesses whose business is selling regulatory and risk management advice to companies (Freeman and Kunreuther 1997; Gunningham and Rees 1997; Ericson, Doyle, and Barry 2003). In the civil sphere regulatory tasks may be undertaken by NGOs, charities, trusts, foundations, advocacy groups, and associations (Bruyn 1999; Hutter and O'Mahony 2004: 2). A deal of research is presently devoted to exploring the workings of non-state regulation and its relationship with state regulation across a variety of domains and also transnationally.

As the sources of regulation and risk management have multiplied, so has research which focuses on the regulatory state and the ways in which regulatory sources are themselves regulated. There are two main literatures here. The first concentrates on the regulation of state regulators and public officials. This literature examines new forms of public management and the growth in the regulation of government and governance (Hood et al. 2004). The second literature considers the concept of meta regulation—that is, the state's oversight of self-regulatory arrangements (Grabosky 1995; Gunningham, Grabosky, and Sinclair 1998; Parker 2002; Scott 2003). These literature of course connect with the accountability literature mentioned above—in particular the literatures on audit, efficiency, and performance.

Risk debates dovetail into these literature. For example, some authors regard risk as a new mode of governance (Condon 2004). The law and regulation are seen as ways of communicating about risk. Indeed forms of risk management may come to be regarded as decentred modes of governance whereby third parties take over from the state in the regulation of risk. For example, according to Ericson, Doyle, and Barry (2003) insurance is a technology of governance beyond the state. They argue that the insurance industry shares similar goals to the state; employs similar methodologies; and is subject to many of the same social forces. Indeed, insurance companies are regarded by some as the original risk experts producing information which is both used by the industry itself and is also a source of exploitation by governments (Freeman and Kunreuther 1993).

This trend has itself led to its own forms of governance—namely, meta risk management, a term Braithwaite (2003) uses to refer to as 'the risk-management of risk management'. This denotes regulators attempting to manage not just their own risk management systems but those of those they regulate. This is a reflexive, systems based approach to regulatory risk management and one which connects with the other key research area, namely, risk regulation and organizations.

Risk Regulation and Organizations

The research foci in this area of risk regulation studies have been upon both public and private sector organizations and their use of risk management approaches.

In Britain the use of risk templates is increasingly influential and public agencies have been under pressure for some time to adopt business practices (James 2001), some of which are discussed under the generic title of the 'New Public Management' (Hood 1991). Part of this move to adopt new management techniques is an emphasis upon risk-based approaches to all public sector departments (Cabinet Office 1999, 2002; NAO 2000). These imperatives manifest themselves in risk regulation regimes through the use of risk assessment tools, especially those derived from natural science and economics (Hood and Jones 1996; Hood, Rothstein, and Baldwin 2001) and in some cases a more general move to risk-based approaches as a way of organizing regulatory activities (Black 2005; Hampton 2005; Hutter 2005). One of the attractions of risk-based regulation is that it is an apparently rational, objective, and transparent way of deploying limited regulatory resources. Thus, its use may be appealed to should a crisis require a need for blame shifting. Institutional imperatives to avoid blame and liability is a key research issue (Horlick-Jones 1996; Hood, Rothstein, and Baldwin 2001; Black 2005; Hutter 2005; Power 2005; and especially Hood 2002). What is not clear from the existing literature are the limits of blame shifting around risk-based models. Too much faith in risk-based systems can be dangerous in itself (Holzer and Millo 2004) and could be counterproductive in a number of ways, blame shifting included.

A traditional risk focus is upon accidents and disasters (see above). Studies of these continue and early discussion so the organizational factors leading to major risk events (Turner 1978; Perrow 1984) have continued and developed. Notable recent examples would be Vaughan's (1996) work on the Challenger accident which underlines the very real need to pay attention to minor anomalies, and communication and the power dynamics within organizations. Work on 'silent disasters' (Beamish 2001) where the consequences of risk events may emerge slowly over time is another important and relatively new area of research activity which emphasizes a strong theme in much of the work on disasters, namely, the ways in which everyday organizational life can incubate risks (Turner and Pidgeon 1997) and the ways in which risky, deviant practices can be normalized (Vaughan 1996). Such discussions feed into how organizations routinely manage risk at an everyday level, for example, their systems for risk identification and management and the tensions which may be involved. Some work focuses on the organizational risk management structures in place (Hutter 2001; Heimer 2005), some on risk personnel (Weait 1994; Power 2005), and some on the tensions which may exist, for example, between production and risk management (Vaughan 1996; Hutter 2001). Increasingly this work emphasizes the dynamic and interactive nature of risk management both with respect to internal organization and the external environment within which organizations operate.

A more recent area of research considers the influence of 'risk speak' on organizational risk management, in particular the emergence of new risk management categories, examples include operational risk and enterprise risk management (Power 2004b) both of which have emerged in corporate and regulatory discussions since the 1990s. Another example of an emerging regulatory category is that of the 'genetically modified' and the associated transnational governance frameworks which have emerged alongside the new category (Lezaun 2006). These frameworks are national and international and relate to examinations of how trans-boundary risks come to be so defined and responded to (Dodd and Hutter 2000).

Transnational Risks

There is increasing awareness of the cross-border effects of risks, most especially involuntary risks such as environmental pollution, nuclear contamination, and financial risks. Most research effort has focused on regulatory responses to these risks. Research has considered the formation and implementation of multilateral agreements between nation states; the activities of transnational forums and organizations such as the OECD and EU; international standard setting has received a deal of attention as has the regulation of global industries, such as telecoms, across different continents. A tension running through these debates is the relative importance of the nation state vis-à-vis more international, even global, forces. Some argue that the nation state has a more restricted role because it has been superseded by supranational organizations. Others argue that it has expanded its role and influence more directly and forcefully in the international context, by becoming not only the exporter of goods but also the exporter of regulatory standards and knowledge. It certainly appears difficult to accept that the role of the nation state is diminishing. What is important is to differentiate among nation states, as some are more powerful than others, notably the USA and Japan. What is also certain is that there is a tension between demands for internationally effective regulations and even handedness on the one hand, and for national economic advantage on the other.[6]

A key issue in these debates is the relationship between risk regulation and trade. For example, what are the transnational effects of regulation? Does risk regulation in one area lead businesses to engage in regulatory shopping so they locate in less regulated areas? The extent to which the regulation and free trade are opposed to each other is a matter of some controversy. The debate thus turns on the effects of regulation on economic competition; this is a subject about which there are strong and very different views. This debate is sometimes characterized as the debate between the 'race to the top' and the 'race to the bottom'. The 'race to the bottom' idea is that stricter standards are the source of competitive disadvantage and will lead companies to move to the lowest cost location. The state response in such a scenario is deregulatory both nationally and internationally. Meanwhile, the 'race to the top' argument maintains that those at the cutting edge of regulation are at a competitive advantage because (in global terms) domestic producers can comply most easily. The state response is a strategic trade policy where the state acts to encourage international regulatory efforts (Porter 1990; Stewart 1993; Vogel 1995). Much of the debate so far focuses on cost benefit analyses, where costs and benefits can be evaluated differently, according to one's standpoint. Little other research has been undertaken on this subject, partly because of the difficulty in getting comparative data and partly because of differential evidential requirements according to standpoint on such a politically controversial subject.

Emerging Issues

The relatively new status of risk regulation studies necessarily implies that many of the research themes and findings discussed in this chapter are in their infancy. There is a pressing need for theoretical development based on empirical work. A number of areas demanding much more in-depth and systematic research have emerged from the above discussion.

First, we need much more detailed and comparative work on risk regulation regimes. More historical, cross-national, and cross-domain studies are essential. A fruitful area for the development of the risk regimes analytic is work on regulation beyond the state which increasingly may be seen as part of a broader risk regulation regime. More detailed consideration of the ways in which state, economic, and civil sources of regulation are able to work together or may hinder each other's efforts is required. This is particularly relevant as some states look to outsource more risk regulation activities and business demands less state intervention.

Second, relatively little attention has been paid to the impact of attempts to widen participation around risk regulation issues. Discussions on this topic are often theoretical and rhetorical (exceptions include Rothstein 2003; Gouldson, Lidskog, and Wester-Herber 2004). There is a dearth of empirical case studies and comparative work which will enable an assessment of what kinds of participation seem to work and the circumstances which foster or inhibit participation. Indeed such research may indicate that participative risk regulation is unhelpful in some situations.

Consideration of the role of risk management within organizations is a third emerging research area, most particularly research that examines how risk management techniques are communicated and implemented within organizations (Hutter and Power 2005). For example, it is not at all clear how many government departments have bought into risk based initiatives or to what extent. An important aspect of this remit is to understand the limitations of risk management approaches, that is, to analyse situations in which they are helpful and when they might be counterproductive. A dimension of this is to research the differential impact of various regulatory sources and tools and to undertake comparative work across different types of organization and domain in the private and public sectors.

A fourth area for development is consideration of the role of experts in risk regulation (Power 2005). Current discussions of expertise are largely confined to science, but there is undoubtedly a need to broaden out the debate to include the relationship between other forms of expertise and regulation. A topical example in light of the Enron and Parmalat difficulties would be the status of the professional advice of accountants. Such discussions include regulation beyond the state as professionals are often incorporated into formal state risk regulation regimes as well as themselves being a focus of regulatory practice. The work of the emerging profession of risk management personnel both inside organizations and outside as consultants is worthy of attention as these personnel increasingly try to professionalize and extend their domains.

Fifth, despite the large literature on globalization, transnational risk regulation studies is still a relatively under researched area. The one area which has attracted a deal of attention is the effects of risk regulation on trading but there is still a deal of empirical research needed on this topic as much of the debate is rhetorical. Kagan and Axelrad (2000) have conducted one of the most broadly international studies to date of multinational corporations and their reactions to national regulatory regimes, but we await any further empirical work of this type. Another perspective on this topic is the trading of risks between countries, for example, of waste products or GM foods. We have some data on the topic (Bruce and Tait 2001), but generally the effects of transnational risk trading on the distribution of risks across the globe is under-researched.

Sixth is a related topic which was signalled in the 1990s as important, yet remains relatively neglected—namely, the social distribution and inequalities of risk (O'Riordan 1983; Short 1984; Tierney 1999). Issues of risk and power are key to risk regulation studies but are often neglected. More direct discussion is necessitated, especially in light of Beck's (1992) proposition that the risks of high modernity are democratic. Consideration needs to be given here to inequalities both within and between nations. Is it the case that all sectors of society suffer the effects of poor risk management equally? And what are the effects of transnational global agreements and regulatory shopping on developing countries—are they able to comply? Do they suffer the effects disproportionately?

As risk regulation studies become more established we might expect more interdisciplinary and international research initiatives to pursue the themes outlined in this section. Risk regulation studies needs closer analysis of the social and political contexts and the broader social and cultural contexts in which risks are understood and experienced. The objective will be to develop and challenge existing theories and connect with other areas of risk research.

Notes

1. The third category cited by Baldwin et al. (ibid) reflects early sociological definitions of social control which are broadly defined and where the words social control and regulation are often used interchangeably and not the category identified here which is more focused and defined.
2. Whilst the mainstream sociological literature on social control gives us important insights into the social control of economic life it is also fair to say that the control of organizations and businesses is relatively neglected by the discipline. The traditional and mainstream social control literature centres on the behaviour of individuals. There is a corporate crime literature strongly related to criminology but until fairly recently very little on regulation. The main focus on the regulation of businesses and markets came, with a few notable exceptions, from economists, political scientists and lawyers in the 1970s (ref Bernstein 1955). And it is here that regulation developed as a more technical term referring to state attempts to regulate economic activities.
3. This has been a traditional focus of risk discussions in American sociology, indeed if ASA Annual Meetings are any barometer of research activity this remains the case. As Turner (1994) cautions there is a need to differentiate between hazards and risks.
4. In 2000 the ESRC Centre for Analysis of Risk and Regulation (CARR) was set up to research precisely these issues and interfaces. See http://www.lse.ac.uk/collections/CARR/
5. Indeed for Majone (1994) it is the rise of these agencies at both state and EU levels which is the defining characteristic of the European regulatory state.
6. The most exhaustive work on global business regulation is Braithwaite and Drahos, 2000. See also Stirton and Lodge, 2002; Thatcher, 2002; Lodge, 2003.

221

References

Baldwin, R. (1997). 'Regulation: After Command and Control', in K. Hawkins (ed.), *The Human Face Of Law: Essays In Honour Of Donald Harris*. Oxford: Clarendon.

_____ Hood, C., and Scott, C. (1998). Socio-*Legal Reader on Regulation*. Oxford: OUP.

Beamish, T. D. (2001). *Silent Spill: The Organization of Industrial Crisis*. The MIT Press.

Beck, U. (1992). *Risk Society*. London: Sage.

Bernstein, M. H. (1955). *Regulating Business by Independent Commission*. Princeton, NJ: Princeton University Press.

Black, J. (2002). *Critical Reflections on Regulation*. CARR Discussion Paper 4.

_____ (2005). 'The Emergence of Risk Based Regulation and the New Public Risk Management in the UK', *Public Law* (Summer issue).

Blockley, D. I. (1996). 'Hazard Engineering', in Hood and Jones (1996), op. cit.

Braithwaite, J. (1982). 'Enforced Self-Regulation: A New Strategy for Corporate Crime Control', *Michigan Law Review*, 80, 1466–507.

_____ (2003). 'Meta Risk Management and Responsive Regulation for Tax System Integrity', *Law and Policy*, 25(1): 1–16.

_____ and Drahos, P. (2000). *Global Business Regulation*. Cambridge: Cambridge University Press.

Breyer, S. (1993). *Breaking the Vicious Circle: Toward Effective Risk Regulation*. Cambridge, MA: Harvard University.

Brickman, R., Jasanoff, S., and Iilgen, T. (1985). *Controlling Chemicals: The Politics of Regulation in Europe and the United States*. Ithaca, London: Cornell University Press.

Bruce, A. and Tait, J. (2001). 'Globalisation and Transboundary Risk Regulation: Pesticides and Genetically Modified Crops', *Health, Risk and Society*, 3(1), March 2001.

Bruyn, S. T. H. (1999). 'The Moral Economy', *Review of Social Economy*, LV11(1): 25–46.

Cabinet Office (1999). *Modernizing Government*. London: HMSO; http://www.cabinet-office.gov.uk/moderngov/download/modgov.pdf

United Kingdom, Cabinet Office (2002). *Risk: Improving Government's Capability to Handle Risk and Uncertainty*. London: Cabinet Office.

Clark, M. (2000). *Regulation: the Social Control of Business between Law and Politics*. Basingstoke, UK: Macmillan.

Clarke, L. and Short, J. F. Jr. (1993). 'Social Organization and Risk: Some Current Controversies', *Annual Review of Sociology*, 19: 375–99.

Cohen, S. (1985). *Visions of Social Control: Crime, Punishment and Classification*. Cambridge: Polity Press.

Condon, M. (2004). 'Technologies of Risk? Regulating Online Investing in Canada', *Law and Policy*, 26, 3(4): 422.

Dodd, N. and Hutter, B. M. (2000). 'Geopolitics and the Regulation of Economic Life', *Law and Policy*, 22(2): 1–24.

Douglas, M. (1985). *Risk: Accountability According to the Social Sciences*. London: Routledge and Kegan Paul.

___ and Wildavsky, A. (1982). *Risk and Culture*. Berkeley, CA: University of California Press.

Ericson, R. V. and Haggerty, K. D. (1997). *Policing The Risk Society*. Toronto: University of Toronto Press.

___ Doyle, A., and Barry, D. (2003). *Insurance as Governance*. Toronto: University of Toronto Press.

Freeman, P. K. and Kunreuther, H. (1997). *Managing Environmental Risk through Insurance*. AEI Press, Kluwer.

Gabe, J. (1995). 'Health, Medicine and Risk: The Need for a Social Approach', in *Medicine, Health and Risk: Sociological approaches*. Oxford: Blackwell, pp. 1–17.

Gaskell, G. and Bauer, M. (eds.) (2001). *Biotechnology 1996–2000: The Years of controversy*. London: Science Museum.

Giddens, A. (1990). *The Consequences of Modernity*. Cambridge: Polity Press.

GM Nation? The Public Debate (2003), http://www.gmnation.org.uk/

Golding, D. (1992). 'A Social and Programmatic History of Risk Research', in Krimsky and Golding (1992), op. cit.

Gouldson, A., Lidskog, R., and Wester-Herber, M. (2004). *The Battle for Hearts and Minds? Evolutions in Organisational Approaches to Environmental Risk Communication*, CARR DP24 http://www.lse.ac.uk/collections/CARR/pdf/DissPaper24.pdf

Gourvish, T. (2003). *Business History and Risk*, CARR DP 12 http://www.lse.ac.uk/collections/CARR/pdf/Disspaper12.pdf

Grabosky, P. N. (1995). 'Using Non-Governmental Resources to Foster Regulatory Compliance', *Governance: An International Journal of Policy and Administration*, 8(4): 527–50.

Gunningham, N. and Rees, J. (1997). 'Industry Self-Regulation: An Institutional Perspective', *Law and Policy*, 19(4): 363–414.

___ Grabosky, P., and Sinclair, D. (1998). *Smart Regulation: Designing Environmental Policy*. Oxford: Clarendon Press.

Gurabardhi, Z., Gutteling, J. M., and Kuttschreuter, M. (2005). 'An Empirical Analysis of Communication Flow, Strategy and Stakeholders' Participation in the Risk Communication Literature 1988–2000', *Journal of Risk Regulation*, 8: 499–511.

Hampton, P. (2005). Reducing Administrative Burdens: effective inspection and auditing. London: HM Treasury.

Hancher, L. and Moran, M. (1989). *Capitalism, Culture and Regulation*. Oxford: Clarendon.

Heimer, C. et al. (2005). 'Risk and Rules: the "legalization" of Medicine', in Hutter and Power (2005), op. cit.

Held, D. (1987). *Models of Democracy*. Cambridge: Polity, in association with Blackwell.

Hilgartner, S. (2000). *Science on Stage: Expert Advice as Public Drama*. Stanford University Press.

Holzer, B. and Millo, Y. (2004). *From Risks to Second-order Dangers in Financial Markets: Unintended Consequences of Risk Management Systems*, CARR DP 29 http://www.lse.ac.uk/collections/CARR/pdf/Disspaper29.pdf

Hood, C. (1991). 'A Public Management for all Seasons', *Public Administration*, 69, 3–19.

——(2002). 'The Risk Game and the Blame Game', *Government and Opposition*, 37(1): 15–37.

——and Jones, D. K. C. (eds.) (1996). *Accident and Design*. London: UCL Press.

——Rothstein, H., and Baldwin, R. (2001). *The Government of Risk*. Oxford: Oxford University Press.

——James, O., Peters, G., and Scott, C. (eds.) (2004). *Controlling Modern Government: Variety, Commonality and Change*. Cheltenham, UK: Edward Elgar (2004).

Horlick-Jones, T. (1996). 'The Problem of Blame', in Hood and Jones (1996), op. cit.

Hutter, B. M. (1988). *The Reasonable Arm of the Law?: The Law Enforcement Procedures of Environmental Health Officers*. Oxford: Clarendon Press.

——(2001). *Regulation And Risk: Occupational Health And Safety On The Railways*. Oxford: Oxford University Press.

——(2005). *The Attractions of Risk-based Regulation: Accounting for the Emergence of Risk Ideas In Regulation*, CARR Discussion paper http://www.lse.ac.uk/collections/CARR/pdf/Disspaper33.pdf

——(forthcoming). 'The Role of Non-State Actors in Regulation', in Folke Schuppert, *Documents on Research in Governance*. Nomos Publishers: Berlin.

——and O'Mahony, J. (2004). *Business Regulation: Reviewing the Regulatory Potential of Civil Society Organisations*, CARR Discussion paper D26.

——and Power, M. K. (eds.) (2005). *Organizational Encounters with Risk*. Cambridge: Cambridge University Press.

Irwin, A. and Wynne, B. (1996). *Misunderstood Science: The Public Reconstruction of Science and Technology*. Cambridge: Cambridge University Press.

James, O. (2001). 'Business Models and the Transfer of Businesslike Central Government Agencies', *Governance*, April, 14(2): 233–52.

Jasanoff, S. (1990). *The Fifth Branch: Science Advisers as Policymakers*. Harvard University Press.

——(1991) 'Cross-National Differences in Policy Implementation', *Evaluation Review*, 15(1): 103–19.

——(2005). 'Restoring Reason: Causal Narratives and Political Culture', in Hutter and Power (2005), op. cit.

——Markle, G. E., Peterson, J. C., and Pinch, T. (eds.) (1995). *Handbook of Science and Technology Studies*. London: Sage.

Jasper, J. W. (1992). 'Three Nuclear Energy Controversies', in D. Nelkin (ed.), *Controversy: Politics of Technical Decisions*. 3rd edn. London: Sage.

Kagan, R. A. and Axelrad, A. L. (2000). *Regulatory Encounters: Multinational Corporations and American Adversarial Legalism*. Berkeley, CA: University of California Press.

Krier, J. E., DeLano, E. W., Noll, R. G., Doyle, M. M. (1990). 'Some Implications of Cognitive Psychology for Risk Regulation', *Journal of Legal Studies*, X1X (June): 747–79.

Krimsky, S. (1992). 'The Role of Theory in Risk Studies', in Krimsky, S. and Golding, D. (eds.) (1992). *Social Theories of Risk*. Westport, CT: Praeger, 3–22.

Lezaun, J. (2006). 'Creating a new Object of Government: Making Genetically Modified Organisms Traceable,' *Social Studies of Science*, 36: 4.

Luhmann, N. (1993). *Risk: A Sociological Theory*. Berlin: de Gruyter.

Majone, G. (1994). *Regulating Europe*. London: Routledge.

Mitnick, B. (1980). *The Political Economy of Regulation*. New York: Columbia University Press.

Moran, M. (2003). *The British Regulatory State*. Oxford: Oxford University Press.

National Audit Office (2000). *Supporting Innovation: Managing Risk in Government Departments*. London: HMSO; http://www.nao.gov.uk/publications/nao_reports/9900864.pdf

National Research Council (1996). *Understanding Risk: Informing Decisions in a Democratic Society*. Washington, DC: National Academy.

Nelkin, D. (ed.) (1985). *The Language of Risk: Conflicting Perspectives on Occupational Health*. Beverly Hills, CA: Sage.

Nelkin, D. (1992). *Controversy: Politics of Technical Divisions*, London: Sage.

Noll, R. G. (1990). 'Reforming Risk Regulation', *Annals of the American Academy of Political and Social Science*, 545.

Noll, R. (1996). 'Reforming Risk Regulation', *Annals of the American Academy of Political and Social Science*, 545, Challenges in Risk Assessment and Risk Management, 165–75.

O'Riordan, T. (1983). 'The Cognitive and Political Dimensions of Risk Analysis', *Journal of Environmental Psychology*, 3: 345–54.

Osborne, D. and Gaebler, T. (1992). *Reinventing Government*. Reading, MA: Addison-Wesley.

Otway, H. J. (1985). 'Regulation and Risk Analysis', in H. Otway and M. Peltu (eds.), *Regulating Industrial Risks—Science, Hazards and Public Protection*. London: Butterworths, pp. 1–19.

Owens, S. (2000). 'Engaging the Public': Information and Deliberation in Environmental Policy', *Environment and Planning*, 32: 1141–8.

Parker, C. (2002). *The Open Corporation: Effective Self-Regulation and Democracy*. Cambridge, Cambridge University Press.

Perrow, C. (1984). *Normal Accidents*. New York: Basic Books.

Phillips Report into BSE (2000) http://www.bse.inquiry.gov.uk

Pidgeon, N., Kasperson, R., and Slovic, P. (eds.) (2003). *The Social Amplification of Risk*. Cambridge: Cambridge University Press.

225

Plough, A. and Krimsky, S. (1987). 'The Emergence of Risk Communication Studies: Social and Political Context Science', *Technology and Human Values*, 12: 4–10.

Pollak, R. A. (1995). 'Regulating Risks', *Journal of Economic Literature*, 33: 179–91.

Poortinga, W. and Pidgeon, N. F. (2003). 'Exploring the Dimensionality of Trust in Risk Regulation', *Risk Analysis*, 961–72.

—— —— (2004). 'Trust, the Asymmetry Principle, and the Role of Prior Beliefs', *Risk Analysis*, 24(6).

Porter, M. E. (1990). *The Competitive Advantage of Nations*. London: Collier Macmillan.

Power, M. (1997). *The Audit Society: Rituals of Verification*. Oxford: Clarendon Press.

——(2004a). *The Risk Management of Everything: Rethinking the Politics of Uncertainty*. London: Demos.

——(2004b). 'Enterprise Risk Management and the Organization of Uncertainty in Financial Institutions', in K. Knorr-Cetina and A. Preda (eds.), *The Sociology of Financial Markets*. Oxford: Oxford University Press.

——(2005). 'The Invention of Operational Risk', *Review of International Political Economy*, 12(1): xxx.

——(2005). 'Organizational responses to risk: the rise of the Chief Officer', in Hutter and Power (2005), op. cit.

Rayner, S. (1991). 'A Cultural Perspective on the Structure and Implementation of Global Environmental Agreements', *Evaluation Review*, 15(1): 75–102.

Reiss, A. (1984). 'Selecting Strategies of Social Control Over Organisational Life', in K. Hawkins and J. Thomas (eds.), *Environment and Enforcement: Regulation and Social Definition of Pollution*. Oxford: Clarendon Press.

Renn, O. (1992). 'Concepts of Risk: A Classification', in S. Krimsky and D. Golding (eds.), *The Social Theories of Risk*. Westport, CN: Praeger.

Rimmington, J. (1992). 'Overview of Risk Assessment', Risk Assessment Conference, Queen Elizabeth II Conference Centre, London.

Rothstein, H. (2003). 'Neglected Risk Regulation: the Institutional Attentuation Phenomenon Health', *Risk and Society*, 5(1): 85–103.

Royal Society (1983). *Risk Assessment: A Study Group Report*. London: Royal Society.

Scott, C. (2003). 'Speaking Softly without Big Sticks: Metaregulation and Public Sector Audit', *Law and Policy*, 25: 203–19.

Short, J. F. Jr (1984). 'The Social Fabric at Risk: Toward the Social Transformation of Risk Analysis', *American Sociological Review*, 49(6): 711–25.

Short, J. and Clarke, L. (eds.) (1992). *Organizations, Uncertainties and Risks*. Boulder, CO: Westview Press.

Shrader-Frechette, K. S. (1991). *Risk and Rationality: Philosophical Foundations for Populist Reforms*. California: California University Press.

Smith, R. and Wynne, B. (eds.) (1989). *Expert Evidence: Interpreting Science in the Law*. London: Routledge.

Stewart, R. B. (1993). 'Environmental Regulation and International Competitiveness', *The Yale Law Journal*, 2039–106.

Stirton, L. and Lodge, M. (2002). 'Embedding Regulatory Autonomy: The Reform of Jamaican Telecommunications Regulation 1988–2001', Carr DP 5; http://www.lse.ac.uk/collections /CARR/pdf/Disspaper5.pdf

Tait, J. (2001). 'More Faust than Frankenstein: The European Debate About the Precautionary Principle and Risk Regulation for Genetically Modified Crops', *Journal of Risk Research*, 4(2), April 2001.

Thatcher, M. (2004). 'Varieties of Capitalism in an Internationalised World: Domestic Institutional Change in European Telecommunications', *Comparative Political Studies*, 37(7): 1–30.

Tierney, K. J. (1999). 'Towards a Critical Sociology of Risk', *Sociological Forum*, 14(2): 215–42.

Turner, B. A. (1978). *Man-made disasters*. London: Wykeham.

—— (1994). 'Causes of Disaster: Sloppy Management', *British Journal of Management*, 5(3): 215–20.

—— and Pidgeon, N. F. (1997). Man-Made Disasters. 2nd edn. Oxford: Butterworth-Heinemann.

Turner, B. (2001). 'Risks, Rights and Regulation: An Overview', *Health, Risk and Society*, 3: 9–18.

Turner, S. (2001). 'What is the Problem with Experts', *Social Studies of Science*, 31(1).

Vaughan, D. (1996). *The Challenger Launch Decision: Risky Technology, Culture and Deviance at NASA*. Chicago, IL: University of Chicago Press.

Vogel, D. (1995). *Trading Up: Consumer and Environmental Regulation in a Global Economy*. Cambridge, MA: Harvard University Press.

—— (2001). *'The New Politics of Risk Regulation in Europe'* CARR DP 3; http://www.lse.ac.uk/collections/CARR/pdf/Disspaper3.pdf

Weait, M. (1994). 'The Role of the Compliance Officer in Firms Carrying on Investment Business', *Butterworth's Journal of International Banking and Financial Law*, 9(8): 381–3.

Weale, A. (1999). *Democracy*. Houndmills, UK: Macmillan.

Wynne, B. (1996). in S. Lash et al. *Risk, Environment and Modernity: Towards a New Ecology*. London: Sage.

11

Social Inequality and Risk

David Abbott, Anwen Jones, and Deborah Quilgars

Introduction

Following the work of such authors as Beck (1992) and Giddens (1991, 1994), there has been considerable academic debate in social policy about the emergence of a risk society (Culpitt 1999; Dingwall 1999; Taylor-Gooby et al. 1999). One important factor is that, in a risk society, the traditional fault-lines of social class are no longer the main divisions in people's ideas about their interests, but that risks, which cut across these lines and may affect all members of society in similar ways, become more important (Taylor-Gooby 2001a). The theory of risk society is important not only because of its intellectual influence but also because these ideas have begun to permeate into, and influence, the policymaking process (Quilgars and Abbott 2000). In Britain, New Labour's 'third way' in welfare, with its emphasis on individual responsibility and the curbing of state intervention, derives its intellectual underpinning from the risk society theory as developed in the UK by Giddens (Giddens 1991, 1994, 1998). Current public policy is influenced by rational choice theory which implies that individuals will not only perceive risks and take responsibility for reducing risk, but that they will do so according to deliberate calculations which will protect their interest. Research suggests, however, that some individuals and groups are more likely to experience risks than others and are less able to plan for, and deal with, contingencies. Research has shown that our society is still unequal, that restructuring of welfare has actually deepened some divisions in society, and that traditional structuring factors continue to shape life experiences (Taylor-Gooby 2001a; Glennerster et al. 2004). This chapter explores issues of inequality and disadvantage in the risk society and questions whether traditional social divisions such as class, gender, and ethnicity are becoming less significant as people become increasingly reflexive and individualized.

Context

The latter half of the twentieth century was one of rapid social change which saw transformation in traditional structures and institutions, including employment patterns and welfare provision. Changes in the global economy, characterized by increasing mobility of capital and the development of new international markets, have had a major impact on Western economies. These changes include globalization and sectoral changes (the decline of manufacturing and growth of the service sector) and labour market deregulation. In the UK, successive Conservative Governments from 1979 to 1996 sought to create a more flexible labour market both through the operation of general economic policies, reducing the rights of employees and, notably, by curbing Trade Union powers. The current Government has introduced some minimum standards within employment relations, for example, the National Minimum Wage and has stated its support for a return to full employment, however, like its predecessors, the current Government remains committed to flexibility in the labour market. The UK labour market is now characterized by increased labour market flexibility, new patterns of working, polarized and more precarious forms of work, intensification of work, and widespread feelings of insecurity (Burchell et al. 1999). Over the same period, successive governments have increasingly curtailed the level of and eligibility for many forms of state provision. Traditionally, the welfare state responded to both unplanned hazards (e.g. unemployment, divorce, and sickness) and planned events (for instance, retirement) but in recent years the state has sought to transfer the responsibility for provision towards individuals and households (McRae 1995; Skinner and Ford 2000). This has been described as a 'new contract for welfare' between the citizen and the state; the main principle of this contract is that 'wherever possible, people are [privately] insured against foreseeable risks and make provision for their retirement' (Department of Social Security 1998: 2). These socio-economic changes, it is argued, have meant that the UK has become an increasingly risky society, especially for its most excluded and disadvantaged citizens.

The issues of poverty and exclusion have been the subject of some of the UK Government's most high profile targets since they came to power in 1997. In particular, the Government has pledged to cut and eventually to 'eradicate' child poverty, and to ensure that within the next two decades no one is disadvantaged by where they live. However, there are no targets for working age poverty, for poverty of the population as a whole, or for overall inequality. Whilst there have been some improvements since 1997, for example, in relative child poverty, which has fallen (but is still above the average for the EU) the UK remains an unequal society. Wheeler et al. (2005), using data from the 2001 Census, examine five issues—health, education, housing, employment, and poverty. The research shows the nature and extent of geographical and social inequality in the UK and demonstrates the continued unequal distribution of resources and prospects across the country and the entire population. They found that poor people with the greatest need for good health care, education, jobs, housing, and transport continue to have the worst access to opportunities and services. Children from less advantaged backgrounds continue to have lower levels of educational attainment and these inequalities lead to lifetime inequalities due to the relationship between education, unemployment, and earnings as well as a range of other outcomes such as general health and psychological well-being (Hobcraft 1998; CASE and HM Treasury 1999; Palmer, Carr, and Kenway 2004).

The UK is divided between 'work-rich' and 'work-poor' areas with geographical location as well as qualifications influencing the chances of obtaining a well-paid job. More than 5 million British men and women of working age are in non-working families, double the number in the 1970s, and there are growing not lessening divides between work-rich and work-poor households. In 2002–3, 12.4 million people (22 per cent of the population) were living in low-income households although this represented a reduction from 14 million in 1996/7 (Palmer, Carr, and Kenway 2004). However, whilst unemployment has reduced among couple households in recent years, there has been much less success in reducing the numbers of people who are economically inactive who want to work, in long-term worklessness due to ill health and disability, and in worklessness among single-adult households. Whilst the proportion of children and pensioners who live in low-income households is falling, the proportion of working age adults without children who live in low-income households has risen over recent years. Being in paid employment does not eliminate the risk of living in poverty, two-fifths of people in low-income working age households now have someone in paid work. Of those who find employment in low-paid work two-fifths no longer have work six months later. More than half of employees on below average incomes are not contributing to a non-state pension (Palmer, Carr, and Kenway 2004).

Commentators (McKnight 2005; Phillips 2005) have recorded how some groups are more insecure and disadvantaged than others, for example:

- Inactivity rates among disabled people remain high (44% of men aged 25–34 and 70% of men aged 55–64) and there remains a large unmet demand to work and high rates of poverty among disabled people;
- Overall, unemployment rates for minority ethnic groups remain significantly higher than for the White population, with Bangladeshi and Black Caribbean males particularly likely to be unemployed (with those in work receiving lower average earnings than White counterparts);
- Despite improvements in female participation rates over time, only 53 per cent of lone parents were employed in 2003;
- Employment rates for men aged 50–64 fell from 84 per cent in 1979 to 64 per cent in 1993;
- Young people have benefited from government employment initiatives and the National Minimum Wage but the unemployment rate for 16–17-year-olds still stands at 21 per cent.

As noted earlier, a key assumption of the risk society thesis is that social change has a common impact across all social groups and that all citizens tend to respond to risks in a similar way. The traditional structures and inequalities such as class, gender, and ethnicity are less significant. According to risk society theories, modern late-industrial societies are in transition, moving from industrial society towards this risk society. In the process of reflexive modernization, more and more areas of life are released from tradition, so that people develop an increasing engagement with both the private and more public aspects of their lives, aspects that were previously governed by taken for granted norms. These developments are what Beck calls 'individualization' (Elliot 2002: 295). The general thrust of individualization theory is that 'given' forms of collective identity have been eroded. Previously existing social forms such as fixed gender roles, inflexible class locations, and masculinist work models disintegrate so that identities are no longer simply ascribed but have to be created by individuals from a range of opportunities and possibilities (Baxter and Britton 2001; Elliot 2002).

In the risk society, traditional political conflicts centred round class, race, and gender are increasingly superseded by new, globalized risk conflicts. Where industrial society is structured through the composition of social classes, the risk society is individualized. This does not mean that social inequalities or structuring of opportunities through such attributes as class, gender, or ethnicity have disappeared. In the early stages of transition from industrial to risk society, risk and class positions tend to merge, leaving the most materially disadvantaged most endangered by risk. The disadvantaged have fewer opportunities to avoid risks because of their lack of resources compared with the advantaged. Nevertheless, risk society theory contends that the influence of traditional markers such as class, gender, and ethnicity are less significant in the risk society; they have become less obvious and acknowledged as affecting life chances as people increasingly make their own choices and become responsible for reflexively creating their own biographies.

The development of a post-traditional order, social reflexivity, and the associated social changes produce a society in which people think about risk and the role of the state in meeting it in a fundamentally different way. In the risk society, individuals question the ability of the state to meet their interests and deal with risk but at the same time, individuals are increasingly confident in their own capacity to cope with the risks they face (Taylor-Gooby 2001a). The nature of welfare citizenship has thus changed as well (Edwards and Glover 2001). For Mythen (2005: 139)

Risk society thesis is concerned not only with the individualisation and routinisation of risk, but also the broader transference of responsibility from institutions to individuals . . . the rolling back of the state in capitalist cultures has led to a tipping of the scales of accountability. As governments divest themselves of responsibility for risk—through privatisation, promotion of private insurance schemes and the withdrawal of state pensions—health risks are converted into baggage to be handled by the individual.

Individuals are pressed into routinely making decisions about education, employment, relationships, identity, and politics and to take responsibility for their actions. The 'semantics of individualization' (Zinn 2002) include now familiar terms such as self-realization, self-control, self-responsibility, and self-management. The arrival of advanced or late modernity, therefore, is not wholly about risk, it is also about an expansion of choice and opportunity to determine one's own future. However, as life courses become (allegedly) dependent on individual decisions, the pressure increases on individuals to make the right choices or be exposed to considerable pressures if they are frequently forced to acknowledge their own responsibility for failure (Zinn 2004).

Key Research Themes

Risk society theories have been criticized for their overly rationalistic and individualistic model of the human subject, for their tendency to generalize and the failure to pay sufficient attention to the role played by class, gender, ethnicity, and nationality in constructing differing risk experiences, in shaping subjectivity and individual life chances (Lash 1993; Alexander 1996; Lupton 1999). However, little empirical research has been conducted that has sought to examine the speculations of risk society theories (Lupton and Tulloch 2002; Mythen 2004). In particular, few studies in the fields of sociology and social policy have specifically examined social divisions and inequality from a risk society perspective (exceptions are Baxter and Britton 2001; Ginn 2001; Taylor-Gooby 2001a). There is recognition within risk research of the importance of cultural and social differences (Lupton 1999; Rohrmann 1999; Lupton and Tulloch 2002; Tulloch and Lupton 2003). To date, however, empirical studies have focused mainly on perceptions and responses to risk and (particularly in youth studies) risk-taking, rather than on differences in the distribution of risk along the lines of disadvantage and inequality. Policy research suggests that differences such as disability, sexuality, and faith (Skeggs 1997; Bottero and Irwin 2003; Burchardt 2003; Molloy, Knight, and Woodfield 2003; Patrick and John, undated) are also significant in shaping life chances but, again, little attention has been paid to these issues within risk research. There is, however, a significant body of empirical work on risk which examines agency, individualization, reflexivity, risk-taking, perceptions of, and responses to, risk, as well as more general empirical work, which indicate the continuing significance of inequality.

Inequality and risk have emerged as issues in a number of studies, particularly in youth studies (Furlong and Cartmel 1997; Green, Mitchell, and Bunton 2000; Mitchell et al. 2001) and in other policy related research, for example, on pensions and the welfare state (Taylor-Gooby et al. 1999; Ginn 2001; Ginn and Arber 2001; Kemp and Rugg 2001). The remainder of the chapter therefore draws on a wider body of literature that demonstrates the continued significance of inequality in the risk society. As it is not possible to provide an exhaustive account of all literature

233

on inequality, the following sections draw on research from three major themes within the life course: youth transition to adulthood; access to and security within the labour market; and older age and retirement. These three themes provide a framework for an examination of risk society theories, particularly in relation to individualization, reflexivity, and the distribution of risk, during the life course. The following sections explore to what extent traditional social structures and divisions continue to shape individual life experiences, perceptions of and responses to risk; to limit reflexivity and constrain choice. Traditional divisions such as social class and inequalities in income and wealth are considered, as are the cross-cutting divisions and differences of gender, age, ethnicity, disability, and sexuality.

Recent Major Findings

Young People and the Transition to Adulthood

The literature on youth transitions seeks to understand the experience of youth and emerging adulthood in societies where the traditional routes from school to work and parental home to independent living have become less secure and fragmented. Furlong and Cartmel (1997) suggest that if the social order has changed and if social structures have weakened then we would expect to find evidence of these changes among young people. They sought to explore whether the traditional parameters which were previously understood as structuring the life chances of young people are still relevant, and the extent to which the terms individualization and risk convey an accurate picture of the changing life contexts of the young (1997: 2) through empirical analysis of the social condition of young people. Vickerstaff (Chapter 9 in this volume) examines similar issues. Furlong and Cartmel examined changes in education, labour market transitions, patterns of dependency, leisure and lifestyle, health, crime and insecurity, and politics and participation. They concluded that radical social changes had taken place and that the experiences of young people growing up in the 1990s are quite different from those encountered by earlier generations but that social divisions that were seen as shaping life chances in the past are still of central importance in understanding structural inequalities in risk society.

The changes in young people's life contexts are closely linked to the transformation of the youth labour market which was part of the broader process of economic change in Western economies. These changes have led to a demand for a better qualified and more highly educated workforce but, although there are more opportunities for training and education for all young people, existing social disadvantages have been maintained. Young people from working class backgrounds and ethnic minorities, in particular, face a new set of disadvantages in the labour market stemming from the development of peripheral employment where new forms of flexible working have increased insecurity and the risk of periodic spells of unemployment (Furlong and Cartmel 1997).

Furlong and Cartmel (1997) and others (Mitchell et al. 2001) accept that collective social identities have weakened and that this is reflected in an individualization of life experiences and a convergence of class cultures. The growth of the service sector and the decline of traditional manu-facturing have been associated with the decline of collectivism among working class youth who now experience, and have to deal with, risk and insecurity on an individual level. Nevertheless, they remain critical of the significance which risk society theories attach to changes in the way individuals interpret the world and subjectively construct social reality, particularly in relation to individual reflexivity.

Life in late modernity involves subjective discomfort and uncertainty. Young people can struggle to establish adult identities and maintain coherent biogra-phies, they may develop strategies to overcome various obstacles, but their life chances remain highly structured with social class and gender being crucial to an understanding of experiences in a range of life contexts. (1997: 109)

Other studies of youth tend to concur that young people face increas-ing risk and uncertainty but that the ways in which these risks are experienced, perceived, and dealt with are still mediated by traditional structures such as class, poverty, gender, disability and ethnicity as well as place. Disabled people, for example, are severely limited in the extent to which they can exercise choice and act reflexively to create their own biographies. Morris (2002) highlights the very significant barriers faced by young disabled people in their transition to adulthood which relate directly to the disabling societal barriers they face. Young disabled people with learning difficulties and/or communication impairments, for example, are often not treated as autonomous, decision-makers. Many have no experience of an independent social life and few opportunities to make friends: they spend most of their time with family or paid carers and have no independent access to transport, telecommunications, or personal assistance over which they have choice and control. Small,

Pawson, and Raghwan (2003) concur and suggest that young adults with learning difficulties rarely get to exercise their choices in the risk society as their relationships are tied so closely to their care and support.

Mitchell et al.'s study (2001) of young people growing up in 'Townsville', a deprived town in the North East of England, examined young people's experiences of risk and identity. They found that young people may live in an increasingly 'timeless' and 'globalized' world, as Furlong and Cartmel (1997) suggest, however, 'local places' and 'spaces' remain a crucial medium and mediator of lived risk experiences, locality and neighbourhood still constitute an important dimension of structured inequality. Subjective feelings of risk are a central feature of young people's lives, together with a perceived lack of collective tradition and security, but perceptions of risk and opportunity are clearly socially constructed in relation to specific cultural contexts (Green et al. 2000). Mitchell et al. (2001) also found that young people pursued individual solutions to wider socio-economic-related insecurities and exclusion, often opting for sometimes individualized and often highly risky solutions to their problems. For example, Green (2004) in a study of young mothers working in prostitution found that for some, the risk of not having enough money to look after their children and be 'good mothers' outweighed the risks of prostitution. Whilst risk might be generated 'at a distance' by global and economic processes, risks are not experienced as such by this group. This leads to what Furlong and Cartmel (1997) call the 'epistemological fallacy of late-modernity'; risks are experienced and addressed individually rather than collectively even though they may result from wider socio-economic pressures beyond the individual.

Kemp and Rugg (2001) draw on risk society theories to examine the impact on young people of the change in housing benefit, specifically the 'single-room rent restriction'.[1] They found most young people were not the well informed, calculating actors assumed by Beck and Giddens; young people were constrained by a lack of knowledge, by social class, and family background. Their degree of choice was heavily constrained by their low income, by the rules governing the housing benefit scheme, and by their imperfect knowledge of those rules. The authors conclude it would be more accurate to say that they were experiencing, not 'biographies of choice', but constrained or 'semi-dependent' biographies.

Risk and uncertainty are features of everyday life for young people who have to negotiate a set of risks that were largely unknown to their parents; this is true irrespective of class or gender (Furlong and Cartmel 1997). As the individualization thesis suggests, these risks and uncertainties are experienced and dealt with in an increasingly individualized way and young people are forced to reflexively negotiate a complex transition to adulthood. At the same time, studies suggest risks are distributed in an unequal fashion and correspond closely to traditional lines of disadvantage which continue to structure life chances (Furlong and Cartmel 1997).

Access to and Security in the Labour Market

In the risk society, the emergence of cyclical global recessions mean that unemployment and job insecurity no longer blight only the poorest and least academically qualified groups in society; the threat of redundancy is universalized, 'you can run into anyone down at the unemployment office' (Beck 1998: 55). In the risk society employment-related risks and opportunities 'are sluiced through the channels of individualization' (Mythen 2005: 133). As the risk regime develops, employers and the state lose structural autonomy and control, traditional collective networks of support and security collapse, and individuals are forced to assume responsibility for shaping their own biographies (Mythen 2004).

For a majority of people, even in the apparently prosperous middle layers, their basic existence and life-world will be marked by economic insecurity. More and more individuals are encouraged to perform as 'Me and Co', selling themselves on the market place. (Beck 2000: 3)

Most commentators agree that there is a consistent trend towards increasing flexibilization, and consequently insecurity and risk of unemployment, in Britain's labour market (Ford 1998; Wheelock 1999; Quilgars and Abbott 2000). However, whilst the labour market may be perceived as a site of general insecurity, empirical evidence suggests that risks continue to be unequally distributed. Labour Force Survey figures showed unemployment rates at six times as great for unskilled workers at 12 per cent in 1997, compared to a low of 2 per cent for professionals (Cebulla et al. 1998). Unskilled workers remain more at risk of recurrent and prolonged periods of unemployment; gender divides between the sexes continue to be reproduced through unequal pay, status, and conditions and the unemployment rate for men from minority groups continues to be disproportionately high. Some working age families in Britain experience combinations of disadvantage which mean that they are almost certain to have no work. These disadvantages include being a lone parent; having low qualifications and skills, being disabled; being aged over 50; living in an area with a high-unemployment rate, and being a member of a minority ethnic group (Berthoud 2003). There is also evidence to suggest that gay men and lesbians face discrimination in the workplace (Sussman 1996; Citizens Advice Bureaux 2003). Keogh, Dodds, and Henderson's (2004) study of working class gay men found that their sexuality had adversely affected their education and employment opportunities, many were unemployed or working in moderately paid jobs that they did not enjoy.

The Government explicitly recognize that the Disabled population in general are doing far less well than non-disabled people in the labour market (Cabinet Office 2005). Burchardt (2003) writes that this disadvantage is by no means random and that those who are already significantly disadvantaged (in terms of, e.g. being poor or having low educational qualifications) are at significantly greater risk of becoming disabled and subsequently experiencing unemployment or reductions in income. Within the population of disabled people overall, those with learning difficulties do even less well. Of an estimated population of 1.2 million, Beyer et al. (2004) suggest that only 35 per cent of adults with learning difficulties are in employment. Williams et al. (2004) highlight the barriers to labour market participation for people with learning difficulties including widely held beliefs that people with learning difficulties are unable to work, severe benefit disincentives, difficulties in accessing transport to get to work, and a lack of information about work options and the rights of disabled people in the workplace.

The risks and uncertainties which, Beck argues, have permeated all walks of life, including work and employment, do not have the same consequences for all. Some individuals have a safety net of their own in the form of highly marketable skills and knowledge, and this gives them the confidence to take risks in relation to their employment and livelihood, for example, giving up well-paid jobs to become self-employed (Tulloch and Lupton 2003). Disadvantaged social groups, however, experience higher levels of unemployment, are more likely to be employed in the peripheral workforce, and continue to habitually live under the spectre of job insecurity (Mythen 2005).

Quilgars and Abbott (2000) explored the issues of how labour market risks are perceived and managed within the workplace and the family. They questioned whether people reflexively reflect on their situations and act on these thoughts to protect themselves and their families as rational choice economic theory would suggest. The research demonstrated that individuals, irrespective of class, age, or gender, believed, as Beck has contended, that the labour market in Britain in the 1990s had become increasingly risky. Similar findings are reported by Taylor-Gooby (2001*a*) in a study of risk and contingency and Tulloch and Lupton (2003) in their study of people's understanding of and responses to risk in Australia and Britain. Respondents in all three studies believed that secure lifetime employment was no longer a certainty, even among highly educated professionals. These studies found that people were reflexive about their labour market positions. They described the changing nature of work, the implications of global and technological change for their security, and their future employment prospects, in some cases demonstrating a good, insightful knowledge of their local labour markets.

One area where risk theory did seem to describe people's experiences was in responses in the workplace. Workers in all types of employment felt relatively powerless in the face of labour market restructuring and globalization (Quilgars and Abbott 2000). Those in non-manual work felt more protected from employment risk with some options open to them to improve their labour market position, but those in manual work had very little personal autonomy in the workplace. What was striking was the highly individualized nature of people's accounts of how they could or could not minimize the risk of unemployment. They spoke of how they, as individuals, had to improve and strengthen their position in whatever way possible, often in competition with others. Collective solutions, most obviously through trade unions, were absent from discussions.

Where risk theory did not reflect Quilgars and Abbott's respondent's (2000) accounts to the same extent was in discussion of financial planning. Evidence from this study supports a growing body of work which demonstrates that people are not as keen to seek individualized solutions as the risk society thesis might suppose. There were a number of reasons for their reluctance: many respondents retained a belief in the role of the state in welfare provision and there was also scepticism of the ability of the private sector to protect them. Research has also found that people find it difficult to estimate the risks of certain events happening to them (such as divorce, ill health, and unemployment) and are often mistaken about their own futures (Rowlingson 2000; Taylor-Gooby 2001*a*). In addition lack of knowledge or financial capability (often, although not always, associated with low educational levels and class) can be a barrier to planning. Even where people are both willing and able to think and plan ahead, their capacity to do so is often limited by economic insecurity and lack of resources. The majority of respondents in the higher socio-economic groups in Quilgars and Abbott's study were heavily involved in financial planning, but for the majority of lower class respondents neither saving nor investment was an option. As one respondent remarked

[Financial planning is] ... *important if you can afford to do it. But if you can't afford to do it, it's no use talking about something that's just a pipe dream.* (Quilgars and Abbott 2000: 28)

The evidence clearly shows a consistent trend towards increasing flexibilization, and consequently insecurity and risk of unemployment, in Britain's labour market. In support of risk society theories, empirical studies suggest that people are reflexive, they consider the risks they face, and how these might be avoided, for example by strengthening their labour market position, often in a highly individualized way. Nevertheless, it is evident that risk and insecurity in the labour market continue to be structured by existing inequalities, and that the ability to behave reflexively, to exercise choice, and to plan for contingencies such as unemployment is highly dependent on socio-economic factors and existing inequalities.

Older Age and Retirement

Theorists of post-modernity have seen older age as a prime site of the agency, choice, and reflexivity that contemporary society allows (Giddens 1991; Beck 1992; Gilleard 1996; Gilleard and Higgs 2000). In the risk society, older people have the opportunity (and the risk) of decisions about who they want to be in retirement and how they will live. 'Retirement has been reinvented as a time of transition to a new life, rather than simply the end of an old one' (Hockey and James 2003: 102). Whilst some commentators focus on the opportunities for older people in the risk society, others focus on the political economy of ageing and the continuity of experiences structured by class, gender, race, and other inequalities. Research on the needs of older people with learning difficulties, for example, suggests that they face great constraints around making choices in older age (as they often do when younger), that they enter residential or nursing care at an earlier age and suffer boredom, and isolation (Foundation for People with Learning Disabilities 2002). Heaphy, Yip, and Thompson (2003) found that amongst older gay men and lesbians, discrimination in the workplace had adversely affected their chances of financial security in old age. An adequate level of income in old age is obviously an important element (in addition to physical, emotional, and mental well-being) in maintaining quality of life but research suggests that recent changes in pension policy will do little to alleviate the relative poverty of many older citizens.

The Government has promised security in retirement for those who cannot afford to provide for themselves and a strengthened private pensions framework for those who can. In return, it expects individuals, wherever possible, to provide for their own retirement (Ring 2003). For Mann (2003: 2)

'... the message is clear; a private pension ensures the consumer is planning and making choices ... people with private pensions want to be in control of their own lives, not dependent on others. Self-reliance is good, dependency bad'.

A climate of risk and uncertainty surrounds pensions and retirement in the UK as pension schemes collapse, final salary schemes are closed to new entrants, and many of those who have taken out personal pensions have seen the value of their savings diminish. Research suggests that it is the less well off who are at most risk, they are likely to have the greatest difficulty in understanding the pensions market, be unable to find or afford advice, and find themselves at greater risk of falling into reliance upon means tested state provision (Ring 2003). Yet it is these very groups, the low to medium earners, that the government is particularly encouraging to make some or more provision.

Poverty and inequality in old age is largely a result of disadvantage, during working life, of low pay, and/or exclusion from the labour market. As Fennell, Phillipson, and Evers (1988: 93) note 'it is in the retirement transition that the individual calls upon the resources he or she has developed during the early and middle phases of the life-cycle.' A measure of exclusion is built into private and occupational pension schemes due to the way the labour market and pension funds operate (see the discussion of insurance in Chapter 2). The inherent limitations include actuarial assumptions based on the length of employment, contribution records and age of retirement, access to the sort of employment that provides a pension, discrimination within, and the imperfections of the labour market and, more recently, employer demands for a more flexible workforce, less full-time employment, and less people on permanent contracts. Most significantly, occupational pensions and provisions based on labour market access offer nothing to those whose work is unpaid—mainly women who remain at greater risk of poverty in old age (Mann 2003).

Ginn (2001) raises the question of whether women's pension prospects are likely to improve in the future. It is clear that the current government expects most mothers of school age children to be in employment, but gaps for child rearing and other caring responsibilities (e.g. for elderly relatives) will continue to reduce the years of pension contributions and also future earnings prospects. In a privatized pension system the lower lifetime earnings of those who undertake caring commitments translate directly into lower pension income. In contrast, state pensions (basic and earnings related) can protect women by compensating for breaks in employment and lower earnings whilst providing family care. If the basic pension is allowed to wither away, increasing numbers of lone older women will face means testing, whilst many working age women are also likely to find their second-tier pension insufficient to compensate for the lower basic pension, drawing them into means testing.

Ginn and Arber (2001) examine the extent of ethnic disadvantage in private pension scheme arrangements and analyse variation according to gender and specific ethnic group, using three years of the British Family Resources Survey, which provides information on over 97,000 adults aged 20–59, including over 5,700 from ethnic minorities. They found both men and women in minority ethnic groups were less likely to have private pension coverage than their white counterparts, but the extent of difference was most marked for Pakistanis and Bangladeshis. A minority ethnic disadvantage in private pension coverage, for both men and women, remained after taking account of age, marital and parental status, years of education, employment variables, class, and income. The research suggests that minority ethnic groups—especially women— will be disproportionately dependent on means-tested benefits in later life, due to the combined effects of low private pension coverage and the policy of shifting pension provision towards the private sector. The short employment records of the largely migrant older ethnic population, discriminatory processes operating in the labour market against ethnic minorities, limited type and availability of jobs in areas of settlement, and lack of language fluency and certain cultural norms may all contribute to a lower lifetime income and hence to poorer pension entitlements in old age compared with the white majority (Ginn and Arber 2001; Pilley 2003). However, there is considerable diversity among different minority ethnic groups: the extent of disadvantage in lifetime earnings relative to the majority white population varies, depending on migration timing and circumstances as well as other factors. Further, since gender and class influence employment participation and pension arrangements, it is likely that structural inequalities exist within each minority ethnic group (Ginn and Arber 2001).

It is clear that in pension provision, as in other areas of welfare policy, there is (and will continue to be) a hierarchy of risk that corresponds with some very traditional forms of social inequality and with different elements of the social division of labour. From this perspective, Giddens' and new Labour's 'third way' appear:

blinkered by traditional definitions of welfare and dependency.... It also returns us to a very traditional road paved with Victorian ideas of self-help and populated by the 'reflexive' professional middle classes...the dismissal of public pensioners (most whom will be working class women) as embedded in a culture of dependency is offensive. It neglects the hierarchy or privileges—and the greater risks—imposed by the different elements of the social division of welfare. (Mann 2003: 14–15)

Emerging Problems and Issues

Empirical evidence suggests that, in accordance with the risk society thesis, individualization is becoming a feature of everyday life. Beck's appreciation of the inherently unstable quality of 'tightrope biographies' resonates with the uncertainties and insecurities faced by many people in western cultures who are faced with the constant demands of planning and shaping their futures and living with uncertainty. However, whilst research studies provide some support for the contention that the broader structuring factors characteristic of industrial society may have weakened somewhat in their influence in the contemporary era, particularly in the move towards individualization, it can be seen that they are still important (Furlong and Cartmel 1997; Lupton 1999: 113; Elliot 2002). Despite promising greater scope for creativity and choice, individualization tends to underplay the influence of structural inequalities that empirical evidence shows still exist and shape the lives of individual actors and groups (Furlong and Cartmel 1997; Taylor-Gooby 2001a, 2001b; Mitchell et al. 2001). However, as these empirical studies suggest, it does appear that whilst many groups and individuals continue to face similar risks as in the past, for example, poverty and unemployment, the way risks are perceived and experienced has changed. In the risk society, inequalities are viewed as individualized, perceived as 'psychological dispositions: as personal inadequacies, guilt feelings, anxieties, conflicts, and neuroses' (Beck 1992: 100).

As individuals assume a greater role in making their own choices then too they assume greater responsibility for the consequences of their choices and actions (Mythen 2004; Zinn 2004). To choose the wrong kind of university degree, occupation, or marriage partner, to become unemployed, or to have an inadequate pension tend to be considered the outcome of an individual's faulty planning or decision-making rather than the outcome of broader social processes (Warde 1994; Lupton 1999; Zinn 2002). Social crises such as mass unemployment are reduced to aggregates of individual failures, a lack of skills on the part of the individual rather than a general decline in demand for labour stemming from world economic recession. The individualization of risk may mean that situations which would once have led to a call for political action are now interpreted as something which can only be solved on an individual level through personal action (Furlong and Cartmel 1997).

The adoption of third way approaches in social policy serves to justify policies which stress individual responsibility but such policies tend to support the interests of groups whose material and cultural resources make them most able to deal with the contingencies of risk society and confront the interests of those groups least able to meet the needs they experience (Taylor-Gooby 2001a). Risk society theory implies value-consensus and social changes are understood as applying equally to all members in society whereas the empirical evidence suggests that some groups are more vulnerable to risks. There is a danger, as Mann (2003) and others have argued, that the needs of the most vulnerable and disadvantaged, those who are unable to behave in a calculating, rational way will be neglected. As noted above, individuals are also likely to be blamed for their decisions, their behaviour, or their inability to save or to meet their own needs.

The attack on 'dependency culture' reveals a hatred of the very idea of dependency and a refusal (and one which also finds support within some radical voices within social policy) to accept that some people need continuing support to cope with their lives. There seems to be real contempt around for people who cannot or will not be 'empowered' at the moment, especially if they are not obviously physically incapacitated in some way. (Hoggett 2001: 44)

The unrelenting reproduction of inequalities in Western Europe suggests that social class remains a significant yardstick of life chances in contemporary society. Access to material resources continues to be the key determinant of action and it is therefore unlikely that the radical restructuring of cultural experience outlined in the risk society thesis has transpired (Elliot 2002; Mythen 2005). Regardless of whether class *identity* has weakened, empirical evidence suggests that the degree and intensity of individualization continues to be mediated by existing inequalities of class, gender, ethnicity, and age as well as other differences such as sexuality and disability. Different social groups are destined to encounter contrasting life experiences, with insecurity and risk being concentrated amongst the poorest and most disadvantaged.

Note

1. The single room rent, which apples only to single claimants under 25 years of age living in privately rented accommodation, is effectively a ceiling on the maximum rent that can be taken into account when housing benefit is calculated. It does not directly affect the amount of rent a landlord can charge which can lead to a shortfall between what a young person receives in benefit and the amount they pay in rent.

References

Alexander, J. (1996). 'Critical Reflections on "Reflexive Modernization"', *Theory, Culture and Society*, 13: 133–8.

Baxter, A. and Britton, C. (2001). 'Risk, Identity and Change: Becoming a Mature Student', *International Studies in Sociology of Education*, vol. 11(1): 87–102.

Beck, U. (1992). *Risk Society*. London: Sage.

—— (1998). *Democracy Without Enemies*. Cambridge: Polity Press.

—— (2000). *Brave New World of Work*. Cambridge: Polity Press.

Berthoud, R. (2003). *Multiple Disadvantage in Employment: A Quantitative Analysis*. York: York Publishing Services.

Beyer, S., Grove, B., Schneider, J., Simons, K., Williams, V., Heyman, A., Swift, P., and Krijnen-Kemp, E. (2004). *Working Lives: The Role of Day Centres in Supporting People with Learning Disabilities into Employment*. London: Department for Work and Pensions (Research Report 23).

Bottero, W. and Irwin, S. (2003). 'Locating Difference: Class, 'Race' and Gender, and the Shaping of Social Inequalities', *The Sociological Review*, 51(4): 463–83.

Burchardt, T. (2003). 'Being and Becoming: Social Exclusion and the Onset of Disability', CASE Report 21, ESRC Centre for the Analysis of Social Exclusion, London School of Economics.

Burchell, B., Day, D., Hudson, M., Lapido, D., Mankelow, R., Nolan, J., Reed, H., Wichert, I., and Wilkinson, F. (1999). *Job Insecurity and Work Intensification: Flexibility and the Changing Boundaries of Work*. York: YPS.

Cabinet Office: Prime Minister's Strategy Unit (2005). *Improving the Life Chances of Disabled People*. London: Strategy Unit.

CASE and HM Treasury (1999). *Tackling Poverty and Extending Opportunity: The Modernisation of Britain's Tax and Benefit System Number Four*. London: HM Treasury.

Cebulla, A., Abbott, D., Ford, J., Middleton, S., Quilgars, D., and Walker, R. (1998). 'A Geography of Insurance Exclusion—Perceptions of Unemployment Risk and Actuarial Risk Assessment'. Paper presented to the Second European Urban and Regional Studies Conference, University of Durham, September.

Citizens Advice Bureaux (CAB) (2003). *Evidence*. London: Citizens Advice Bureaux, April.

Culpitt, I. (1999). *Social Policy and Risk*. London: Sage.

Department of Social Security (1998). *A New Contract for Welfare: Partnerships in pensions*. London: The Stationery Office.

Dingwall, R. (1999). 'Risk Society: The Cult of Theory and the Millennium?' *Social Policy and Administration*, 33(4): 474–91.

Edwards, R. and Glover, J. (eds.) (2001). *Risk and Citizenship: Key Issues in Welfare*. London: Routledge.

Elliot, A. (2002). 'Beck's Sociology of Risk: A Critical Assessment', *Sociology*, 36(2): 293–315.

Fennell, G., Phillipson, C., and Evers, H. (1988). *The Sociology of Old Age*. Milton Keynes: Open University Press.

Ford, J. (1998). *Risks, Home Ownership and Job Insecurity*. London: Shelter.

Foundation for People with Learning Disabilities (2002). *Today and Tomorrow: The Report of the Growing Older with Learning Disabilities Programme*. London: The Foundation for People with Learning Difficulties.

Furlong, A. and Cartmel, F. (1997). *Young People and Social Change: Individualisation and Risk in Late Modernity*. Buckingham, UK: Open University Press.

Giddens, A. (1991). *Modernity and Self Identity. Self and Society in the Late Modern Age*. Oxford: Polity Press.

——(1991). *Modernity and Self-Identity*. Cambridge: Polity Press.

——(1994). *Beyond Left and Right*. Cambridge: Polity Press.

——(1998). *The Third Way: the Renewal of Social Democracy*. Cambridge: Polity Press.

Gilleard, C. (1996). 'Consumption and Identity in Later Life: Toward a Cultural Gerontology', *Ageing and Society*, 16: 489–98.

——and Higgs, P. (2000). *Cultures of Ageing*. Harlow: Pearson Education Ltd.

Ginn, J. (2001). From Security to Risk: Pension Privatisation and Gender Inequality, Catalyst Working Paper (http://www.catalystforum.org.uk/pubs/paper3.html).

——and Arber, S. (2001). 'Pension Prospects of Minority Ethnic Groups: Inequalities by Gender and Ethnicity', *British Journal of Sociology*, 52(3): 519–39.

Glennerster, H., Hills, J., Piachaud, D., and Webb, J. (2004). *One Hundred Years of Poverty and Policy*. York: The Joseph Rowntree Foundation.

Green, E. (2004). 'Risky Identities: Young Women Doing Street Prostitution and "Doing Motherhood"', in W. Mitchell, R. Bunton, and E. Green (eds.), *Young*

People, Risk and Leisure: Constructing Identities in Everyday life. Basingstoke, UK: Palgrave Macmillan.

——Mitchell, W., and Bunton, R. (2000). 'Contextualising Risk and Danger: An Analysis of Young People's Perceptions of Risk', *Journal of Youth Studies*, 3: 109–26.

Heaphy, B. T., Yip, A. K. T., and Thompson, D. (2003). 'The Social and Policy Implications of Non-heterosexual Ageing', *Quality in Ageing*, 4(3): 30–5.

Hobcraft, J. (1998). *Intergenerational and Life-Course Transmission of Social Exclusion: Influences of Childhood Poverty, Family Disruption and Contact with the Police*. CASE paper 15, Centre for Analysis of Social Exclusion, London: London School of Economics.

Hockey, J. and James, A. (2003). *Social Identities Across the Life Course*. London: Palgrave Macmillan.

Hoggett, P. (2001). 'Agency, Rationality and Social Policy', *Journal of Social Policy*, 30(1): 37–56.

Kemp, P. and Rugg, J. (2001). 'Young People, Housing Benefit and the Risk Society', *Social Policy and Administration*, 35(6): 688–700.

Keogh, P., Dodds, C., and Henderson, L. (2004). *Working Class Gay Men: Redefining Community, Restoring Identity*. London: Sigma Research.

Lash, S. (1993). 'Reflexive Modernization: The Aesthetic Dimension', *Theory, Culture and Society*, 10: 1–23.

Lupton, D. (1999). *Risk*. London: Routledge.

——and Tulloch, J. (2002). 'Risk is Part of Your Life: Risk Epistemologies Among a Group of Australians', *Sociology*, 36(2): 317–34.

Mann, K. (2003). 'The Schlock and the New: Risk, Reflexivity and Retirement', in C. Bochel and N. Ellison et al. (eds.), *Social Policy Review*, 15, Bristol: Policy Press/Social Policy Association.

McKnight, A. (2005). 'Employment: Tackling Poverty Through "Work for Those Who Can"', in J. Hills and K. Stewart (eds.), *A More Equal Society?* Bristol, CT: The Policy Press, pp. 23–46.

McRae, H. (1995). 'There's a Bit of Sting in all of Us', *The Independent*. 19 October: 21.

Mitchell, W. A., Crawshaw, P., Bunton, R., and Green, E. (2001). 'Situating Young People's Experiences of Risk and Identity', *Health, Risk and Society*, 3(2): 217–33.

Molloy, D., Knight, T., and Woodfield, K. (2003). *Diversity in Disability: Exploring the Interactions Between Disability, Ethnicity, Age, Gender and Sexuality*. London: Corporate Document Services.

Morris, J. (2002). *Moving into Adulthood: Young Disabled People Moving into Adulthood*. York: Joseph Rowntree Foundation. http://www.jrf.org.uk/Knowledge/findings/foundations/512.asp.

Mythen, G. (2004). *Ulrich Beck: A Critical Introduction to the Risk Society*. London: Pluto Press.

Mythen, G. (2005) 'Employment, Individualisation and Insecurity: Rethinking the Risk Society Perspective', *The Sociological Review*, 53(1): 129–49.

Palmer, G., Carr, J., and Kenway, P. (2004). *Monitoring Poverty and Social Exclusion 2004*, http://www.poverty.org.uk/reports/mpse2004.pdf

Patrick, A. and John, S. (undated). *Poverty and Social Exclusion of Lesbians and Gay Men in Glasgow*. Glasgow: Glasgow City Council, http://www.womens-library.org.u./ povertystudy.htm

Phillips, C. (2005). 'Ethnic Inequalities Under New Labour: Progress or Entrenchment?', in J. Hills and K. Stewart (eds.), *A More Equal Society?*. Bristol: The Policy Press, pp. 189–208.

Pilley, C. (2003). 'Immigrants and Financial Services: Literacy, Difficulty of Access, Needs and Solutions', Special Report for the FinLit project on Financial Education and Poverty Prevention in Europe. Institut Für Finanzdienstleistungen, Hamburg (unpublished).

Quilgars, D. and Abbott, D. (2000). 'Working in the Risk Society', *Community, Work and Family*, 3(1): 15–36.

Ring, P. (2003). ' "Risk" and UK Pension Reform', *Social Policy and Administration*, 37(1): 65–81.

Rohrmann, B. (1999). *Risk Perception Research*, Arbeiten zur Risiko-Komunication Heft 69, University of Jülich.

Rowlingson, K. (2000). *Fate, Hope and Insecurity: Future Orientation and Forward Planning*. London: Policy Studies Institute.

Skeggs, B. (1997). *Formations of Class and Gender*. London: Sage.

Skinner, C. and Ford, J. (2000). *Planning, Postponing or Hesitating: Understanding Financial Planning*. York: Centre for Housing Policy.

Small, N., Pawson, P., and Raghavan, R. (2003). 'Choice Biography' and the Importance of the Social, *British Journal of Learning Disabilities*, 31: 159–65.

Sussman, T. (1996). 'Gay Men in the Workplace: Issues for Mental Health Counsellors', *Journal of Gay, Lesbian and Bisexual Identity*, 1(3): 193–211.

Taylor-Gooby, P. (2001a). 'Risk, Contingency and the Third Way: Evidence from BHPS and Qualitative Studies', *Social Policy and Administration*, 35(2): 195–211.

—— (2001b). 'Complex Equalities: Redistribution, Class and Gender', in R. Edwards and J. Glover (eds.), *Risk and Citizenship*. London: Routledge.

—— Dean, H., Munro, M., and Parker, G. (1999). 'Risk and the Welfare State', *British Journal of Sociology*, 50(2): 177–95.

Tulloch, J. and Lupton, D. (2003). *Risk and Everyday Life*. London: Sage.

Warde, A. (1994). 'Consumption, Identity-Formation and Uncertainty', *Sociology*, 28(4): 877–98.

Wheeler, B., Shaw, S., Mitchell, R., and Doling, D. (2005). 'The Relationship Between Poverty, Affluence and Area', *Findings*. Joseph Rowntree Foundation, September.

Wheelock, J. (1999). 'Fear or Opportunity? Insecurity in Employment', in J. Vail, J. Wheelock, and M. Hill (eds.), *Insecure Times: Living with Insecurity in Contemporary Society*. London: Routledge.

Williams, V., Tarleton, B., Watson, D., and Johnson, R. (2004). *Nice Job—if You Can Get it: Work and People with Learning Difficulties*. Bristol, CT: Norah Fry Research Centre.

Zinn, J. (2002). 'Conceptual Considerations and an Empirical Approach to Research on Processes of Individualisation', Forum Qualitative Sozialforschung/Qualitative Social Research, 3,1, http://www.qualitative-research.net/fqs-texte/1-02/1-02zinn-e.htm

_____ (2004). 'Health, Risk and Uncertainty in the Life-Course: A Typology of Biographical Certainty Constructions', *Social Theory and Health*, 2(3): 199–221.

12

The Media and Risk

Emma Hughes, Jenny Kitzinger, and Graham Murdock

The Context: Media Attention and 'Expert' Assessment

The column inches of newspaper space and the minutes of television time devoted to risk rarely neatly parallel scientifically defined hierarchies. A death from an aeroplane accident is 6,000 times more likely to make the front page than a death from cancer, and nuclear accidents receive far greater attention than the fatalities caused by smoking (Greenberg et al. 1989). Nor do patterns of media attention parallel the actual trajectory of any particular threat. For example, coverage of salmonella poisoning dramatically decreased, whilst actual incidents increased (Miller and Reilly 1995). Conversely, coverage of river pollution has risen whilst pollution levels have declined (Dunwoody and Peters, 1992: 206). Observing these variations risk professionals are often tempted to complain that journalists exaggerate risks that pose little threat to the public and play down those that do. This ignores the very different roles the two groups play. Professional risk assessment is in the business of calculating how likely a threat is (probability) and how widespread its effects will be (magnitude). Unlike pre-modern notions of 'fate' or 'misfortune' however, contemporary ideas of risk also involve discussions of controllability and preventability, and this inevitability places them firmly in the social and political arena raising difficult questions of accountability and blame.

Historically, journalists have been assigned three major roles in modern democracies; providing full, reliable, and disinterested information on developments that affect collective life; organizing an open arena for voicing and debating public anxieties and concerns; and operating as a watchdog on the performance of corporate and governmental power centres, checking for failures, evasions, and abuses. These roles are now performed in a context in which publics in western democracies have become progressively mistrustful of both politicians and experts (particularly those employed by governments or major corporations) and increasingly concerned about the implications of techno-scientific developments both for the environment and for human health (Beck 1992). They suspect those in power of pursuing their own sectional or professional agendas rather than upholding the public interest (Petts, Horlick-Jones, and Murdock 2001). Consequently, a great deal of risk coverage is taken up with scrutinizing scientific innovations, company activities, and government policies. During the 2001 anthrax attacks in the USA, for example, the press took the opportunity to assess 'the strengths and weaknesses of the nation's public health infrastructure [and] the political and policy backgrounds against which this infrastructure operates' (Winett and Lawrence 2005: 3).

The issue of preparedness (or lack of it) for future anthrax attacks was pushed onto the public agenda by suspected terrorist action, but media attention can also be prompted by more broadly based political action. Mazur's work, for example, has shown that the degree of media interest in nuclear power paralleled the number of participants in the largest anti-nuclear demonstration in each year (cited in Dunwoody and Peters 1992: 206–7). In both cases coverage was picking up on the social and political concerns of readers and audiences. Rather than seeing the media's role as a simple 'mirror' for expert definitions and assessments of risk these writers argue that it is entirely appropriate that news coverage should take account of issues around risk management, accountability, justice, and the possibilities for action, rather than simply focus on the likelihood or magnitude of a threat (Lichtenberg and MacLean 1991: 165–7).

Major Research Themes: Modelling Mediation—Transportation and Construction

These disagreements about the way media should operate in complex democracies are indicative of a deeper division between two very different models of how mediated communication works, which have led to two different traditions of research. Professional risk managers and researchers have tended to see media as transportation systems whose main role is to disseminate the risk information and assessments arrived at by experts with the minimum amount of alteration, interference, and 'noise'. Borrowing metaphors from engineering they envisage newspapers and broadcasting stations as relay posts transmitting messages about risk to individual receivers who then decode and assimilate them. Even in its more sophisticated variants, represented by the influential social amplification of risk (SARF) model developed by Kasperson and his collaborators (see Kasperson and Kasperson 1996), this model cannot deal adequately with the complex social and symbolic organization of risk communication. In transportation accounts the media system is all too often presented as a black box, an undifferentiated institutional nexus, rather than a highly differentiated field of action in which media organizations compete for audience time and attention in clearly demarcated markets, tabloid and broadsheet, commercial and public service, governed by different rules, requirements, and pressures. The emphasis on information transfer and the dominant metaphor of 'message' relay is too one dimensional to catch the way additional layers of meaning are generated by the connotations carried by key phrases and images. Audiences are viewed primarily as individuals rather and as members of social networks embedded in specific social location that offer access to particular kinds of resources for interpretation and response (see Murdock, Petts, and Horlick-Jones 2003). As a result the transportation approach has tended to be replaced by approaches which emphasize the part played by different actors and forces in the social construction of media messages.

In this conception, risk communication is seen as a continual process of construction. Journalists and programme makers produce risk accounts out of the materials obtained through established routines of surveillance, search, and assembly. Language and imagery combine on the page or on the screen to assemble a range of meanings. Audiences draw on their stock of interpretive resources to develop their own interpretations and then take them for discursive outings in the course of everyday talk and argument. Since most recent research on risk communication has worked with some variant or other of this constructionist approach, it forms the main focus for this chapter. We review recent research across these three areas, examining the role of journalists and institutions in making the news, the interaction between the imagery which informs media messages and the reality communicated, and the role of audiences in actively contributing to the interpretation of media output.

Recent Findings: Making the News

The news media are both complex organizations working with finite resources and tight deadlines and (with the major exception of public broadcasting organizations) commercial businesses competing for audiences and advertisers. These two institutional features combine to shape the routine coverage of risk in powerful and predicable ways and help to determine *which* risks attract attention, *how, when, who, why*, and *under what conditions*. In examining how these decisions get to be made, researchers have identified two key factors; the organization of the production process (particularly the imperative of meeting daily deadlines) and the way the relations between journalists and their sources are organized; and journalists' professional conceptions of what makes a 'good' story (the features that make an event newsworthy and the properties of an impactful image, photograph, or piece of film).

Sources and Relations

Source–journalist relations have a major impact on how stories are initially defined or 'framed'. The initial British press stories voicing concerns about GM foods and crops, for example, frequently referred to the earlier BSE (Mad Cow disease) crisis (Murdock 2004). By establishing this parallel they invited readers to look for a repeat of the government's prevarication, deception, and perceived lack of concern with public health. This frame gained ground because there was no settled scientific consensus on the long-term impacts of GM foods. Since the evidence was itself at issue (Hargreaves and Ferguson 2000) demands from the government and the established scientific community for factual accuracy in reporting made little headway and the way was left open for critical and oppositional voices to set the agenda. Eventually, the government was forced to respond to public concern by establishing an independent national debate on the issues, *GM Nation?*, supported by a series of sustained investigations into possible impacts (see Understanding Risk Team 2004).

This remains however an exception. Generally, research shows that the media privilege 'official sources': (Stallings 1990; Scahnne and Meier 1992) and that press releases and announcements of policy initiatives are a key source of news stories. Releasing information at pre-arranged press conferences with carefully arranged deadlines consolidates the power of official voices. Information that can be attributed to an 'official' source is less likely to be scrutinized for validity than information from 'alternative' sources. Journalists will often rely on the 'bureaucratically visible' rather than those with most direct expertise (Shepherd 1981; Dunwoody and Peters 1992). They may also feel freer to present 'contentious' statements if these can be identified as official. A lack of policy events will often mean a lack of media interest. Journalists and editors interviewed in the mid 1990s, for example, commented that genetics was not a 'big news story' because of the lack of legislation, and those talking about BSE commented that as 'nothing was happening' it was no longer of media interest (Kitzinger and Reilly 1997).

Where reporting about risks involves a crisis, such as a sudden flash flood, this privileging of official voices is likely to be even more prominent and journalists will often seek out an 'information-csar', relying on a single official source which they feel to be reliable and trustworthy (Schanne and Werner 1992: 152). In the face of tight deadlines in a 'disaster' journalists will turn to those agencies seen to have responsibility for a specific topic. Early reports therefore may frame the crisis in ways which exclude the perspectives of 'opposition groups', except where there are established patterns of contact (Stallings 1990; Freudenburg et al. 1996).

However, journalists may shift the ground rules once the immediate crisis is past and they redefine a story as a 'risk story'. They may then become more critical of official sources, concerned about motives and open to treating different positions as legitimate (Dunwoody and Peters 1992). They may also take more account of the speaker's willingness to go beyond formal risk assessment statements to comment on political problems and solutions. Sources on different sides of a debate may differ in their willingness to do this. If official sources are seen to 'hold back' on journalists, they will be more prepared to seek out alternative opinions and give a platform to 'mavericks' (Kitzinger and Reilly 1997).

Journalist-source relations are not shaped solely by journalists' choices and preferences, however. The resources commanded by 'claims makers' seeking (or responding) to media attention also play a major role. Government and corporate sources have bigger budgets and teams of dedicated PR people. This enables them to stay in the definitional contest to frame issues for longer. In the first phase of US press coverage of silicone breast implants in the 1990s, for example, coverage focused on the health risks and featured testimony from women who alleged they had been damaged. Following a major public relations campaign by the leading manufacturer, Corning, however, later coverage was dominated by industry assurances that implants were safe (Powers and Andsager 1999). Also, as Hansen argues, in his case study of Greenpeace's occupation of the redundant Brent Spar oil platform designed to prevent Shell from sinking it in the North Sea, whilst critical voices can command news attention for their claims through dramatic, highly visual, actions they have much more difficulty controlling the way their claims are framed and inflected by individual newspapers. Whereas the left of centre tabloid, the *Daily Mirror,* hailed Shell's decision not to sink the rig as a 'Victory For the People', the conservative broadsheet, the *Daily Telegraph,* attacked it as 'A Triumph for the Forces of Ignorance' (Hansen 2000). Governments on the other hand often have less room for manoeuvre than corporations and the efficacy of official sources may be undermined by bureaucratic and political restrictions (inhibiting them from providing a quick and 'quotable' response to journalists' enquiries). Alternative sources may have 'better' resources in terms of being able to process requests quickly, provide vivid quotes, and produce 'human interest' stories or dramatic demonstrations that make for good pictures (Kitzinger 1998; Miller et al. 1998).

These requirements stem from a wider set of journalistic conceptions of what makes a good story. These 'news values' are shared by reporters working in widely different news organizations and help account for the relatively stability of general patterns of risk coverage.

Constructing Newsworthiness

The media will tend to focus on risks which kill or injure many people at one time (e.g. a plane crash), rather than those which have a cumulative effect over the year (e.g. car crashes) (see Singer and Endreny 1987; Hansen 1994). Routine sources of danger (such as traffic accidents) are less newsworthy than sudden catastrophes and unusual risks are more attractive than common risks (Dunwoody and Peters 1992: 205). Reporting also tends to be 'event' orientated rather than issue orientated (Kristiansen 1988). A crisis such as a famine will attract attention; the process which leads up to this crisis has little media value (a tendency which has dire consequences for commitments to prevent, rather than simply respond to, such problems).

The reporting of risk is also influenced by the pace at which a threat unfolds and how evidence is marshalled and procedures launched as 'news events'. Long-term and continuous developments (such as environmental degradation) have less chance of breaking into news production cycles because journalists are concerned with the 'news of the day' (Hansen 1991). A geographically bounded event—such as an oil spill—will also provide a more media friendly crisis than one without a 'news centre'. To counter these structural biases environmental activists have become skilled at creating news events that fit compressed time frames whilst highlighting longer term risks and which offer journalists dramatic images that encapsulate the core arguments and allow people to visualize an invisible or hidden risk. During the campaign against the commercial planting of GM crops in Britain, protest groups around the country invaded fields hosting trial plantings and ripped up crops dressed in the same kind of white protection suits as those worn by the workers who entered the Chernobyl nuclear power station after fire had destroyed the reactor. By establishing an instantly recognizable association between the alleged health and environmental impacts of GM and the proven environmental contamination and cancer clusters caused by the failure the Chernobyl plant these highly photogenic costumes created a powerful image of widespread, long-lasting, contamination (Murdock 2004).

Another key factor influencing media attention, particularly in the tabloid press, is the existence of a 'human angle' to the story, a personal face to the tragedy (Hansen 1994). News stories about risk often feature personal accounts—the soldier claiming to suffer from gulf war syndrome, the parents who believe their child's autism was caused by vaccination, and the father who protests that the allegations of abuse made against him by his adult daughter are liable to be false memories induced by psychoanalysis. The ability of personal accounts to engage audience interest can get a risk onto the news agenda in spite of official denials (Kitzinger 1998; Boyce 2005). However, the other side of this coin is that when a risk is still hypothetical and there are no proven victims to talk to, a story is less attractive to journalists. For example, it was not until journalists could interview people suffering from the brain disease associated BSE that media attention fully re-focused on the problem (Kitzinger and Reilly 1997). Emerging diseases with long gestation periods may thus not attract media attention until it is 'too late'.

Journalists' judgements about the perceived relevance of a risk will be influenced by the degree of cultural, political, or geographical proximity of the threat to themselves and their perceived audiences (Adams 1986; Lichtenberg and MacLean 1991; Kitzinger 1998). For example, when 52 people died in a terrorist attack in the London underground and on a bus in July 2005 this received front page coverage across the UK media. The dead and injured were honoured and commemorated by an official two minute silence and the threat of future attacks discussed at length. However, far less attention is paid to the threats posed to civilians in other countries. In Iraq, for example, almost twenty-five thousand civilians were killed between March 2003 and 2005—the equivalent of the London bombings every two days, day in, day out, for three years. These deaths barely registered in the UK media (in contrast to reports of every death of a British soldier involved in the conflict) (Kirby and Davies 2005).

The cultural obsession with celebrity also structures risk reporting, particularly in tabloid titles, ensuring that risks which impact on stars and public personalities are likely to get more attention than those that simply affect the 'ordinary person'. As a consequence, we may come to know about the threat of different diseases through the lens of celebrity afflictions (Rogers and Chang 1991). *Where* the tragedy strikes, and *to whom*, is therefore a key factor in determining the extent of attention it receives. Although the cross-national reach of the contemporary mass media offers a potential basis for the emergence of an increasing global civil cosmopolitan sensibilities in ways which support environmental responsibilities (Szerszynski and Toogood 2000) in practice reporting about risk often gets caught up in discourses of national (or ethnic or religious) self-interest. Risks are often portrayed as originating elsewhere and crossing national borders through immigration and tourism ('terrorism'), imports and smuggling (proscribed GM materials), or bird migration (avian flu).

Who is identified as a *source* of threat is also significant in determining the extent of media interest often a problematic aspect of media reporting. This can be illustrated by looking at the risk to children of murder or sexual assault. Research shows that journalists are much more interested in the threat posed by strangers than that posed by relatives. The abduction and murder of children by strangers is cause for national shock and alarm. But headlines such as: 'WEEP, 3 children murdered in 100 hrs as Britain sinks to a new low' (*Sun*, 14 August 1991) ignore the evidence that 150 to 200 children meet their death every year at the hands of their own mother or father. One child is killed in this way every few days, year in, year out (NSPCC 1992). Stranger-danger stories, however, have far greater appeal to journalists. They offer a clear 'other' to be made a villain of the piece— 'the predatory paedophile' and the random and public nature of such attacks makes every reader or viewer feel that their child is potentially at risk from the 'pervert on the loose'. By contrast, journalists see cases of abduction or sexual assault by relatives as less palatable to their listeners, readers, or viewers (see Kitzinger 2004).

As we noted earlier, questions of accountability and blame often feature prominently in risk reporting. The ability to blame someone (an official, an institution, the government) may be an important criterion in attracting the media to a story (Sandman, Weinstein, and Klotz 1987).

257

Scientific uncertainty is not necessarily attractive to journalists, but controversy *is* (Kitzinger and Reilly 1997). Media interest tends be heightened where there is overt conflict between stakeholders (Peters 1995), perceived government failures, or clear evidence of vested interests promoting a particular position or attempting to silence or discredit oppositional voices (Miller and Reilly 1995). By the same token, a story may disappear from public view once blame is seen to lie at the door of ordinary individuals rather than experts or those in authority. For example, the salmonella in eggs story was 'resolved' once *consumers* rather than *producers* were seen to be at fault (Miller and Reilly 1995).

Recent Findings

From Actuality to Fiction

Up until now we have concentrated on news reporting of risk since that is what most of the research to date has focused on. However, if we want to understand how risk is represented in contemporary public culture and how these representations provide resources for everyday understandings and misunderstandings it is vital to take account of non-news media, particularly fiction. Whilst in some ways the *news* media are ill adapted for addressing potential risks (as opposed to crises or disasters which have already occurred) fiction is a rich mine of imagery and narratives about the future and a major cultural space in which to explore issues of ethics, power, and responsibility. A systematic comparison of how human genetic research was represented in news and fiction over one year found that fictional formats were much more able to represent aspects of the ethical and social conflict around genetic developments and that it was through fiction, rather than news reporting, that the media most thoroughly explored some of the challenges that new genetic knowledge might present to individuals in the future (Kitzinger et al. 2000). This is an exception however. To date, comparatively little systematic research has been done in this area by scholars interested in risk, but we can usefully sketch in some of the key issues by looking more closely at the most famous popular fiction of risk, Mary Shelley's *Frankenstein*.

Originally published in 1818 it was adapted for the stage five years later as, *Presumption: Or the Fate of Frankenstein*, and has enjoyed continued currency in western popular culture ever since, providing the basis for countless comic books, cartoons, films, and fancy dress costumes

(Graham 2002). In the process it has become 'the governing myth of modern biology' (Turney 1998: 3), a readily available reservoir of images and discourse that has been drawn on in successive debates on the implications of the next wave of genetic research and its applications.

As the GM debate in Britain illustrates, it offered powerful symbolic ammunition to critics of incorporating GM ingredients into foodstuffs and allowing commercial plantings. Protesters dressed as the monster appeared on demonstrations and picket lines. The tag 'Frankenstein Foods' achieved widespread currency in news reports and formed the basis of the public campaign against GM launched by the *Daily Mail*, Britain's second largest circulation national daily paper. Another best selling daily, the *Daily Mirror*, drew on the image of Baron Frankenstein's obsessive pursuit of his project and his total disregard for other people's opinion, to produce a font page lampooning Tony Blair's support for the GM industry. Headed, 'The Prime Monster: Fury as Blair says: I eat Frankenstein Food 'and it's Safe'' it carried a digitally manipulated portrait of the Prime Minister in the image of the monster made famous by Boris Karloff in the 1931 film of the story (Murdock 2004).

Frankenstein is the pre-eminent tale of science overreaching its proper limits and of reason producing technologies that their creators can no longer control. It belongs firmly in the Gothic tradition of narratives that challenged the Enlightenment ideal of 'progress' with its axial assumption that the practical application of scientific breakthroughs would produce a continuous stream of individual benefits and social betterment. Later science fictions, however, were as likely to be utopian as dystopian. When Gernsbach, the founder of modern science fiction, launched his magazine *Amazing Stories* in 1926, he set out to champion progressivism and technological benevolence (Graham 2002: 27). This positive deployment of futuristic images is still very much in play in contemporary discussions. For example, in the debates about the risks of changing the law to allow embryos to be used in stem cell research it was proponents of these moves, not their opponents, who referred to science fiction scenarios (Kitzinger and Williams 2005).

Understanding Risk

The webs of meanings offered by media accounts and representations of risk, both factual and fictional, provide one of the key sources that people can draw on in developing their own understandings and responses. As we mentioned at the outset however, constructionist accounts of sense making see this process as always and everywhere thoroughly social. Instead of looking for direct relations between individualized consumption and personalized responses this approach explores how mediated accounts intersect with grounded experience and vernacular knowledge, how people's present responses are shaped by their past biographies, and how provisional interpretations are continually tested, modified, or confirmed through everyday conversation and argument. The guiding image is of diverse publics with a variety of 'biographical and social histories' drawing on 'a number of circuits of communication in facing a wide range of risks' in a diversity of concrete circumstances (Tulloch and Lupton 2001: 5; Tulloch and Lupton 2003).

In this approach the notion of a simple 'hypodermic' effect on our perceptions is decisively rejected and the media's role in informing public responses to risk is seen as part of more complex sociocultural process. We come to risk stories already 'primed with culturally learned assumptions and weightings' (Douglas 1992: 58; cited in Lutpon 1999: 37) and we have other sources of knowledge, which rather than being dismissed as superstition or ignorance can be seen as 'lay expertise' (Wynne 1996). Attention to micro-narratives of how people assess risk shows that our responses are reflective and strongly shaped by both our social location (Tulloch and Lupton 2003: 132) and our negotiations of our self-identity (as belonging or not belonging to an at risk group) (Macgill 1989). This does not mean, however, that the media are without influence or that their impact is impossible to identify.

Media-oriented research suggests that the *quantity* of media coverage accorded to different types of risk can help inform how we think about safety and danger by helping to set the agenda for concern informing different waves of public anxiety at different points—concern shifting from worries about particular diseases, to the 'problem' of 'young people today', illegal drugs or the threats associated with the internet or terrorism. Sometimes the sheer amount of media attention to the potential of a risk can set the agenda, even if the bulk of reporting concludes that the risk is negligible. This was clearly the case in the flurry of attention to the safety of the MMR (mumps, measles, and rubella) vaccine. The very fact that the media gave extensive attention to debates about the vaccine's safety, even if most coverage came down on the side of the vaccine, raised questions about a previously routinely accepted medical procedure. By getting people to think about the MMR vaccine the media set the scene for a change in take-up rates that, policymakers feared, could lead to a disease epidemic (Petts and Niemeyer 2004: 13; Boyce 2005).

Usually, however, it is not just a question of the *extent* of reporting, the *nature* of the coverage is also significant. Research exploring what people recall from media reports, how they relate to media representations, and how they use these materials in constructing their own sense of risks is a vital part of understanding the media's role and reveals a much more multi-layered and complicated picture than simply exploring the media's agenda setting role.

Research into our 'geographies of fear' suggests that the media impact on where we feel threatened, and by whom (and how we defend ourselves against, or attack, those who we identify as being a threat). For example, media reporting routinely associates mental illness with random violent assaults when the evidence shows that they are much more likely to injure themselves than other people. Empirical research with audiences suggests that, in the absence of news offering alternative images of the mentally ill, this link increases fear and misunderstanding (Philo 1996). Similarly the media often associate mental illness, mental disability, or 'deviance' (such as being gay) with paedophilia. This not only makes it hard for a woman to believe that her respectable, socially skilled, and apparently 'normal' husband might be capable of abuse but also feeds into vigilante attacks on gay men or those with mental illness or disabilities (Kitzinger 2004).

There is often a strong disjuncture between the patterns of violence logged by police statistics or in-depth academic research and those mapped out by news reporting. For example, news reports tend to focus on the threat to women out alone at night, yet it is young men who are most likely to be attacked in the street, whilst women are more vulnerable in their own homes (Weaver, Carter, and Stanko 2000). A similarly skewed picture is presented by the coverage of child sexual abuse. Ninety-six per cent of newspaper articles about how to protect children focus on threats from strangers whilst only 4 per cent even partially address abuse by fathers, uncles, step-fathers, brothers, and other family members, the most common category of abuse identified through organizations which work with children (Kitzinger 2004). Focus groups with members of the public suggest that the sheer quantity of coverage devoted to children being abducted can bring stranger-danger to the forefront of our thinking. It also shows that stranger-danger stories may be particularly memorable for readers because parents may identify with the distress of the distraught family and the outrage of the shocked community. The iconographic image of the abducted child in their school uniform, released by the police, may strike a chord with every viewer; indeed, they probably have a similar school photograph on their own mantelpiece. The setting of the search, from the play ground to surrounding waste land, could be 'anywhere'. The narrative structure of stranger abductions is also very powerful—readers eagerly follow the story as the police first announce that the child is missing, the search proceeds, the parents appeal for his or her safe return, and finally, all too often, the body is then found and the search for the murderer begins. The figure of the threatening other is also very easy to process. The predatory paedophile is a monster of common imagination.

However, simply to blame the media for the widespread focus on 'stranger-danger' rather than other forms of sexual abuse, including incest, is to ignore the role of other factors in the forming of our fears. Media accounts of children being abducted and sexually assaulted by strangers are important in making us fear the threat that strangers can pose to children but a constructionist approach also alerts us to the possible importance of other circuits of communication. The circulation of everyday knowledge in routine conversation between friends and acquaintances is also key in supporting the focus on some sources of threat, and not others. The 'social currency' of different types of risk knowledge (the extent to which it is publicly shared or not) may also play a role in shaping everyday understandings of risk. When an unknown man behaves suspiciously around children (e.g. hanging around outside a school offering sweets) this becomes a matter for public knowledge. The head teacher may send out letters of warning and parents will exchange their concerns outside the school gate. By contrast, when a child is discovered to have been sexually abused within a family this is usually kept a closely guarded secret.

As the above thumbnail sketch around stranger-danger suggests, there are some common factors which seem to impact on how people receive risk narratives. These include the power of visual images and specific phrases, the use of narrative drama, the impact of personal accounts, and the role of identification. Although none of these factors should be seen as acting in isolation they each merit sustained investigation.

Sometimes a picture is worth a thousand words. Indeed, sometimes images may undercut messages presented in the text or narration of a news story or broadcast. For example, the dramatic and recurring image of people dying of AIDS wasting away, which was so often displayed in the early days of the AIDS crisis, undermined health education attempts to inform the public that people with HIV usually display no symptoms at all (Miller et al. 1998). Similarly, in-depth research into how people responded to a documentary about nuclear power found that the disturbing and 'unnatural' image of a steaming pond next to a nuclear power station conveyed a powerful sense of threat to viewers, even when the narrator explained that the steam was produced by the hot water used in the cooling towers (Corner et al. 1990).

As we noted in our discussion of 'Frankenstein Foods' the promotion of specific labels, phrases, and words can be powerful carriers of ideas about risk. For example, the precise (or imprecise) language used in media discussion of disease risks can help to inform how people think about transmission. In the early days of the AIDS crisis journalists routinely wrote about the risk of 'body fluids' (preferring not to specify terms such as 'semen' which might be unpalatable over the breakfast table). One consequence of this language was that it left some people believing that HIV could easily be spread via saliva. After all, they argued, saliva must be dangerous because it is a body fluid. Again, though, the role of broader cultural categories needs to be considered. If the term body fluids alone were shaping perceptions, then tears should be seen as equally dangerous. The fact that they were not suggests other factors were also coming into play such as deep cultural ideas about purity and pollution.

The way in which an account is organized as a narrative may be as important as the details of what is said. For example, a documentary examining leukaemia clusters around the nuclear power plant Sellafield was told through an account of one family's quest for understanding and justice around their child's illness. This structure proved crucial in shaping how people related to the documentary. Corner and his colleagues argue that the family tragedy scenario prevented people assimilating other information and debate even when it is clearly included in a text. They conclude: 'the sheer power of the depiction it offered of one family's tragedy, backed up by the programme's own "dark" framing of the industry ... tended to crystallise meanings at the lower level for our respondents, leaving the wider reach of speculation relatively unassimilated' (Corner et al. 1990: 100).

Overlapping with this last point is the observation that personal accounts may sometimes be more effective in making people think about risk than facts and statistics. For example, Boyce found that what made people 'think twice' about vaccinating their own children often had very little to do with the 'facts' presented in the media about the risks of MMR. Instead, parents were often profoundly moved by the powerful testimony from parents who believed their children's autism was caused by the vaccine (Boyce 2005). Similarly research into media coverage of 'inherited breast cancer' found that women were sometimes barely aware of the scientific research and discoveries in this area. However, they vividly recalled, and had engaged with, fictionalized and factual presentations of human interest stories about 'breast cancer families'. Few women in this research had taken in the front page news that specific 'breast cancer' genes had been discovered. What they *did* recall were the tragic tales of whole families 'cursed' by breast cancer and the traumatic decision facing some women considering prophylactic mastectomies. It was these personal accounts which helped to shape their own risk assessments (Henderson and Kitzinger 1999).

The final key aspect of media coverage we wish to highlight here overlaps with this and concerns issues of imaginative identification and empathy.

Earlier in this chapter we mentioned that journalists seek to craft risk stories they consider 'relevant' and with which readers/viewers might identify. However, identification involves active audience involvement and requires the mobilization of complex levels of cultural categorization.

For example, in the early days of the AIDS crisis, the disease was presented as 'belonging' to particular, socially marginalized, risk groups, particularly gay men. This allowed people to insulate themselves from a sense of being at risk even if they were engaged in high-risk behaviour. As long as they refused the associated identity they could feel immune from the virus (Miller et al. 1998). The mode of presentation (via the concept of risk groups), and the moralistic dimensions of AIDS discourses (associating the disease with deviance) combined with pre-existing social categories and people's own identity management strategies to create a particular type of media 'effect' for some people.

Similarly complex processes of identification, or distancing, are evident in women's responses to statistics about male violence. This was clearly demonstrated in some responses to the Zero Tolerance campaign, the first major advertising initiative in Britain designed to highlight the risks of sexual abuse and challenge social attitudes towards assaults against women and girls. One retired woman, reacting to a campaign statement that almost 50 per cent of female murder victims are killed 'by their partner or ex-partner', suggested that the victims must be mainly prostitutes murdered by their clients. The figures were therefore, she explained, not applicable to 'ordinary people'. Similarly other participants in this research argued that the statistics publicized by campaign about the high incidence of rape were not as bad as they might seem. This was because, they argued, they must include 'bogus' cases such as 'date rapes' or incidents where women have 'led the man on'.

As this example shows, statistics about the frequency of a threat are not simply accepted by people and translated into an understanding of risk. They 'negotiate' with statistics drawing on prevailing stereotypes and mythologies. Faced with publicity highlighting endemic sexual violence, some respondents nevertheless managed to keep rape and assault as the preserve of stranger-danger or to see it as a misfortune that only happens to women who 'ask for it'.

Issues of identification are not self-evident. In the aftermath of the London underground bombings, for example, much was made of 'British identity'. However, a sense of being British does not preclude identifying with people from other nations. The concept of the universal Muslim community, the Ummah, for example, cuts across geographic and national boundaries. Disproportionate concern about a 'home grown' tragedy can thus be seen as hypocritical. As 'Ali', a young Luton man commented, when interviewed about the bombings:

[the West] are grieving 52 people who died in London, but I've been grieving the death of thousands of children in Palestine, in Chechnya, in Kashmir, in Iraq, since I was 15.

Technological changes which allow access to transnational media can support such identification. As Ali went on to comment:

It's not just the BBC and ITV any more, we have al-Jazeera, we have the internet. We live in a globalised society. The world had become a smaller village. If something happens to innocent people in Iraq, the Muslims of Luton will know about it and feel that grief. (quoted in Akbar and Duff 2005)

Emerging Research Approaches: From Active to Interactive Audiences

As we have noted, the main shift in research in this field has been towards constructionist approaches. These have tended to focus on how readers and viewers draw on their stocks of cultural resources to interpret or 'decode' particular media texts (a documentary, a soap opera, a feature film, or a news bulletin) and how their understandings are modified or confirmed through conversation and argument. This emphasis has produced a dominant image of media audiences as continuously 'active', selecting, comparing, connecting, debating, and judging. With the growing ubiquity of the Internet, however, this description only tells part of the story. Audiences are moving from being active to becoming interactive. More and more people are shifting between the television screen and newspaper page and the World Wide Web with increasing frequency and fluidity, checking accounts, locating additional information, following links to other sources, and dipping into the debates on bulletin boards. Some are contributing as well as accessing material, helping to develop online information resources, writing web logs ('blogs') publicizing their experiences and opinions, and posting images shot on camera phones or compact digital video cameras. In some cases, these amateur pictures, of the immediate aftermath of the London bombings or the initial devastation caused by the Indonesia Tsunami, are the only eye witness record we have of major risk events.

Almost all print and broadcast news organizations now have web pages as do the government agencies, corporations, scientific and professional organizations, social movements, and campaigning groups that source the news machine. This development is still in the process of formation but it is already clear that it has the capacity to alter flows of public knowledge about risk and control over the communication process in fundamental ways raising urgent new research questions.

The increasing ubiquity of the Internet shifts the balance between expert knowledge, everyday experience, and personal testimony and increases opportunities for public participation in debates around shared risks. This has contradictory implications. On the one hand it could reinforce the shift towards more populist forms of news-making as news organizations in an increasingly competitive marketplace use enhanced public 'feedback' as the basis for campaigns tailored to popular preoccupations and misconceptions. On the other, by requiring both media and risk professionals to rethink their roles and to see representations and accounts of risk as increasingly collective and collaborative constructions rather than finished products manufactured behind closed doors and 'released' for public consumption, it strengthens moves towards more open deliberation on key issues. Exploring these possibilities requires sustained research mapping emerging patterns of peer-to-peer activity and interaction on the web, and tracing how they intersect with established institutionalized systems of public communication.

A focus on modes of participation, however, can all too easily obscure the persistence of substantial inequalities in access to and use of the Internet and the continuing exclusion of significant numbers of the elderly and those in poverty. Nor are these 'Digital Divides' simply a matter of income. They are also the outcome of differential access to key social and cultural resources (see Murdock and Golding 2004). Addressing these exclusions presents urgent tasks both for public policy and for research. We need to look in detail at the factors that support active information searching and participation in key risk areas.

By alerting us to the fact that perceptions and interpretations alone are rarely the sole or even sometimes the major determinates of responses to risk. The issue of Digital Divides introduces a second and broader research agenda there are socio-economic pressures beyond communication issues. A consumer may be concerned about GM products, but buy them because they are cheaper, a homeless male prostitute may exchange immediate access to accommodation, for the more distant fear of HIV. To develop a full understanding of the media's role in constructing risks we need always to keep such contexts and questions of power firmly in mind. Media research in this field must be firmly integrated with research across these issues.

References

Adams, W. (1986). 'Whose Lives Count? TV Coverage of Natural Disasters', *Communication*, 36(2): 113–22.

Akbar, A. and Duff, O. (2005). 'Muslim Leaders Pledge to Root Out the Extremists in Their Community … But in Luton, Summit is Treated with Contempt', *The Independent*, 20 July 2005: 8–9.

Beck, U. (1992). *Risk Society: Towards a New Modernity*. London: Sage.

Boyce, T. (2005). *Sowing the Seeds of Doubt: the MMR and Autism Story*, PhD. Thesis, University of Wales at Cardiff.

Corner, J., Richardson, K. and Fenton, N. (1990). *Nuclear Reactions: Forms and Response in 'Public Issue' Television*. London: J. Libbey.

Douglas, M. (1992). *Risk and Blame. Essays in Cultural Theory*. London: Routledge.

Dunwoody, S. and Peters, H. P. (1992). 'Mass Media Coverage of Technological and Environmental Risks', *Public Understanding of Science*, 1: 199–230.

Freudenburg, W., Coleme, C.-L., Gonzale, J., and Helgeland, C. (1996). 'Media Coverage of Hazard Events: Analyzing Assumptions', *Risk Analysis*, 16(1): 31–42.

Graham, E. L. (2002). *Representations of the Post/Human: Monsters, Aliens and Others in Popular Culture*. New Brunswick, New Jersey: Rutgers University Press.

Greenberg, M., Sachsman, D., Sandman, P., and Salmone, K. (1989). 'Risk, Drama and Geography in Coverage of Environmental Risk by Network TV', *Journalism Quarterly*, 66(2): 267–76.

Hansen, A. (1991). 'The Media and the Social Construction of the Environment', *Media, Culture and Society*, 13(4).

_____ (ed.) (1994). *The Mass Media and Environmental Issues*. Leicester, UK: Leicester University Press.

_____(2000). 'Claims-Making and Framing in British Newspaper Coverage of the "Brent Spar" Controversy', in Stuart Allen et al. (eds.), _Environmental Risks and the Media_. London: Routledge, pp. 55–72.

Hargreaves, I. and Ferguson, G. (2000). _Bridging the Gulf of Understanding Between the Public, the Media and Science_. Economic and Social Research Council.

Henderson, L. and Kitzinger, J. (1999). 'The Human Drama of Genetics: "Hard" and "Soft" Media Representations of Inherited Breast Cancer', _Sociology of Health and Illness_, 21(5): 560–78.

Kasperson, R. E. and Kasperson, J. X. (1996). 'The Social Amplification and Attenuation of Risk', _The Annals of the American Academy of Political and Social Science_, 545: 95–105.

Kirby, T. and Davies, E. (2005). 'Revealed: Iraq's Civilian Death Toll: 24,865', _The Independent_, 20th July 2005: 1.

Kitzinger, J. (1998). 'The Gender-politics of News Production: Silenced Voices and False Memories', in C. Carter, G. Branston, and S. Allan, (eds.), _News, Gender and Power_. London: Routledge.

_____(2004). _Framing Abuse: Media Influence and Public Understanding of Sexual Violence Against Children_. London: Pluto Press.

_____and Williams, F. (2005). 'Forecosting Scientific Futures: legitimising hope and calming fears in the embryo stem cell debate', _Social Science and Medicine_, 61: 731–40.

_____Henderson, L., Smart, A., and Eldridge, J. (2000). _Final Report to the Wellcome Trust_. London: The Wellcome Trust.

_____and Reilly, J. (1997). 'The Rise and Fall of Risk Reporting', _The European Journal of Communication_, 12(3): 319–50.

Kristiansen, C. (1988). 'The British Press's Coverage of Health: An Antagonistic Force', _Media Information Australia_, 47: 56–60.

Lichtenberg, J. and MacLean, D. (1991). 'The Role of the Media in Risk Communication', in R. Kaperson and P. Stallen (eds.), _Communicating Risks to the Public: International Perspectives_. London: Kluwere.

Lupton, D. (1999). _Risk_. London: Routledge.

Macgill, S. (1989). 'Risk Perception and the Public: Insights from Research Around Sellafield', in J. Brown (ed.), _Environmental Threats: Perceptions, Analysis and Management_. London: Belhaver Press, pp. 48–66.

Miller, D. and Reilly, J. (1995). 'Making an Issue of Food Safety: The Media, Pressure Groups and the Public Sphere', in D. Maurer and J. Sobal (eds.), _Eating Agendas: Food and Nutrition as Social Problems_. New York: Aldine de Gruyter.

Miller, D. et al. (1998). _The Circuit of Mass Communication: Media Strategies, Representation and Audience Reception in the AIDS Crisis_. London: Sage.

Murdock, G. (2004). 'Popular Representation and Postnormal Science: The Struggle over Genetically Modified Foods', in Sandra Braman (ed.), _Biotechnology and Communication: The Meta-Technologies of Information_. Mahwah, NJ: Lawrence Erlbaum Associates, pp. 227–59.

____ and Golding, P. (2004). 'Dismantling The Digital Divide: Rethinking The Dynamics of Participation and Exclusion', in Andrew Calabrese and Colin Sparks (eds.), *Toward a Political Economy of Culture: Capitalism and Communication in the 21st Century*. Lanham. Rowman and Littlefield, pp. 244–60.

____ Petts, J. and Horlick-Jones, T. (2003). 'After Amplification: Rethinking the Role of the Media in Risk Communication', in Nick Pigeon, Roger Kasperson, and Paul Slovic (eds.), *The Social Amplification of Risk*. Cambridge: Cambridge University Press, pp. 156–78.

NSPCC (1992). *The NSPCC Fort Park*. London: NSPCC.

Peters, H. (1995). 'The Interaction of Journalists and Scientific Experts: Co-operation and Conflict Between two Professional Cultures', *Media, Culture and Society*, 17(1): 31–48.

Petts, J., Horlick-Jones, T., and Murdock, G. (2001). *Social Amplification of Risk: The Media and the Public*. London: The Health and Safety Executive. Contract Research Report 329/2001.

____ and Niemeyer, S. (2004). 'Health Risk Communication and Amplification', *Health, Risk and Society*, 6: 7–23.

Philo, G. (ed.) (1996). *The Media and Mental Distress*. Harlow: Longman.

Powers, A. and Andsager, J. L. (1999). 'How Newspapers Framed Breast Implants in the 1990s', *Journalism and Mass Communications Quarterly*, 76(3): 551–64.

Roger and Chang (1991).

Sandman, P., Weinstein, N., and Klotz, M. (1987). *Environmental Risk and the Press*. Oxford: Transaction books.

Schame, M. and Werner, M. (1992). 'Media Coverage of Risk: Results from Content Analysis', in Durant, J. *Museums and the Public Understanding of Science*. London: Science Museum Publications.

Shepherd, G. (1981). 'Selectivity of Sources Reporting the Marijuana Controversy', *Journal of Communication* 31: 134.

Singer, E. and Endreny, P. (1987). 'Reporting Hazards: Their Benefits and Costs', in *Journal of Communication* 37(3): 10–26.

Stallings, R. (1990). 'Media Discourse and the Social Construction of Risk', *Social Problems*, 37(1): 80–95.

Szerszynski, B. and Toogood, M. (2000). 'Global Citizenship: The Environment and the Media', in S. Allan et al. (eds.), *op cit*, pp. 218–28.

Tulloch, J. and Lupton, D. (2001). 'Risk, the Mass Media and Personal Biography', *European Journal of Cultural Studies*, 4(1): 5–27.

____ ____ (2003). *Risk and Everyday Life*. London: Sage.

Turney, J. (1998). *Frankenstein's Footsteps: Science, Genetics and Popular Culture*. New Haven, CT: Yale University Press.

Understanding Risk Team (2004). *A Deliberative Future?: An Independent Evaluation of the GM Nation? Debate*. University of East Anglia. Department of Environmental Science.

Weaver, C. K, Carter, C., and Stanko, E. (2000). 'The Female Body at Risk': Media, Sexual Violence and the Gendering of Public Environments', in S. Allan et al. (eds.), *op cit*, pp. 171–83.

Winett, L. B. and Lawrence, R. G. (2005). 'The Rest of the Story: Public Health, the News, and the 2001 Anthrax Attacks', *Press/Politics*, 10(3): 3–25.

Wynne, B. (1996). 'May the Sheep Safely Graze? A Reflexive View of the Expert-lay Knowledge Divide', in S. Lash, B. Szerszinski, and B. Wynne (eds.), *Risk, Environment and Modernity: Towards a New Ecology*. London: Sage, pp. 44–83.

13

Social and Public Policy: Reflexive Individualization and Regulatory Governance

Peter Taylor-Gooby

The Context: Two Perspectives on Risk in Social Policy Research

Welfare states are currently undergoing rapid change as part of the broader social shifts associated with the transition from a modernity structured around neo-Keynesian nation state capitalism towards a more globalized, post-Fordist, and individualized future. The developments in the UK associated with the emergence of New Labour and of a third way social policy are at the forefront of these shifts, and this chapter focuses particularly on this country. These changes are reflected in risk-research in this field. Social policy is about the meeting of social need under particular circumstances: mass democracy, modern industry, and particular patterns of family and household life. The needs on which policy focuses are those not met through employment or family and household dependency and care.

Recent developments in the context of social policy have led to increasing pressure on the capacity of national governments to meet such needs effectively on a mass scale. To simplify, the demands on welfare states are rising (as a result of ageing populations, increases in the numbers of single person households, greater fluidity in family life and flexibility in employment, and innovations in medical technology). This is happening just at a time when the capacity of governments to provide is declining (as globalization and more open international markets in goods, labour and finance intensify pressures to cut spending and maintain competitiveness) and as voters in the advanced welfare states become more inclined to question high taxes and social contributions, and as growing inequalities impose pressures on the willingness of the electorate to pay for services which they see as going to more distant groups (see Barr 1998: 12–13; Ferrera and Rhodes 2000; Scharpf and Schmidt 2000; Pierson 2001; Taylor-Gooby 2001 for discussion). The outcome is a duality in policy which has led to two corresponding streams of research.

Mass services tend to be cut back; means-tested support and private services play a greater role. Welfare state ideologies stress the responsibility of the individual for her own welfare. At the same time, the mechanisms directed specifically at vulnerable and high-risk groups who are unable to manage their own needs effectively and concerned to identify and manage those risks are sharpened and extended. Social policy is about constraining one aspect of the role of the state (mass provision) whilst expanding another (regulation of the lives of the vulnerable). This reflects contrary trends in the experience of risk and uncertainty: citizens are more likely to experience uncertainty in the course of their lives, as a result of shifts in work, family life, and in social expectations about the capacity of government to manage these shifts. At the same time, some aspects of life grow more secure: life expectancy continues to increase, living standards to rise, and opportunities to communicate, travel, and become acquainted with other cultures expand. Greater individualization and greater control have both stimulated research interest.

This leads to a puzzle in modern analysis of risk and public policy. On one hand, a great deal of work is concerned to chart the recent trajectory of the development of the welfare state from a social insurance, mass protective model to one which stresses the activation of individuals to tackle risks on their own behalf, with appropriate support (Barr 1998; Ewald 2002; Jessop 2002). This fits with a logic which interprets current social changes as a transition away from circumstances of confident stable growth, industrialism, and nuclear families, mainly supported by a breadwinner's earnings. The new direction is one in which changes in work and work patterns, household structures, and the complex international shifts at the economic, political, and cultural level summed up as globalization presage greater uncertainty about the life course and increasingly stringent limitations on the capacity of the nation state to manage the problems that individuals face. This model stresses the transition from certainty to uncertainty in people's understanding of their lives and sees the welfare state as responding in parallel fashion, by reducing its predictable mass service provision, but expanding the supportive services it provides to enable individuals to identify, pursue, and grasp the opportunities available to them (Beck, Bonss, and Lau 2003: 6).

On the other hand, a parallel analysis points out that, although mass social insurance systems are no longer expanding, and privatized or means-tested individualized services are, it is not obvious that the importance of the actuarial calculations through which life-course risks were precisely assessed, central to the traditional welfare state approach to risk during the expansive period of modern society, has declined in social policy. Modern techniques of risk-rating, risk assessment, and risk-management are pursued in child protection, in the management of those with mental health problems, of asylum seekers, of the frail elderly, of homeless people, and of other groups in order to identify the vulnerable accurately, to assess the cost benefit of interventions, and to target resources upon them cost effectively (Leonard 1997; Kemshall 2002; Denny, 2006).

Risk-research in social policy thus contains examples of both the shift from a *modern* to a *reflexive risk society* (Giddens 1994, 1998), and the expansion of *technocratic governance* (Dean 1999). It is this duality and the rapid pace of change in welfare state policies which provides a rich field for the application of theoretical models and also for extensive data gathering to test and refute them. It also provides opportunities for confusion and debate between those who emphasize the move to social uncertainty or to social management, towards independent activation or to the control of individual behaviour, to greater responsibility or to regulation, since both are happening at once.

Research Themes

Social and public policies deal with needs in two spheres of people's lives: the private sphere of family care and intimate relationships, and the more public market sphere of paid employment, income, and poverty. The broad approaches of risk society and governance and regulation have led to a focus on particular themes within these areas, and to a redrawing of the boundaries between them. As expectations of individual proactivity and responsibility for achieving outcomes and managing risks for the mass of the population grow stronger, some areas shift to the private sector; research in fields as diverse as pensions and access to paid work increasingly concerns individual values and motivations. At the same time, the behaviour of particular groups in what was formerly a private arena of life enters the public sphere. The risks encountered in child and elder care, health-related activities such as smoking, diet, and exercise become matters of public concern. The focus of mental health services shifts from integration of those defined as mentally ill into the community to the identification of vulnerable or dangerous groups and the concentration of available resources onto these cases. On the one hand, interest in how individuals manage their lives in risk society grows. On the other, new techniques of governance for vulnerable and threatening groups become the focus of attention. We will examine some key findings in these areas.

Major Findings

The main currents of research activity in relation to the risks dealt with in social and public policy concern the two main areas affected by the new policy stance: the private sphere of family and care, and the public sphere of work and incomes. We also discuss briefly research on state policies for medicine and health (for a broader perspective, see Chapter 8). This area straddles private and public spheres, and brings out the collision of interventionism and individualization.

Family and Care: Individual Responsibility and Surveillance and Regulation

The context of research in this area is greater diversity in family forms, a shift towards female employment, and an expansion of private care. Since the 1970s divorce rates and single parenthood have doubled and cohabitation trebled. The proportion of mothers in paid work has trebled, whilst male employment has fallen by 14 per cent (ONS 2004, Figures 2.11, 2.14, Table 2.4; Williams, 2004: 15). Day care for children has tripled since the early 1990s, roughly half in day nurseries and almost all private (ONS 2003, Table 8.21). Elder care provision has roughly doubled, most of it private, whilst residential accommodation has declined sharply (ONS 2004, Tables 8.1, 8.2). As a result of these changes, the pattern of risks faced during the life course and their incidence for different social groups have shifted.

Research falls into two general categories: work which analyses current shifts in terms of greater self-oriented individualization in the ways people live their lives, and work which stresses the re-emergence of 'moral rationalities', of reciprocity, and of 'compassionate realism' in relationships. In relation to risks in the area of the family and social care, the chief contrast between the two main approaches lies in understanding of the impact of a greater diversity of sexual relationships and in family life on the risks people anticipate and how they respond to them: individualization is interpreted as leading towards a liberation from traditional roles and obligations, so that 'the ethic of individual self-fulfilment and achievement is the most powerful current in modern society' (Beck and Beck-Gersheim 2002: 22; see Williams 2004: 56 and chapters 3 and 4).

On the other, a stream of empirical research examining family relationships in the context of divorce and re-partnering concludes that 'the shape of commitments is changing, but there is no loss of commitment' (see Finch 1989 and Williams 2004: 8 for a detailed account of processes whereby such commitments are negotiated). This process is understood in terms of people's greater involvement in 'moral reasoning about care'. Such consideration includes recognition of the responsibility and capacity to pursue the role of 'energetic moral agents' (p. 42) in negotiating relationships and commitments in terms of what is the 'proper thing to do' (p. 8). In short, the transition is from a situation in which people asked 'what ought I to do?' in relation to a received system of moral rules, to one in which they consider 'How best can I manage this?'. The new practical ethics are based on respect for others, being non-judgemental and openness to reciprocity in a constructed system of moral negotiation.

This issue has important policy relevance. A stream of policy-related arguments presses for greater regulation of more individualized lifestyles. From this perspective, Deacon argues that 'welfare ... has to delineate, reaffirm and at times enforce the obligations that people have to their families, their neighbours and to the wider communities in which they live' (2004a, 2004b: 22). Sacks calls for 'clear connections between rights and responsibilities' (1997: 233). In policy, such assumptions have led to the establishment of a Child Support Agency with the role of enforcing the financial obligations of absent parents to their children and to a wide range of schemes to promote good quality parenting and from childminders and day nurseries within a national childcare strategy (DfES 1998). Government identifies lifestyle changes as generating risks which it needs to address.

The regulatory aspects of these policies can be located within an overall economic strategy, led by the Treasury, which is concerned to promote high levels of employment. In relation to childcare, this strategy is expressed in policies to mobilize mothers into paid work, which include contributions towards the costs of childcare for low-income parents through the Child Tax Credit. The Sure Start strategy has invested in the provision of day nurseries in areas of high social deprivation and encouraged provision elsewhere (DfES 1998). These policies are highly targeted on low-income groups, but represent a substantial investment in the UK context, where intervention in the area of family responsibilities has traditionally been limited.

One area where the issue of how far government should adopt a regulatory as opposed to an enabling stance in relation to family care has provoked considerable debate is that of social security for lone parents. The New Deal for Lone Parents (the main system of means-tested support for this group) has developed an increasingly forceful approach, including invitations and then requirements to attend interviews at which claimers will be encouraged to take paid work, and at which the income gap between wages and benefits for those in work and the benefits for those out of work are stressed. Duncan and Edwards in a national qualitative study (1999) show how the assumptions behind this policy fit with the values of most lone parents. However, a minority, particularly among lower social class white people, value mother-care particularly highly. They follow a different moral rationality from the incentive driven individualism implicit in the policy of attaching markedly higher incomes to paid work. The result is that they are penalized in the current policy framework. Benefits for those who remain outside the labour market to provide mother-care remain low to enhance employment incentives. One approach identifies the key issue as lack of access to work, and the key risk that lone parent families run as poverty; the other focuses more on the risk of lack of access to mother-care faced by their children when their mothers take jobs.

Paid Work, Inequality, and Poverty

The themes of support and empowerment for more proactive citizens versus regulation of individualist behaviour also emerge in policies in the area of employment and access to opportunities, one of the central themes of New Labour policy. A key aspect of the third way approach is the promotion of social justice in an unequal market-based society through greater access to opportunities. This is immediately apparent in the area of paid work and the risk of gaining access to the labour market. As globalization and technological change reduce the availability of unskilled labour in developed countries, entry into paid work for low-skilled young people is becoming increasingly problematic. The main policies include both market incentives and the regulation of behaviour on the one hand, and the expansion of supported opportunity on the other. The former area includes New Deals for various groups with weak access to employment, legislation to impose a minimum wage, and to establish an extensive range of means-tested Tax Credit support to enhance incentives for the low paid in one of the most unequal wage-structures in Europe (Luxembourg Income Study 2004), and cut-backs in the out-of-work benefits available for those of working age, so that unemployment benefit is replaced with a time-limited Job-Seeker's Allowance and access to Incapacity Benefit constrained. Tax credits for those in work, the childcare strategy, and a cautious expansion of the maternity and paternity benefit regime can also be seen as enhancing opportunities.

Government has also restructured pensions, the largest spending area of social security. The shifts continue a long-term process of shifting from state to private provision (DSS 1998) and involve promoting various private investment systems, whilst state pensions are more heavily targeted through means-testing and tax credits. Research into the impact of these policies has shown:

- Growth of employment, reflecting general economic buoyancy, but particularly marked among young mothers, young people, and those with disabilities, indicating that policies to enhance the employability of these groups have enjoyed some success; (NAO 2002: 6; Treasury/DTI 2003; charts 2.4, 2.5; for more detailed discussion see Taylor-Gooby 2004: ch. 3);

- Little change in the level of economic activity, sickness, and disability being the main factors preventing men of working age from working and home responsibilities for women (ONS 2002: 69);

- A decline in poverty, especially among families with children, which reverses a 20-year trend to rising poverty levels (DWP 2004: 4);

- Inequality, which has increased sharply since the late 1970s, shows no sign of falling as incomes at the top end continue to rise (Hills 2004: 69–70);

- Policies to expand the role of private pensions have been relatively unsuccessful; as available schemes prove unattractive, company schemes continue to decline, and individual savings rates remain low

(Pensions Policy Institute 2003). Pressures on the new means-tested state pensions credit are forecast to continue to rise, possibly to 80 per cent of all pensioners by 2050 (Clark and Emmerson 2002).

The evidence on the mixed successes and limitations of the new policies has stimulated research on caring relationships and the motivations of carers, incentives, and paid employment and on trajectories of poverty. Care issues and the emergence of the two strands of individualization in risk society and of governance in areas which had previously been seen as part of a private sphere are discussed above. The pattern of research in relation to the risks that face people in the areas of work, employment, and poverty is broadly similar. On the one hand, the extent to which people become increasingly individualized, their judgements and the choices they make in these areas are subject to examination. On the other, the key issues are seen as the processes of management and control of access to paid work.

In relation to work incentives, a series of surveys by Dean and others (e.g. 1999, 2002*a*, 2002*b*) analyses work motivations and patterns of employment among groups of employed and unemployed people in particular regional labour markets. The results show a range of orientations to paid work, but stress the significance of a 'dependency trap' in which those on benefits feel that access to higher-paid employment is denied them. Using different methods based on micro-simulation from an elaborate model of the tax and benefit system, Brewer, Clark, and Myck also conclude that 'the overall effect on labour supply is uncertain, but it is probably small' (2001: 1).

Further work discuses welfare fraud, in the context of the individualized assumption that those faced with choices between work and benefits will make decisions governed by incentives. Fraud is a strong concern of government (in line with the individual incentive approach to work motivations) and has led, for example, to the setting up of a welfare fraud group in the Treasury under the Paymaster General. Most research, however, indicates that the problem is relatively small and confined to particular groups (Rowlingson et al. 1997; Rowlingson and Whyley 1998). Much of the discussion is confused by statistics which count overpayments of benefit as fraud and multiply known fraud by substantial weightings on the assumption that it is the tip of an iceberg of undetected fraud (Dean and Melrose 1995). A review of quantitative and qualitative work shows that while public concern exists it has not 'reached high levels' (Williams, Hill, and Davies 2004: 2).

In relation to poverty and the success of government initiatives in poverty reduction most research is cautiously positive. However, two issues may be identified. First, government policies operate in a context which is favourable, since economic conditions ensure relatively high employment and upward pressures on incomes, but even in this context, the targets set are unlikely to be reached (Dickens 2002; Sutherland, Sefton, and Piachaud 2003; Walker and Wiseman 2003). Second, the advances are made through policies that ensure substantially lower incomes for those who do not succeed in gaining paid work. The fact that overall engagement in paid work has not risen indicates that there is an obstinate core of poverty which the new programmes will be unable to tackle (Hasluck 2000; Piachaud and Sutherland 2002). This leads to interest in the operation of the new measures to direct those out of work into paid employment.

Central to the new approach is the 'single gateway' for all able-bodied claimants (Maxwell and Kenway 2000: 31; Butcher 2002). This includes assessment of benefit entitlement, reinforcement of obligations to enter activation programmes, counselling and advice about the impact of 'make work pay' benefits on incomes in work, and the opportunities available on training schemes and in local labour markets, to press home the duties associated with the linkage of welfare state rights to citizen responsibilities. The process includes a contract between claimant and the benefits service about job-search behaviour and benefit rights. As research at the CRSP centre in Loughborough indicates, a major issue is that 'the partners to the contract are not equal. Users need to be empowered to ensure that the state fulfils its side of the contract' (CRSP 1999: 7). This area of work reflects the governance of social security claimers and the processes whereby new state systems intensify control (Hill 1999: 106).

In pensions, the unwillingness of many individuals to invest privately has stimulated work on motivations and expectations in this field, and on government policies designed to influence behaviour. Work which focuses on individualization and choice shows high levels of mistrust of both private and public providers, combined with unrealistic expectations of the retirement incomes that existing contributions will produce (Rowlinson 2002; DWP 2003; Taylor-Gooby and Hastie 2003). The outcome is that the choices pursued do not further the public policy goal of adequate mass pensions.

In relation to governance and control, a further concern is the extent to which privatization policies will disadvantage groups who are already weak by market standards, intensifying the risks that these groups face. Ginn points out the problems that women, often with career and contributions records interrupted by years spent child-rearing, face (Ginn 2004: 129–32); Hills discusses low-income groups (2004: 362–3). These arguments have led to new proposals for pension reform, and the field is currently at the centre of policy debate (PPI 2003; ESRC 2004; Hills 2004).

Medicine, Health, and Health Promotion

The twin agenda of reflexivity and governance emerge prominently in the arena of health care. On the one hand, a well-established stream of research in sociology argues that individuals take greater responsibility for their own health and are more inclined to challenge the judgements and assumptions of professionals and state agencies (see, for a review, Alaszewski and Horlick-Jones 2003; Horlick-Jones 2004). On the other, the view that individuals will wish to take greater responsibility for their own health has led to measures intended to influence the choices that people make and research into the way in which lay publics respond to professional advice on health risks (Kemshall 2002: 44–52). Broader research interest in the body reflects the division between individual proactivity in body-management and medicalized regulation (see Twigg 2005).

There is considerable evidence that individuals are discriminating in their use of health advice. The simplistic view that, in risk society, the expert is simply devalued, as Giddens and others sometimes suggest (see, e.g. Giddens 1994: 95) and the equally simplistic view that the authority of experts is unquestioned are both limited. Thus, Ward, Bissell, and Noyce show that 'mapping the contours of consumer ideas about risk becomes a complex project in which people [shift] back and forth ... between docile and reflexive approaches' (2000: 148). Similarly Williams and Calnan suggest 'people are not simply passive or active, dependent or independent, believers or sceptics. Rather they are a complex mixture of all these things ...' (1996: 264). Nettleton's view of the new health promotion agenda incorporates both expertise and lay response: 'a range of risks are presented by the experts and it is up to individuals to calculate the likely consequences of certain actions to themselves' (1997: 208).

In this context, government policy has shifted to place health promotion (resting heavily on changes in consumer behaviour) at the forefront of its health agenda. A series of government pronouncements (*The Health of the Nation*, DH 1992, *Our Healthier Nation*, DH 1999, and *Choosing*

Health, DH 2004) stress the importance of lifestyle changes in relation to tobacco smoking, alcohol consumption, healthier diets, and exercise as of central importance to improvements in people's health. This strand of policy builds on research that is well-summarized in Cabinet Office papers (Halpern et al. 2003). Relevant policies include both support and empowerment of active citizens, and also measures to direct and regulate behaviour.

Information is made available through a range of means including a major web and phone-based NHS direct advice and information service, warnings on cigarette packets, and guidelines for healthy alcohol consumption and exercise regimes. At the same time, tobacco advertising is circumscribed, anti-smoking advertising becomes increasingly compelling, pressure is brought to bear on food manufactures to reduce salt and sugar and introduce healthier prepared foods, and alcohol advertising is limited and underage smoking and drinking are to be curbed. Exercise schemes for older people and other at risk groups are to be established. This programme includes elements of both activation of individuals and regulation of behaviour—more marked in relation to tobacco than alcohol. It straddles both aspects of state policies to risk (Petersen 1997).

Emerging Problems and Issues

The chief issues to emerge from this brief review of current research are that

- A reorientation of public policy is underway, which responds to the increased individualization of a reflexive risk society;
- At the same time, the new policies also regulate and govern groups seen as most likely to be at risk themselves or to create risks for others.

These shifts have stimulated the rapid development of new avenues in research. Five issues are perhaps most pressing.

First, it is clear that the operation of public policy incentives and patterns of motivation in relation to individual behaviour is imperfectly understood (Frey 1997; Le Grand 2003). While economic psychology has generated a considerable volume of work on motivations and on how economic rationality can be modified in a laboratory setting, it is simply unclear how far values and assumptions associated with citizenship, traditional welfare states, and the expectations of what the government will provide relate to such rationality in particular everyday life contexts (see Taylor-Gooby 2000, Chapter 1, for a discussion).

Second, globalization and the growing importance of cross-national relationships at economic, political, and cultural levels are extensively discussed in the literature. However, apart from specific fields such as European public policy (e.g. Wallace and Wallace 2000; Richardson 2001), there is relatively little analysis of the role of these relationships and their influence on policy. A number of studies examine globalization and in general conclude that the impacts are both positive and negative, but broaden the range of issues relevant to policy (e.g. Yeates 2001; George and Wilding 2002; George and Page 2004). The new journal *Global Social Policy* seeks to provide a focus for this field. There is some work on the influence of international actors in particular policy areas—for example, the extent to which WTO agreements on the service sector and on government provision as competition to private providers will impact on social care provision. In addition a considerable quantity of work has analysed migration issues and the social policy treatment of refugees (Bloch and Levy 1999; Kaye 1999; Burnett and Peel 2001; Ungerson 2003). However, the theoretical importance given to this field, particularly by risk society analysts, suggests that more work will emerge in the future.

Third, an established tradition in social and public policy analysis has examined the impact of policies on different social groups, paying particular attention to social class divisions, and, more recently, to gender and ethnic divisions (see Titmuss 1958; Williams 1989). Increasingly other divisions by age, sexuality, and region attract attention. Work which focuses on risk often pays surprisingly little attention to these issues, treating the population as homogenous in relation to risk (see chapter 11). Thus, an important strand in theoretical approaches writes in terms of social changes understood as affecting all individuals in broadly similar ways (e.g. Giddens 1994, 1998; Bauman 1998; Mythen 2005). A considerable volume of empirical work makes generalizations on the basis of studies of particular groups (Irwin, Simmons, and Walker 1999; Ewald 2002; Petts and Niemeyer 2004) and this is often a preferred method in psychological work (e.g. Eiser 2004). The different impact of risks and policies to meet them on different groups in a risk society merits attention (see Vail, Wheelock, and Hill 1999: ch. 1). In addition, governance and surveillance approaches often deal with the extent to which government manages poor and vulnerable minorities. This raises the question of how new forms of management regulate lives at the bottom in the interests of other social groups (Kemshall 2002: 130).

Fourth, the emergence of new patterns of risk in the course of people's lives has led to new political agenda: the risks to individual welfare of being unable to get adequate care support for children or frail elderly kin so that one can pursue paid work, of being unable to access secure employment in a rapidly changing labour market, or of failing to gain reliable provision from private or voluntary providers, are now far more salient than they once were. The politics of public policy appears to operate differently in this additional welfare domain. Traditional welfare states were driven essentially by class politics (Baldwin 1990; Huber and Stephens 2001). In the case of new social risks the groups directly affected (lone parents, unskilled people who find difficulty getting jobs, poorer groups) are smaller and often transitory, so that corresponding mass constituencies do not exist (Bonoli 2002). As a result, outcomes are more likely to be directed by other actors, often governments concerned to mobilize the labour force into employment or employers who wish to cut labour costs (Taylor-Gooby 2004: ch. 9). The area of new social risks is now emerging onto the research agenda, with implications for understanding shifts in the politics of social policy.

Nonetheless, issues about risk and social and public policy are beginning to play a substantial role in research. The new directions are summed up in two recent and very different books. Le Grand's *Motivation, Agency and Public Policy* (2003) provides a detailed review of relevant behavioural economic research to reinforce the case for 'well-designed public services, ones that employ market-type mechanisms but do not allow unfettered self-interest to dominate altruistic motivations' (2003: 168). He argues that if market and quasi-market systems are designed appropriately, they can effectively empower individuals against service providers or other more privileged citizens. The upshot is that governments do not need to operate through the authoritative interventionism typical of the neo-Keynesian model to achieve welfare goals. Welfare states are still possible in a more individualist risk society. The resources of the economic psychology of behaviour in response to risk and of the public administration of experiments in quasi-market design are used to buttress the argument.

Kemshall's *Risk, Social Policy and Welfare* (2002) is written more from the perspective of governance and regulation. It examines policy shifts in health care, child protection, and mental health services to investigate how far 'risk is replacing need as the key organizing principle in health and personal social services' (p. 22). In health care the health promotion agenda and growth of the private sector, in child protection the increasing use of various administrative tools to identify high-risk children and concentrate resources on them and in mental health and community care, comparable approaches which focus on individuals who may be a danger to themselves and others are charted. The key conclusions are that 'responsibilization is the price of citizenship and inclusion' in the emerging welfare framework, and that 'individuals and ... communities are increasingly responsible for the generation and prudent use of their own welfare resources (active rather than passive welfare). ... Techniques, strategies and mechanisms ... have changed with the times and the objectives ... have been reconstituted from social solidarity to control and discipline, to diversity management' (2002: 130).

These studies seek to take forward research overviews in, respectively, the individual responsibility and the state regulation approaches that are head and tail of the new welfare state settlement. They show how new directions in research are becoming established in work on social and public policy at a theoretical and a practical level. This field offers rich opportunities to test analytically based claims about social change and transitions from modernity. The opportunity to do this is now being taken up.

References

Alaszewski, A. and Horlick-Jones, T. (2003). *Risk and Health: Research Review and Priority Setting*, Report for MRC and ESRC.

——— Harrison, L., and Manthorpe, J. (1998). *Risk, Health and Welfare*. Buckingham: Open University Press.

Baker, T. and Simon, J. (2002). *Embracing Risk: The Changing Culture of Insurance and Responsibility*. Chicago: University of Chicago Press.

Baldwin, P. (1990). *The Politics of Social Solidarity*. Cambridge: Cambridge University Press.

Barr, N. (1998). *The Economics of the Welfare State*. Oxford: Oxford University Press.

Bauman, Z (1998). *Work, Consumerism and the New Poor*. Buckingham: Open University Press.

Beck, U. and Beck-Gernsheim, E. (2002). *Individualisation, Institutionalised Individualism and its Social and Political Consequences*. London: Sage.

——— Bonss, W., and Lau, C. (2003). 'The Theory of Reflexive Modernity', *Theory, Culture and Society*, 20(2): 1–33.

Bloch, A. and Levy, C. (eds.) (1999). *Refugees, Citizenship and Social Policy in Europe*. Basingstoke: Macmillan.

Bonoli, G. (2002). *The Politics of New Social Risks*. Presented at APSA, Boston.

Brewer, M., Clark, T., and Myck, M. (2001). *Credit Where It's Due*, Institute for Fiscal Studies, Commentary no 86.

Burnett, A. and Peel, M. (2001). 'Asylum-Seekers and Refugees in Britain', *BMJ*, 322: 544–7.

Burrows, R. and Loader, B. (eds.) (1994). *Towards a Post-Fordist Welfare State?*. London: Routledge.

Butcher, T. (2002). *Delivering Welfare*. Buckingham: Open University Press.

Clark, T. and Emmerson, C. (2002). *The tax and benefit system and the incentive to invest in a SH pension*, IFS bulletin 28.

CRSP (1999). *Briefings*. University of Loughborough.

Deacon, A. (2004*a*). 'An Ethic of Mutual Responsibility?', in C. Beem and L. Mead (eds.) *Welfare Reform and Political Theory*. New York: Russell Sage.

——(2004*b*). 'An Ethic of Mutual Responsibility?', in C. Beem and L. Mead (eds.), *Welfare Reform and Political Theory*. New York: Russell Sage.

Dean, H. and Melrose, M. (1999). 'Poverty, Riches and Social Citizenship', in J. Macmillan Hills (2004), *Inequality and the State*. Oxford: Oxford University Press, 2004.

————'Fiddling the Social: Understanding Benefit Fraud', *Benefits*, 14: 17–18, September 1995.

——and Shah, A. (2002*a*). 'Insecure Families and Low-Paying Labour Markets: Comments on the British Experience', *Journal of Social Policy*, 31(1): 61–80.

——(2002*b*). 'Business Versus Families: Whose Side is New Labour On?', *Social Policy and Society*, 1(1): 3–10.

Dean, M. (1999). *Governmentality*. London: Sage.

Denay, D. (2006). *Risk and Society*. London: Sage, p. 280.

DfES (1998). *Meeting the Childcare Challenge* cmnd 3959, HMSO, London.

DH (1992).*The Health of the Nation*, HMSO, London.

——(1999). *Saving Lives: Our Healthier Nation*, Cm 4386, HMSO, London.

——(2004). *Choosing Health*, Cm 4135, HMSO, London.

Dickens, R. (2002). 'Is Welfare to Work Sustainable?', *Benefits*, 10: 2.

DoH (2000). 'The NHS Plan -*The Government's Response to the Royal Commission on Long term Care*, (7/11-02).

DSS (1998). *A New Contract for Welfare*, cm 3805, London: HMSO.

Duncan, S. and Edwards, R. (1999). *Lone Mothers, Paid Work and Gendered Moral Rationalities*. London: Macmillan.

DWP (2003). *Pensions 2002: Public Attitudes to Pensions and Savings for Retirement*, research report no 193, by Victoria Mayhew.

——(2004). *Households Below Average Income, 1994/5–2002-3*, HMSO, London.

ESRC (2004). *Pensions, Pensioners and Pensions Policy*, Economic and Social Research Council, Swindon.

Eiser, R. (2004). *Public Perception of Risk*, Foresight paper, OST.

Ewald, F. (2002). 'The return of Descartes' malicious demon', in T. Baker and J. Simon (eds.), *Embracing Risk*. Chicago: University Press.

Ferrera, M. and Rhodes, M. (2000). 'Recasting European Welfare States' and 'Building a Sustainable Welfare State', *West European Politics*, 23(2), 1–10, 257–82.

Finch, J. (1989). *Family Obligations and Social Change*. Cambridge: Polity.

Frey, B. (1997). *Not Just for the Money*. Cheltenham: Edward Elgar.

George, V. and Page, R. (2004). *Global Social Problems*. Cambridge: Polity Press.

——and Wilding, P. (2002). *Globalisation and Human Welfare*. London: Palgrave.

Giddens, A. (1994). *Beyond Left and Right*. Cambridge: Polity Press.
——(1998). *The Third Way*. Cambridge: Polity Press.
Ginn, J. (2004). 'European Pension Privatisation', *Social Policy and Society*, 3(2): 123–34.
Halpern, D., Bates, C., and Beales, G., with Heathfield, A. (2003). *Personal Responsibility and Behaviour Change*, Cabinet Office Strategy Unit.
Hasluck, C. (2000). *The New Deal for Young People*, Research and Development Report, ESR41, Sheffield.
Hill, M. (1999). 'Insecurity and Social Security', in J. Vail, J. Wheelock, and M. Hill (eds.), *Insecure Times*. London: Routledge.
Hills, J. (2004). 'National Insurance, State Pensions and the Future', *Journal of Social Policy*, 33(3): 347–72.
Hood, C., Rothstein, H., Baldwin, R. et al. (2000). *The Government of Risk: Understanding Risk Regulation Regimes*. Oxford: Oxford University Press.
Horlick-Jones, T. (2004). 'Experts in Risk ... Do They Exist?', *Health, Risk and Society*, 6: 1.
Huber, E. and Stephens, J. (2001). *Development and Crisis of the Welfare State*. Chicago: Chicago University Press.
Irwin, Q., Simmons, P., and Walker, G. (1999). 'Faulty Environments and Risk Reasoning', *Environment and Planning A*, 31(3): 1311–26.
Jessop, B. (2002). *The Future of the Capitalist State*. Cambridge: Polity Press.
Kaye, R. (1999). 'The Politics of Exclusion', *Contemporary Politics*, 5(1): 25–45.
Kemshall, H. (2002). *Risk Social Policy and Welfare*. Buckingham: Open University Press.
Le Grand, J. (2003). *Motivation, Agency and Public Policy*. Oxford: Oxford University Press.
Leonard, P. (1997). *Postmodern Welfare*. London: Sage.
Luxembourg Income Study (2004). *Income Inequality Tables* at http://www.lisproject.org/keyfigures/ineqtable.htm, consulted November 2004.
Maxwell, S. and Kenway, P. (2000). Poverty Briefing no 9, *CPAG*.
Mythen, G. (2005). 'Employment, Individualisation and Insecurity', *Sociological Review*, 33(1): 129–49.
National Audit Office (2002). *The New Deal for Young People* HCP 639 2001–2.
Nettleton, S. (1997). 'Governing the Risky Self', in A. Petersen and R. Bunton (eds.), *Foucault, Health and Medicine*. London: Routledge.
ONS (2002). *NDLP: statistical release to September 2002*.
——(2003). *Social Trends no 33*, HMSO, London.
——(2004). *Social Trends no 34*, HMSO, London.
Pensions Policy Institute (2003). *The Pensions Landscape*, PPI, London.
Petersen, A. (1997). 'Risk, Governance and the New Public Health', in A. Petersen and R. Bunton (eds.), *Foucault, Health and Medicine*. London: Routledge.
Petts, J. and Niemeyer, S. (2004). 'Health Risk Communication and Amplification', *Health, Risk and Society*, 6(1): 7–23.

Piachaud, D. and Sutherland, H. (2002). 'Child Poverty', in Hills, Piachaud and Le Grand (2002), *Understanding Social Exclusion*. Oxford: Oxford University Press, pp. 141–54.

Pierson, P. (ed.) (2001). *The New Politics of the Welfare State*. Oxford: Oxford University Press.

Richardson, J. (2001). *European Union*. London: Routledge.

Rowlingson, K. (2002). 'Private Pension Planning: The Rhetoric of Responsibility, the Reality of Insecurity', *Journal of Social Policy*, 31(4), October, 623–42.

——and Whyley, C. (1998). 'The Right Money to the Right People?' Fighting Fraud, Reducing Error and Tackling Non-Take-Up' *Benefits*, 21, January.

——, Whyley, C., Newburn, T. and Berthoud, R. (1997). *Social Security Fraud: the Role of Penalties*. London: TSO.

Sacks, J. (1997). *The Politics of Hope*. London: Jonathon Cape.

Scharpf, F. and Schmidt, V. (eds.) (2000). *Welfare and Work in the Open Economy: Diverse Responses to Common Challenges*. Oxford: University Press.

Sutherland, H., Sefton, T., and Piachaud, D. (2003). *Poverty in Britain: The Impact of Government Policy Since 1997*. Cambridge: Cambridge University Press.

Taylor-Gooby, P. (ed.) (2001). *Welfare States under Pressure*. London: Sage.

——and Hastie, C. (2003). 'Paying for "World Class" Services: A British Dilemma', *Journal of Social Policy*, 32(2): 271–88.

—— (2004). *New Risks, New Welfare*. Oxford: Oxford University Press.

Titmuss, R. (1958). 'The Social Division of Welfare' in *Essays on the Welfare State*, George, Allen and Unwin, London.

Treasury/DTI, Balancing Work and Family Life, 2003, HMSO, London.

Twigg, J. (2005). *The Social Politics of the Body: Food, Health and Social Care*. Basingstoke: Palgrave.

Ungerson, C. (2003). 'Commodified Care Work in European Labour Markets', *European Societies*, 5(4): 377–96.

Vail, J., Wheelock, J., and Hill, M. (eds.) (1999). *Insecure Times*. London: Routledge.

Walker, R. and Wiseman, M. (2003). 'Making Welfare Work', *International Social Security Review*, 56, no 1.

Wallace, H. and Wallace, W. (2000). *Policy-making in the EU*. Oxford: Oxford University Press.

Ward, P., Bissell, P., and Noyce, P. (2000). 'The Uncertain world of the Consumer', in P. Taylor-Gooby (ed.) (2000), *Risk, Trust and welfare*. Basingstoke: Macmillan.

Williams, F. (1989). *Social Policy*. Cambridge: Polity Press.

—— (2004). *Rethinking Families*, Calouste Gulbenkian Foundation, London.

Williams, S. and Calnan, M. (1996). 'Modern Medicine and the Lay Populace in ate Modernity', in Williams and Calnan (eds.), *Modern medicine, Lay perspectives and Experiences*. London: UCL Press.

Williams, T., Hill, M., and Davies, R. (2004). *Attitudes to the Welfare State and the Response to Reform*, DWP Research Report no 88.

Yeates, N. (2001). *Globalisation and Social Policy*. London: Sage.

Index